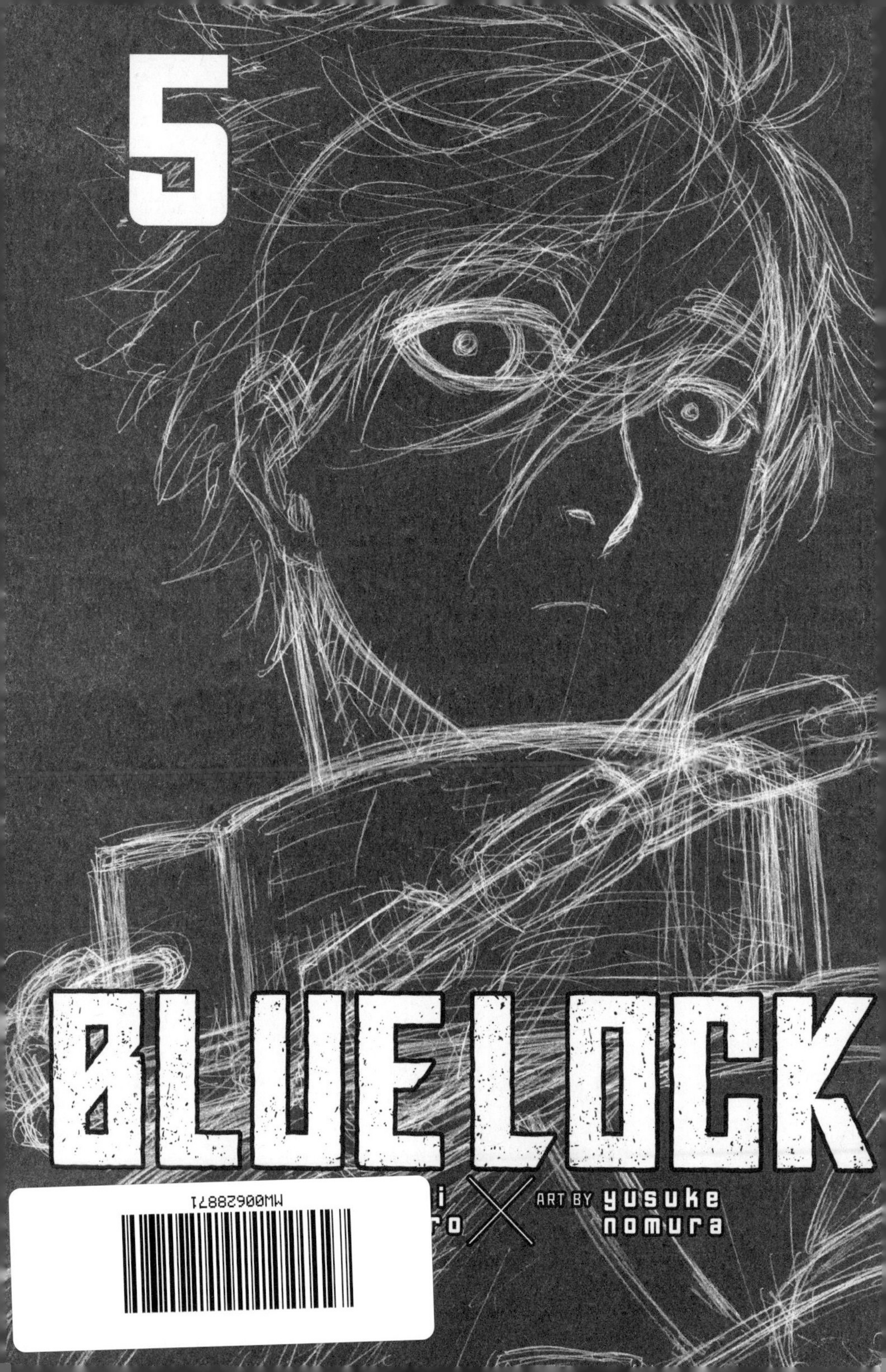
5
BLUE LOCK
ART BY yusuke nomura

# CONTENTS

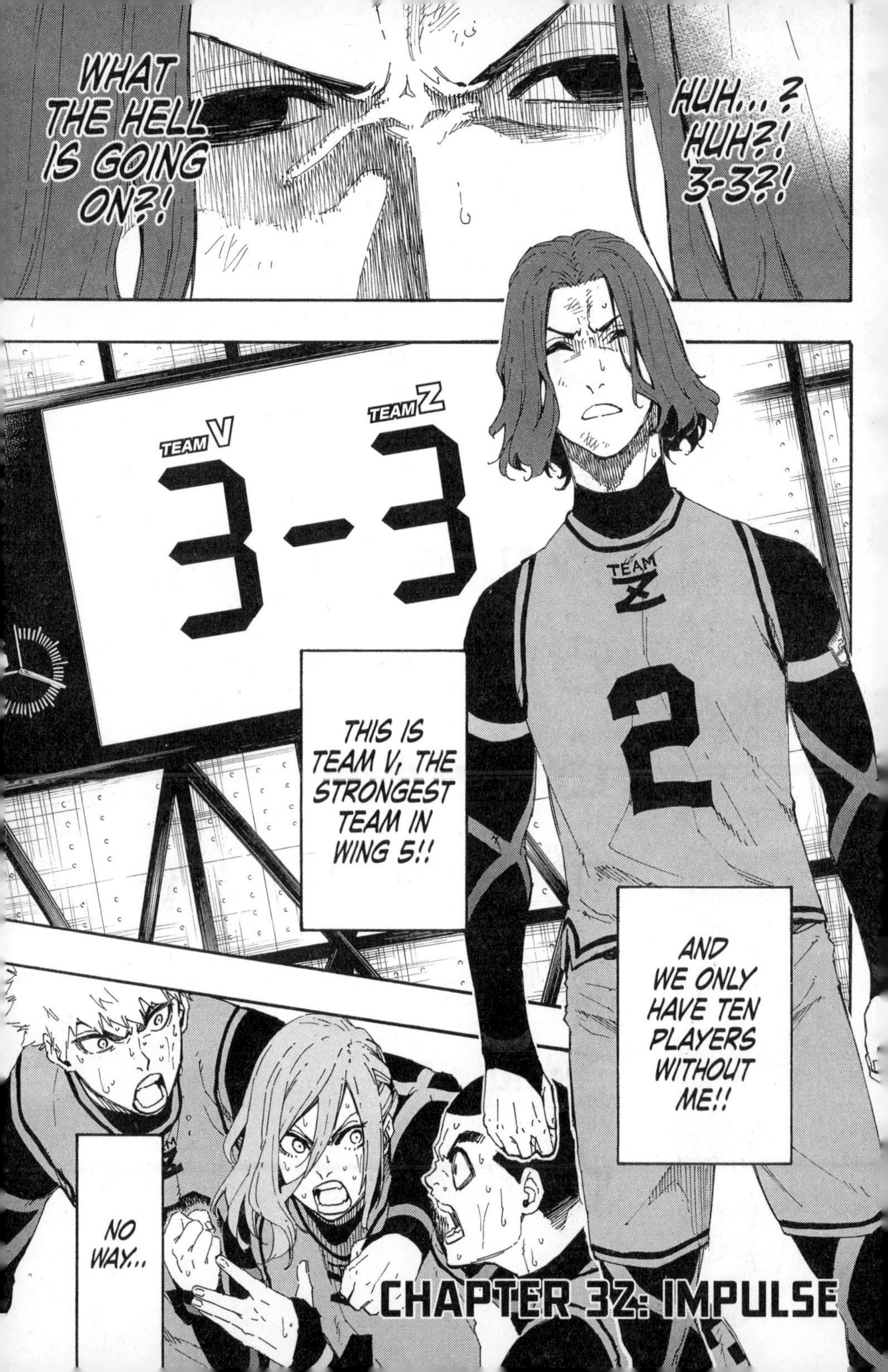
HUH...? HUH?! 3-3?!
WHAT THE HELL IS GOING ON?!
TEAM V
3-3
TEAM Z
THIS IS TEAM V, THE STRONGEST TEAM IN WING 5!!
AND WE ONLY HAVE TEN PLAYERS WITHOUT ME!!
NO WAY...
CHAPTER 32: IMPULSE

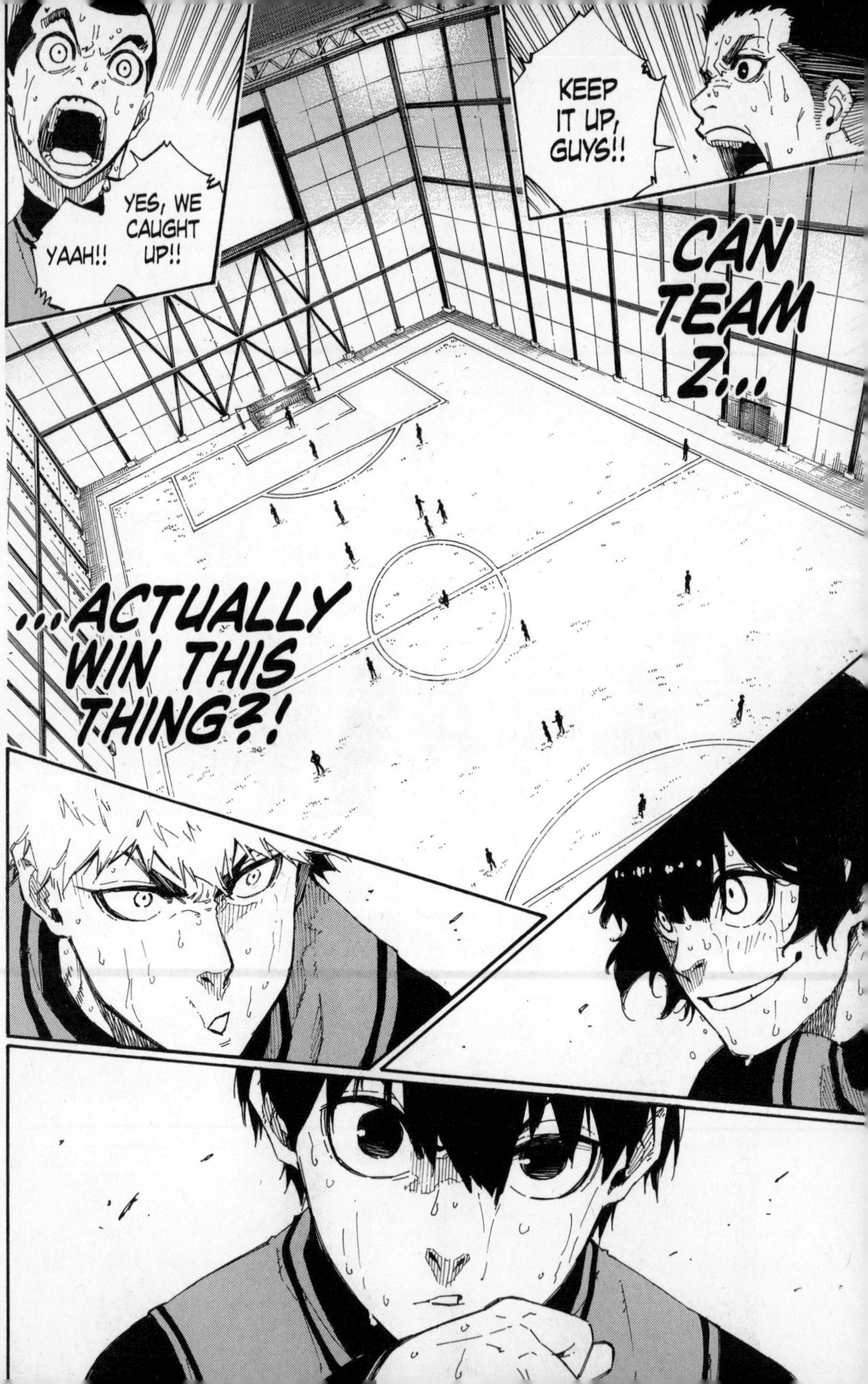
KEEP IT UP, GUYS!!
YES, WE CAUGHT UP!!
YAAH!!
CAN TEAM Z...
...ACTUALLY WIN THIS THING?!

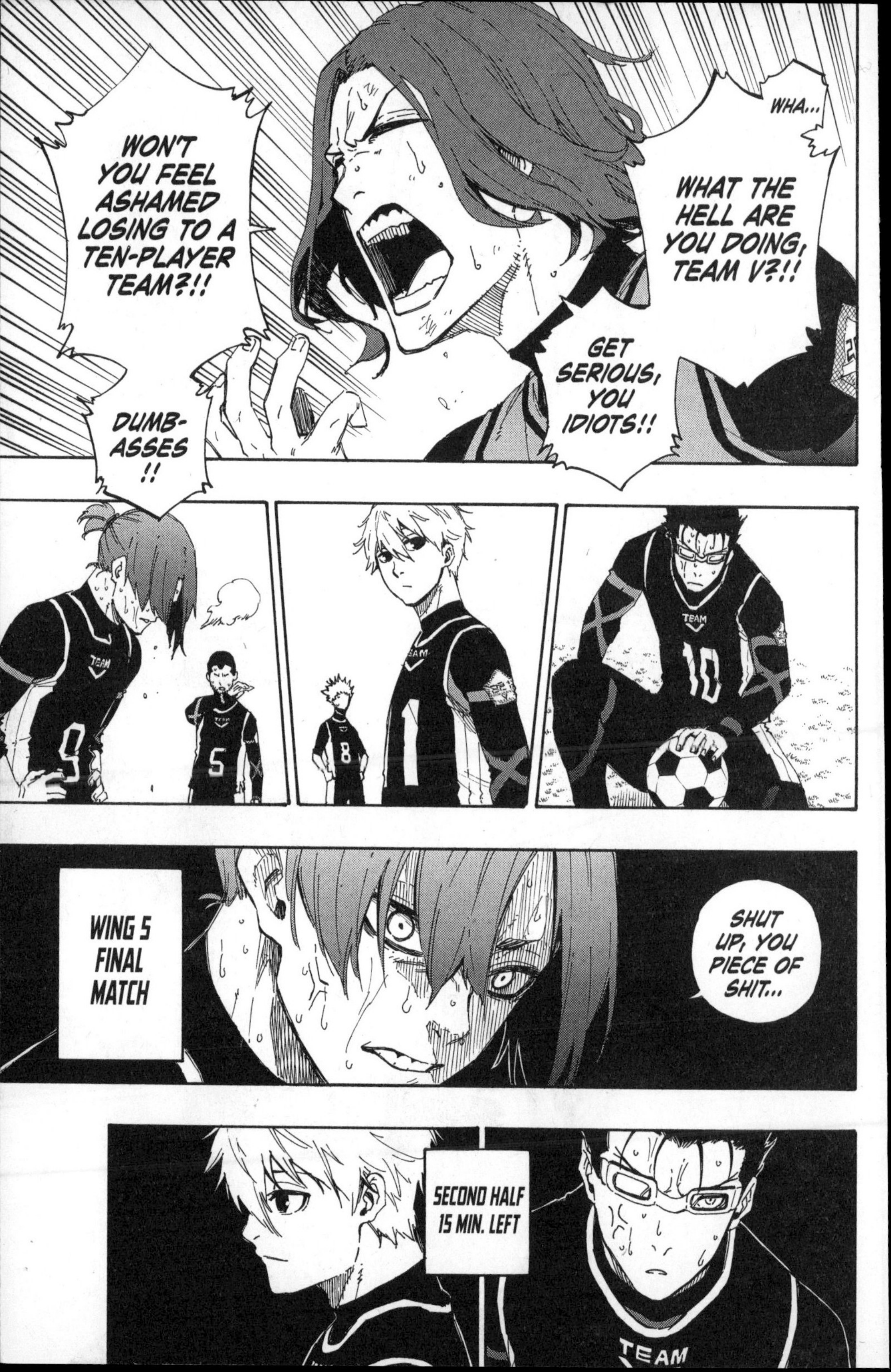
WHA...
WHAT THE HELL ARE YOU DOING, TEAM V?!!
GET SERIOUS, YOU IDIOTS!!
WON'T YOU FEEL ASHAMED LOSING TO A TEN-PLAYER TEAM?!!
DUMB-ASSES!!
SHUT UP, YOU PIECE OF SHIT...
WING 5 FINAL MATCH
SECOND HALF 15 MIN. LEFT

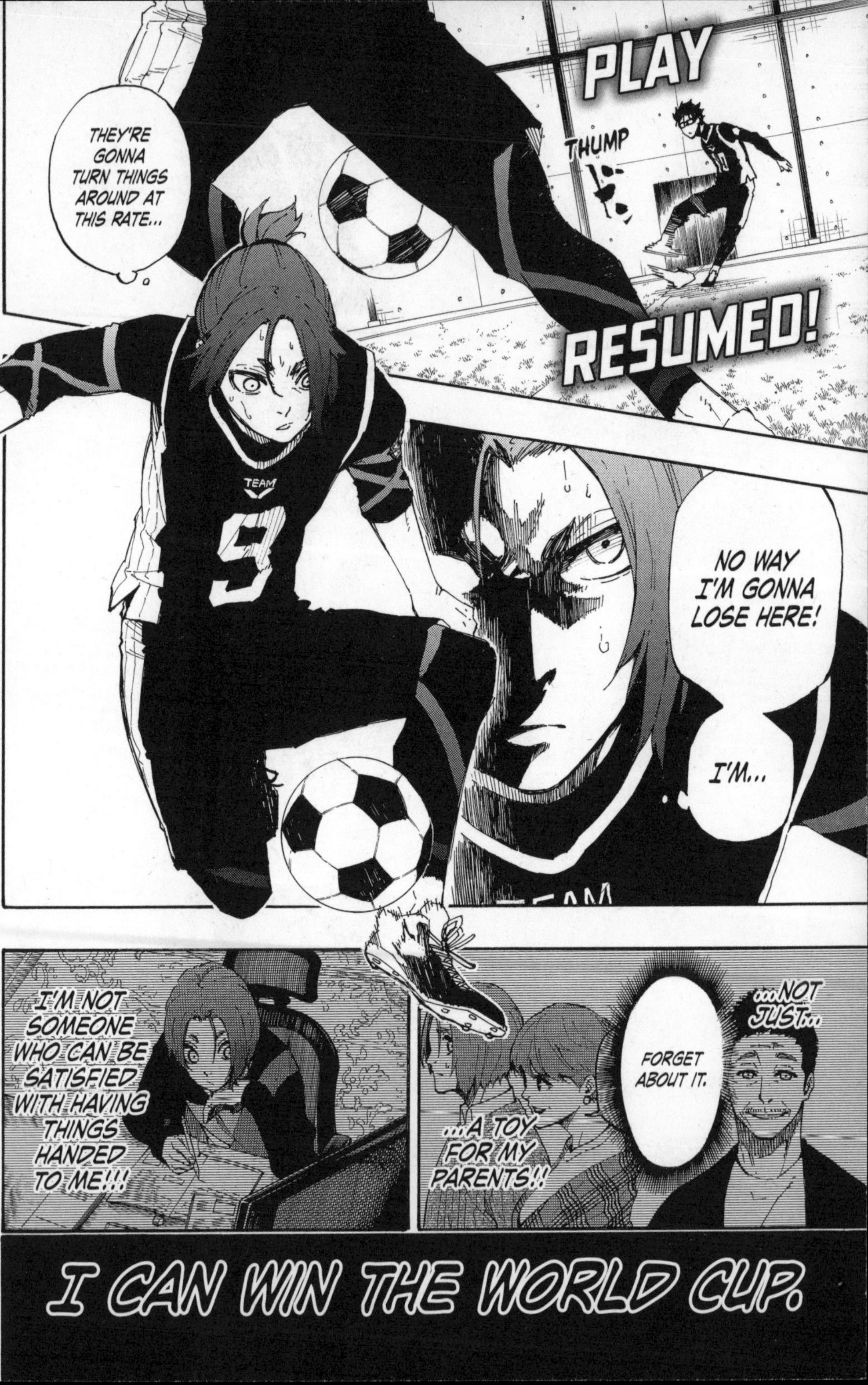
PLAY
THUMP
RESUMED!
THEY'RE GONNA TURN THINGS AROUND AT THIS RATE...
NO WAY I'M GONNA LOSE HERE!
I'M...
...NOT JUST...
FORGET ABOUT IT.
...A TOY FOR MY PARENTS!!
I'M NOT SOMEONE WHO CAN BE SATISFIED WITH HAVING THINGS HANDED TO ME!!!
I CAN WIN THE WORLD CUP.

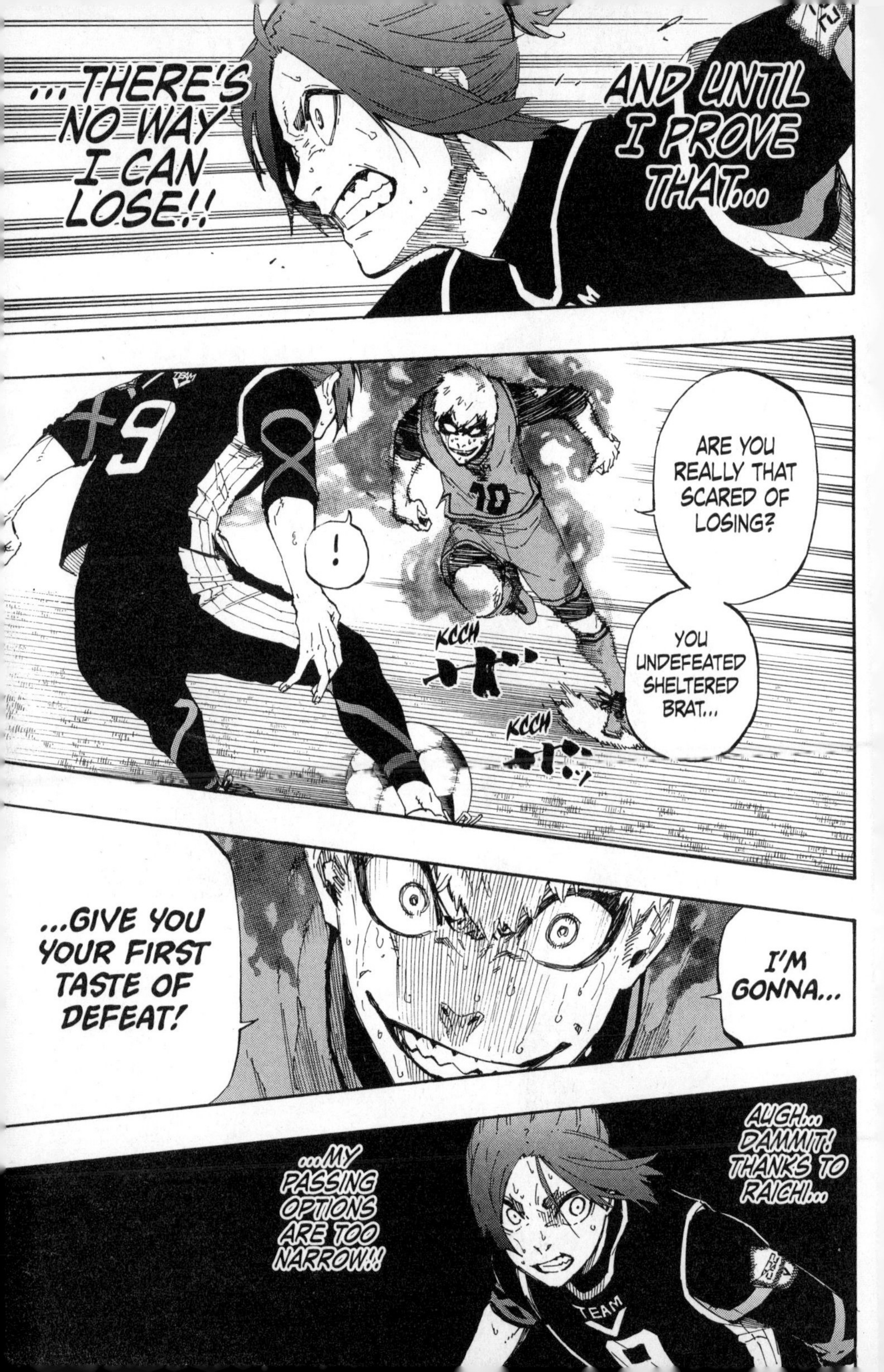
AND UNTIL I PROVE THAT...
...THERE'S NO WAY I CAN LOSE!!
ARE YOU REALLY THAT SCARED OF LOSING?
YOU UNDEFEATED SHELTERED BRAT...
!
KCCH
KCCH
I'M GONNA...
...GIVE YOU YOUR FIRST TASTE OF DEFEAT!
AUGH... DAMMIT! THANKS TO RAICHI...
...MY PASSING OPTIONS ARE TOO NARROW!!

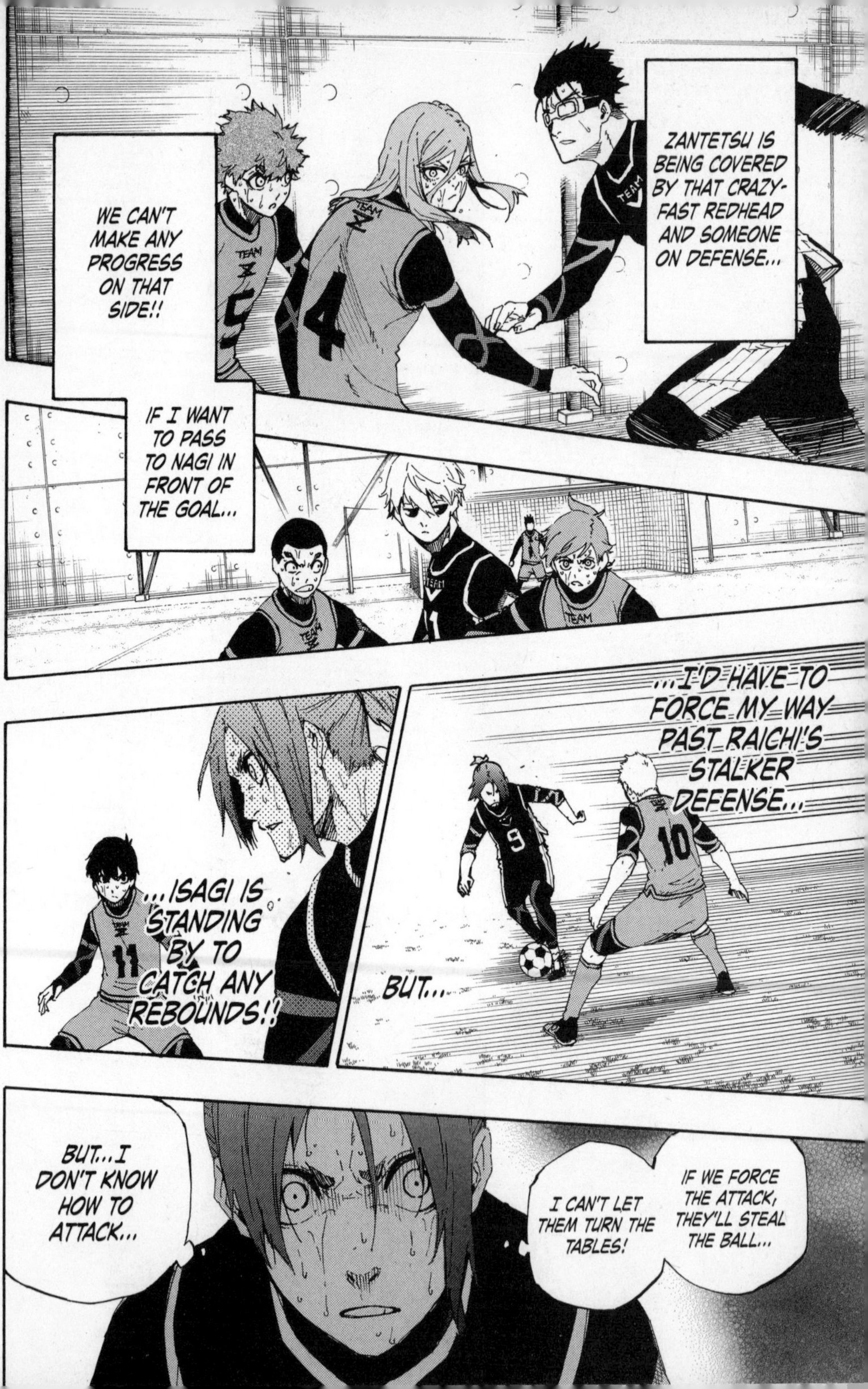
ZANTETSU IS BEING COVERED BY THAT CRAZY-FAST REDHEAD AND SOMEONE ON DEFENSE...
WE CAN'T MAKE ANY PROGRESS ON THAT SIDE!!
IF I WANT TO PASS TO NAGI IN FRONT OF THE GOAL...
...I'D HAVE TO FORCE MY WAY PAST RAICHI'S STALKER DEFENSE...
BUT...
...ISAGI IS STANDING BY TO CATCH ANY REBOUNDS!!
IF WE FORCE THE ATTACK, THEY'LL STEAL THE BALL...
I CAN'T LET THEM TURN THE TABLES!
BUT...I DON'T KNOW HOW TO ATTACK...

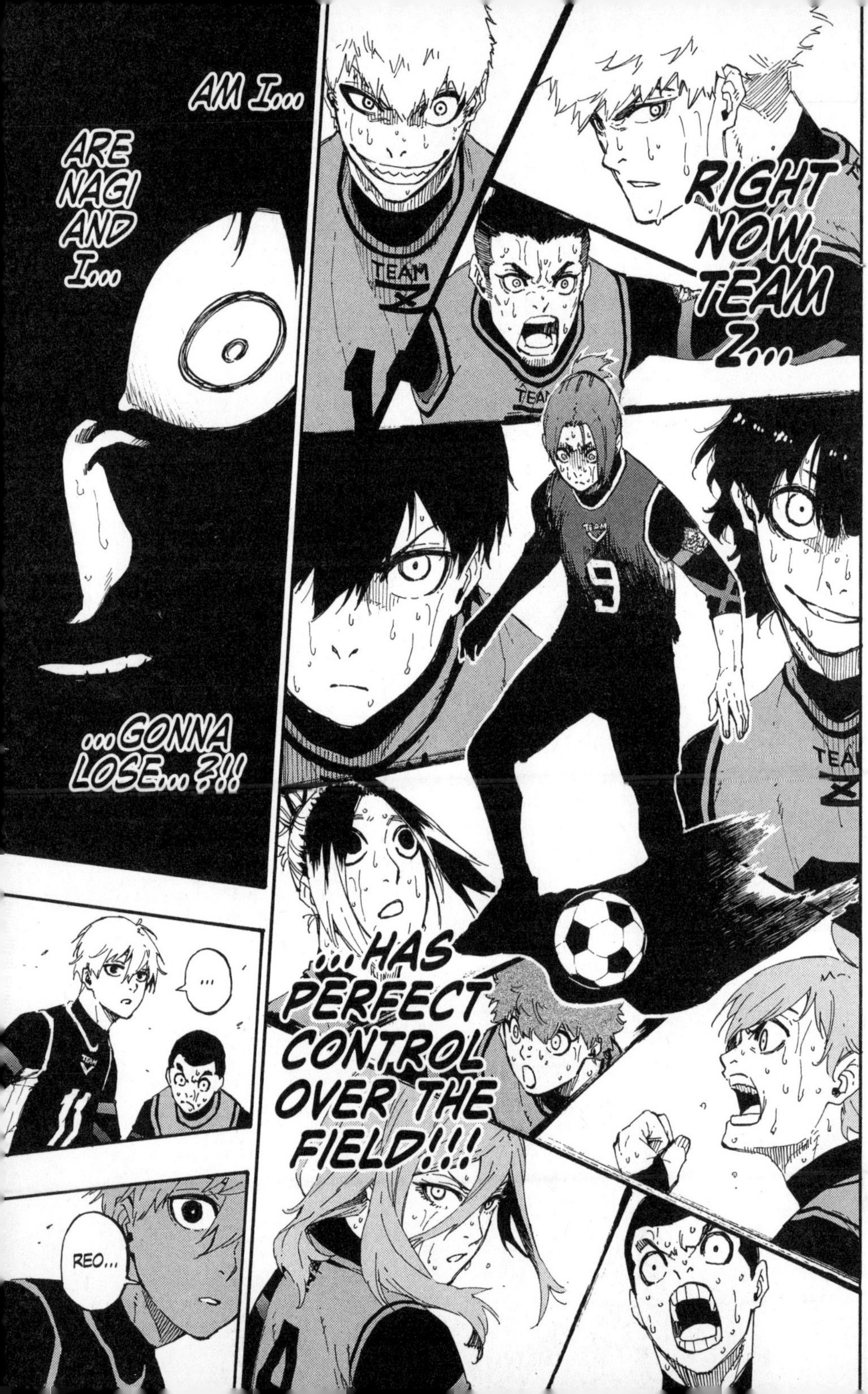
RIGHT NOW, TEAM Z...
...HAS PERFECT CONTROL OVER THE FIELD!!!
AM I...
ARE NAGI AND I...
...GONNA LOSE...?!!
...
REO...

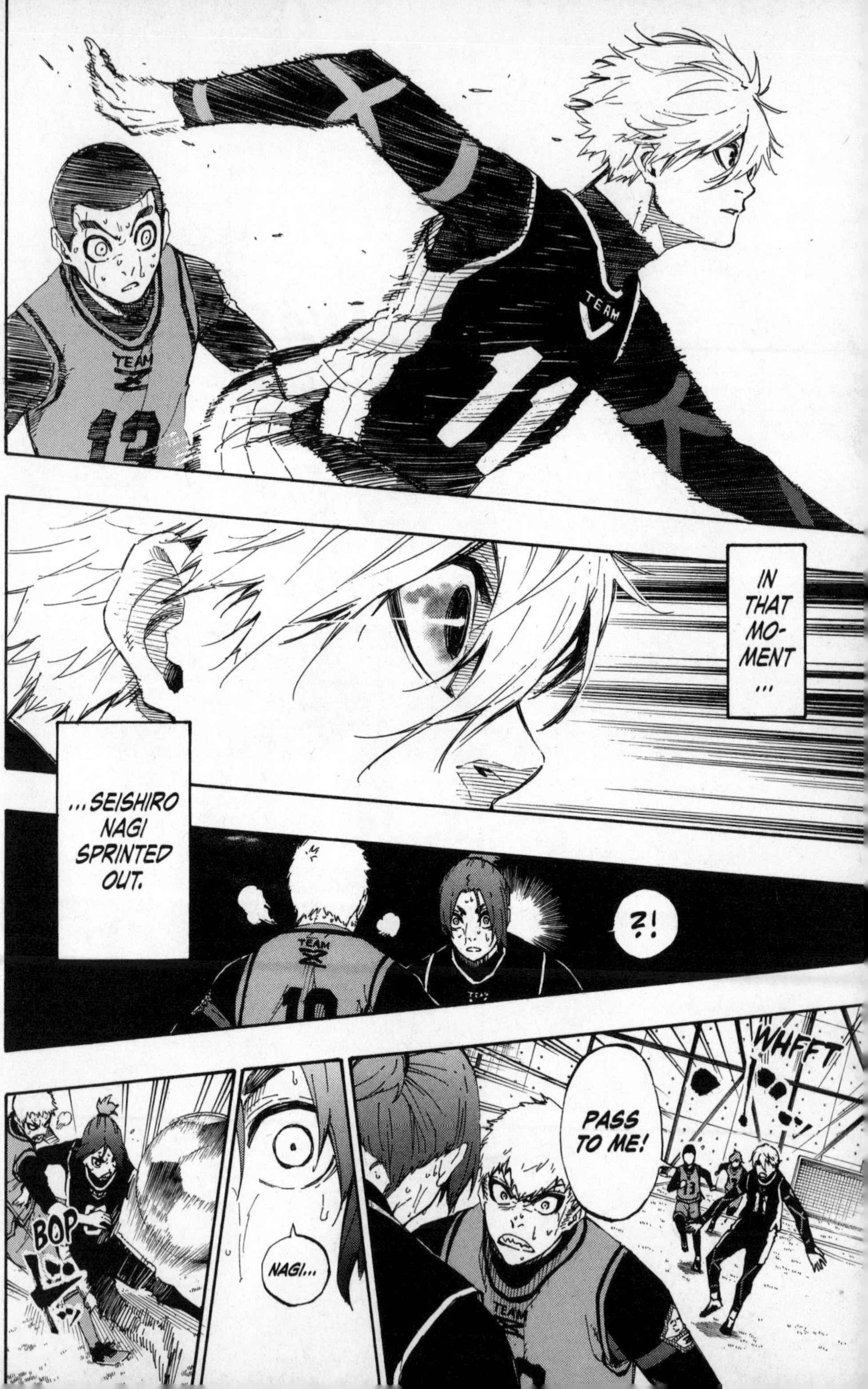
IN THAT MO- MENT ...
...SEISHIRO NAGI SPRINTED OUT.
?!
WHFFT
PASS TO ME!
NAGI...
BOP

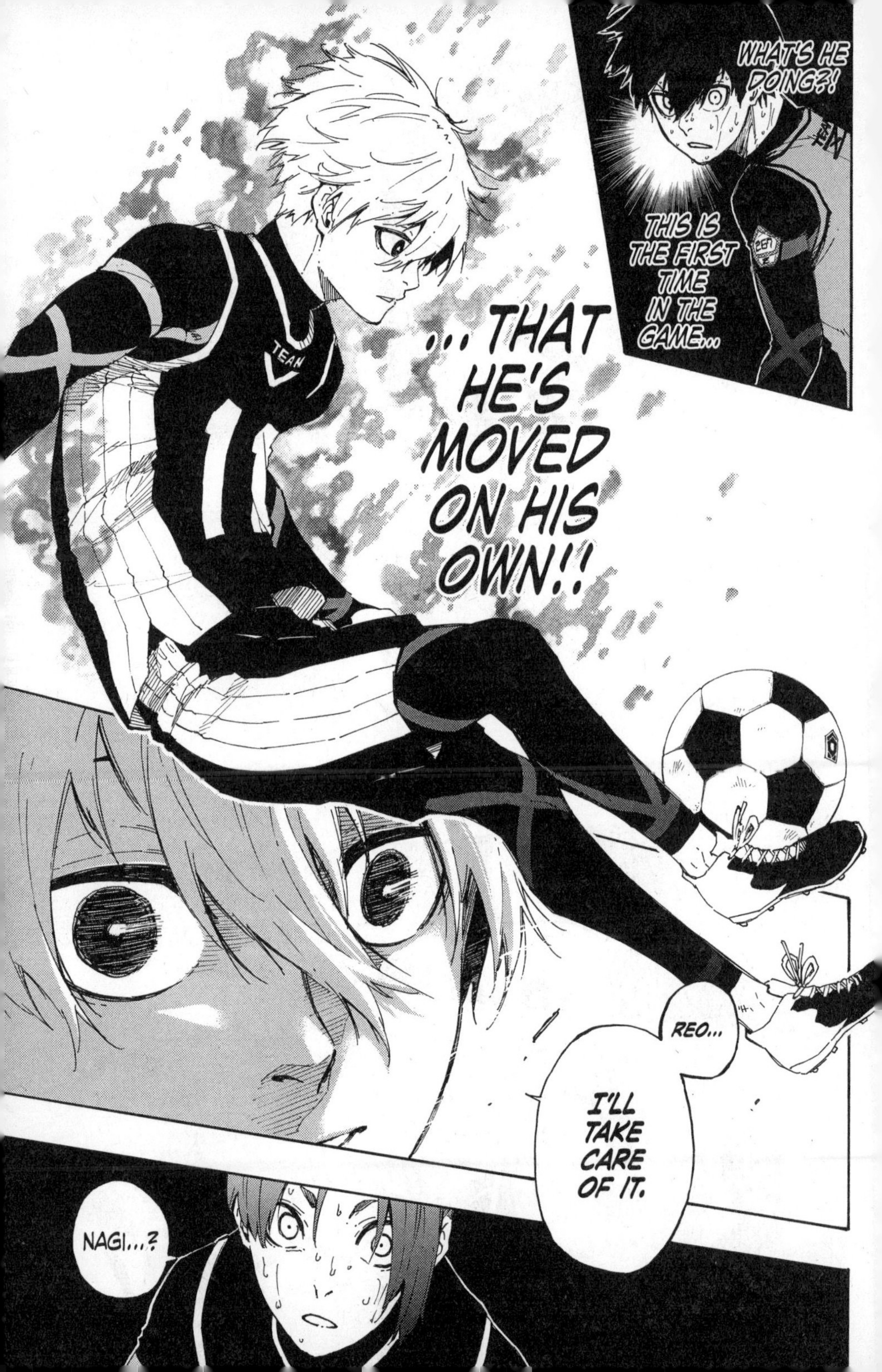
WHAT'S HE DOING?!
THIS IS THE FIRST TIME IN THE GAME...
...THAT HE'S MOVED ON HIS OWN!!
REO...
I'LL TAKE CARE OF IT.
NAGI...?

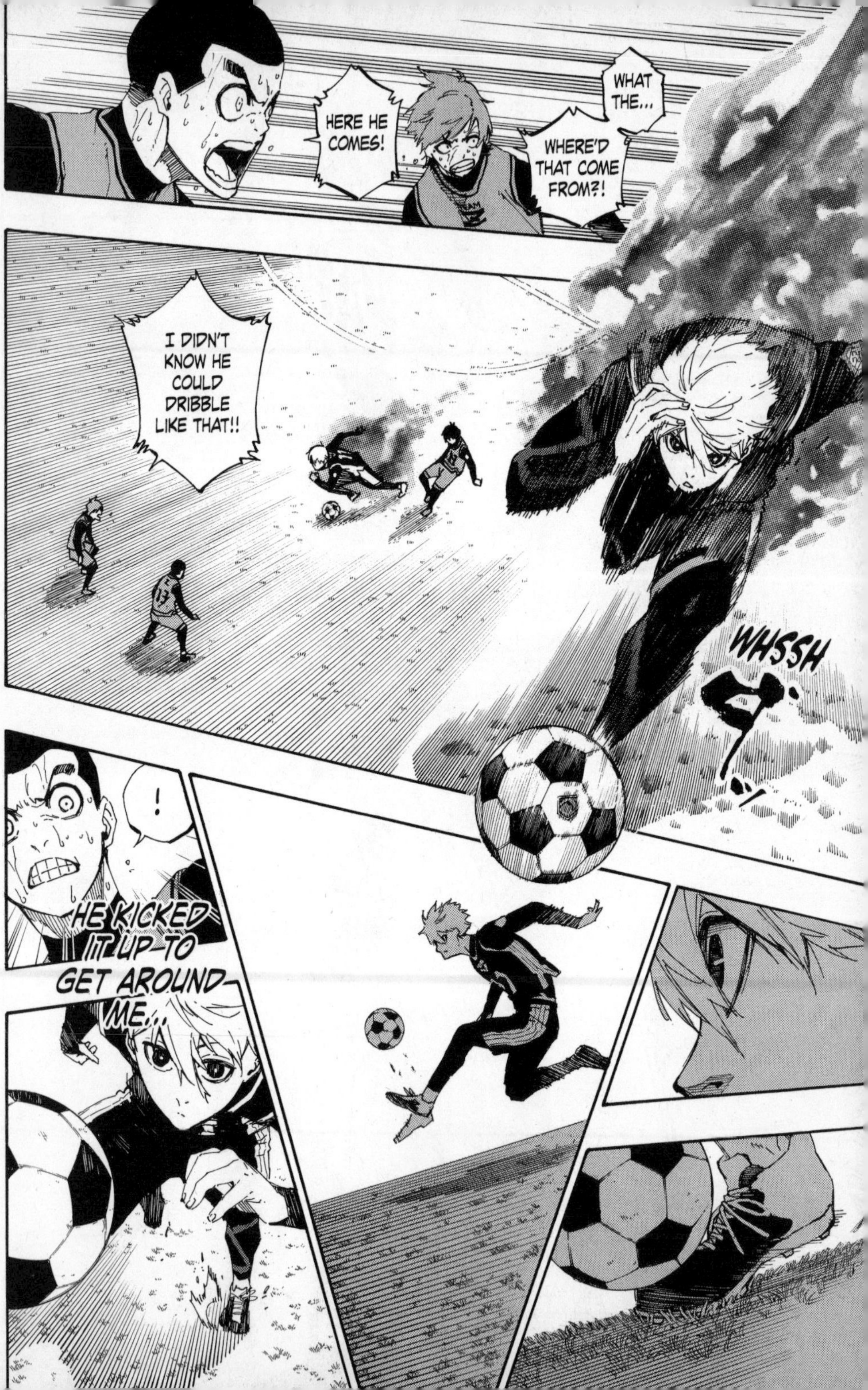
WHAT THE...
WHERE'D THAT COME FROM?!
HERE HE COMES!
I DIDN'T KNOW HE COULD DRIBBLE LIKE THAT!!
WHSSH
!
HE KICKED IT UP TO GET AROUND ME...

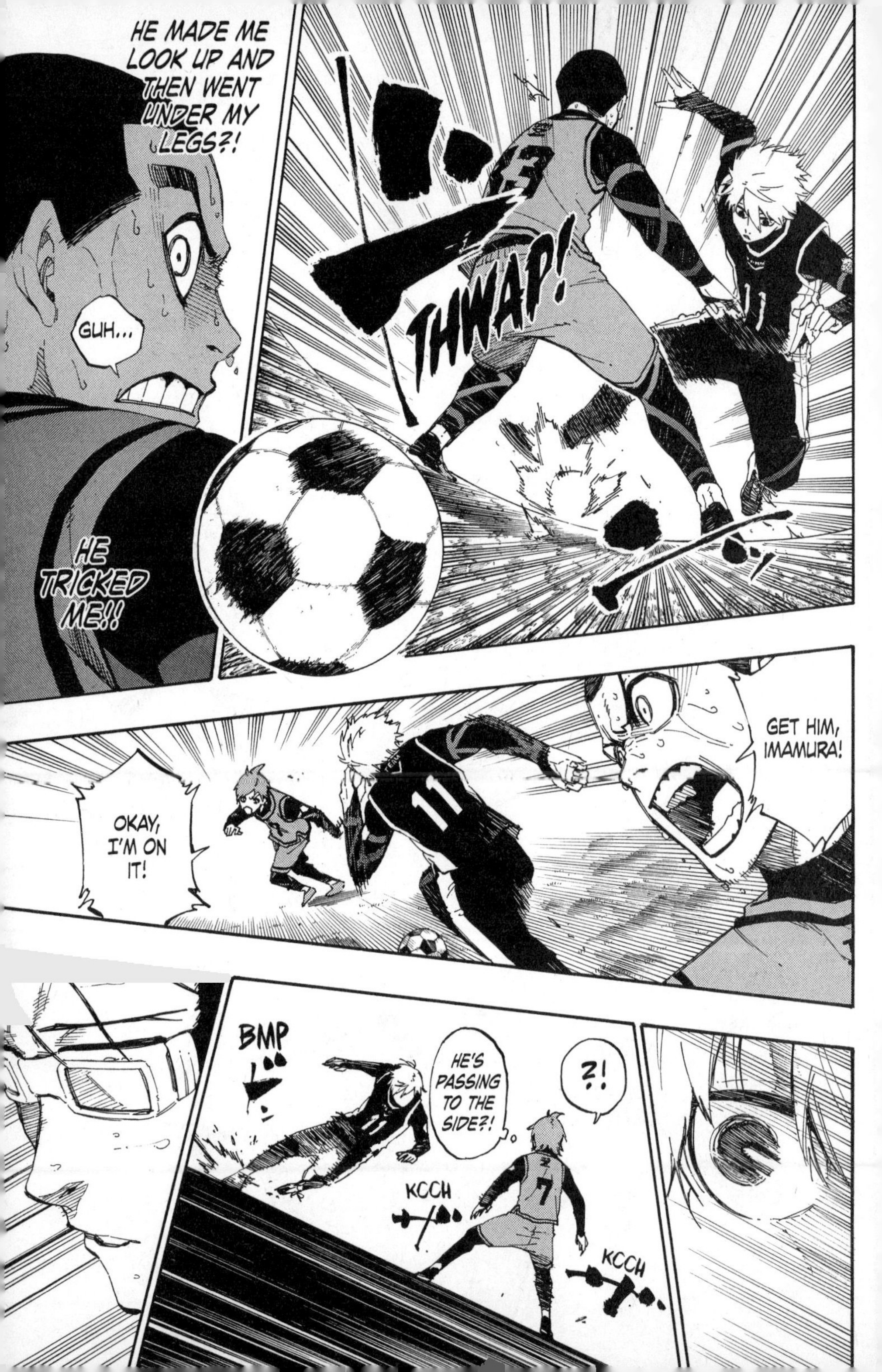
THWAP!
HE MADE ME LOOK UP AND THEN WENT UNDER MY LEGS?!
GUH...
HE TRICKED ME!!
GET HIM, IMAMURA!
OKAY, I'M ON IT!
?!
HE'S PASSING TO THE SIDE?!
BMP
KCCH
KCCH

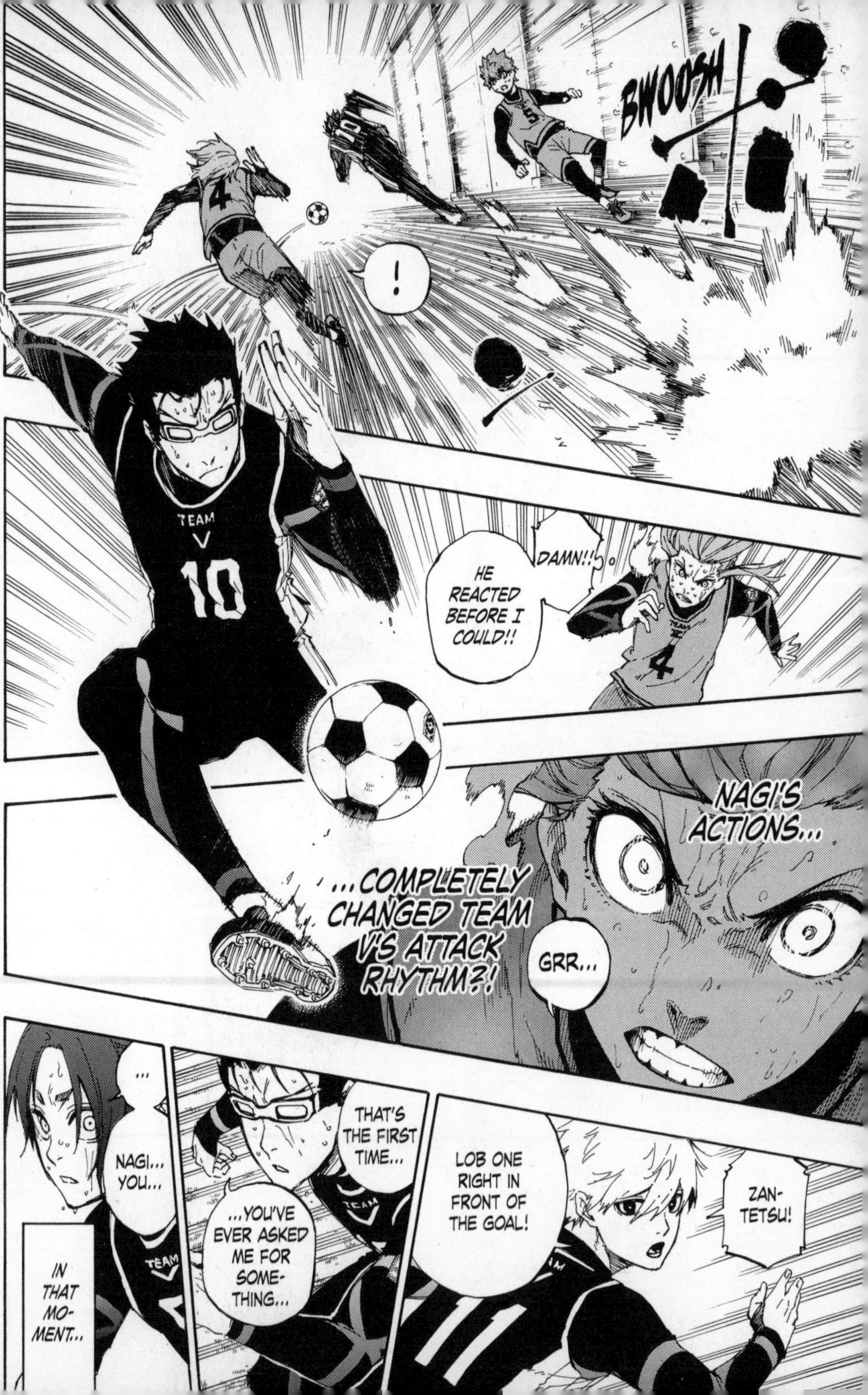
BWOOSH
!
DAMN!!
HE REACTED BEFORE I COULD!!
NAGI'S ACTIONS...
...COMPLETELY CHANGED TEAM V'S ATTACK RHYTHM?!
GRR...
ZAN-TETSU!
LOB ONE RIGHT IN FRONT OF THE GOAL!
THAT'S THE FIRST TIME...
...YOU'VE EVER ASKED ME FOR SOME-THING...
...
NAGI... YOU...
IN THAT MOMENT...

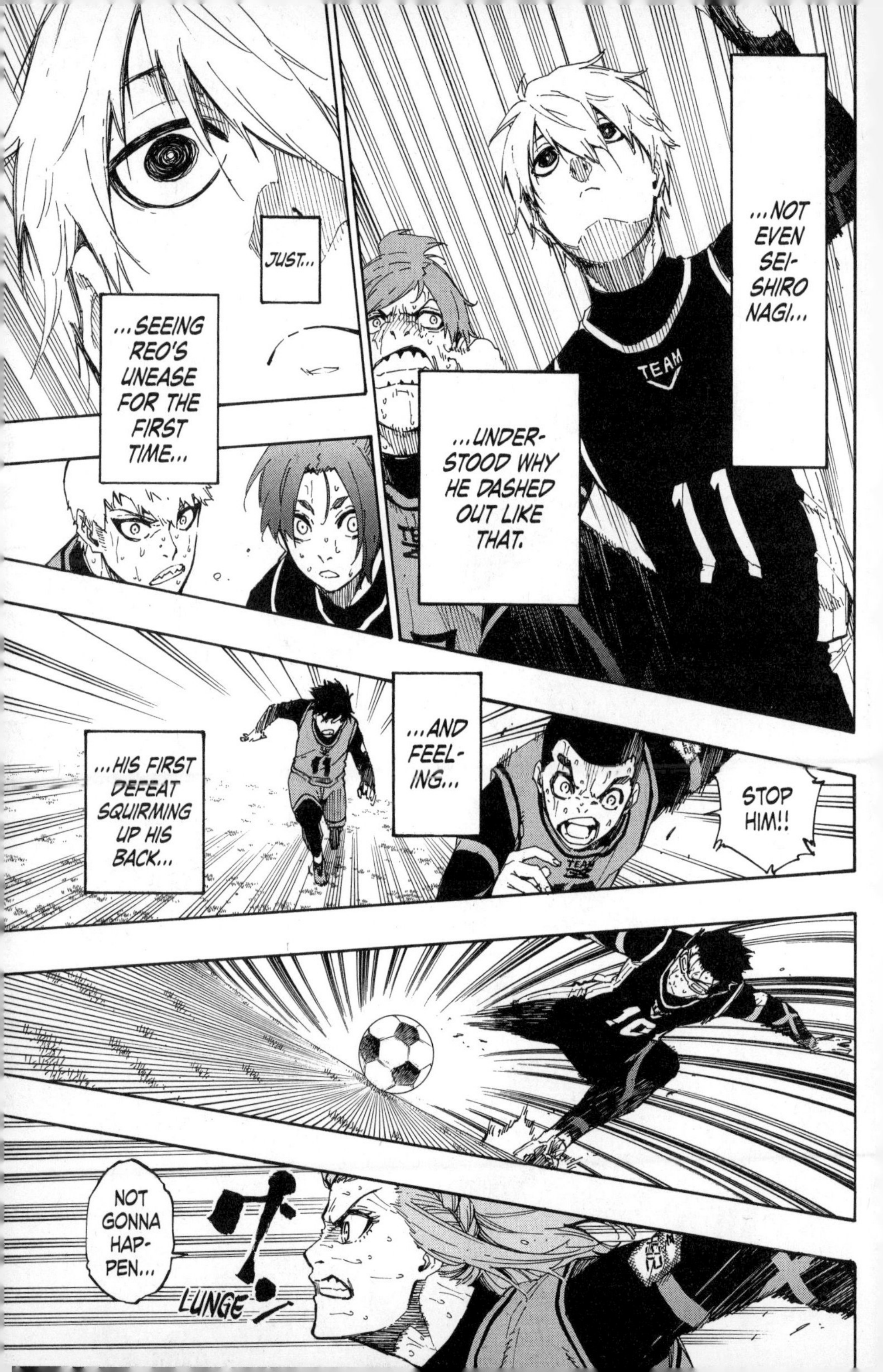

...NOT EVEN SEI-SHIRO NAGI...
...UNDER-STOOD WHY HE DASHED OUT LIKE THAT.
JUST...
...SEEING REO'S UNEASE FOR THE FIRST TIME...
TEAM
STOP HIM!!
...AND FEEL-ING...
...HIS FIRST DEFEAT SQUIRMING UP HIS BACK...
LUNGE
NOT GONNA HAP-PEN...

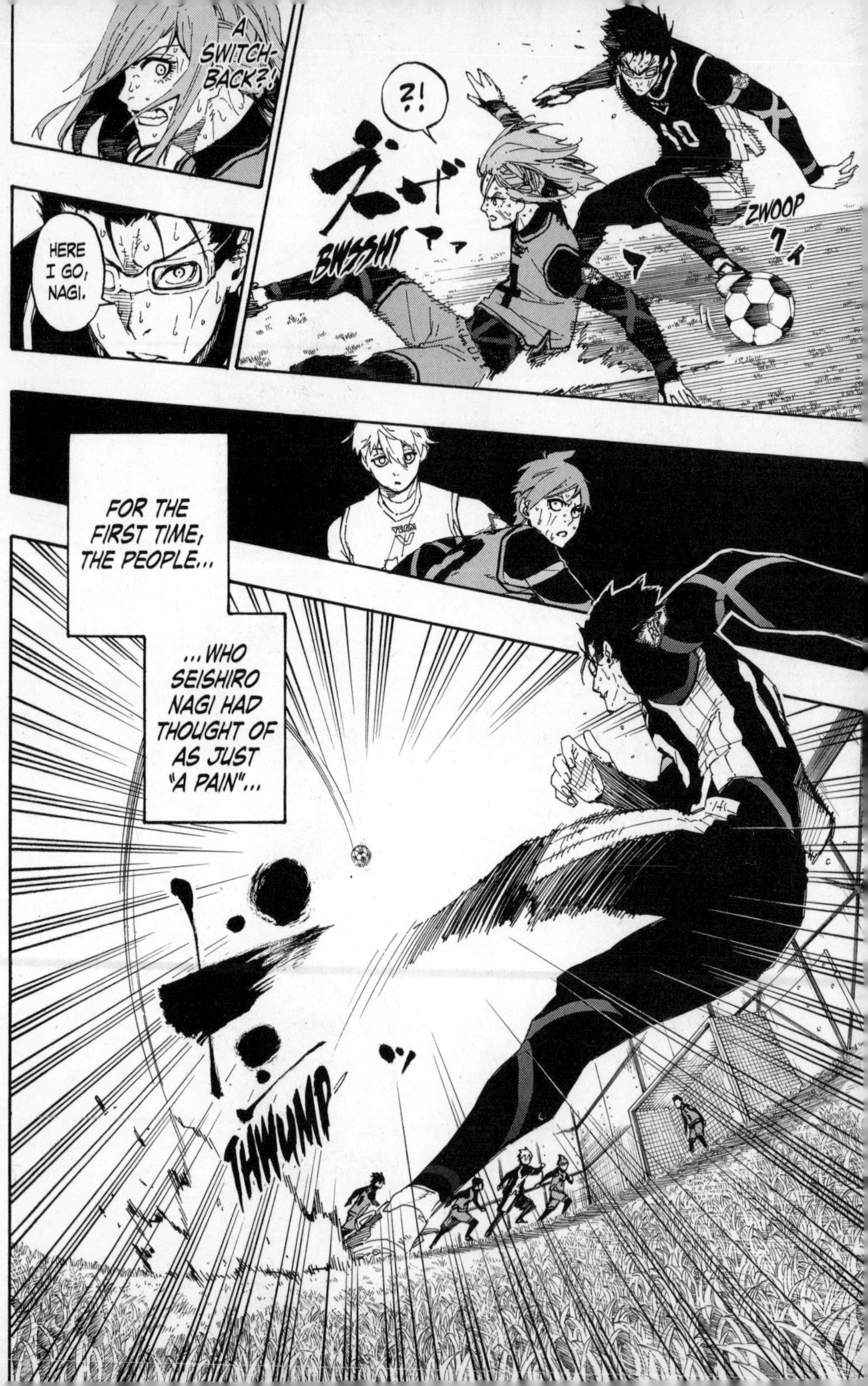
?!
BWSSHT
ZWOOP
A SWITCH-BACK?!
HERE I GO, NAGI.
FOR THE FIRST TIME, THE PEOPLE...
...WHO SEISHIRO NAGI HAD THOUGHT OF AS JUST "A PAIN"...
THWUMP

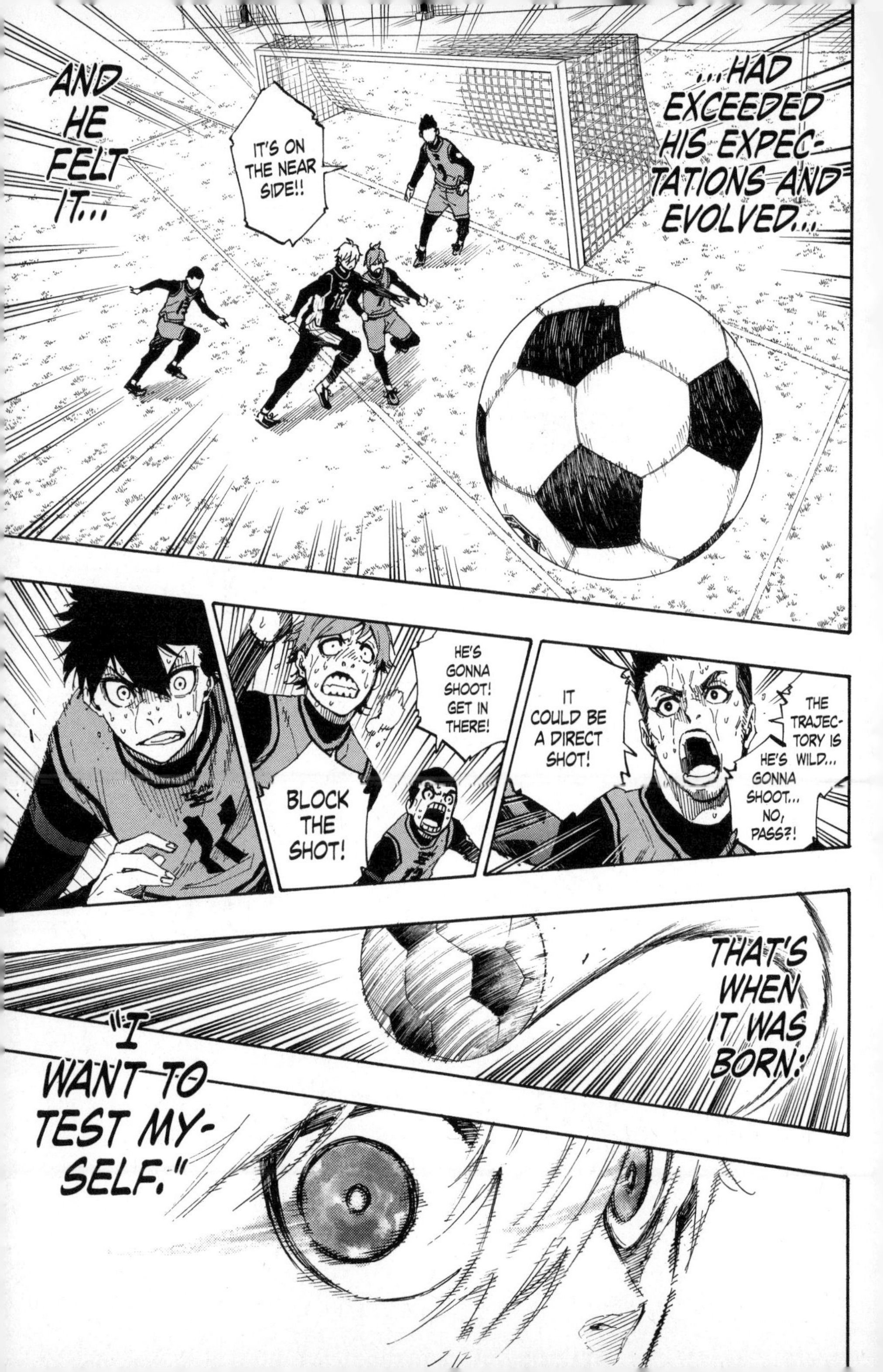
...HAD EXCEEDED HIS EXPEC-TATIONS AND EVOLVED...
IT'S ON THE NEAR SIDE!!
AND HE FELT IT...
THE TRAJEC-TORY IS WILD...
HE'S GONNA SHOOT... NO, PASS?!
IT COULD BE A DIRECT SHOT!
HE'S GONNA SHOOT! GET IN THERE!
BLOCK THE SHOT!
THAT'S WHEN IT WAS BORN:
"I WANT TO TEST MY-SELF."

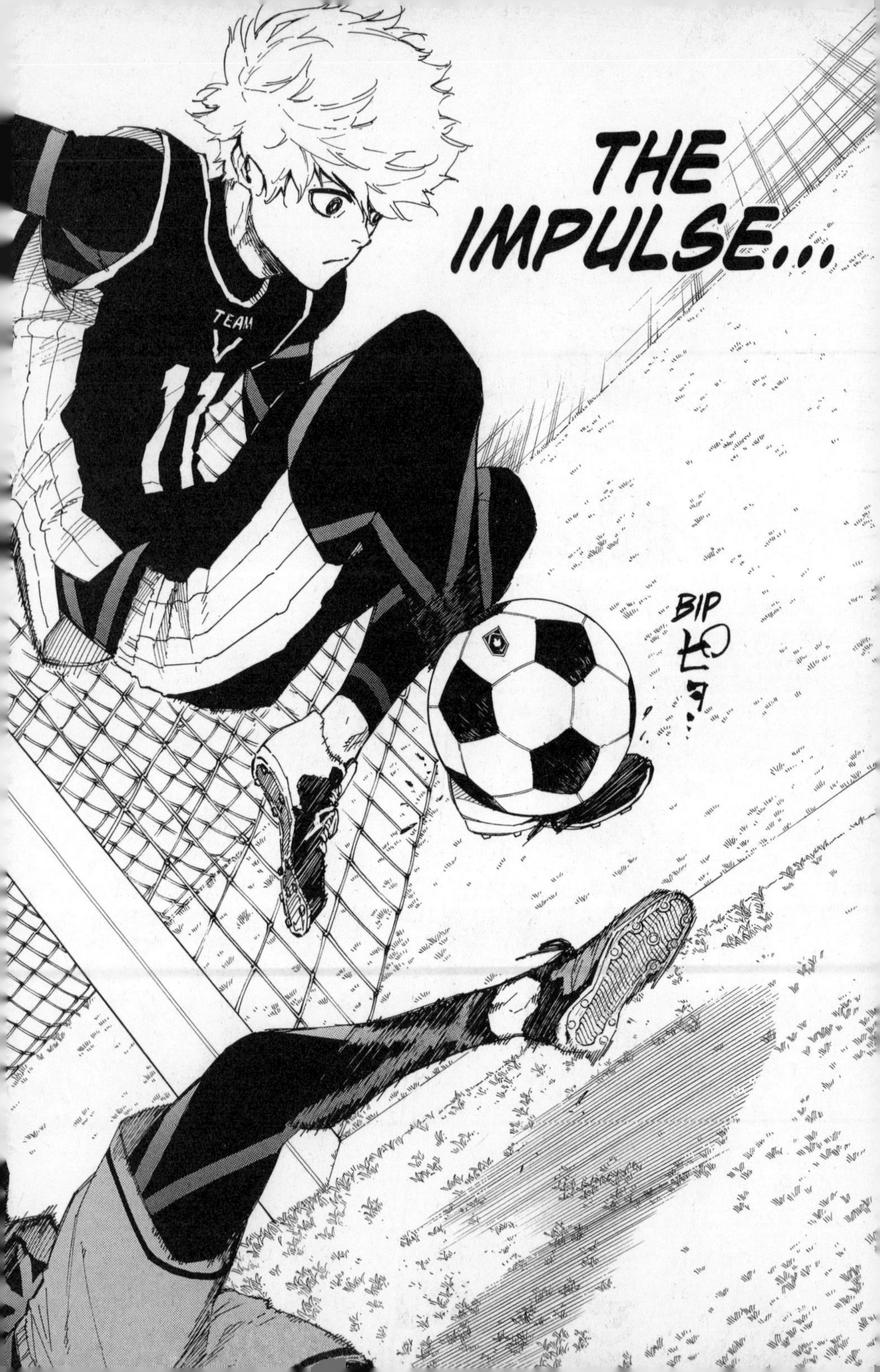
THE IMPULSE...
TEAM
BIP
ピタ…

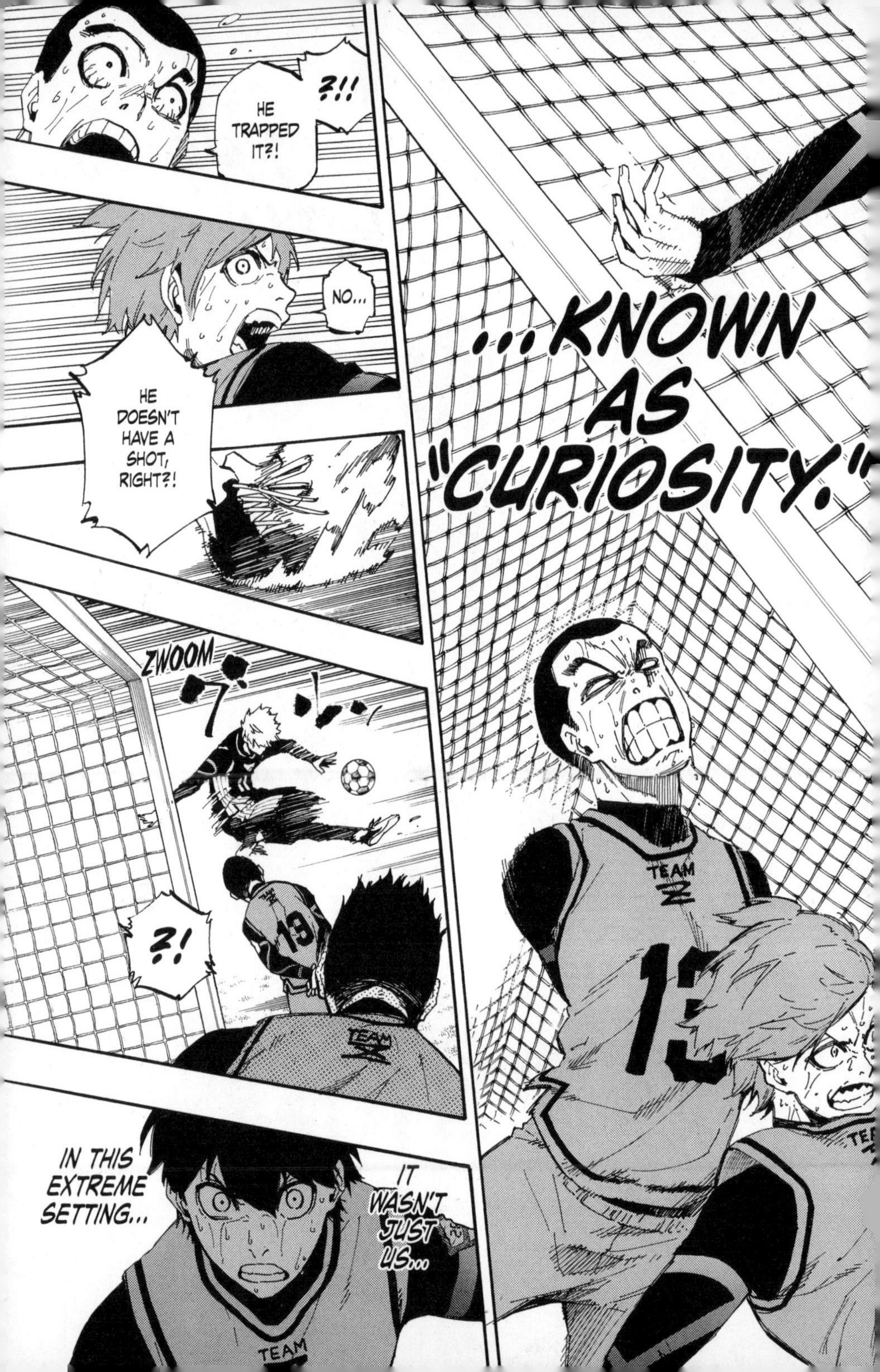
...KNOWN AS "CURIOSITY."
?!!
HE TRAPPED IT?!
NO...
HE DOESN'T HAVE A SHOT, RIGHT?!
ZWOOM
?!
TEAM Z
IT WASN'T JUST US...
IN THIS EXTREME SETTING...
TEAM

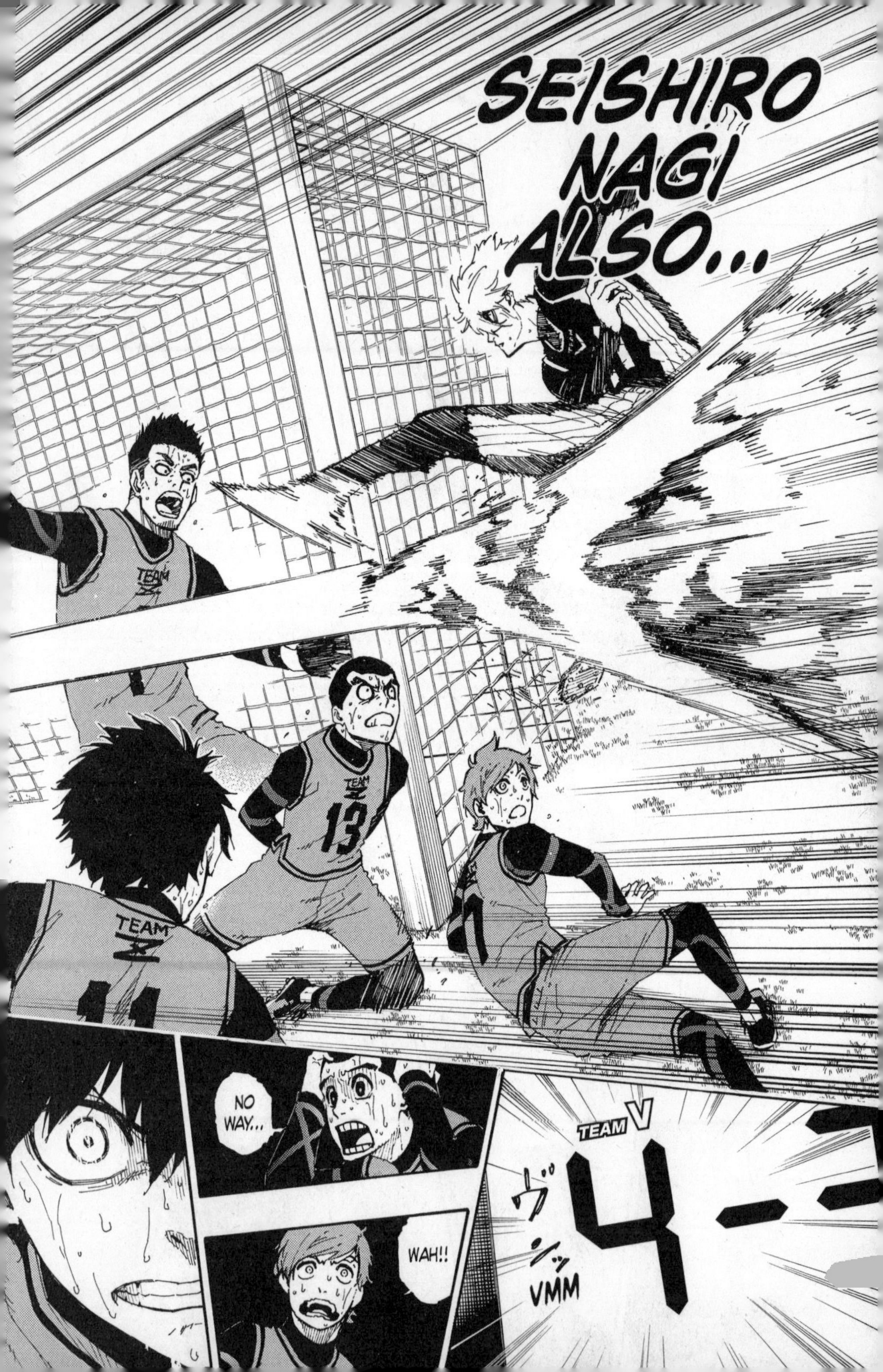

SEISHIRO NAGI ALSO...
TEAM V
4-
VMM
NO WAY...
WAH!!

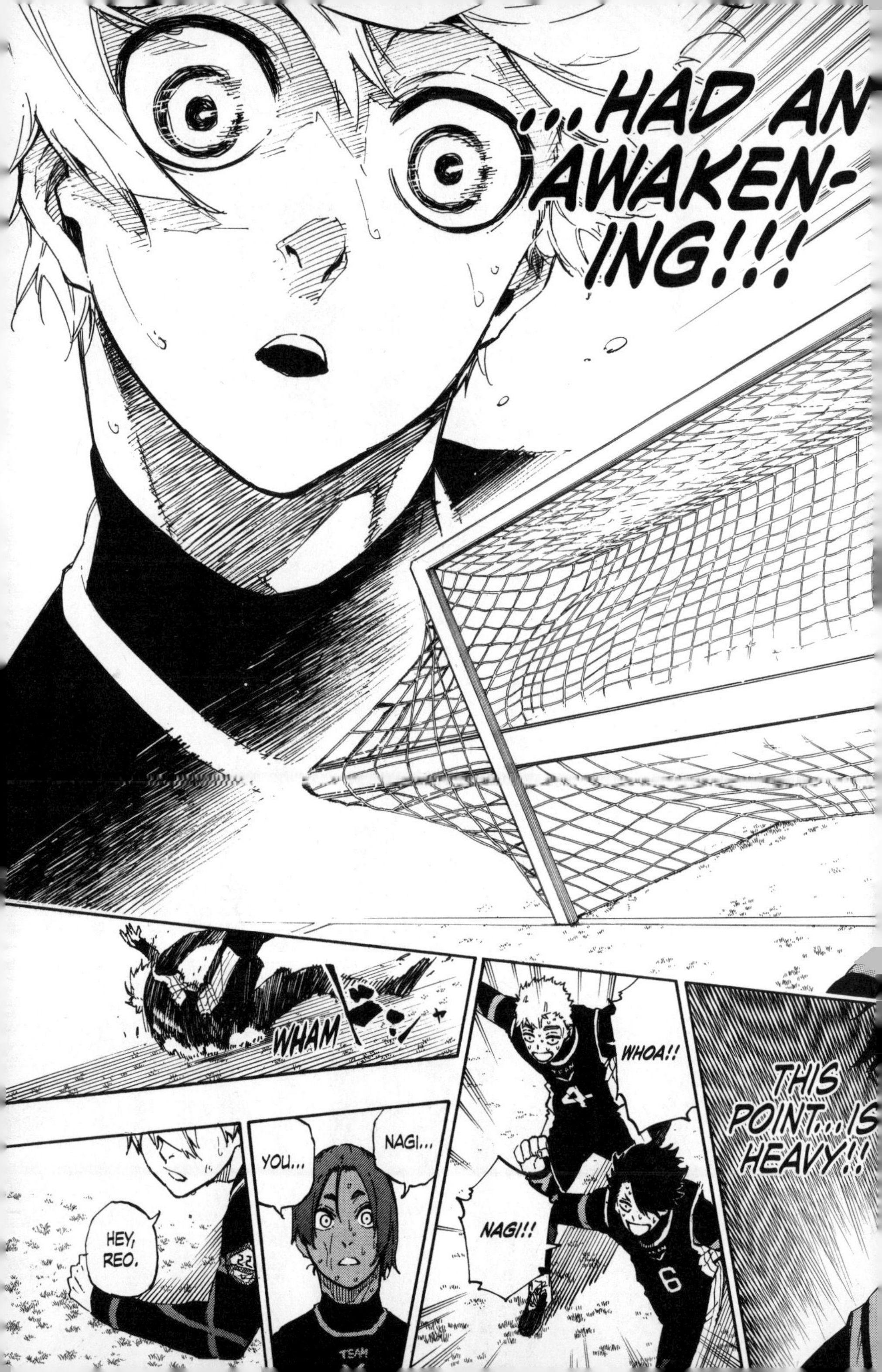
...HAD AN AWAKEN-ING!!!
THIS POINT...IS HEAVY!!
WHOA!!
NAGI!!
WHAM
NAGI...
YOU...
HEY, REO.

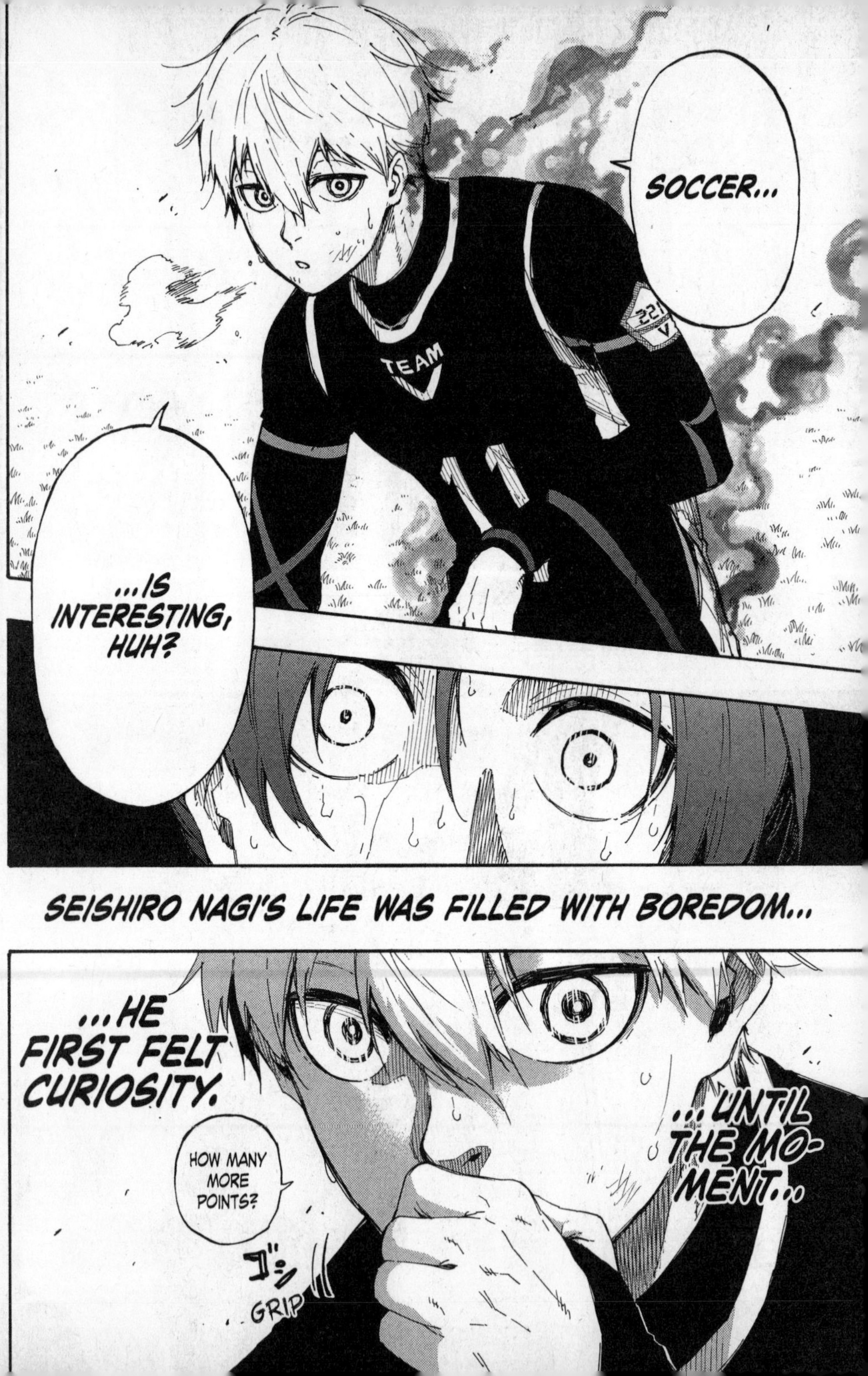
SOCCER...
...IS INTERESTING, HUH?
SEISHIRO NAGI'S LIFE WAS FILLED WITH BOREDOM...
...UNTIL THE MO-MENT...
...HE FIRST FELT CURIOSITY.
HOW MANY MORE POINTS?
GRIP

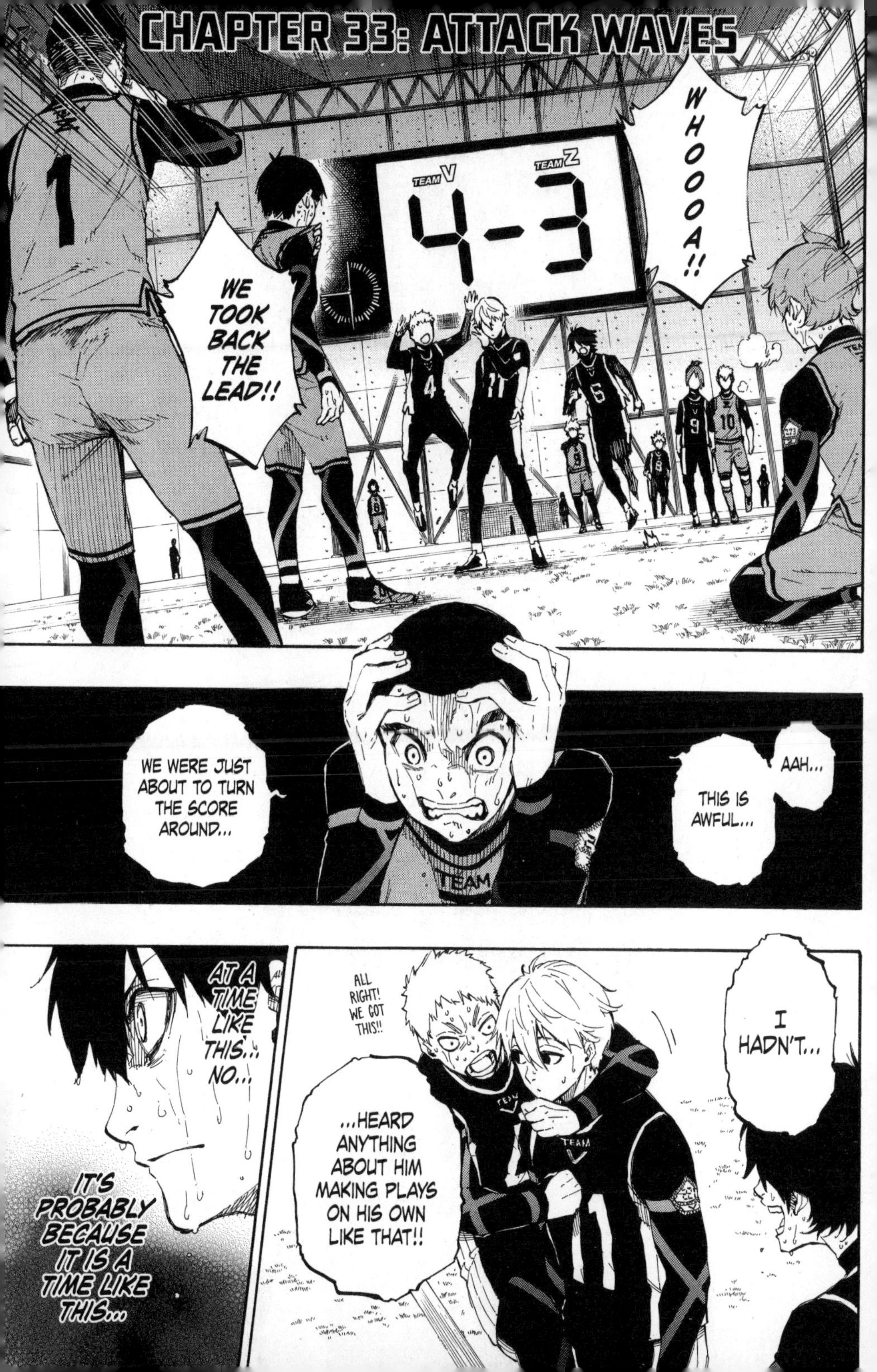
CHAPTER 33: ATTACK WAVES
TEAM V TEAM Z
4-3
WHOOOOA!!
WE TOOK BACK THE LEAD!!
AAH...
THIS IS AWFUL...
WE WERE JUST ABOUT TO TURN THE SCORE AROUND...
I HADN'T...
...HEARD ANYTHING ABOUT HIM MAKING PLAYS ON HIS OWN LIKE THAT!!
ALL RIGHT! WE GOT THIS!!
AT A TIME LIKE THIS... NO...
IT'S PROBABLY BECAUSE IT IS A TIME LIKE THIS...

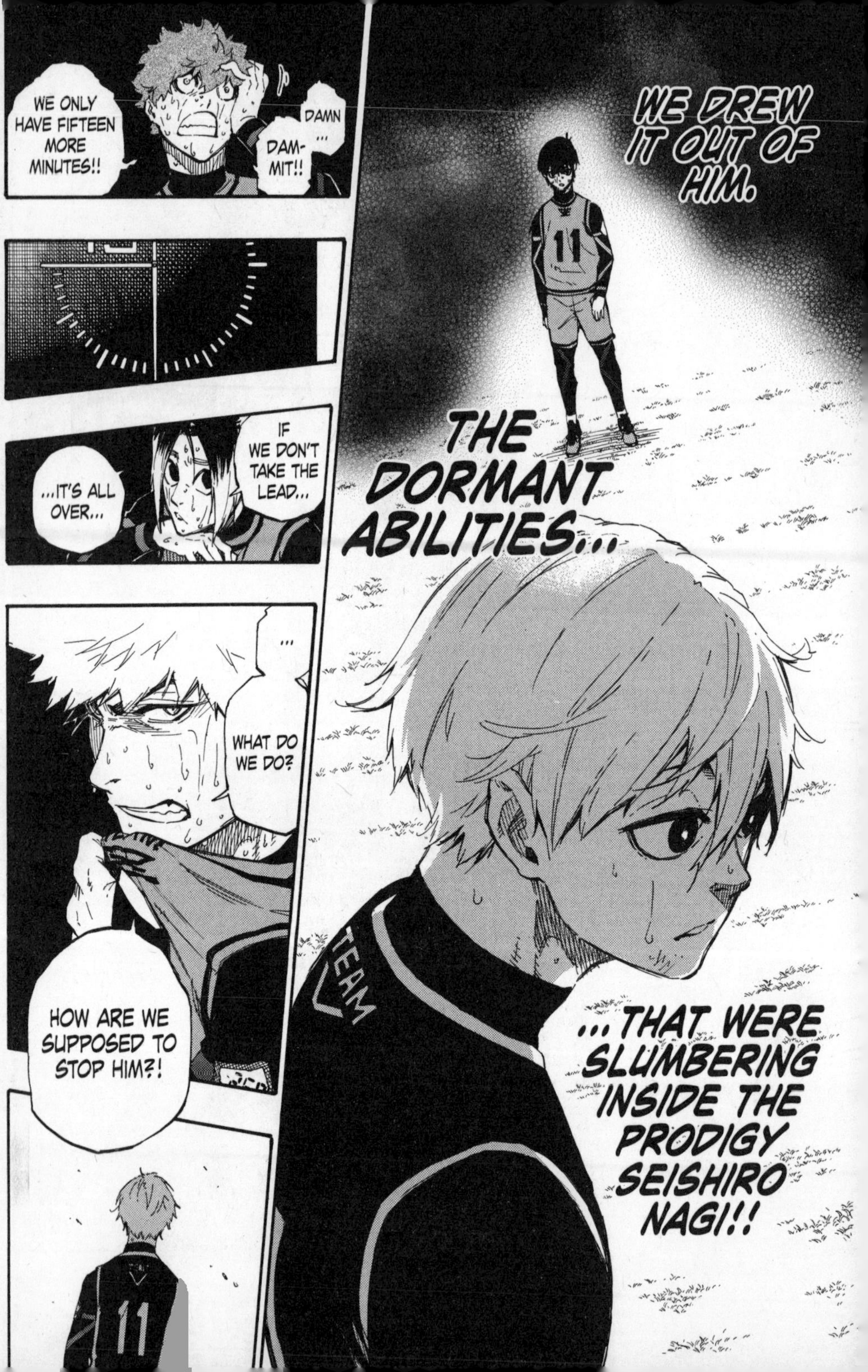
WE DREW IT OUT OF HIM.
THE DORMANT ABILITIES...
...THAT WERE SLUMBERING INSIDE THE PRODIGY SEISHIRO NAGI!!
DAMN...
DAM-MIT!!
WE ONLY HAVE FIFTEEN MORE MINUTES!!
IF WE DON'T TAKE THE LEAD...
...IT'S ALL OVER...
...
WHAT DO WE DO?
HOW ARE WE SUPPOSED TO STOP HIM?!

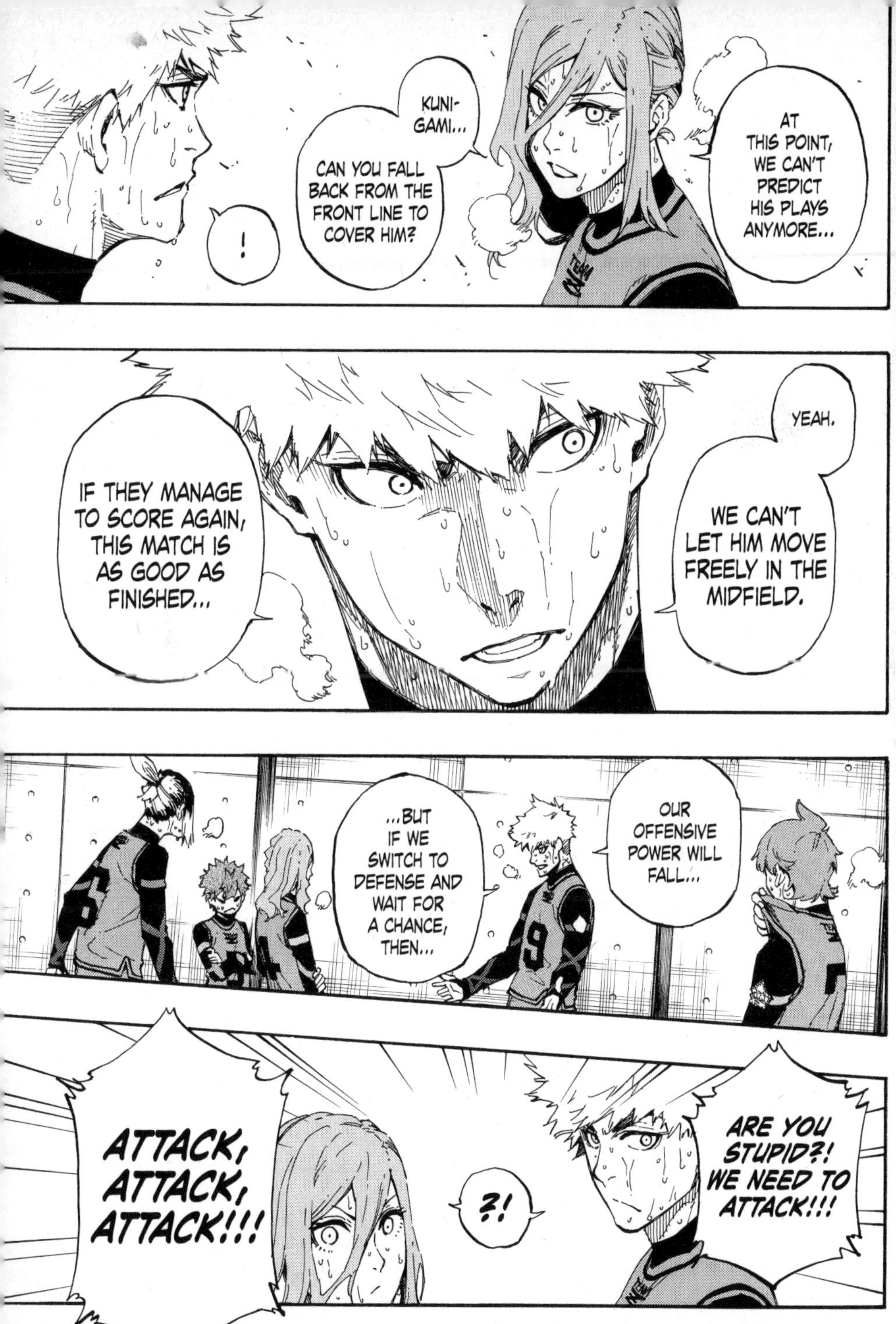
AT THIS POINT, WE CAN'T PREDICT HIS PLAYS ANYMORE...
KUNI-GAMI...
CAN YOU FALL BACK FROM THE FRONT LINE TO COVER HIM?
!
YEAH.
WE CAN'T LET HIM MOVE FREELY IN THE MIDFIELD.
IF THEY MANAGE TO SCORE AGAIN, THIS MATCH IS AS GOOD AS FINISHED...
OUR OFFENSIVE POWER WILL FALL...
...BUT IF WE SWITCH TO DEFENSE AND WAIT FOR A CHANCE, THEN...
ARE YOU STUPID?! WE NEED TO ATTACK!!!
?!
ATTACK, ATTACK, ATTACK!!!

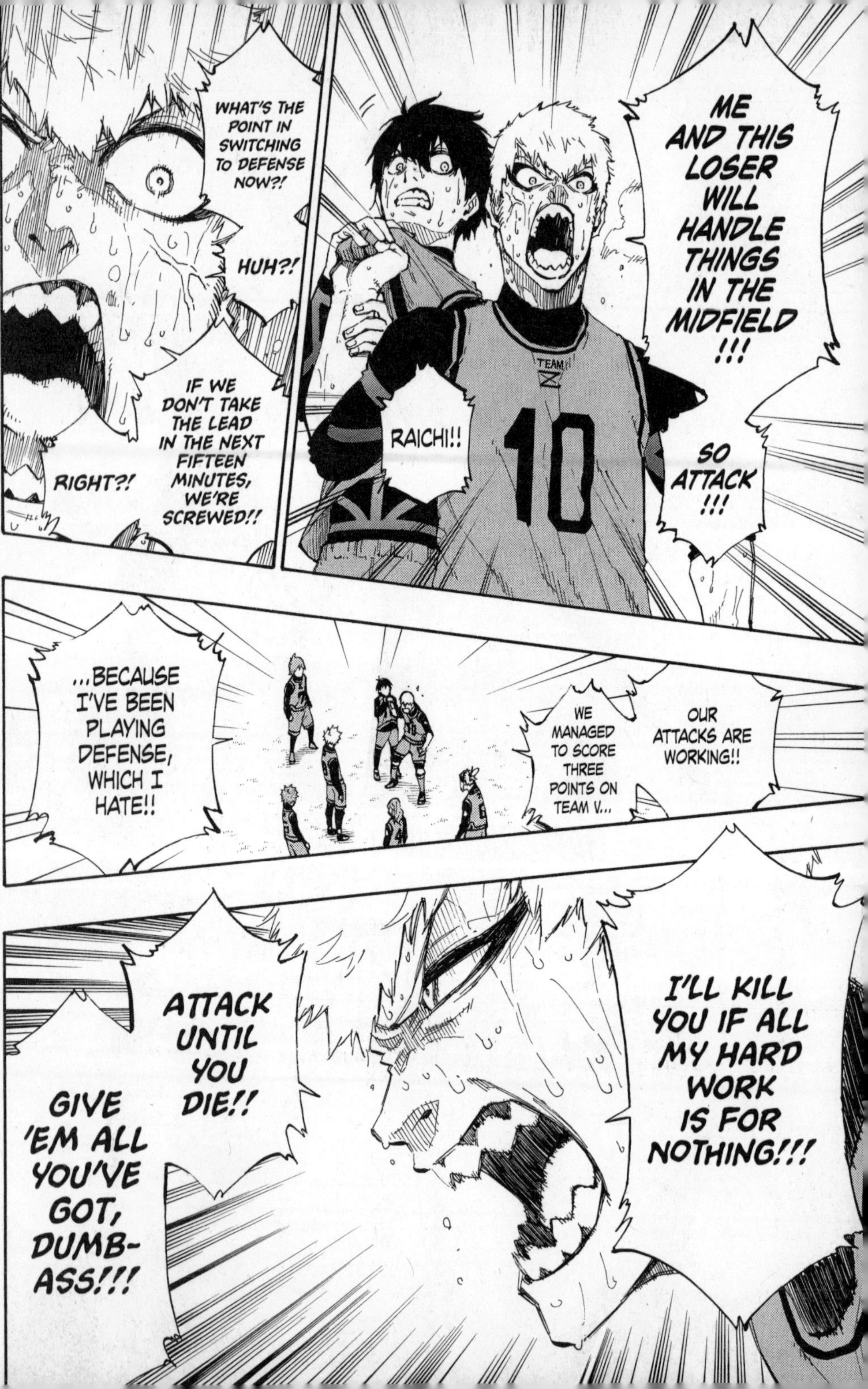
ME AND THIS LOSER WILL HANDLE THINGS IN THE MIDFIELD!!!
SO ATTACK!!!
RAICHI!!
WHAT'S THE POINT IN SWITCHING TO DEFENSE NOW?!
HUH?!
IF WE DON'T TAKE THE LEAD IN THE NEXT FIFTEEN MINUTES, WE'RE SCREWED!!
RIGHT?!
OUR ATTACKS ARE WORKING!!
WE MANAGED TO SCORE THREE POINTS ON TEAM V...
...BECAUSE I'VE BEEN PLAYING DEFENSE, WHICH I HATE!!
I'LL KILL YOU IF ALL MY HARD WORK IS FOR NOTHING!!!
ATTACK UNTIL YOU DIE!!
GIVE 'EM ALL YOU'VE GOT, DUMB-ASS!!!

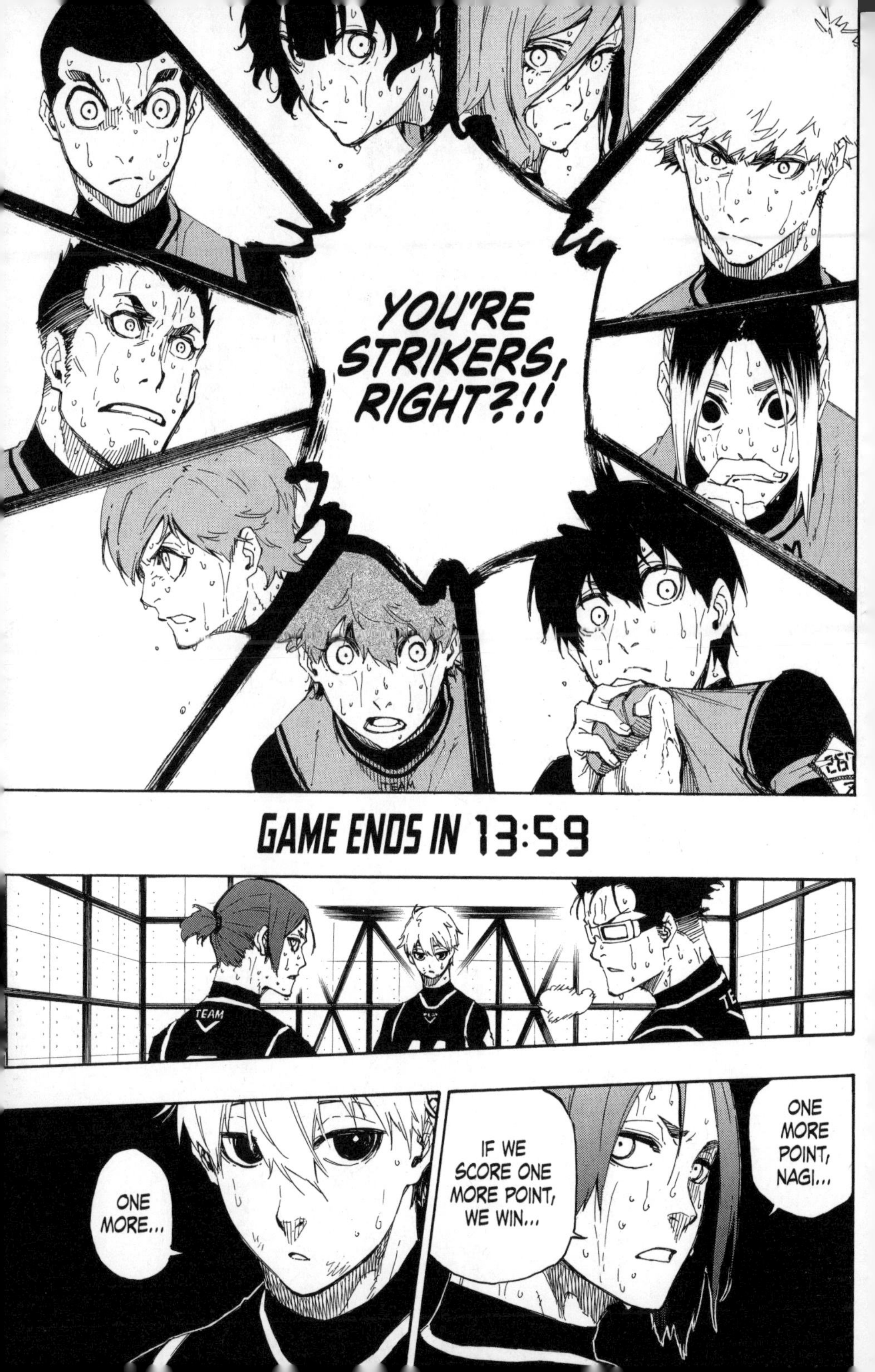
YOU'RE STRIKERS, RIGHT?!!
GAME ENDS IN 13:59
ONE MORE POINT, NAGI...
IF WE SCORE ONE MORE POINT, WE WIN...
ONE MORE...

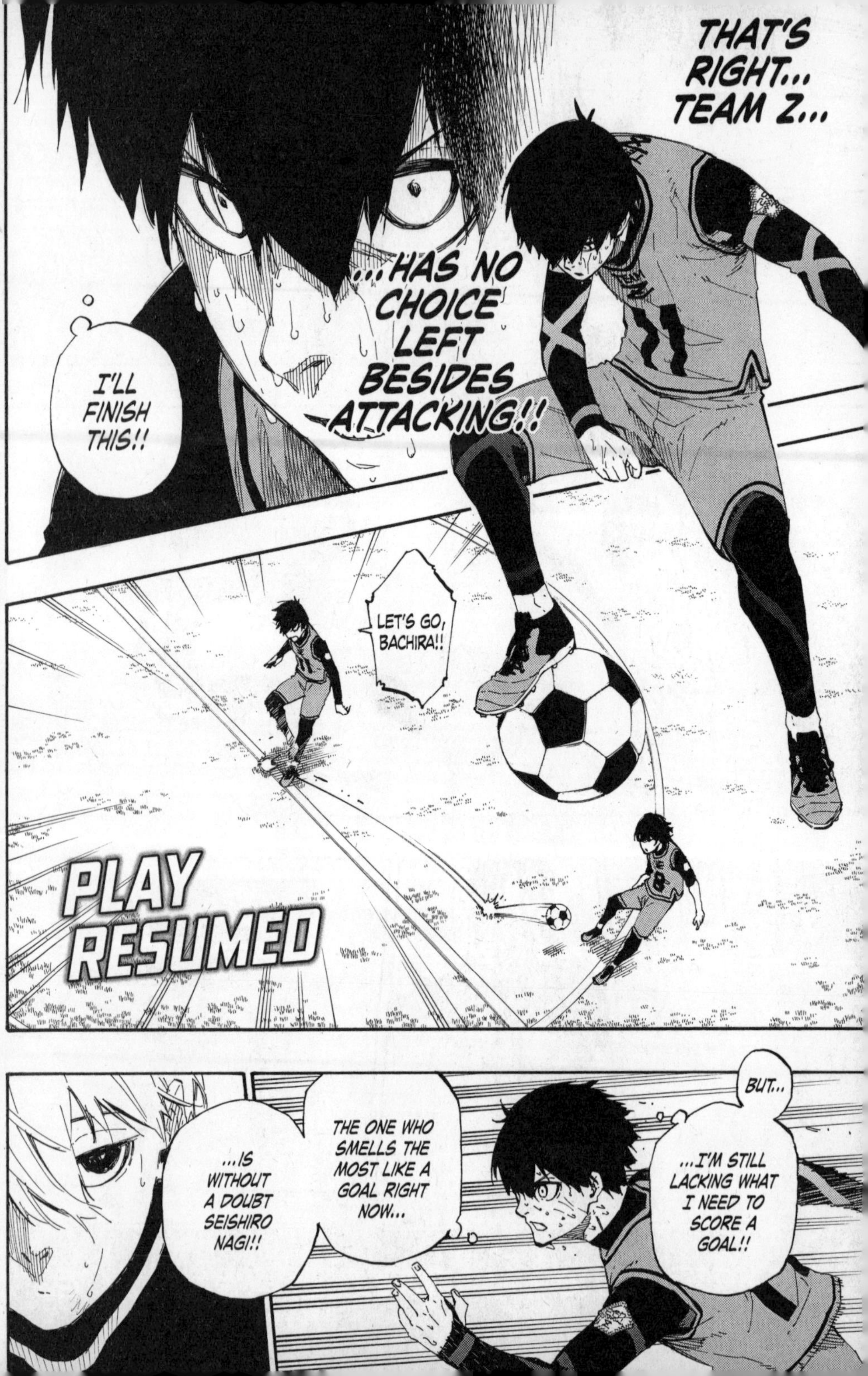
THAT'S RIGHT... TEAM Z...
...HAS NO CHOICE LEFT BESIDES ATTACKING!!
I'LL FINISH THIS!!
LET'S GO, BACHIRA!!
PLAY RESUMED
BUT...
...I'M STILL LACKING WHAT I NEED TO SCORE A GOAL!!
THE ONE WHO SMELLS THE MOST LIKE A GOAL RIGHT NOW...
...IS WITHOUT A DOUBT SEISHIRO NAGI!!

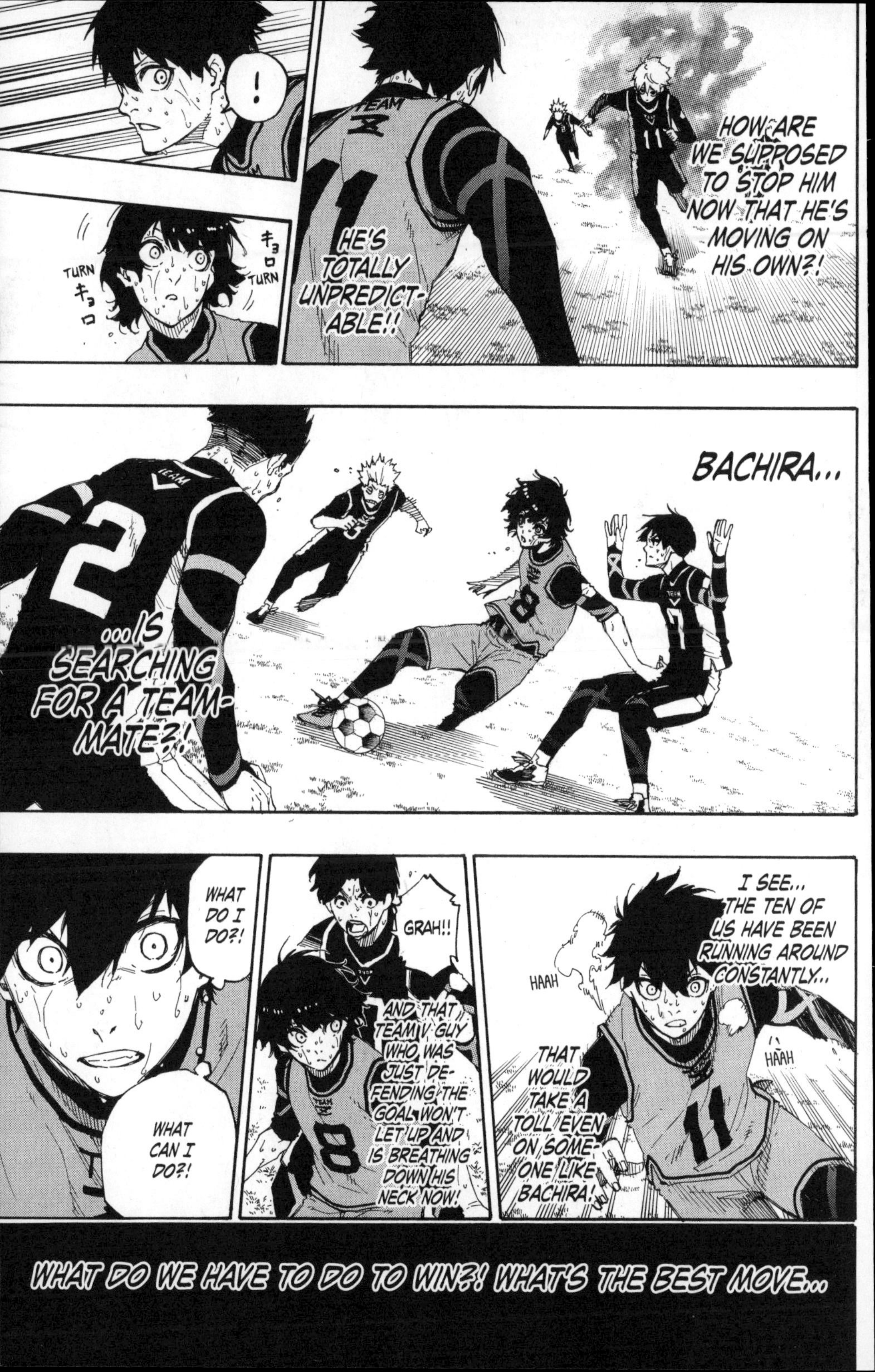
HOW ARE WE SUPPOSED TO STOP HIM NOW THAT HE'S MOVING ON HIS OWN?!
HE'S TOTALLY UNPREDICTABLE!!
!
キョロ TURN
TURN キョロ
BACHIRA...
...IS SEARCHING FOR A TEAMMATE?!
I SEE... THE TEN OF US HAVE BEEN RUNNING AROUND CONSTANTLY...
HAAH
HAAH
THAT WOULD TAKE A TOLL EVEN ON SOMEONE LIKE BACHIRA!
GRAH!!
AND THAT TEAM V GUY WHO WAS JUST DEFENDING THE GOAL WON'T LET UP AND IS BREATHING DOWN HIS NECK NOW!
WHAT DO I DO?!
WHAT CAN I DO?!
WHAT DO WE HAVE TO DO TO WIN?! WHAT'S THE BEST MOVE...

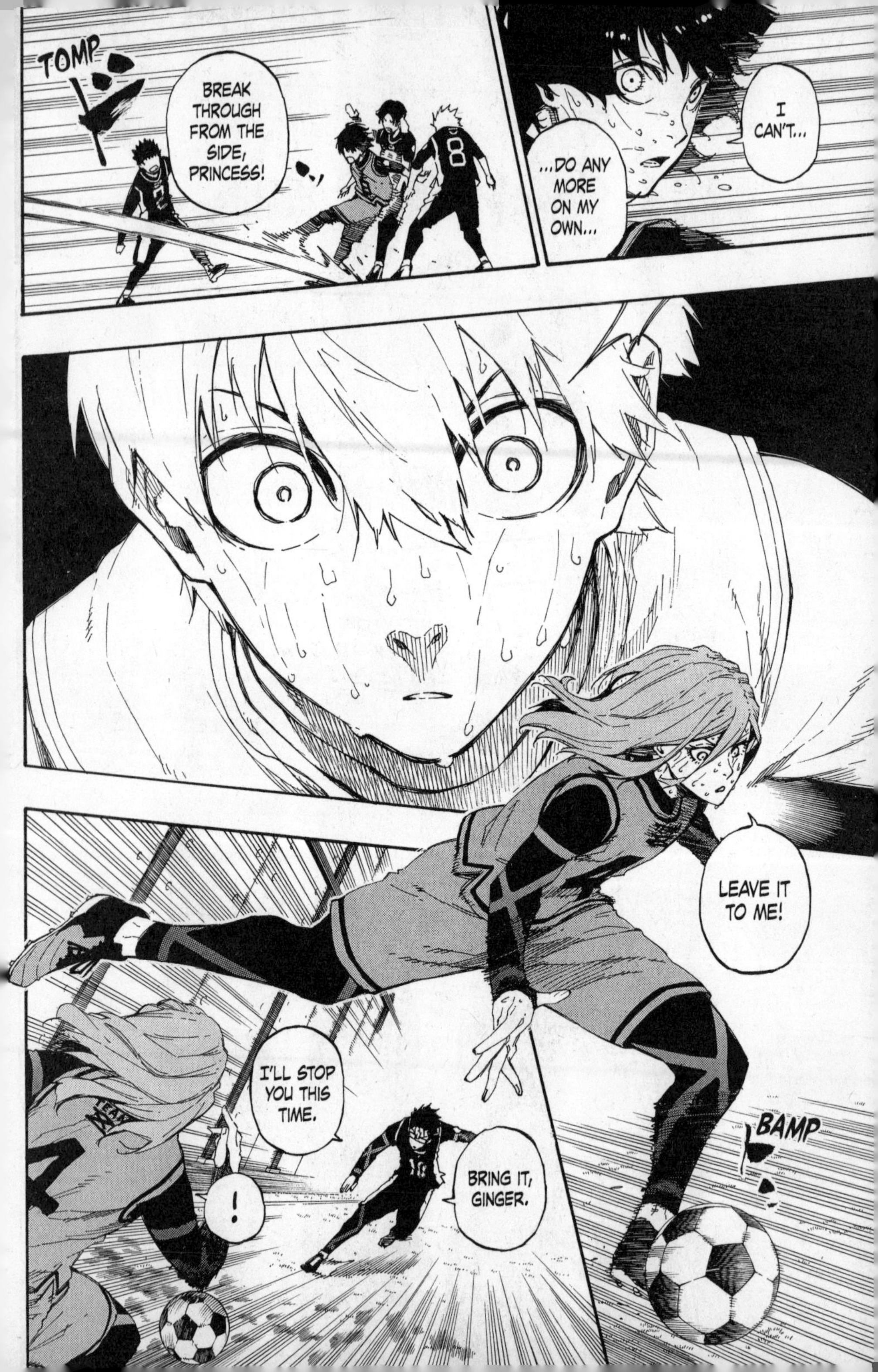
I CAN'T...
...DO ANY MORE ON MY OWN...
TOMP
BREAK THROUGH FROM THE SIDE, PRINCESS!
LEAVE IT TO ME!
BAMP
BRING IT, GINGER.
I'LL STOP YOU THIS TIME.
!

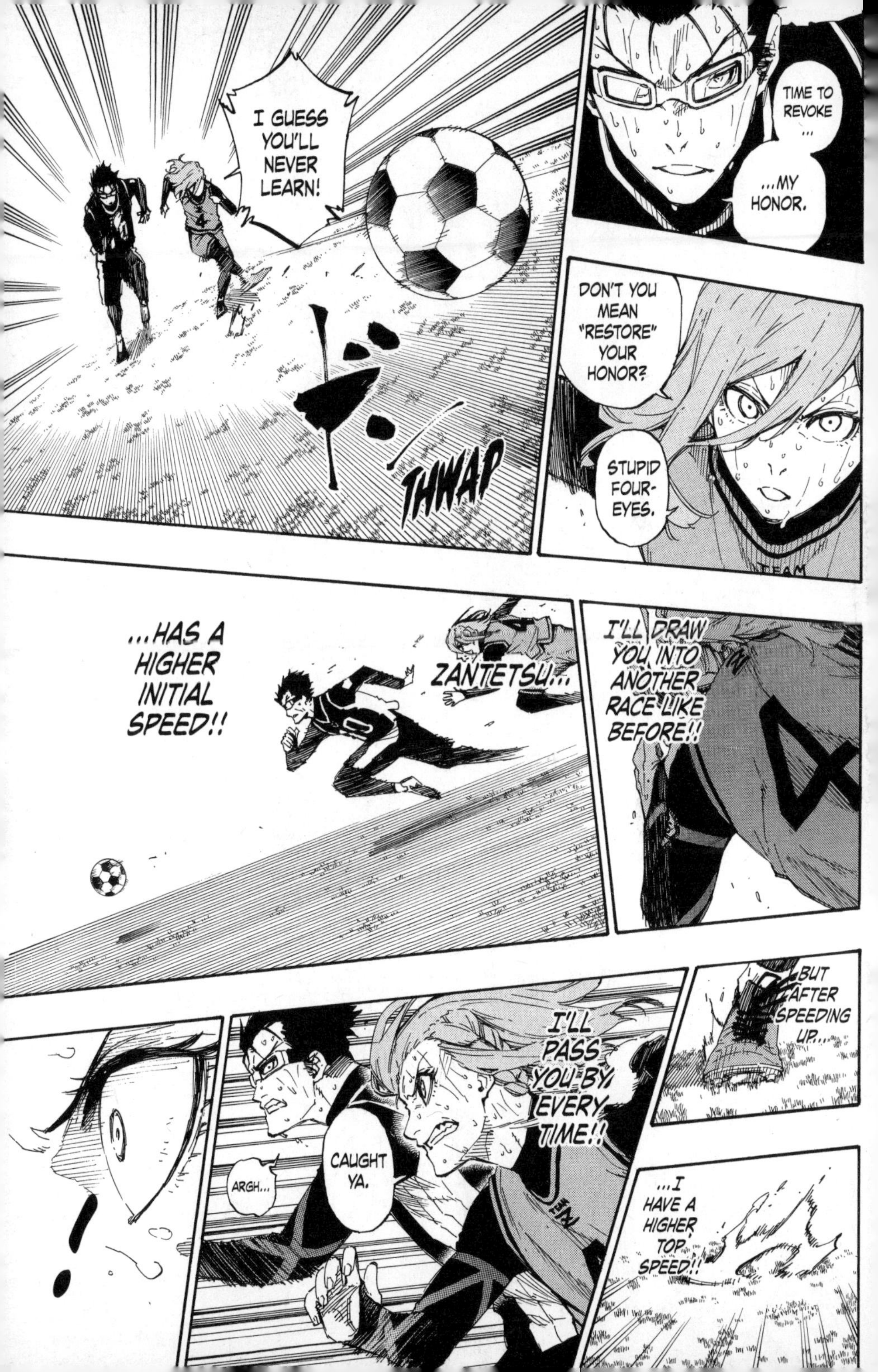
TIME TO REVOKE ...
...MY HONOR.
DON'T YOU MEAN "RESTORE" YOUR HONOR?
STUPID FOUR-EYES.
I GUESS YOU'LL NEVER LEARN!
THWAP
I'LL DRAW YOU INTO ANOTHER RACE LIKE BEFORE!!
ZANTETSU...
...HAS A HIGHER INITIAL SPEED!!
BUT AFTER SPEEDING UP...
...I HAVE A HIGHER TOP SPEED!!
I'LL PASS YOU BY EVERY TIME!!
CAUGHT YA.
ARGH...

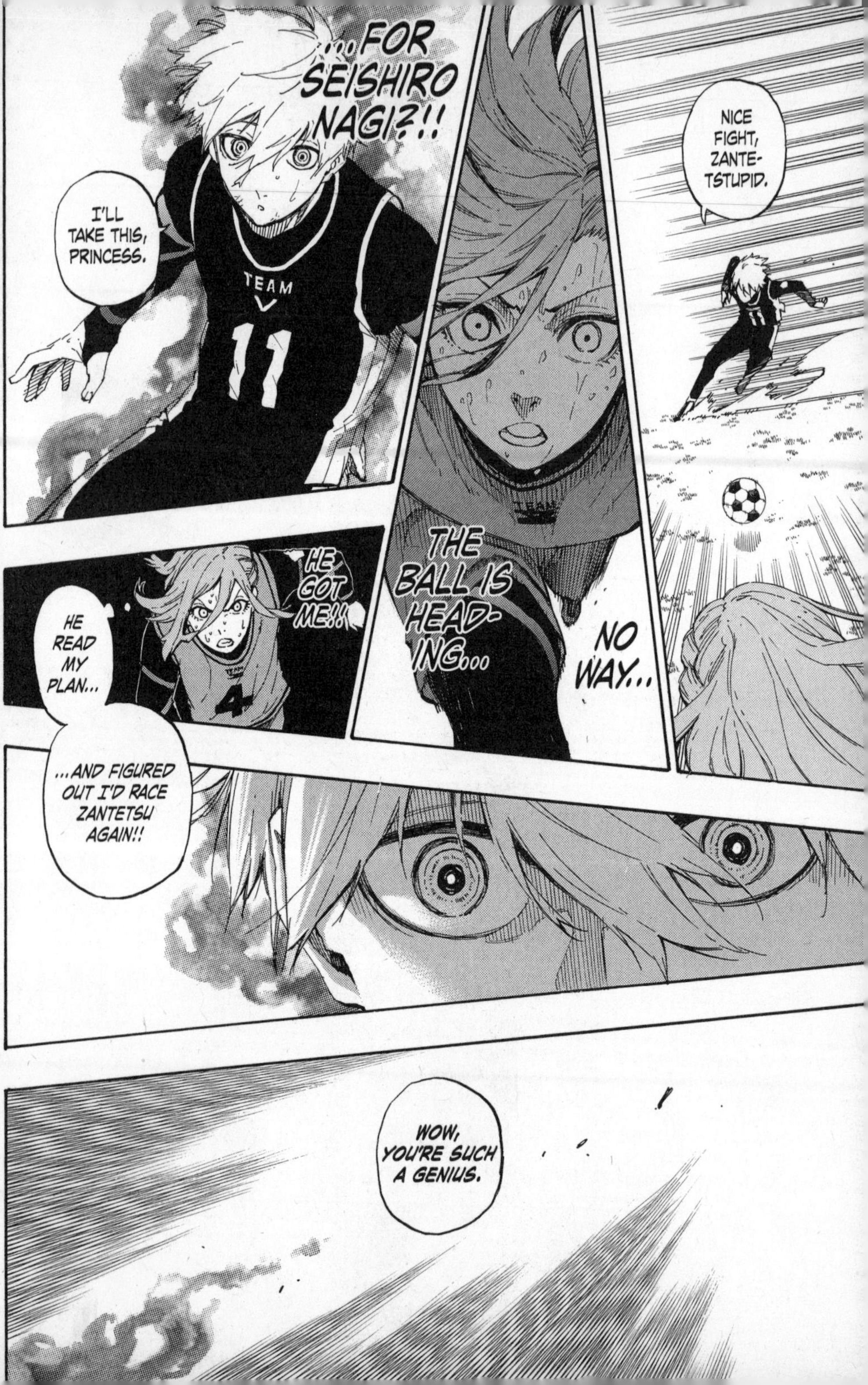
NICE FIGHT, ZANTE-TSTUPID.
THE BALL IS HEAD-ING...
NO WAY...
...FOR SEISHIRO NAGI?!!
I'LL TAKE THIS, PRINCESS.
HE GOT ME!!
HE READ MY PLAN...
...AND FIGURED OUT I'D RACE ZANTETSU AGAIN!!
WOW, YOU'RE SUCH A GENIUS.

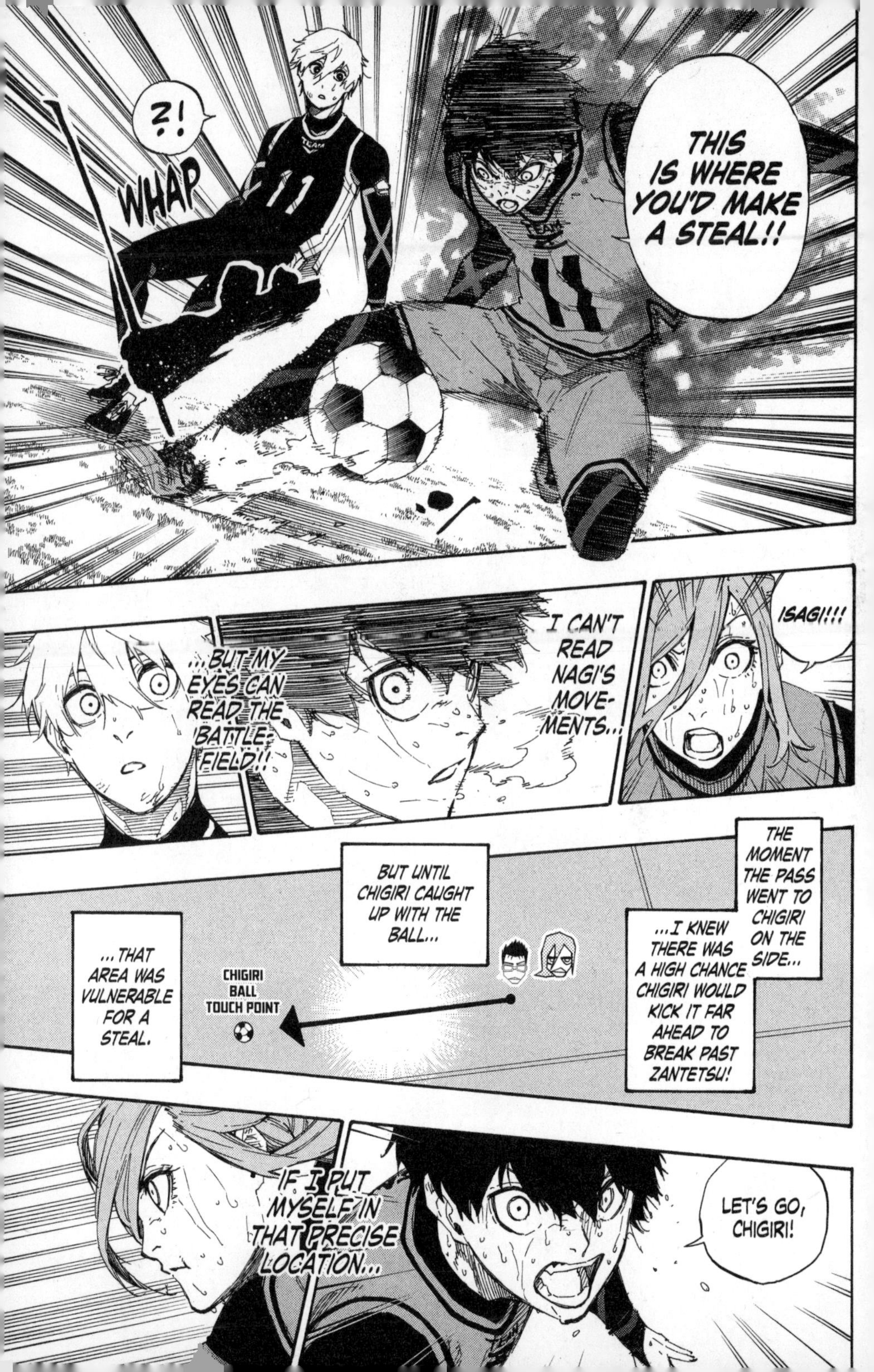
THIS IS WHERE YOU'D MAKE A STEAL!!
?!
WHAP
ISAGI!!!
I CAN'T READ NAGI'S MOVEMENTS...
...BUT MY EYES CAN READ THE BATTLEFIELD!!
THE MOMENT THE PASS WENT TO CHIGIRI ON THE SIDE...
...I KNEW THERE WAS A HIGH CHANCE CHIGIRI WOULD KICK IT FAR AHEAD TO BREAK PAST ZANTETSU!
BUT UNTIL CHIGIRI CAUGHT UP WITH THE BALL...
CHIGIRI BALL TOUCH POINT
...THAT AREA WAS VULNERABLE FOR A STEAL.
LET'S GO, CHIGIRI!
IF I PUT MYSELF IN THAT PRECISE LOCATION...

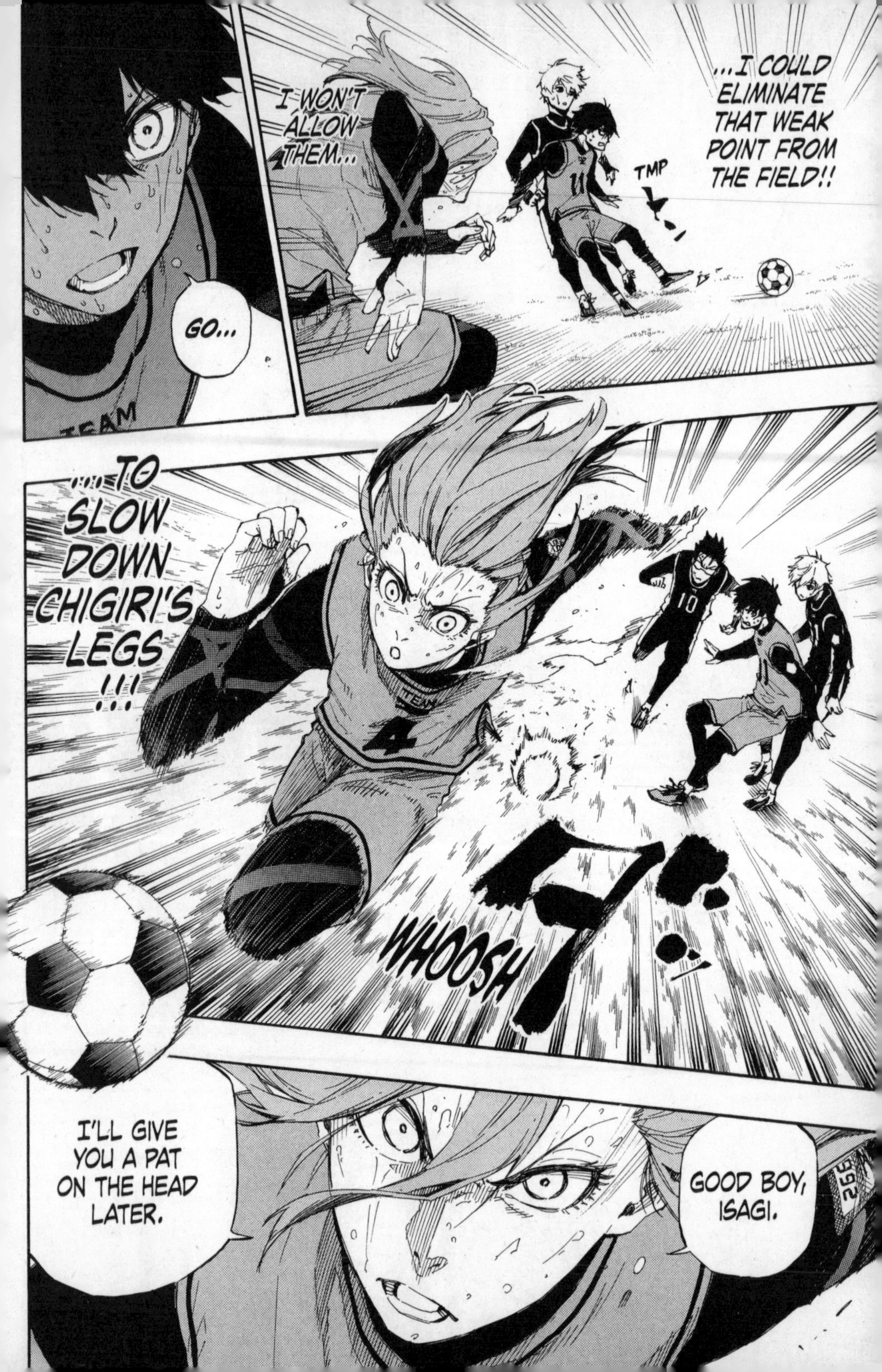
...I COULD ELIMINATE THAT WEAK POINT FROM THE FIELD!!
TMP
I WON'T ALLOW THEM...
GO...
TEAM
...TO SLOW DOWN CHIGIRI'S LEGS !!!
TEAM
WHOOSH
GOOD BOY, ISAGI.
I'LL GIVE YOU A PAT ON THE HEAD LATER.

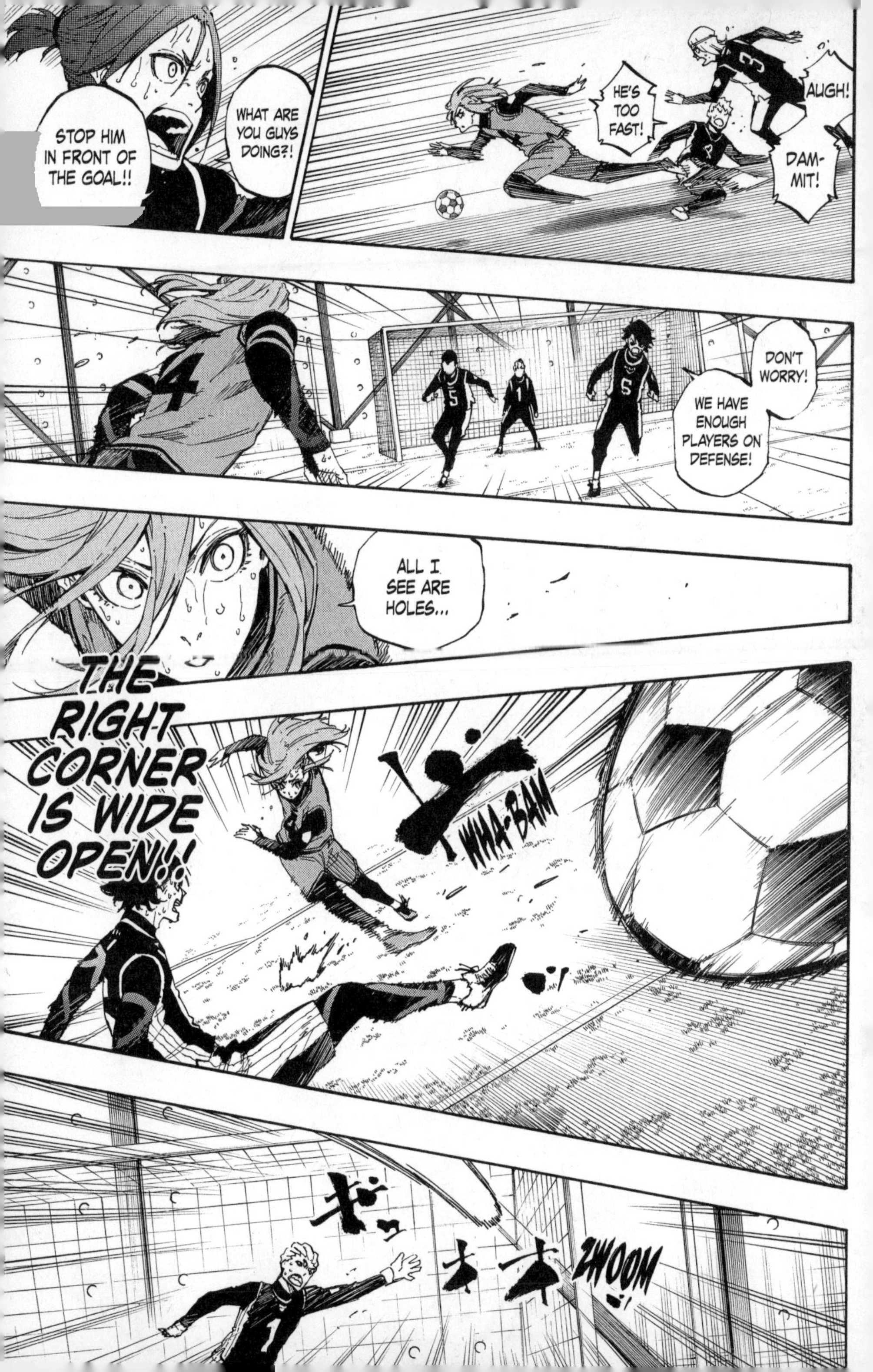
AUGH!
HE'S TOO FAST!
DAM-MIT!
WHAT ARE YOU GUYS DOING?!
STOP HIM IN FRONT OF THE GOAL!!
DON'T WORRY!
WE HAVE ENOUGH PLAYERS ON DEFENSE!
ALL I SEE ARE HOLES...
WHA-BAM
THE RIGHT CORNER IS WIDE OPEN!!
ZWOOM

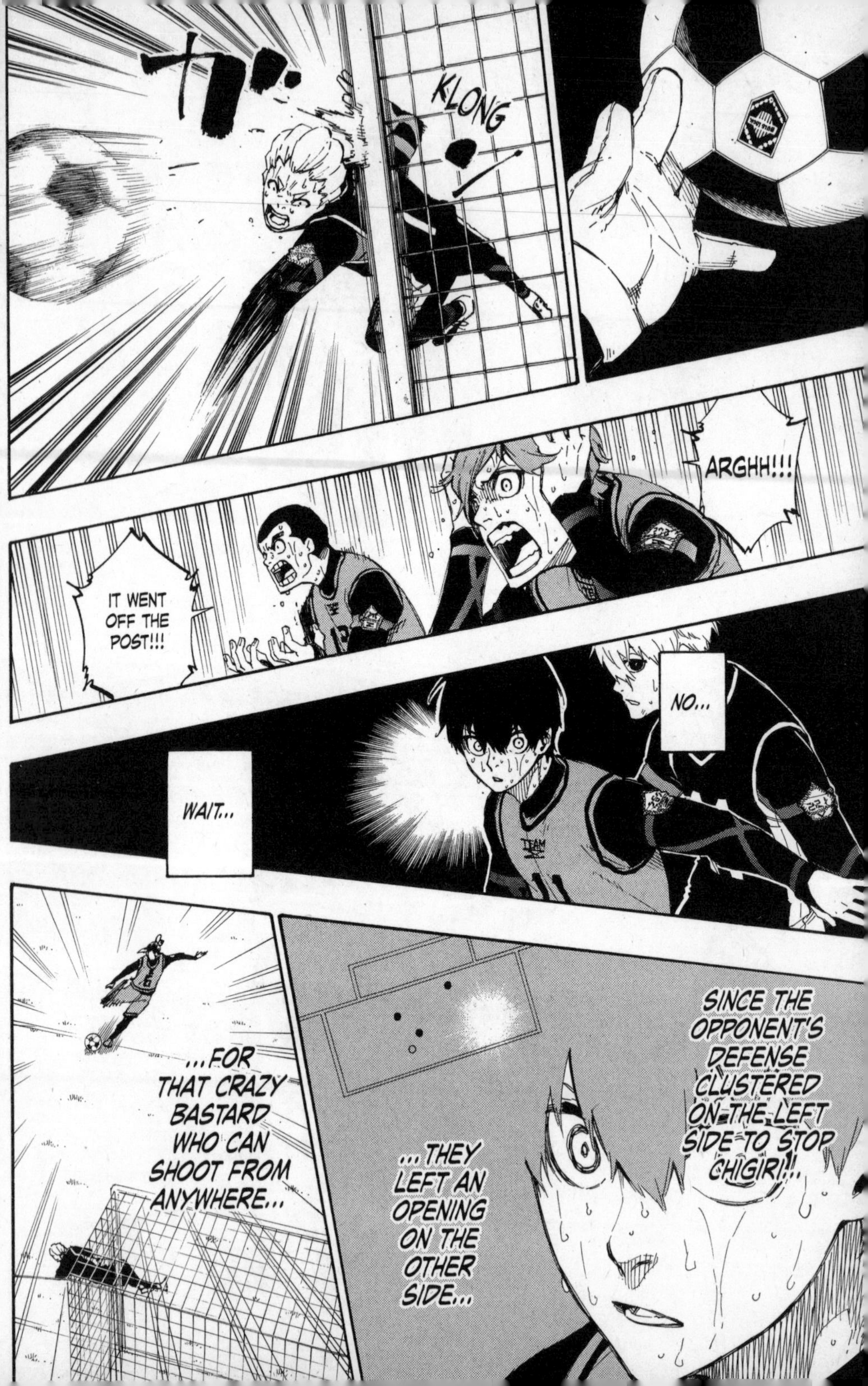
KLONG
ARGHH!!!
IT WENT OFF THE POST!!!
NO...
WAIT...
SINCE THE OPPONENT'S DEFENSE CLUSTERED ON THE LEFT SIDE TO STOP CHIGIRI!!...
...THEY LEFT AN OPENING ON THE OTHER SIDE...
...FOR THAT CRAZY BASTARD WHO CAN SHOOT FROM ANYWHERE...

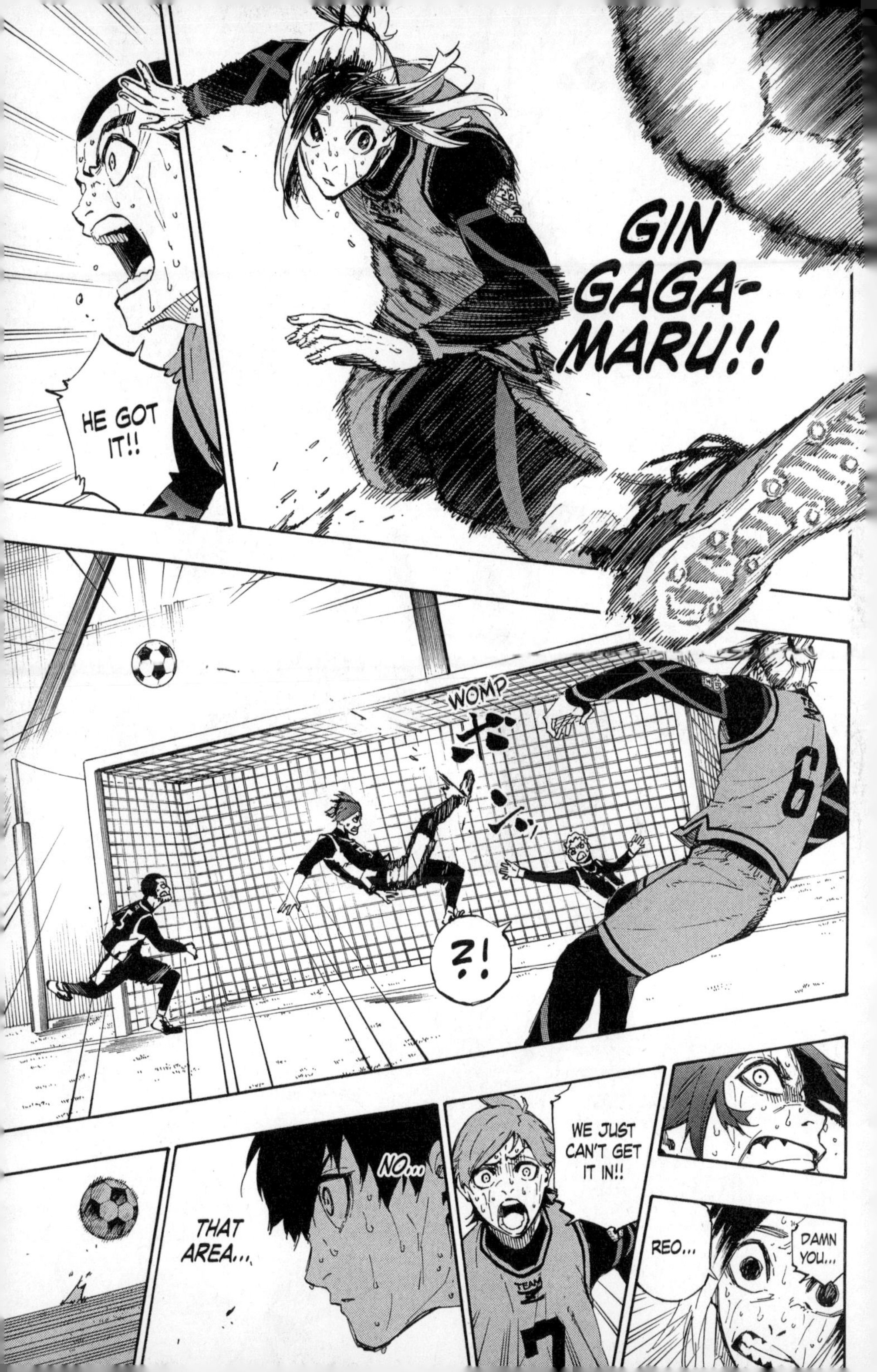
GIN GAGA-MARU!!
HE GOT IT!!
WOMP
?!
DAMN YOU...
REO...
WE JUST CAN'T GET IT IN!!
NO...
THAT AREA...

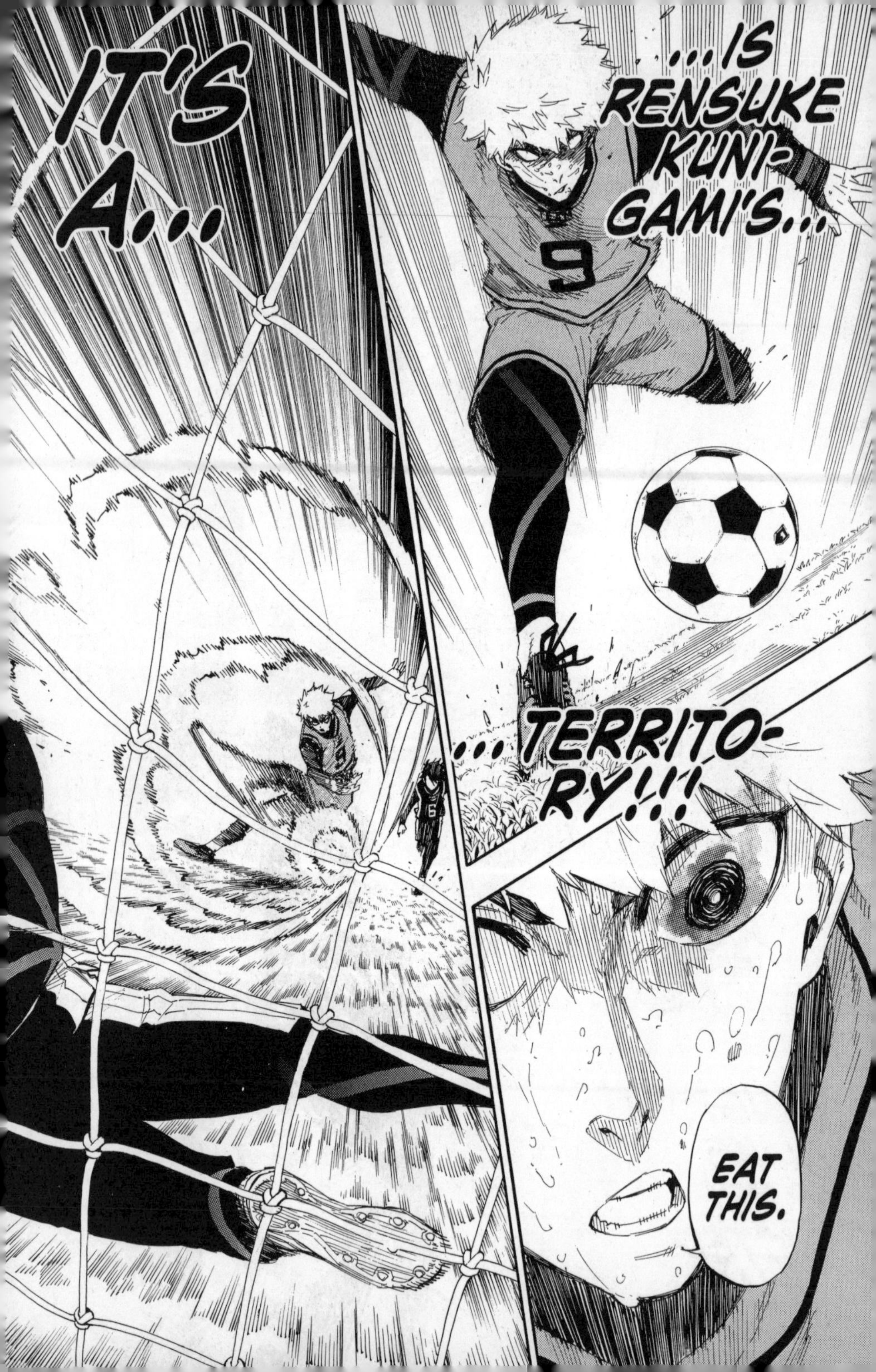
...IS RENSUKE KUNI-GAMI'S...
...TERRITO-RY!!!
EAT THIS.
IT'S A...

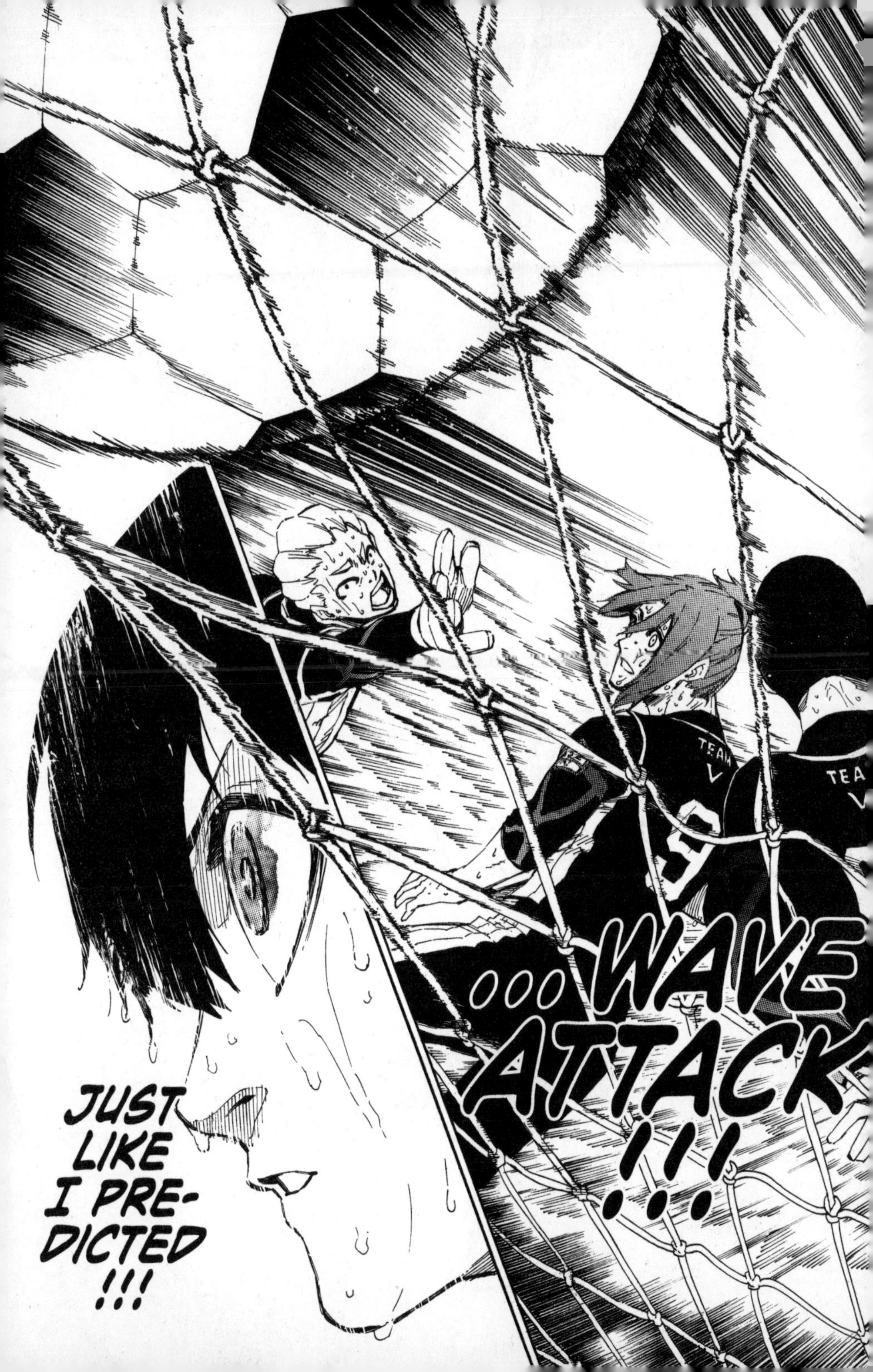
...WAVE ATTACK!!!
JUST LIKE I PRE-DICTED!!!

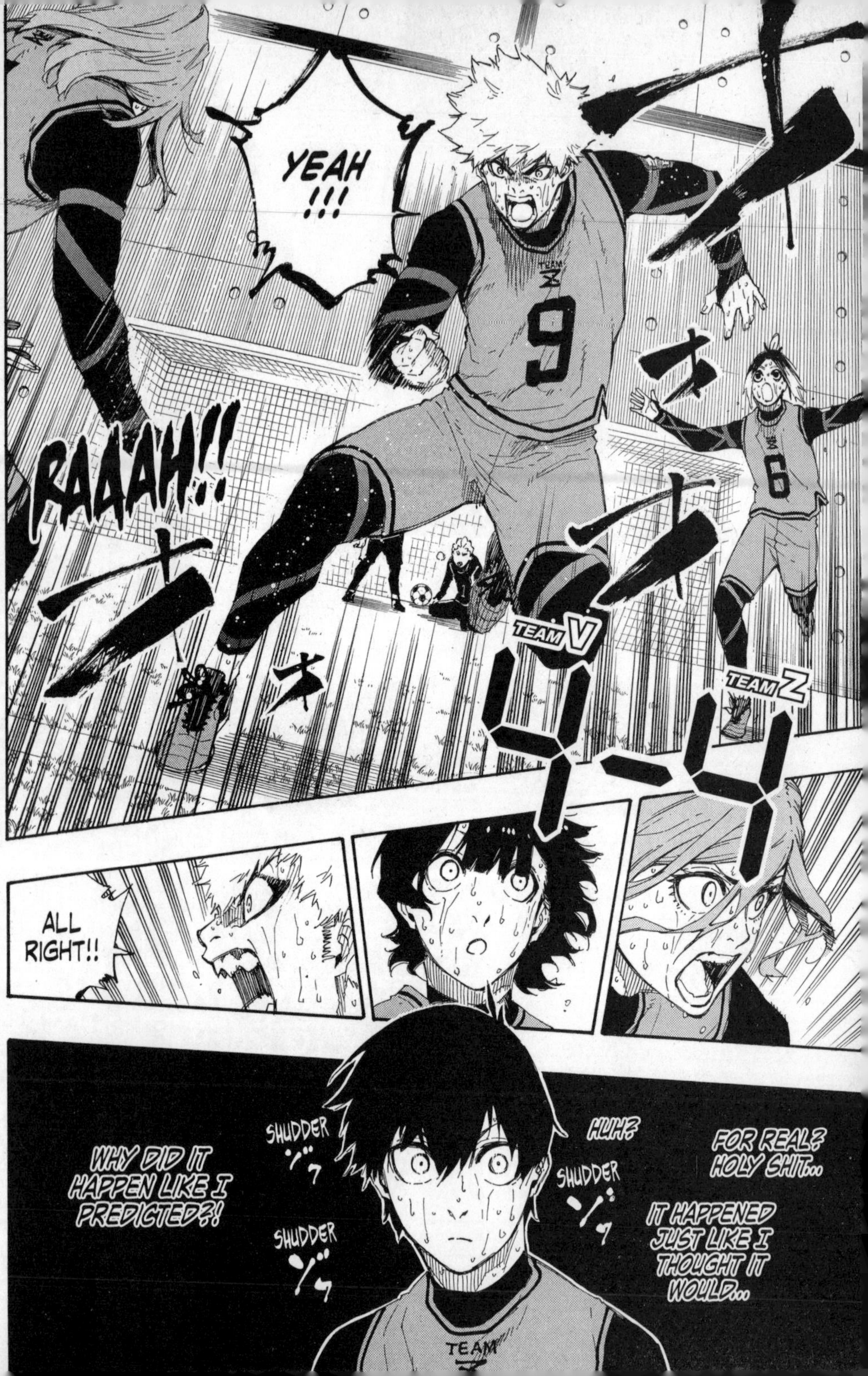
YEAH!!!
RAAAH!!
TEAM V
4-4
TEAM Z
ALL RIGHT!!
FOR REAL? HOLY SHIT...
IT HAPPENED JUST LIKE I THOUGHT IT WOULD...
HUH?
SHUDDER
SHUDDER
SHUDDER
WHY DID IT HAPPEN LIKE I PREDICTED?!

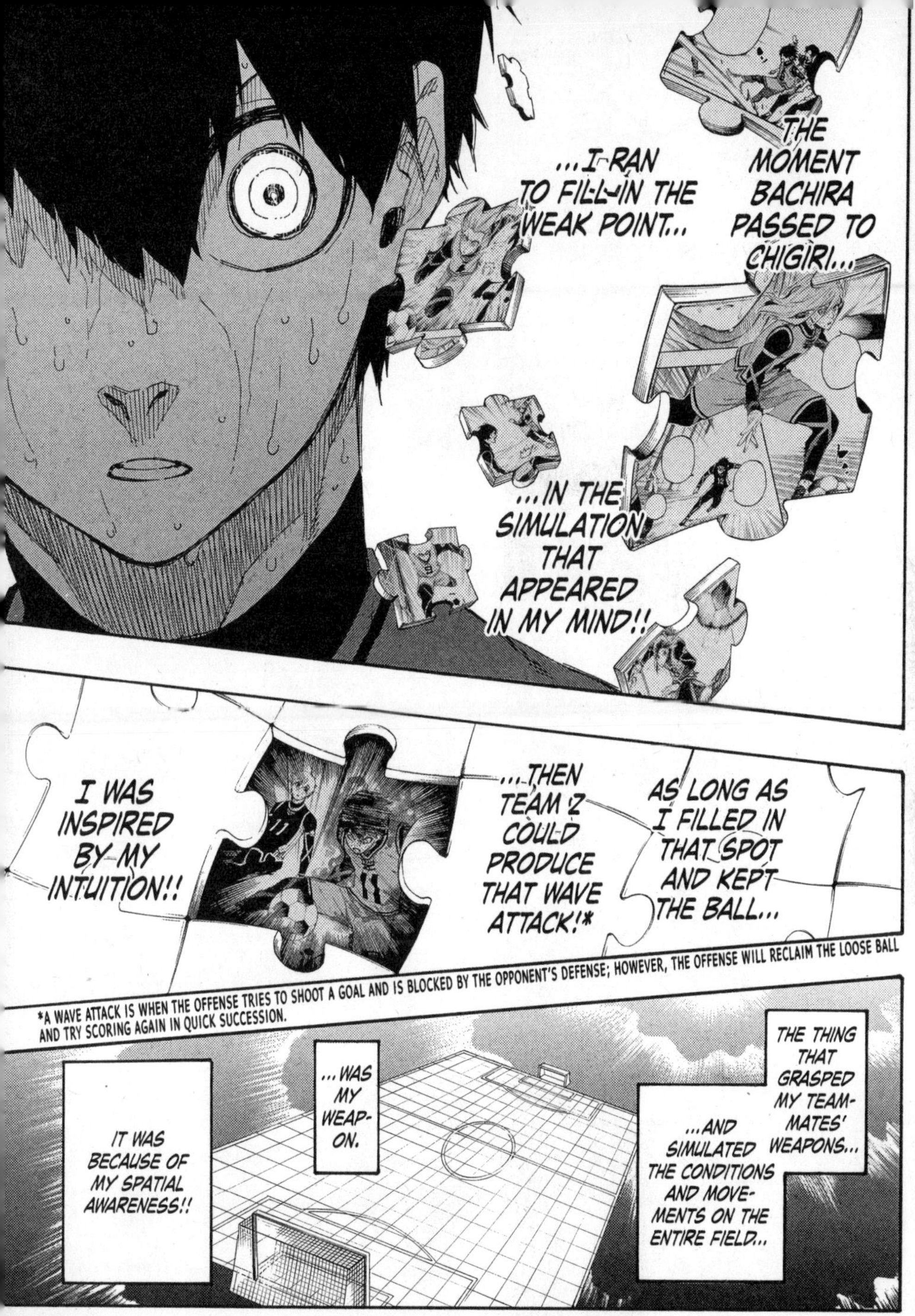
THE MOMENT BACHIRA PASSED TO CHIGIRI...
...I RAN TO FILL-IN THE WEAK POINT...
...IN THE SIMULATION THAT APPEARED IN MY MIND!!
AS LONG AS I FILLED IN THAT SPOT AND KEPT THE BALL...
...THEN TEAM Z COULD PRODUCE THAT WAVE ATTACK!*
I WAS INSPIRED BY MY INTUITION!!
*A WAVE ATTACK IS WHEN THE OFFENSE TRIES TO SHOOT A GOAL AND IS BLOCKED BY THE OPPONENT'S DEFENSE; HOWEVER, THE OFFENSE WILL RECLAIM THE LOOSE BALL AND TRY SCORING AGAIN IN QUICK SUCCESSION.
THE THING THAT GRASPED MY TEAMMATES' WEAPONS...
...AND SIMULATED THE CONDITIONS AND MOVEMENTS ON THE ENTIRE FIELD...
...WAS MY WEAPON.
IT WAS BECAUSE OF MY SPATIAL AWARENESS!!

THAT'S IT... I JUST NEED TO USE IT LIKE THAT...!

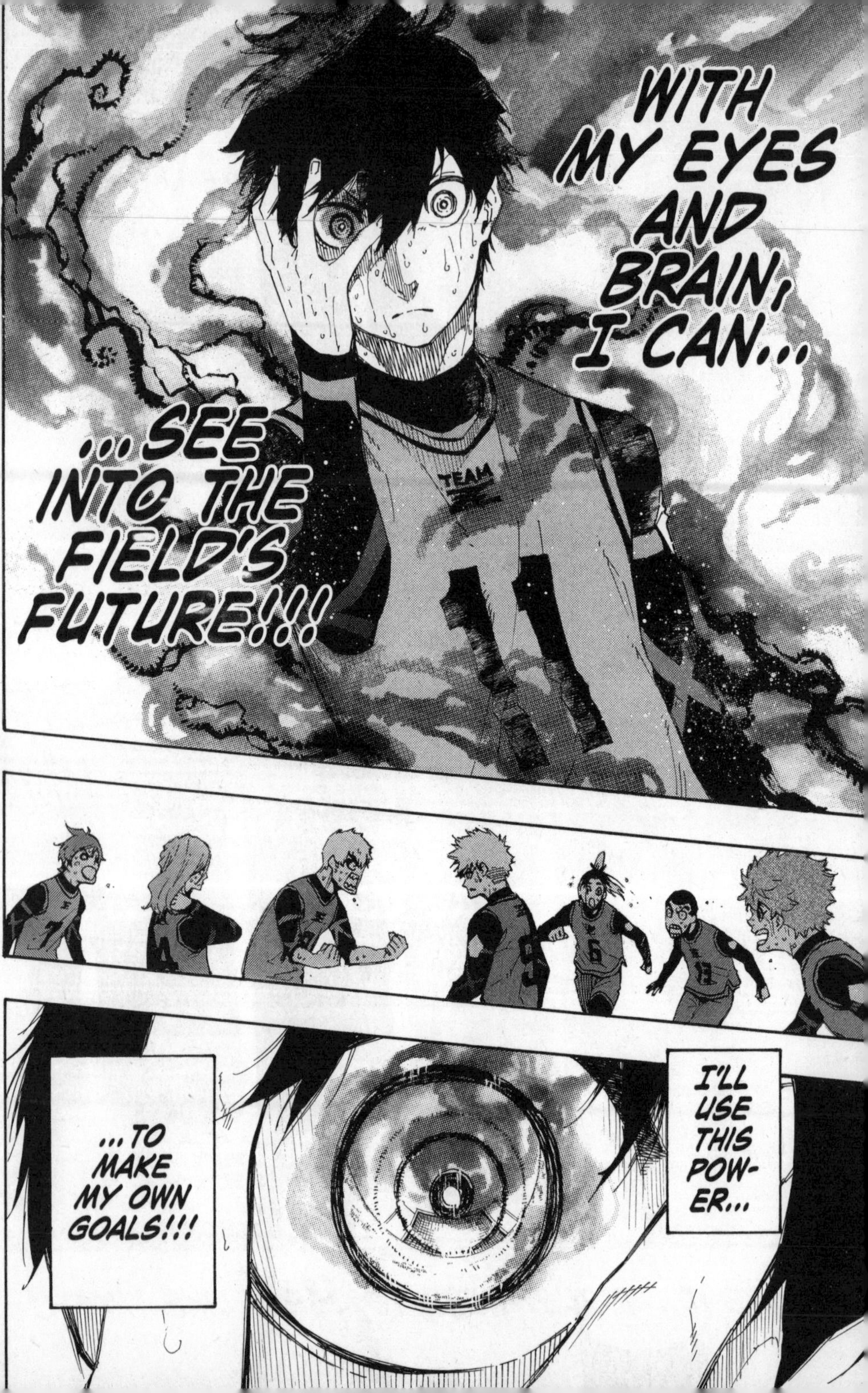
WITH MY EYES AND BRAIN, I CAN...
...SEE INTO THE FIELD'S FUTURE!!!
I'LL USE THIS POW-ER...
...TO MAKE MY OWN GOALS!!!

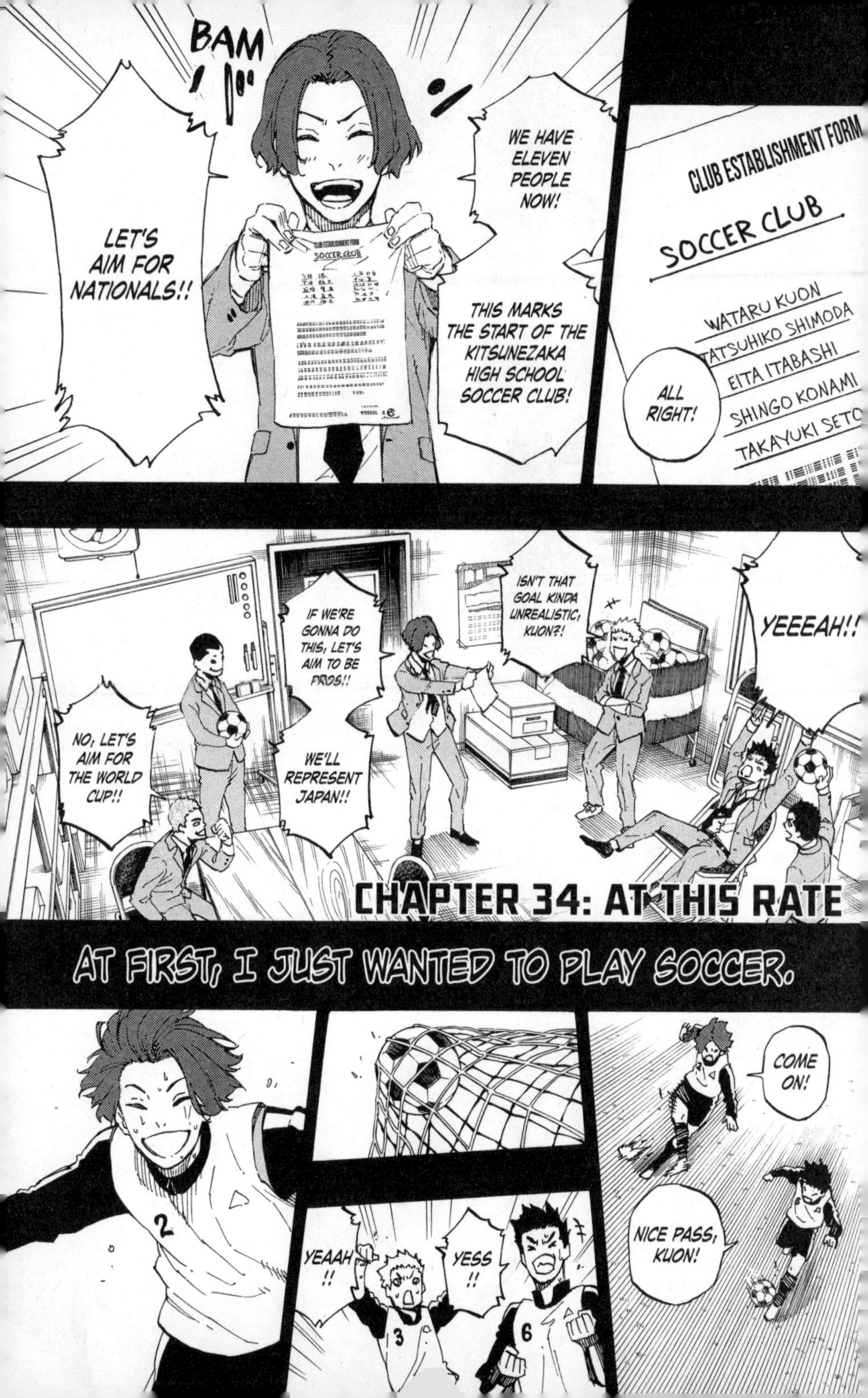
CLUB ESTABLISHMENT FORM
SOCCER CLUB
WATARU KUON
TATSUHIKO SHIMODA
EITA ITABASHI
SHINGO KONAMI
TAKAYUKI SETO
ALL RIGHT!
BAM
WE HAVE ELEVEN PEOPLE NOW!
LET'S AIM FOR NATIONALS!!
THIS MARKS THE START OF THE KITSUNEZAKA HIGH SCHOOL SOCCER CLUB!
YEEEAH!!
ISN'T THAT GOAL KINDA UNREALISTIC, KUON?!
IF WE'RE GONNA DO THIS, LET'S AIM TO BE PROS!!
WE'LL REPRESENT JAPAN!!
NO, LET'S AIM FOR THE WORLD CUP!!
CHAPTER 34: AT THIS RATE
AT FIRST, I JUST WANTED TO PLAY SOCCER.
COME ON!
NICE PASS, KUON!
YESS!!
YEAAH!!

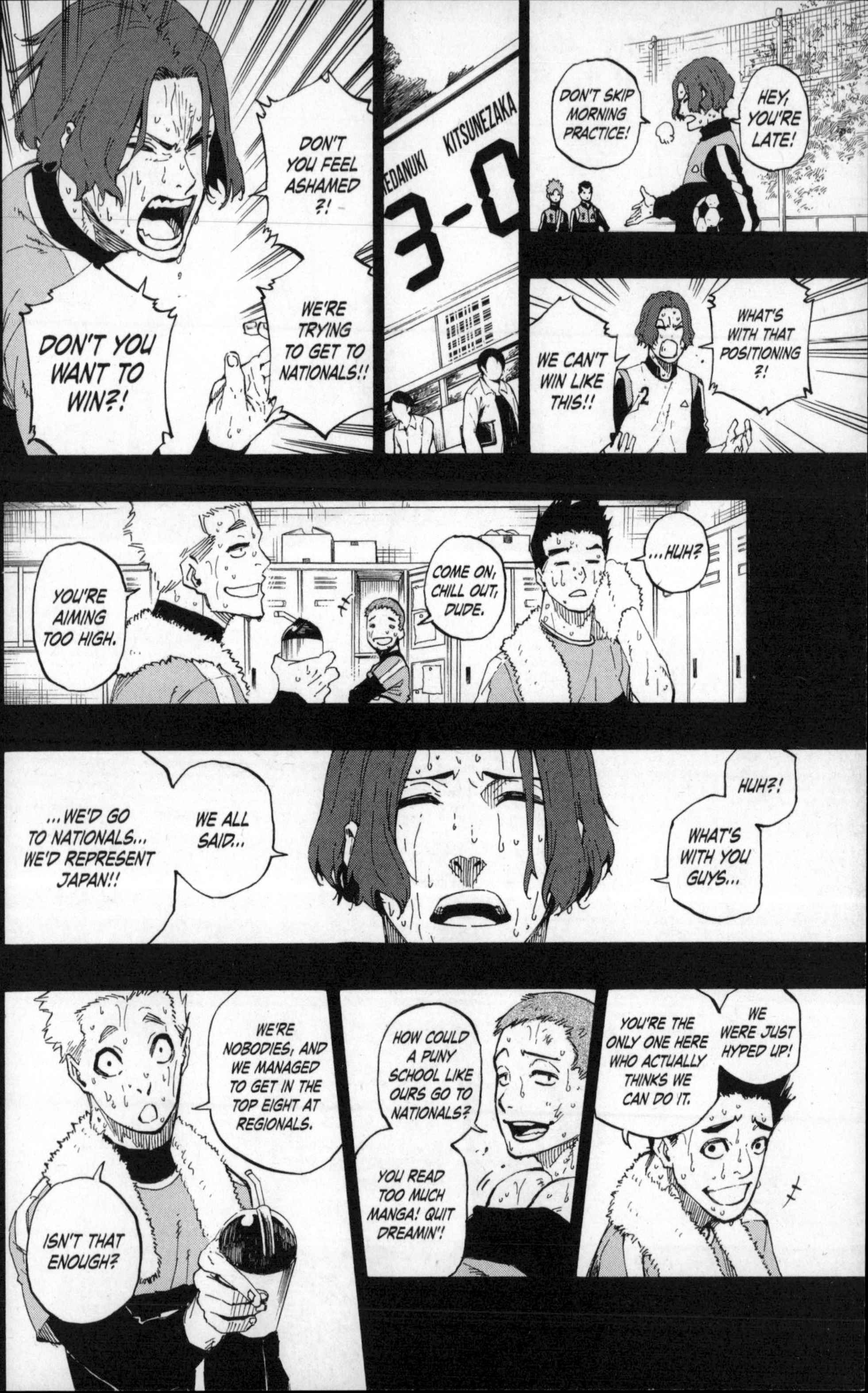
HEY, YOU'RE LATE!
DON'T SKIP MORNING PRACTICE!
WHAT'S WITH THAT POSITIONING?!
WE CAN'T WIN LIKE THIS!!
KITSUNEZAKA
EDANUKI
3-0
DON'T YOU FEEL ASHAMED?!
WE'RE TRYING TO GET TO NATIONALS!!
DON'T YOU WANT TO WIN?!
...HUH?
COME ON, CHILL OUT, DUDE.
YOU'RE AIMING TOO HIGH.
HUH?!
WHAT'S WITH YOU GUYS...
WE ALL SAID...
...WE'D GO TO NATIONALS... WE'D REPRESENT JAPAN!!
WE WERE JUST HYPED UP!
YOU'RE THE ONLY ONE HERE WHO ACTUALLY THINKS WE CAN DO IT.
HOW COULD A PUNY SCHOOL LIKE OURS GO TO NATIONALS?
YOU READ TOO MUCH MANGA! QUIT DREAMIN'!
WE'RE NOBODIES, AND WE MANAGED TO GET IN THE TOP EIGHT AT REGIONALS.
ISN'T THAT ENOUGH?

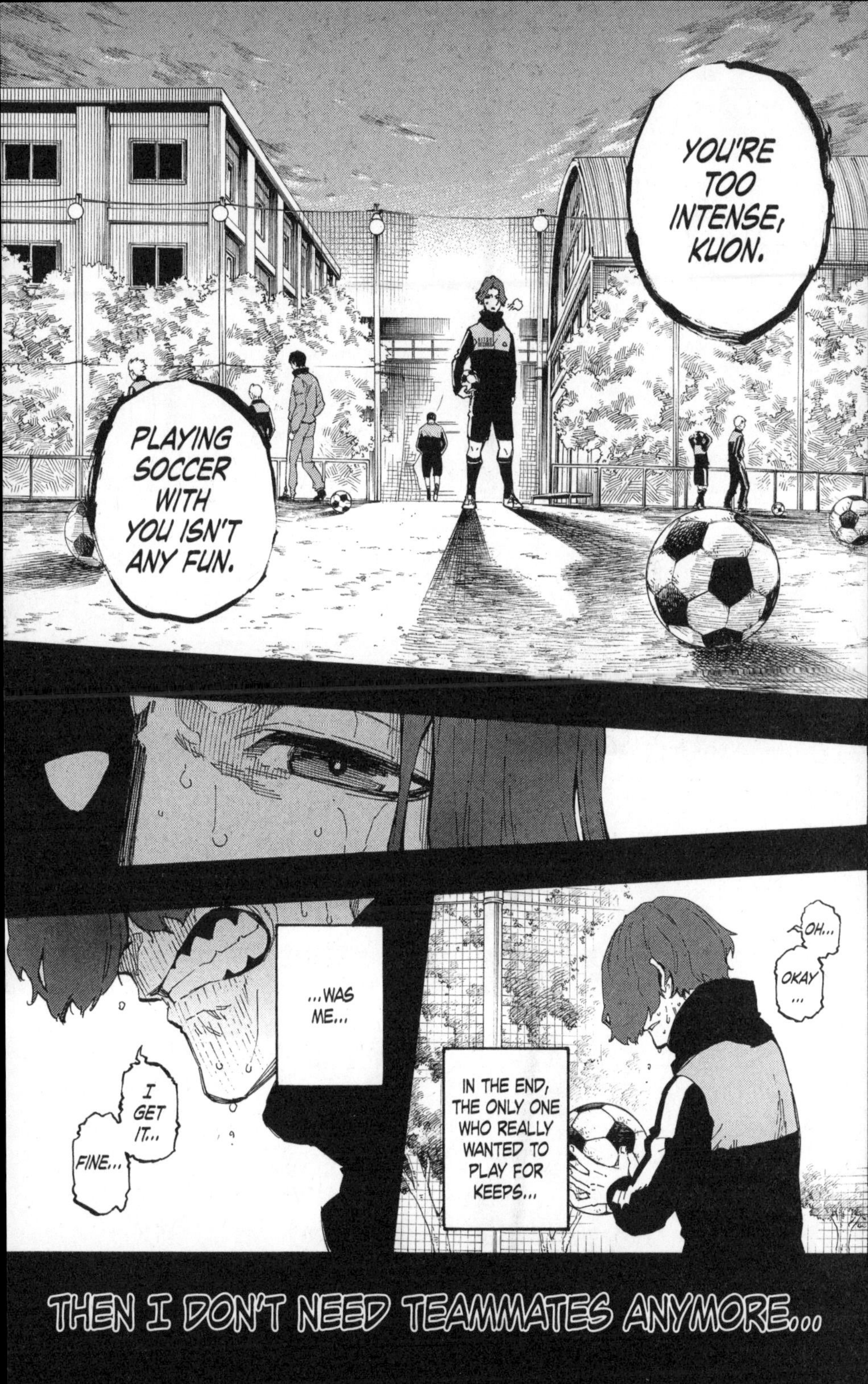
YOU'RE TOO INTENSE, KUON.
PLAYING SOCCER WITH YOU ISN'T ANY FUN.
OH...
OKAY...
IN THE END, THE ONLY ONE WHO REALLY WANTED TO PLAY FOR KEEPS...
...WAS ME...
I GET IT...
FINE...
THEN I DON'T NEED TEAMMATES ANYMORE...

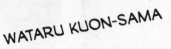

WATARU KUON-SAMA

YOU'VE BEEN SELECTED FOR A SPECIAL PLAYER TRAINING PROGRAM

THERE'S SOMEONE WHO ACKNOWLEDGES MY TALENT.

THIS IS WHERE I NEED TO FIGHT...

I'M NOT THE MEDIOCRE TYPE WHO LETS THEIR DREAMS STAY DREAMS!!

EVEN IF I END UP ON MY OWN... NO MATTER WHAT METHODS I USE...

...I'LL PLAY TO WIN!!!

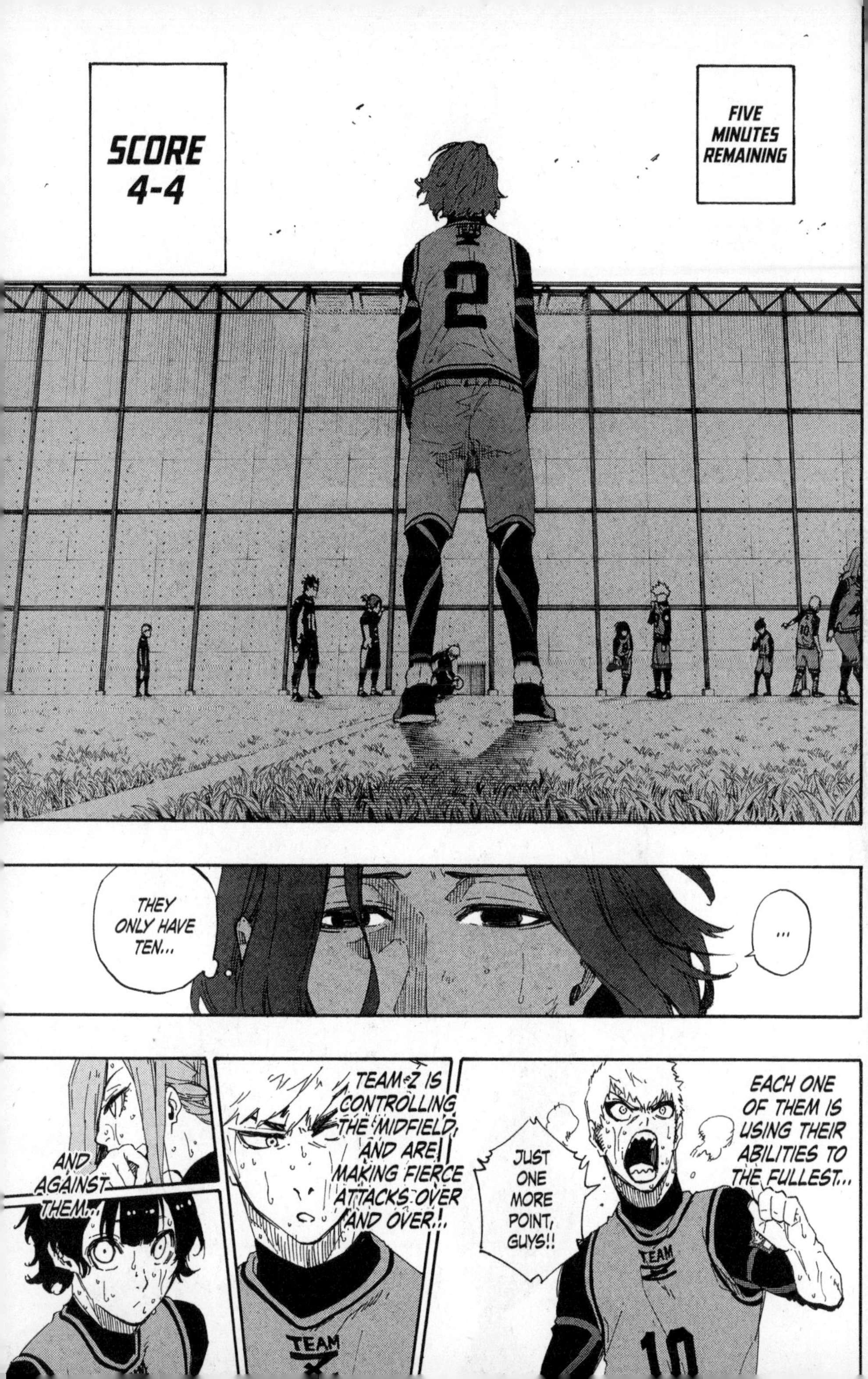
FIVE MINUTES REMAINING
SCORE 4-4
...
THEY ONLY HAVE TEN...
EACH ONE OF THEM IS USING THEIR ABILITIES TO THE FULLEST...
JUST ONE MORE POINT, GUYS!!
TEAM Z IS CONTROLLING THE MIDFIELD, AND ARE MAKING FIERCE ATTACKS OVER AND OVER...
AND AGAINST THEM...

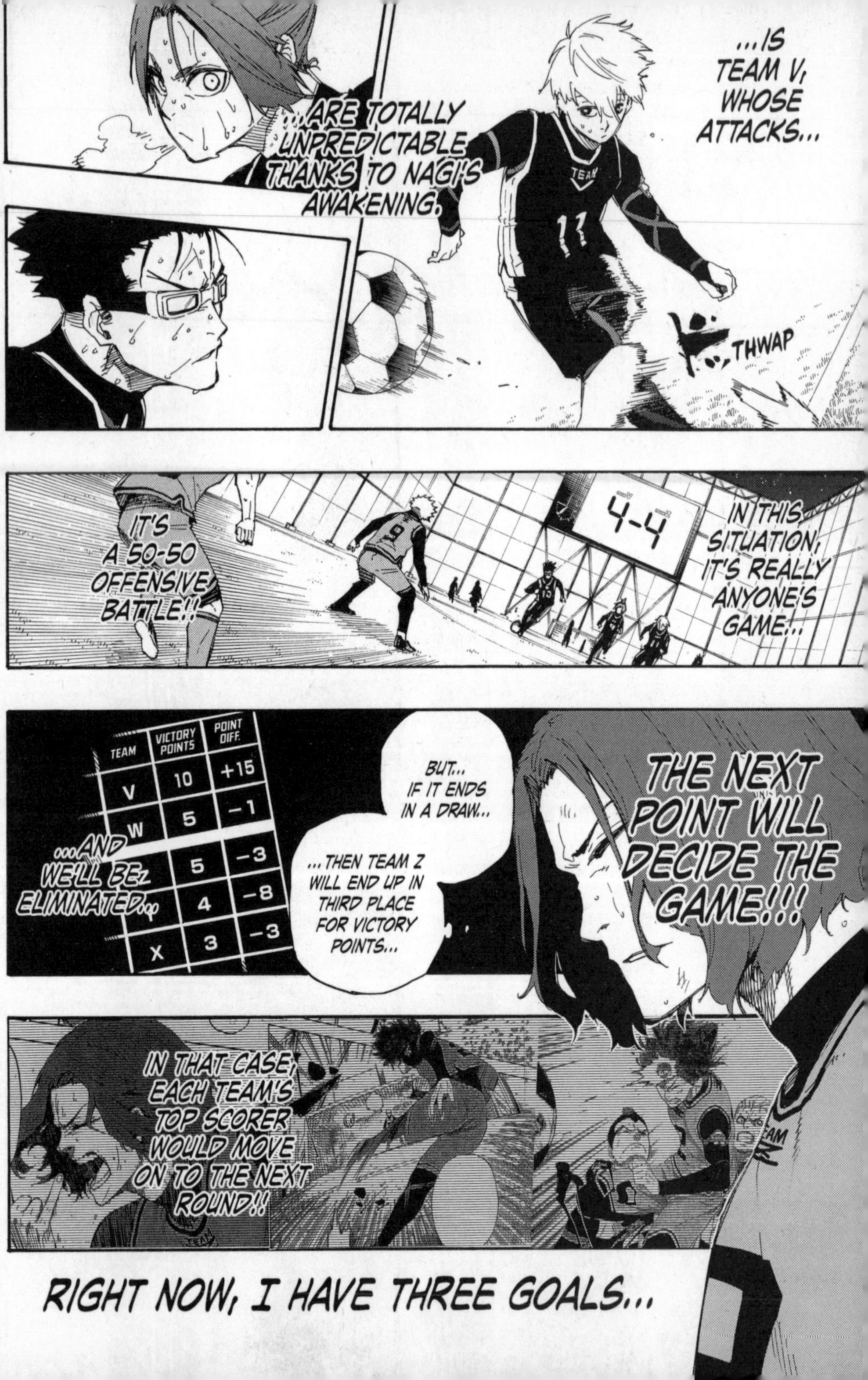
...IS TEAM V, WHOSE ATTACKS...
...ARE TOTALLY UNPREDICTABLE THANKS TO NAGI'S AWAKENING.
TEAM
THWAP
IN THIS SITUATION, IT'S REALLY ANYONE'S GAME...
4-4
IT'S A 50-50 OFFENSIVE BATTLE!!
THE NEXT POINT WILL DECIDE THE GAME!!!
BUT... IF IT ENDS IN A DRAW...
...THEN TEAM Z WILL END UP IN THIRD PLACE FOR VICTORY POINTS...
TEAM
VICTORY POINTS
POINT DIFF.
V 10 +15
W 5 −1
5 −3
4 −8
X 3 −3
...AND WE'LL BE ELIMINATED...
IN THAT CASE, EACH TEAM'S TOP SCORER WOULD MOVE ON TO THE NEXT ROUND!!
RIGHT NOW, I HAVE THREE GOALS...

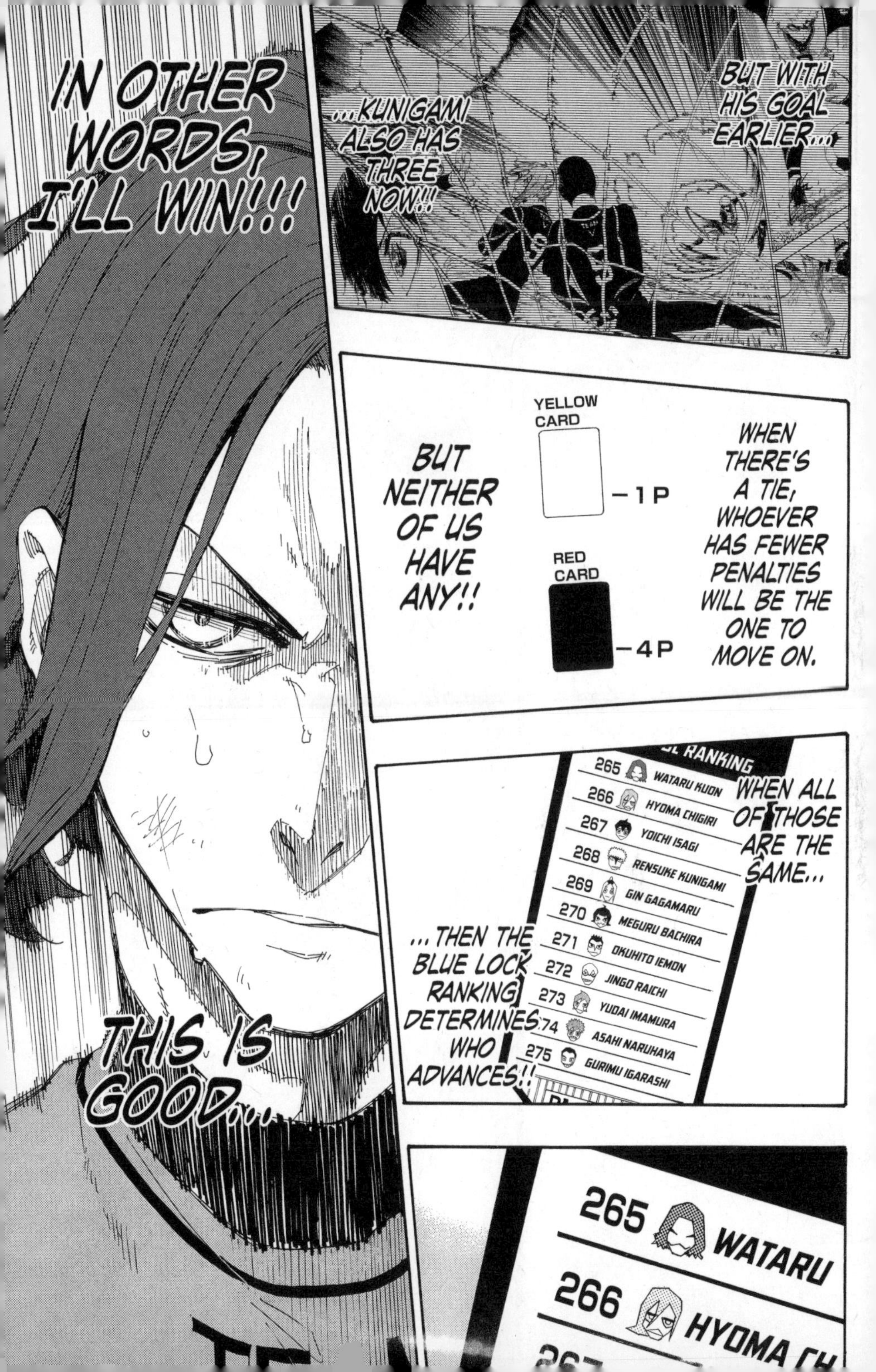
BUT WITH HIS GOAL EARLIER...
...KUNIGAMI ALSO HAS THREE NOW!!
WHEN THERE'S A TIE, WHOEVER HAS FEWER PENALTIES WILL BE THE ONE TO MOVE ON.
YELLOW CARD
−1P
RED CARD
−4P
BUT NEITHER OF US HAVE ANY!!
WHEN ALL OF THOSE ARE THE SAME...
265 WATARU KUON
266 HYOMA CHIGIRI
267 YOICHI ISAGI
268 RENSUKE KUNIGAMI
269 GIN GAGAMARU
270 MEGURU BACHIRA
271 OKUHITO IEMON
272 JINGO RAICHI
273 YUDAI IMAMURA
74 ASAHI NARUHAYA
275 GURIMU IGARASHI
...THEN THE BLUE LOCK RANKING DETERMINES WHO ADVANCES!!
265 WATARU
266 HYOMA
IN OTHER WORDS, I'LL WIN!!!
THIS IS GOOD...

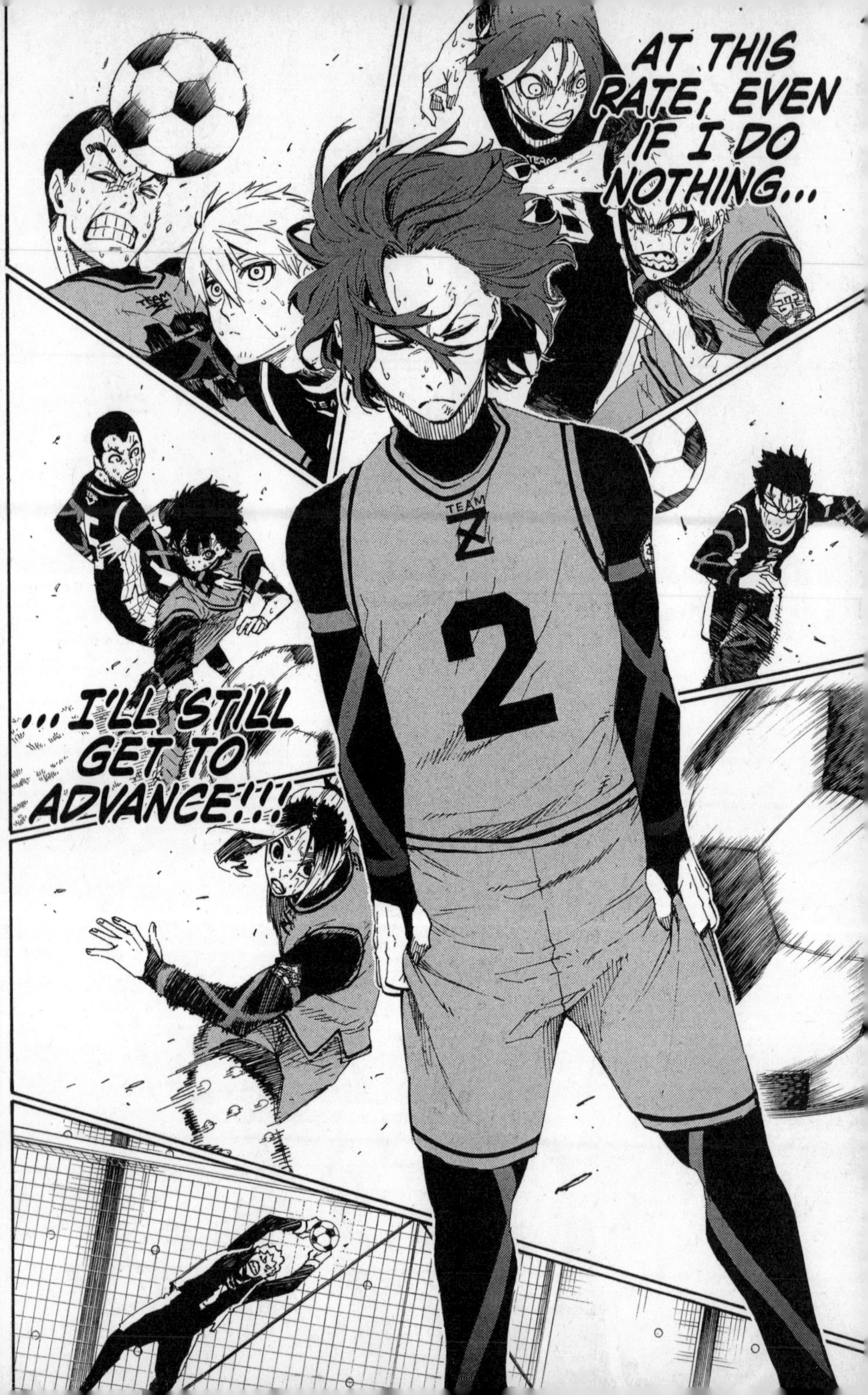
AT THIS RATE, EVEN IF I DO NOTHING...
...I'LL STILL GET TO ADVANCE!!!

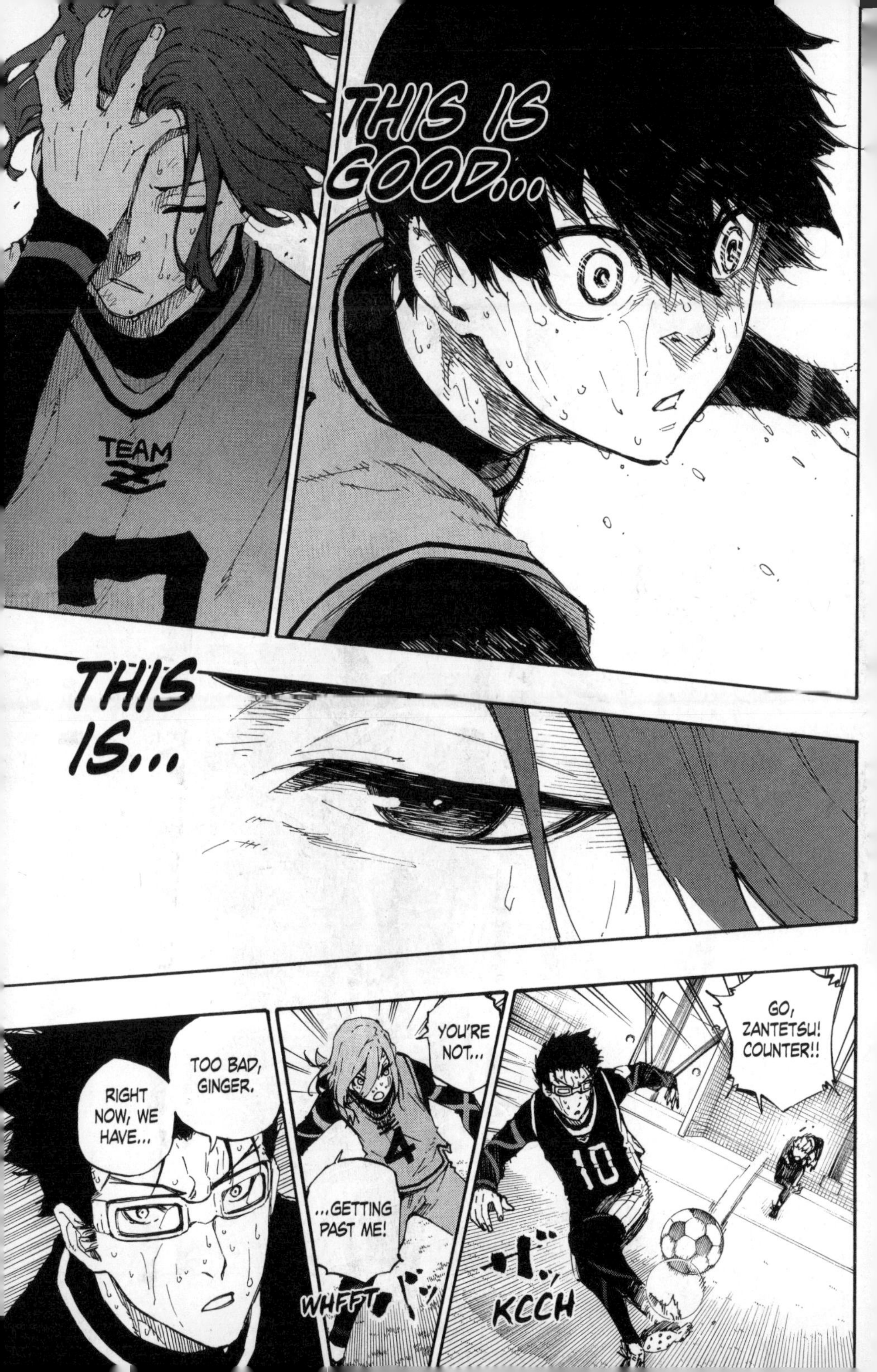
THIS IS GOOD...
THIS IS...
GO, ZANTETSU! COUNTER!!
KCCH
YOU'RE NOT...
...GETTING PAST ME!
WHFFT
TOO BAD, GINGER.
RIGHT NOW, WE HAVE...

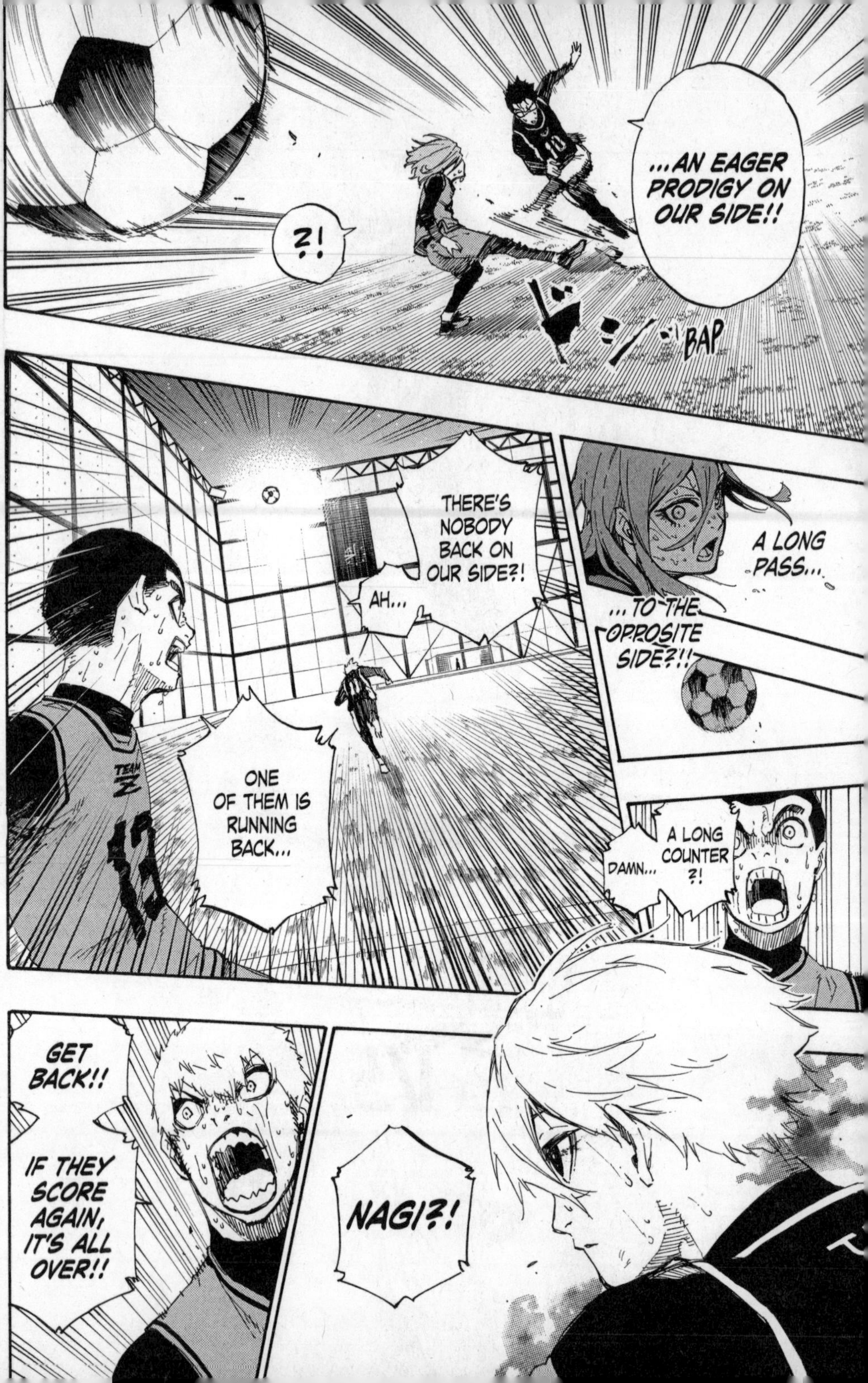
...AN EAGER PRODIGY ON OUR SIDE!!
?!
BAP
A LONG PASS...
...TO THE OPPOSITE SIDE?!!
A LONG COUNTER?!
DAMN...
THERE'S NOBODY BACK ON OUR SIDE?!
AH...
ONE OF THEM IS RUNNING BACK...
NAGI?!
GET BACK!!
IF THEY SCORE AGAIN, IT'S ALL OVER!!

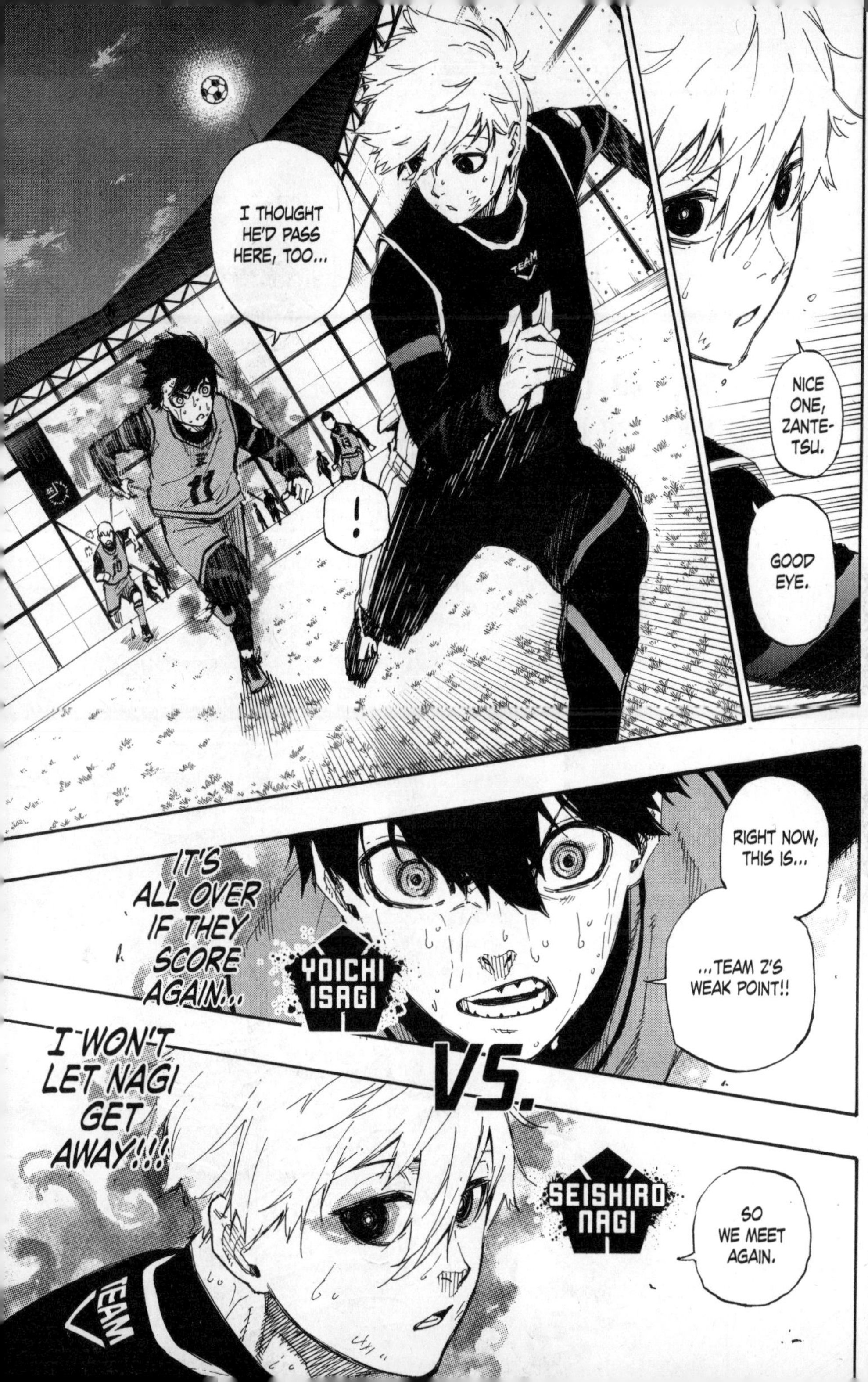

NICE ONE, ZANTE-TSU.
GOOD EYE.
I THOUGHT HE'D PASS HERE, TOO...
!
RIGHT NOW, THIS IS...
...TEAM Z'S WEAK POINT!!
IT'S ALL OVER IF THEY SCORE AGAIN...
YOICHI ISAGI
VS.
SO WE MEET AGAIN.
SEISHIRO NAGI
I WON'T LET NAGI GET AWAY!!!

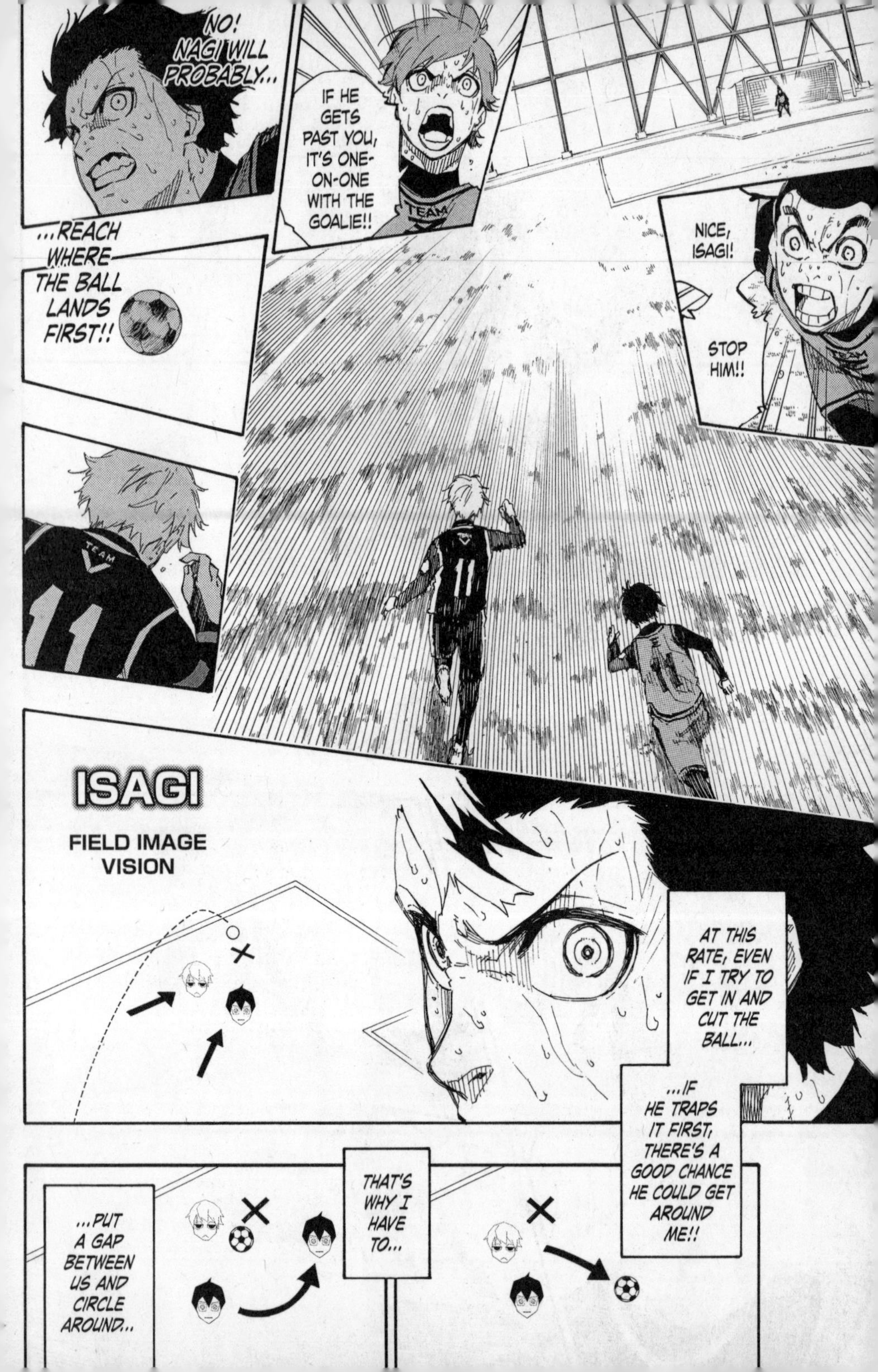
NICE, ISAGI!
STOP HIM!!
IF HE GETS PAST YOU, IT'S ONE-ON-ONE WITH THE GOALIE!!
NO! NAGI WILL PROBABLY...
...REACH WHERE THE BALL LANDS FIRST!!
AT THIS RATE, EVEN IF I TRY TO GET IN AND CUT THE BALL...
ISAGI
FIELD IMAGE VISION
...IF HE TRAPS IT FIRST, THERE'S A GOOD CHANCE HE COULD GET AROUND ME!!
THAT'S WHY I HAVE TO...
...PUT A GAP BETWEEN US AND CIRCLE AROUND...

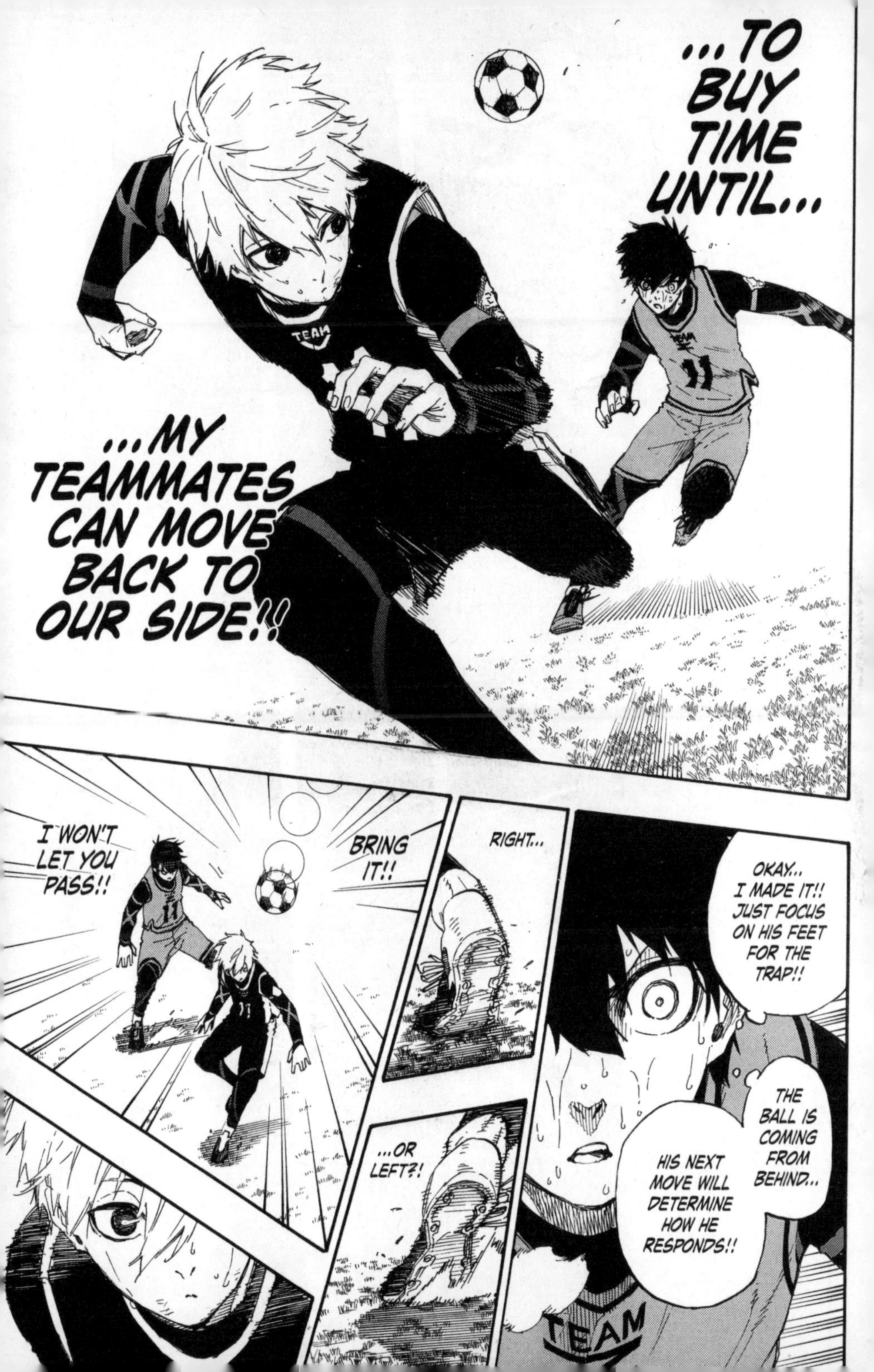

...TO BUY TIME UNTIL...
...MY TEAMMATES CAN MOVE BACK TO OUR SIDE!!
OKAY... I MADE IT!! JUST FOCUS ON HIS FEET FOR THE TRAP!!
THE BALL IS COMING FROM BEHIND...
HIS NEXT MOVE WILL DETERMINE HOW HE RESPONDS!!
RIGHT...
...OR LEFT?!
BRING IT!!
I WON'T LET YOU PASS!!
TEAM

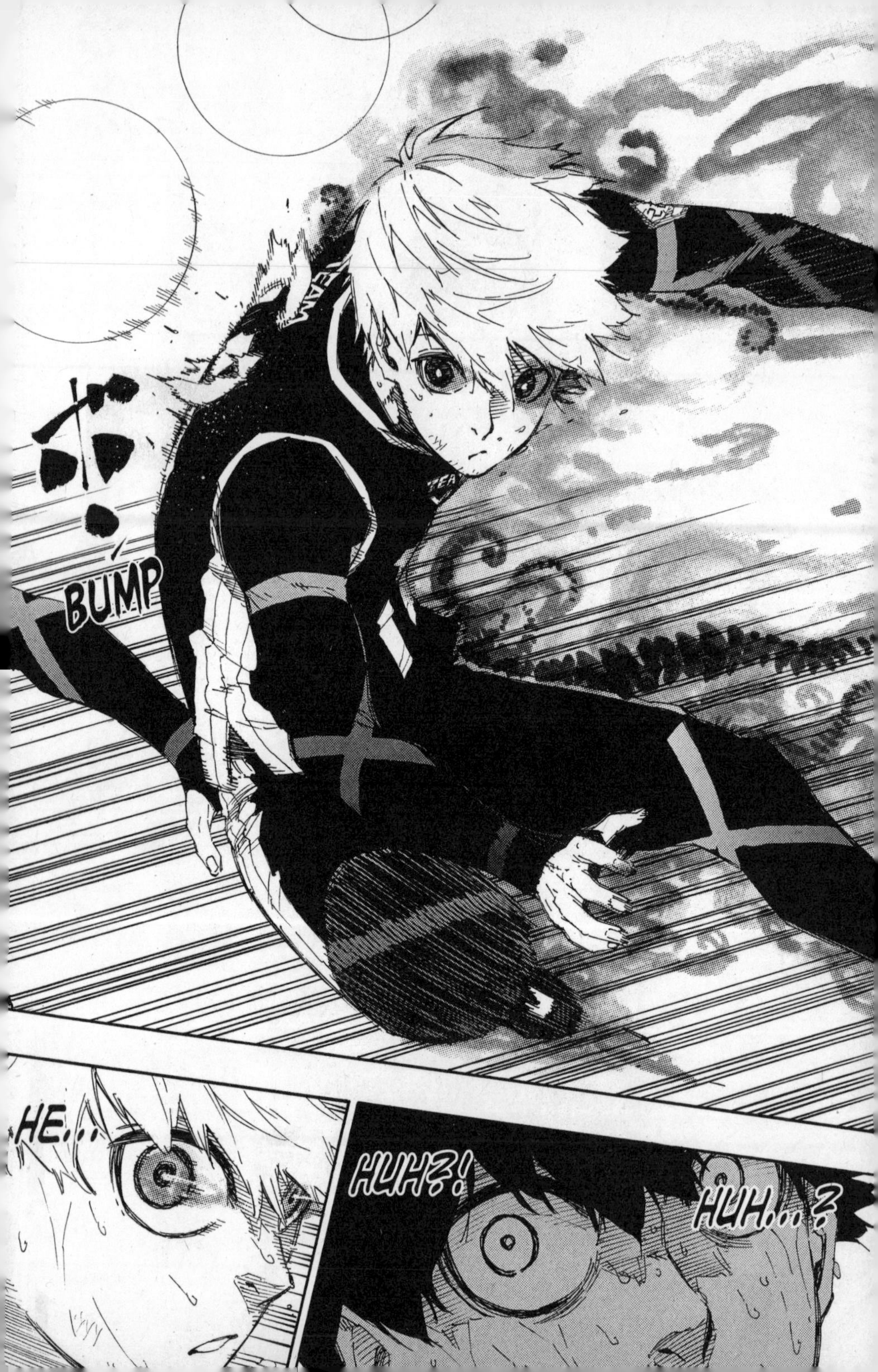
BUMP
HUH...?
HUH?!
HE...

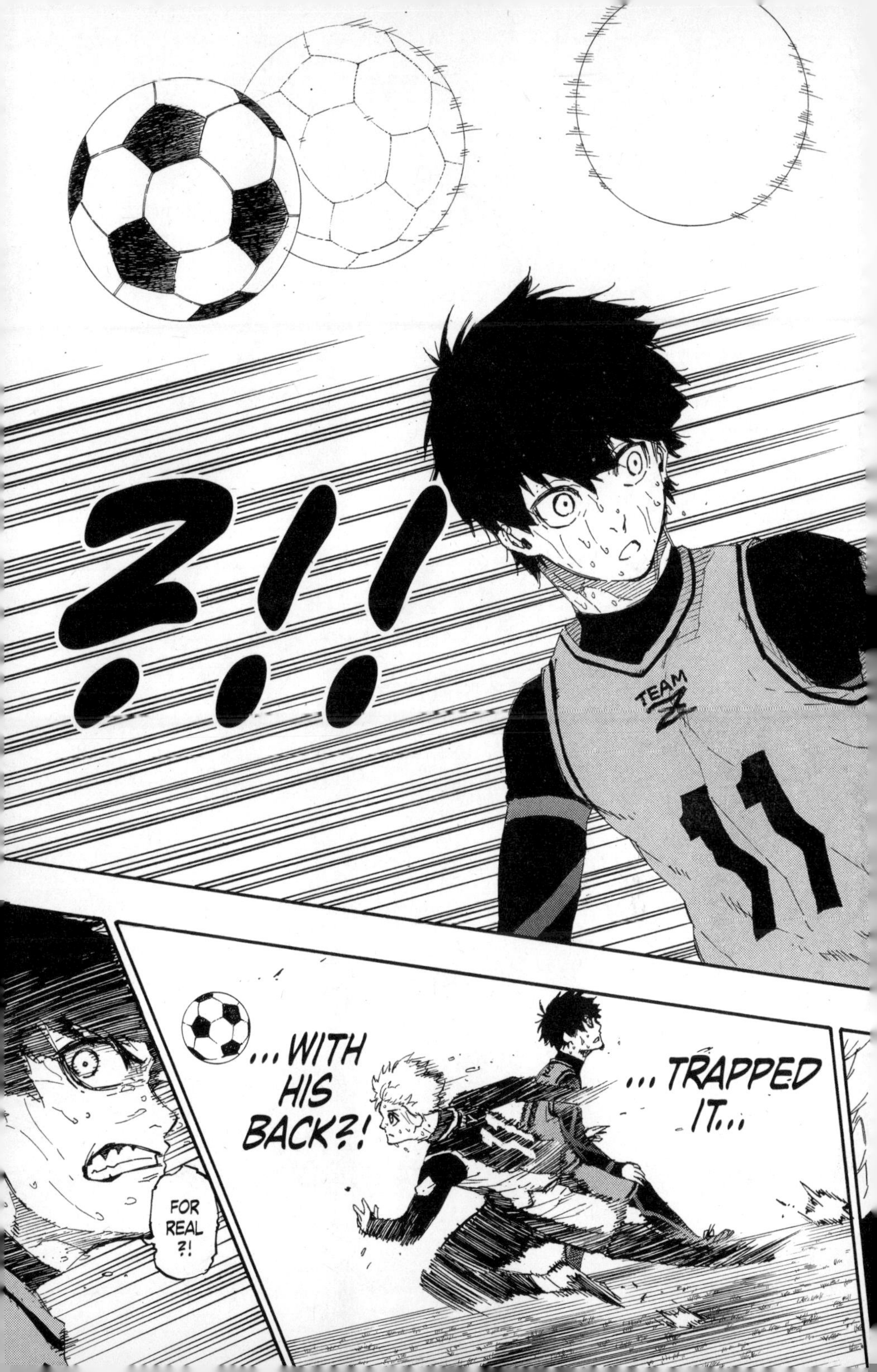
?!!
...TRAPPED IT...
...WITH HIS BACK?!
FOR REAL ?!

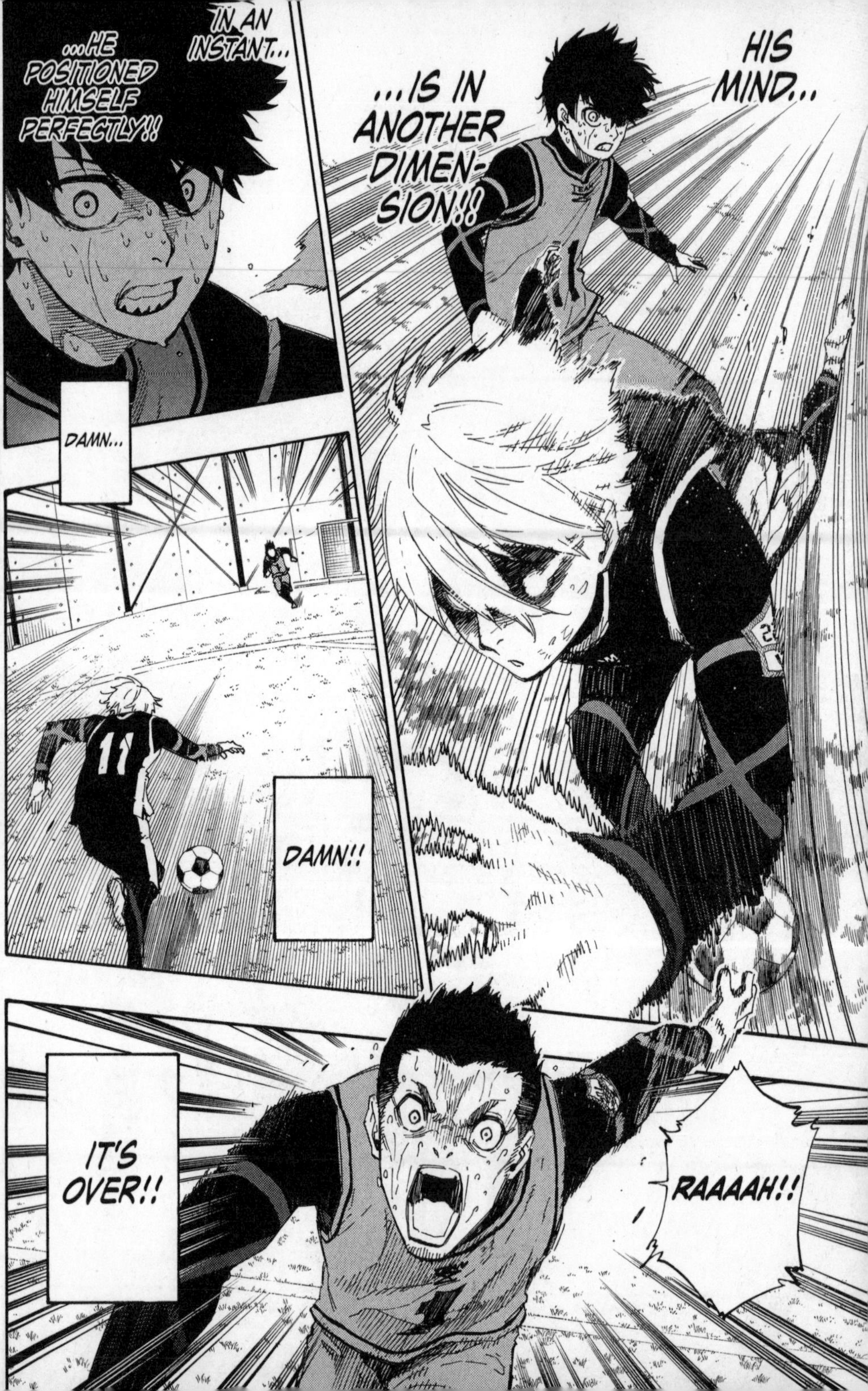
HIS MIND...
...IS IN ANOTHER DIMENSION!!
IN AN INSTANT...
...HE POSITIONED HIMSELF PERFECTLY!!
DAMN...
DAMN!!
RAAAAH!!
IT'S OVER!!

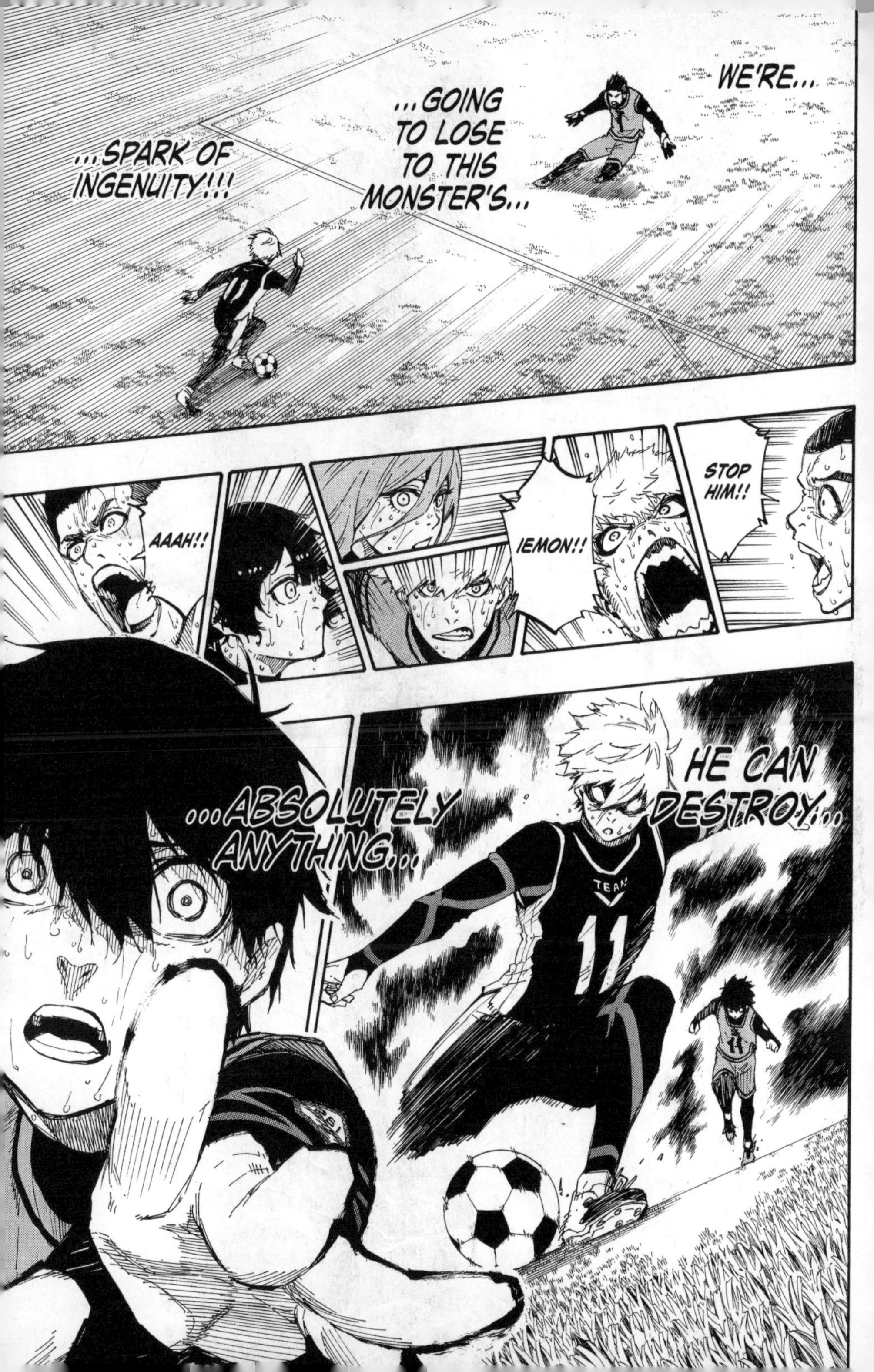
WE'RE...
...GOING TO LOSE TO THIS MONSTER'S...
...SPARK OF INGENUITY!!!
STOP HIM!!
IEMON!!
AAAH!!
HE CAN DESTROY...
...ABSOLUTELY ANYTHING...
TEAM
11

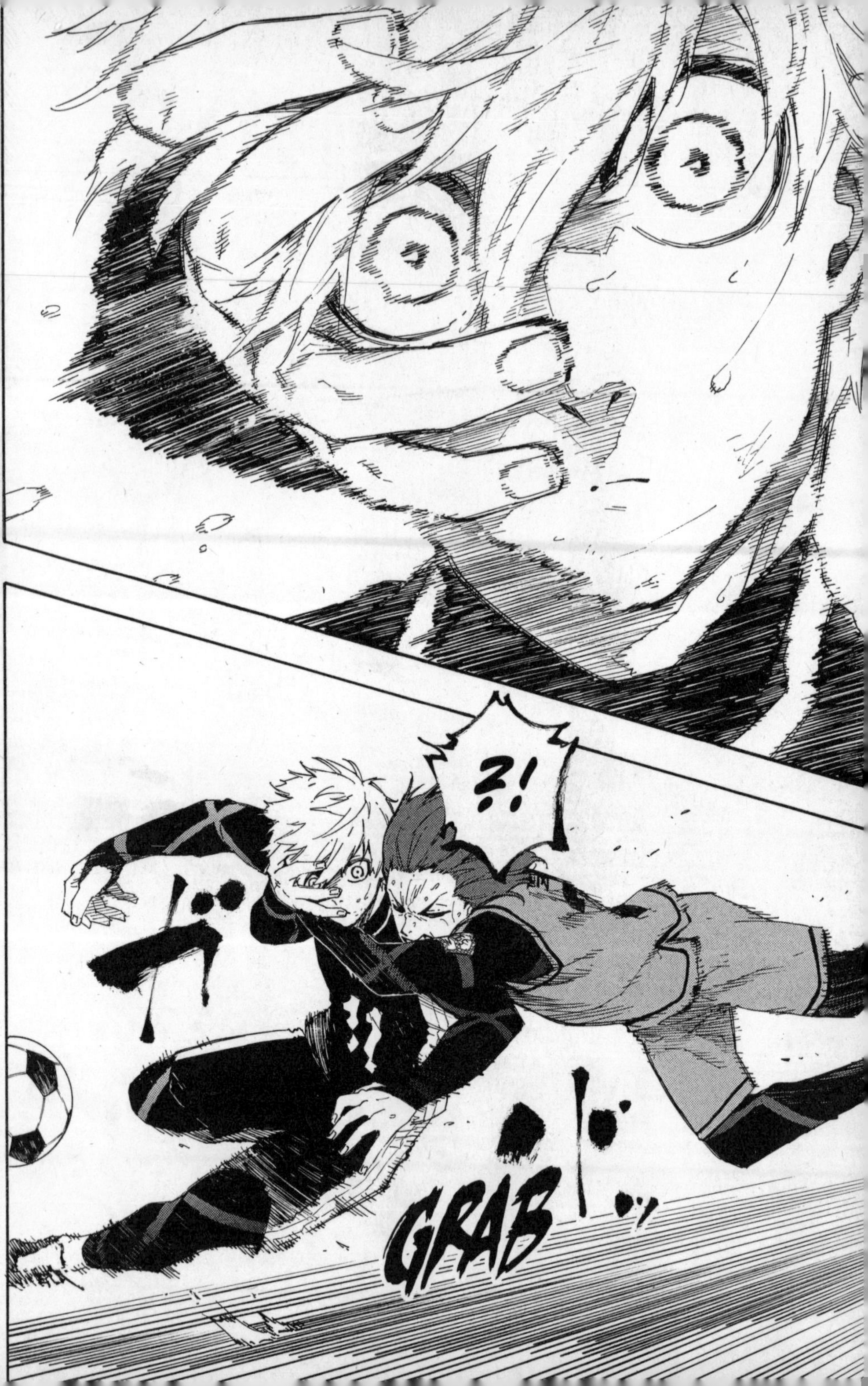
?!
GRAB

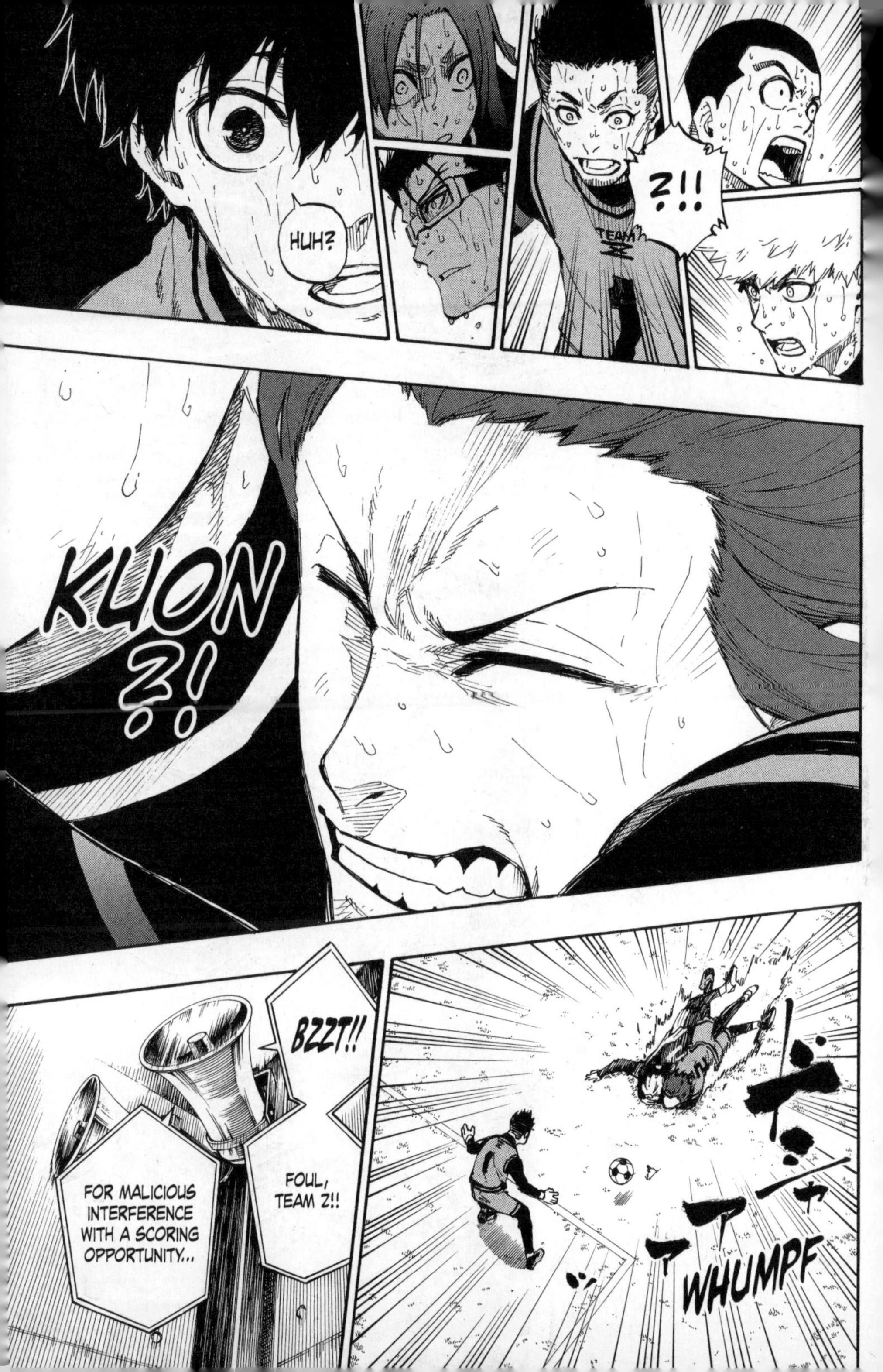
?!!
HUH?
KUON ?!
WHUMPF
BZZT!!
FOUL, TEAM Z!!
FOR MALICIOUS INTERFERENCE WITH A SCORING OPPORTUNITY...

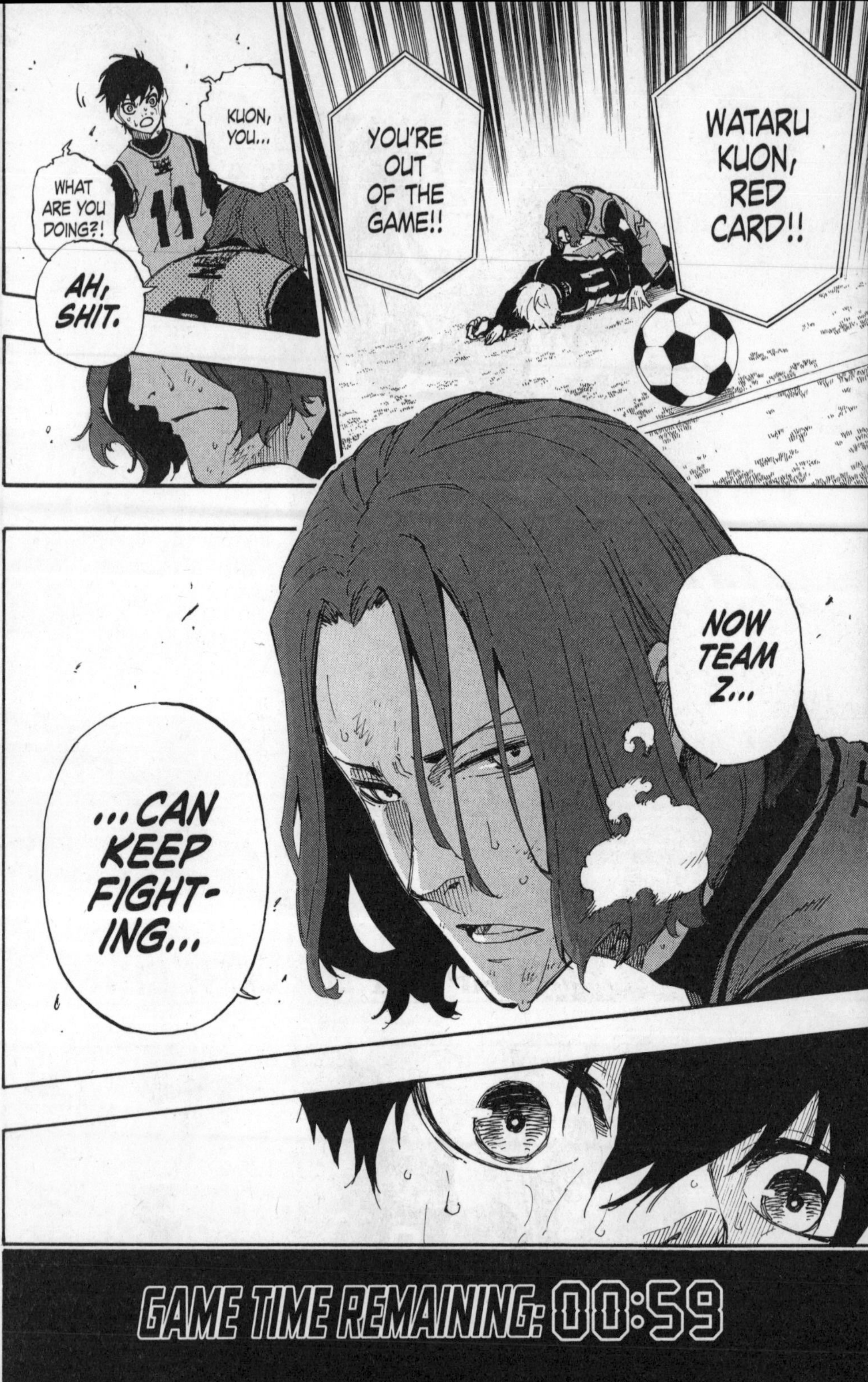
WATARU KUON, RED CARD!!
YOU'RE OUT OF THE GAME!!
KUON, YOU...
WHAT ARE YOU DOING?!
AH, SHIT.
NOW TEAM Z...
...CAN KEEP FIGHT-ING...
GAME TIME REMAINING: 00:59

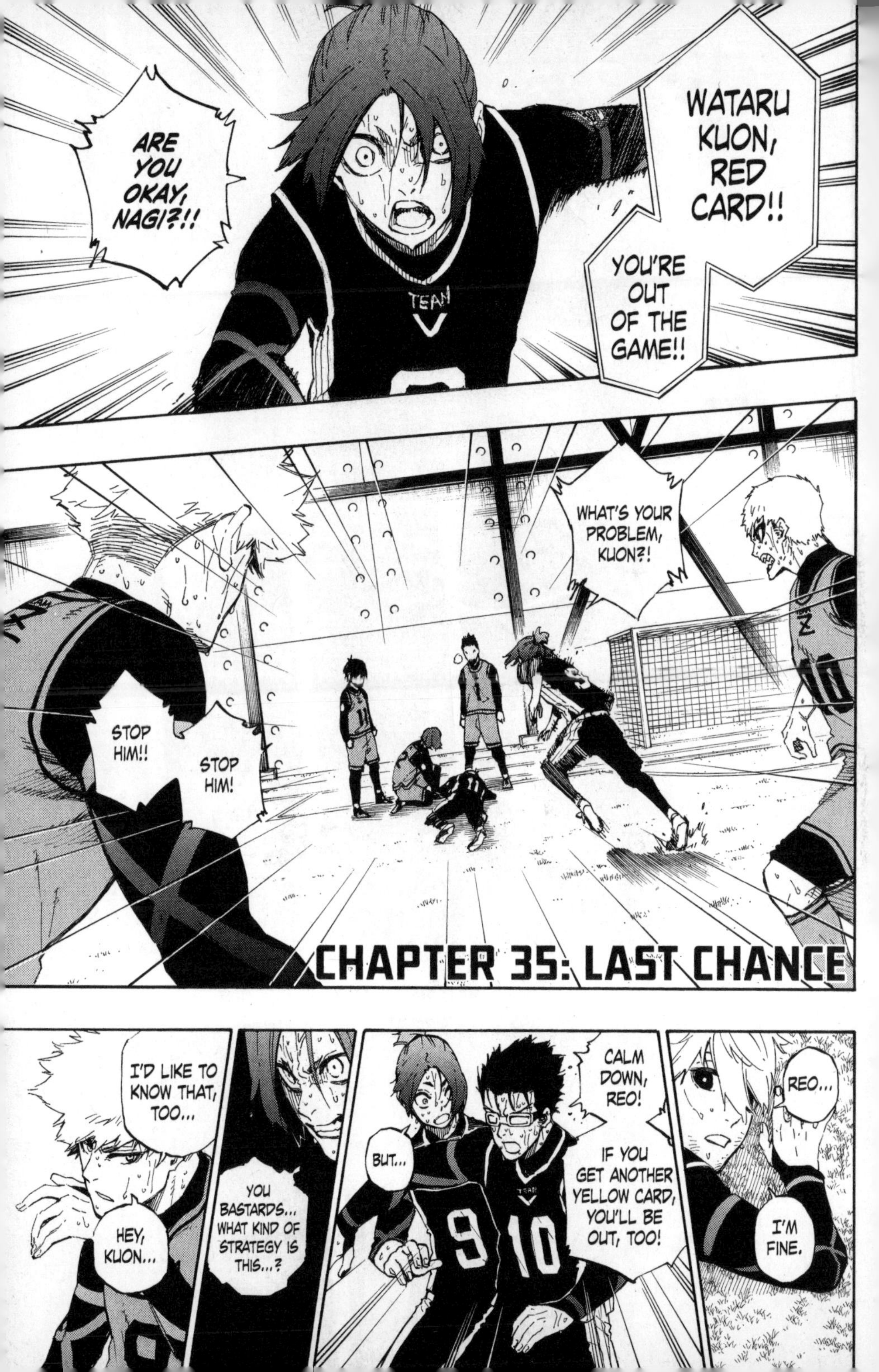
WATARU KUON, RED CARD!!
YOU'RE OUT OF THE GAME!!
ARE YOU OKAY, NAGI?!!
WHAT'S YOUR PROBLEM, KUON?!
STOP HIM!
STOP HIM!!
CHAPTER 35: LAST CHANCE
REO...
I'M FINE.
CALM DOWN, REO!
IF YOU GET ANOTHER YELLOW CARD, YOU'LL BE OUT, TOO!
BUT...
YOU BASTARDS... WHAT KIND OF STRATEGY IS THIS...?
I'D LIKE TO KNOW THAT, TOO...
HEY, KUON...

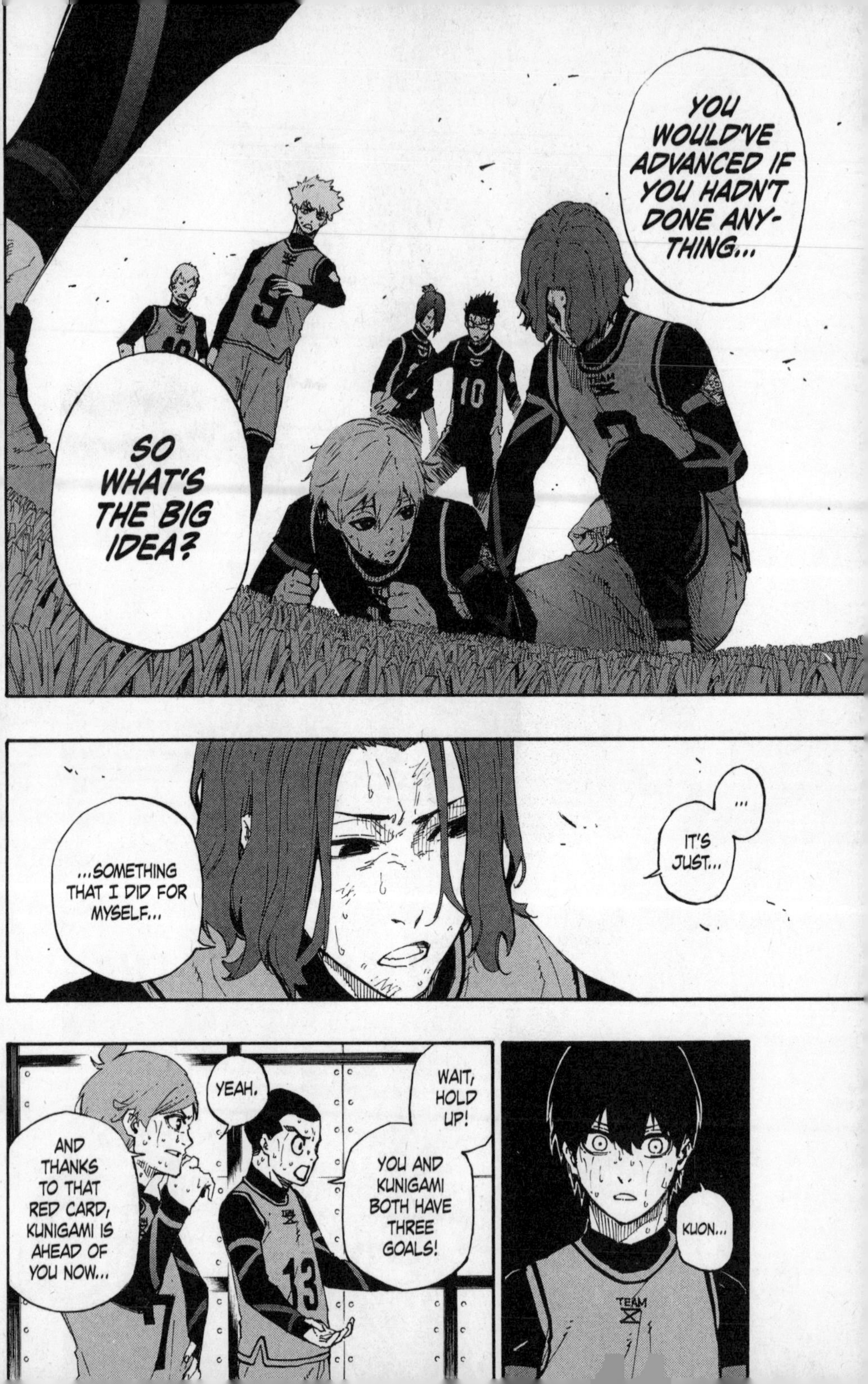
YOU WOULD'VE ADVANCED IF YOU HADN'T DONE ANYTHING...
SO WHAT'S THE BIG IDEA?
...
IT'S JUST...
...SOMETHING THAT I DID FOR MYSELF...
KUON...
WAIT, HOLD UP!
YOU AND KUNIGAMI BOTH HAVE THREE GOALS!
YEAH.
AND THANKS TO THAT RED CARD, KUNIGAMI IS AHEAD OF YOU NOW...

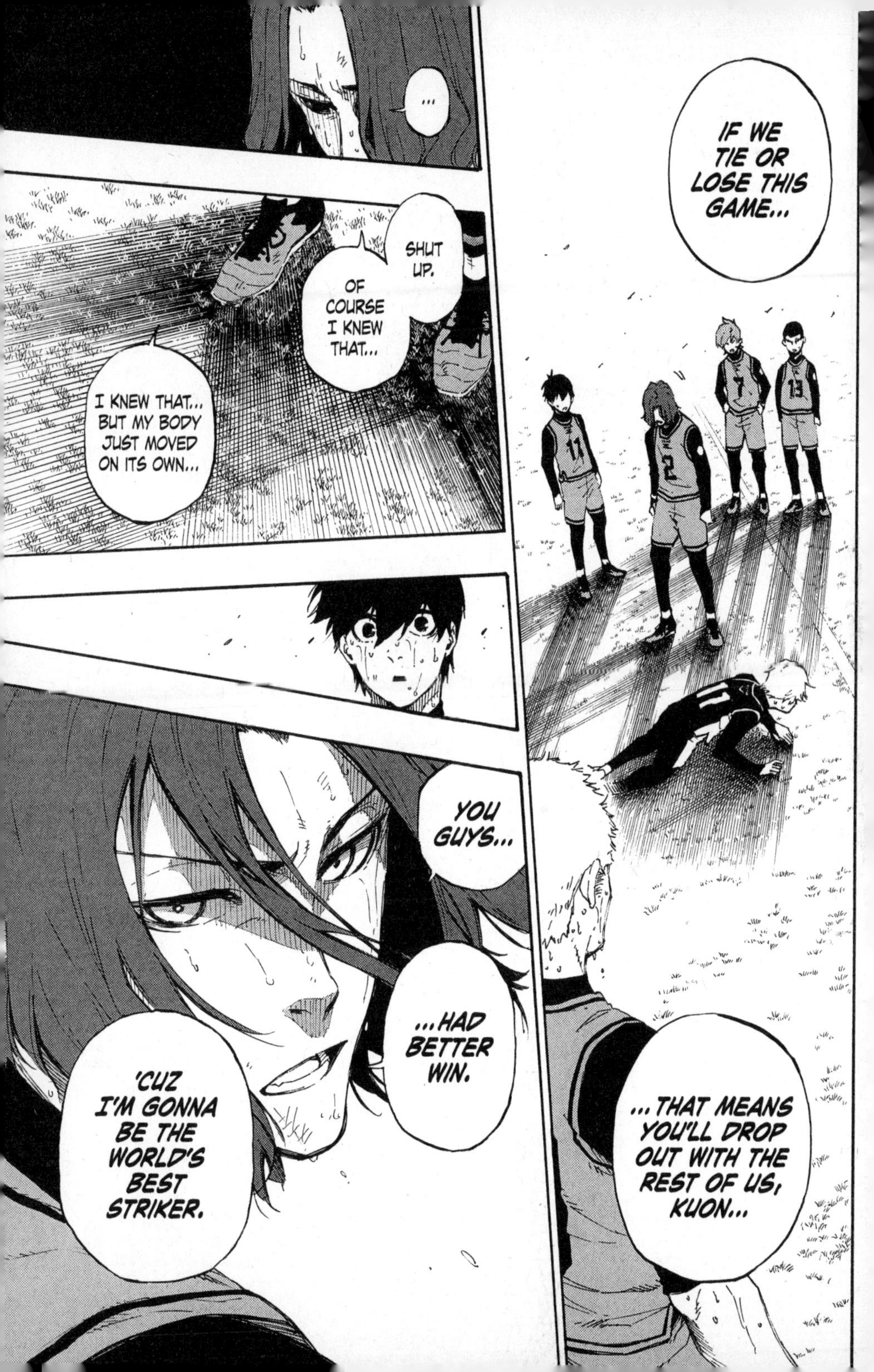
IF WE TIE OR LOSE THIS GAME...
...THAT MEANS YOU'LL DROP OUT WITH THE REST OF US, KUON...
...
SHUT UP.
OF COURSE I KNEW THAT...
I KNEW THAT... BUT MY BODY JUST MOVED ON ITS OWN...
YOU GUYS...
...HAD BETTER WIN.
'CUZ I'M GONNA BE THE WORLD'S BEST STRIKER.

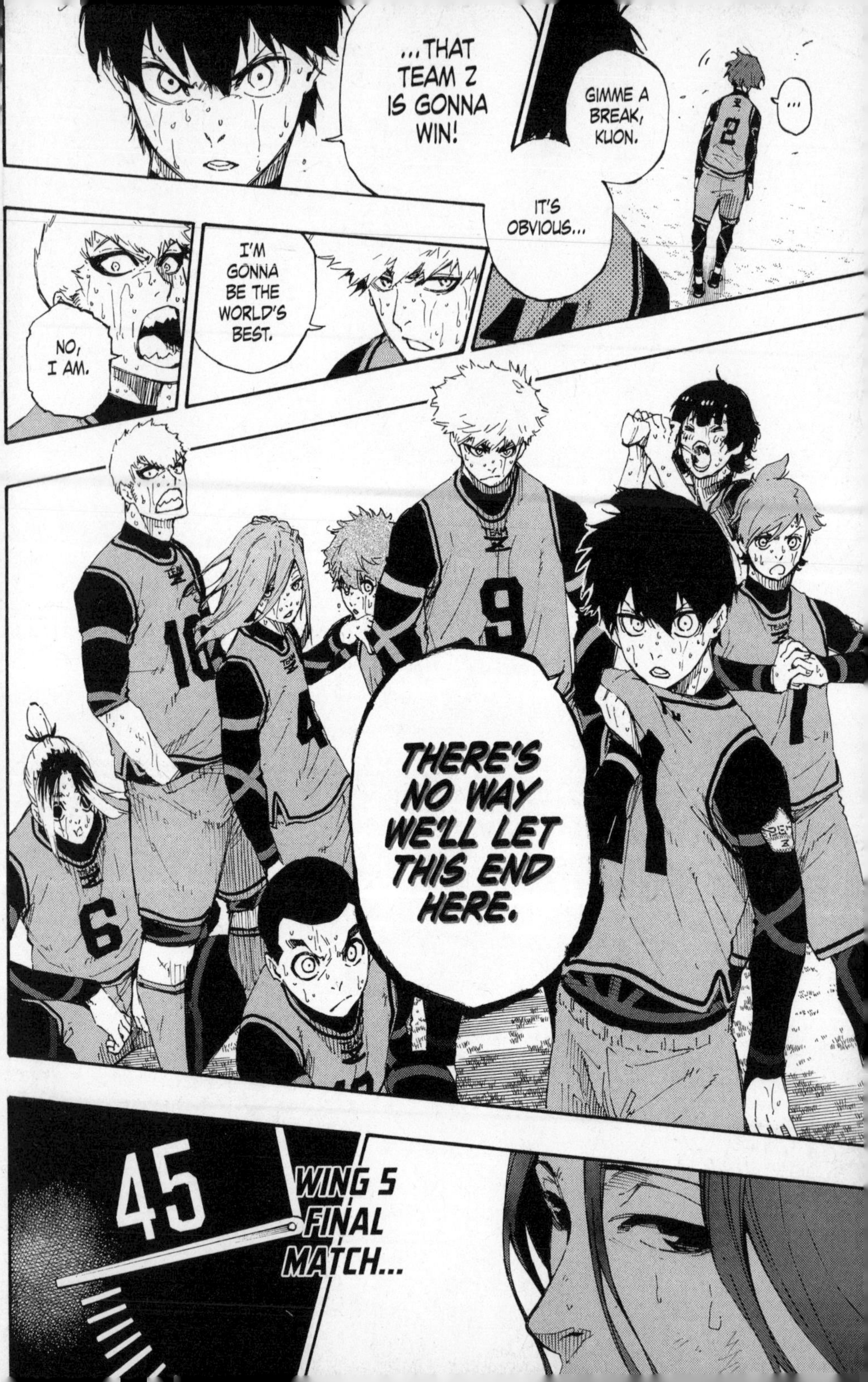
...
GIMME A BREAK, KUON.
IT'S OBVIOUS...
...THAT TEAM Z IS GONNA WIN!
I'M GONNA BE THE WORLD'S BEST.
NO, I AM.
THERE'S NO WAY WE'LL LET THIS END HERE.
45
WING 5 FINAL MATCH...

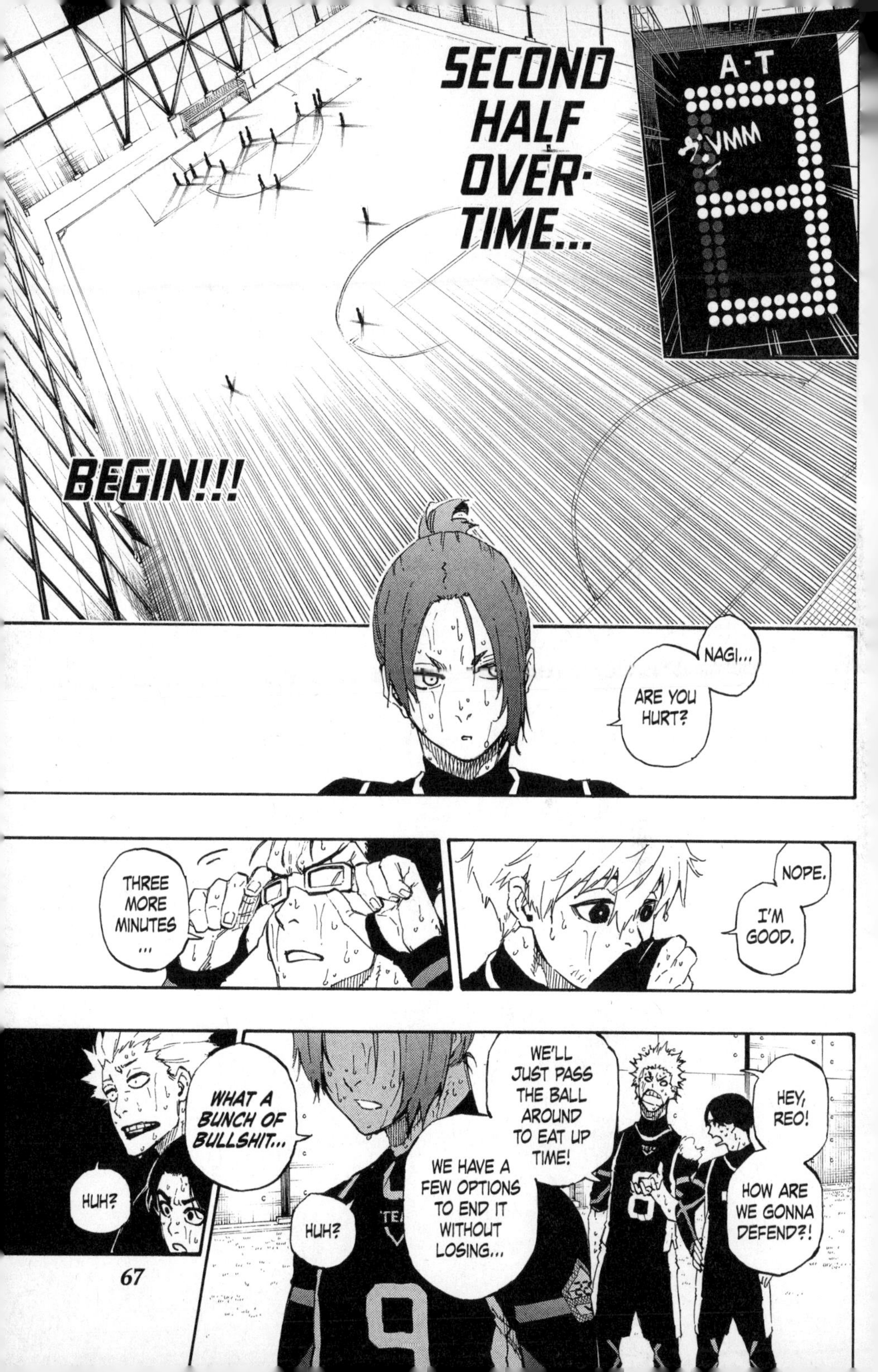
A-T
VMM
SECOND HALF OVER-TIME...
BEGIN!!!
NAGI...
ARE YOU HURT?
NOPE.
I'M GOOD.
THREE MORE MINUTES ...
HEY, REO!
HOW ARE WE GONNA DEFEND?!
WE'LL JUST PASS THE BALL AROUND TO EAT UP TIME!
WE HAVE A FEW OPTIONS TO END IT WITHOUT LOSING...
HUH?
WHAT A BUNCH OF BULLSHIT...
HUH?

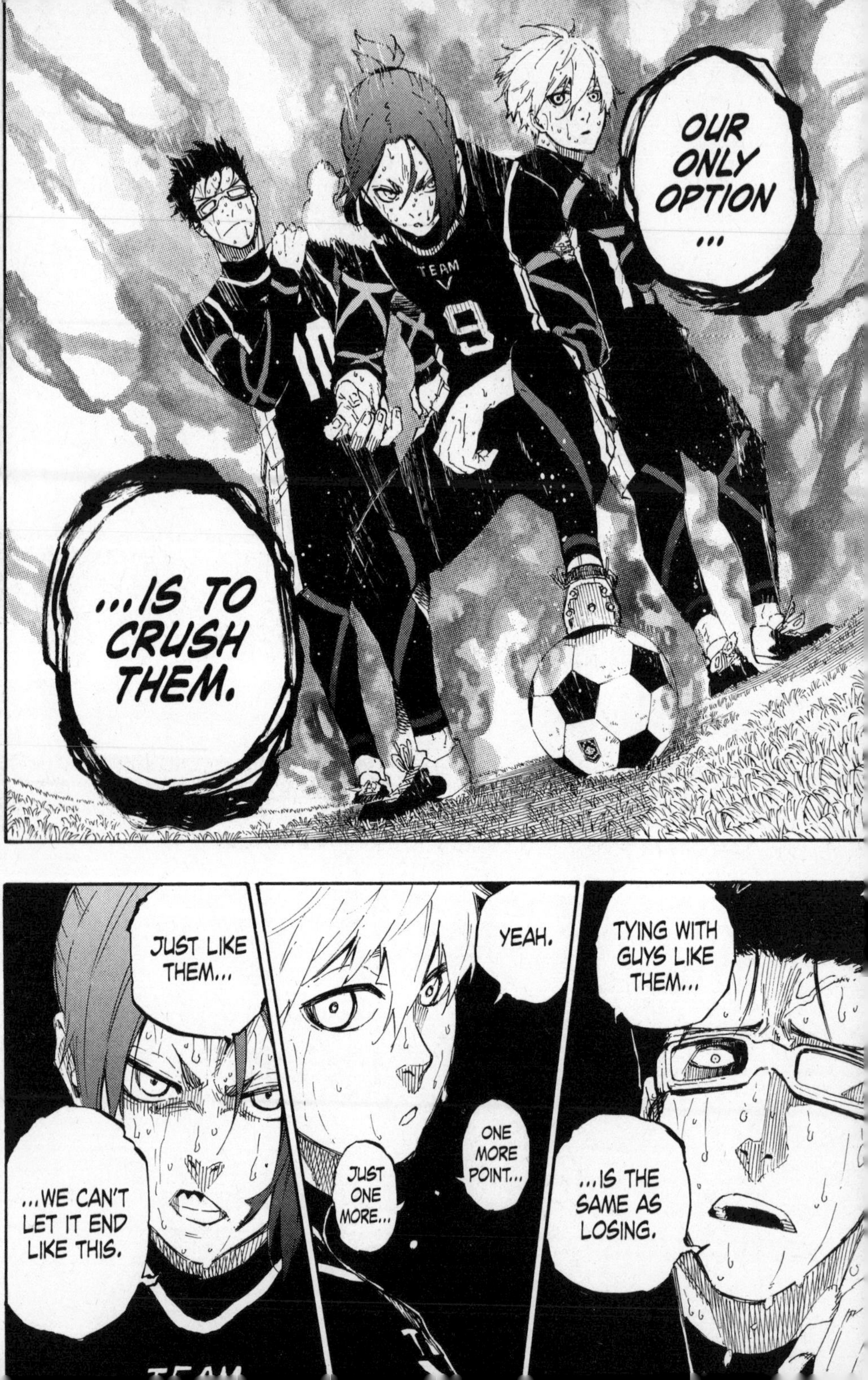
OUR ONLY OPTION ...
...IS TO CRUSH THEM.
TYING WITH GUYS LIKE THEM...
...IS THE SAME AS LOSING.
YEAH.
ONE MORE POINT...
JUST ONE MORE...
JUST LIKE THEM...
...WE CAN'T LET IT END LIKE THIS.

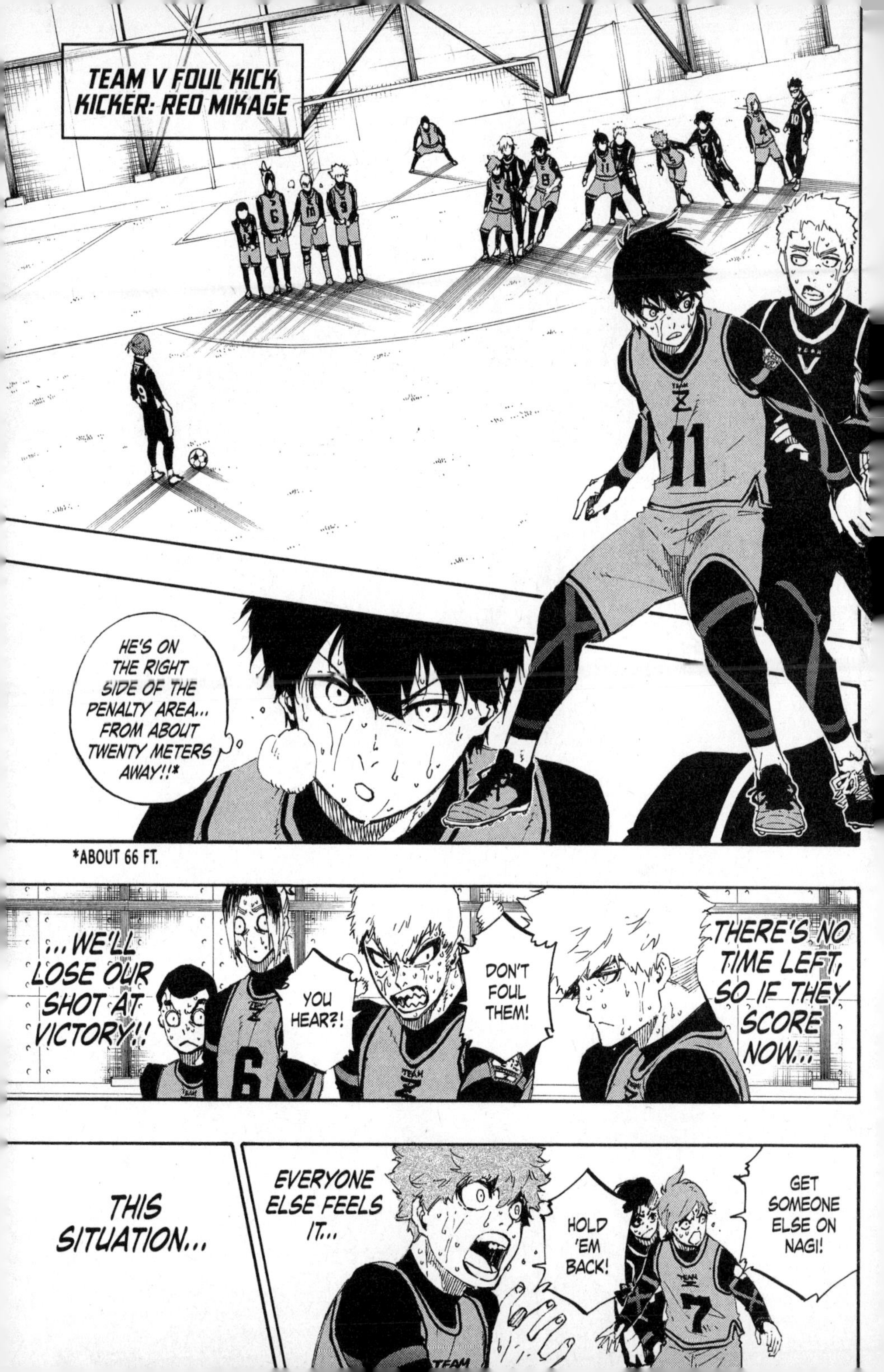
TEAM V FOUL KICK
KICKER: REO MIKAGE
HE'S ON THE RIGHT SIDE OF THE PENALTY AREA... FROM ABOUT TWENTY METERS AWAY!!*
THERE'S NO TIME LEFT, SO IF THEY SCORE NOW...
DON'T FOUL THEM!
YOU HEAR?!
...WE'LL LOSE OUR SHOT AT VICTORY!!
GET SOMEONE ELSE ON NAGI!
HOLD 'EM BACK!
EVERYONE ELSE FEELS IT...
THIS SITUATION...
*ABOUT 66 FT.

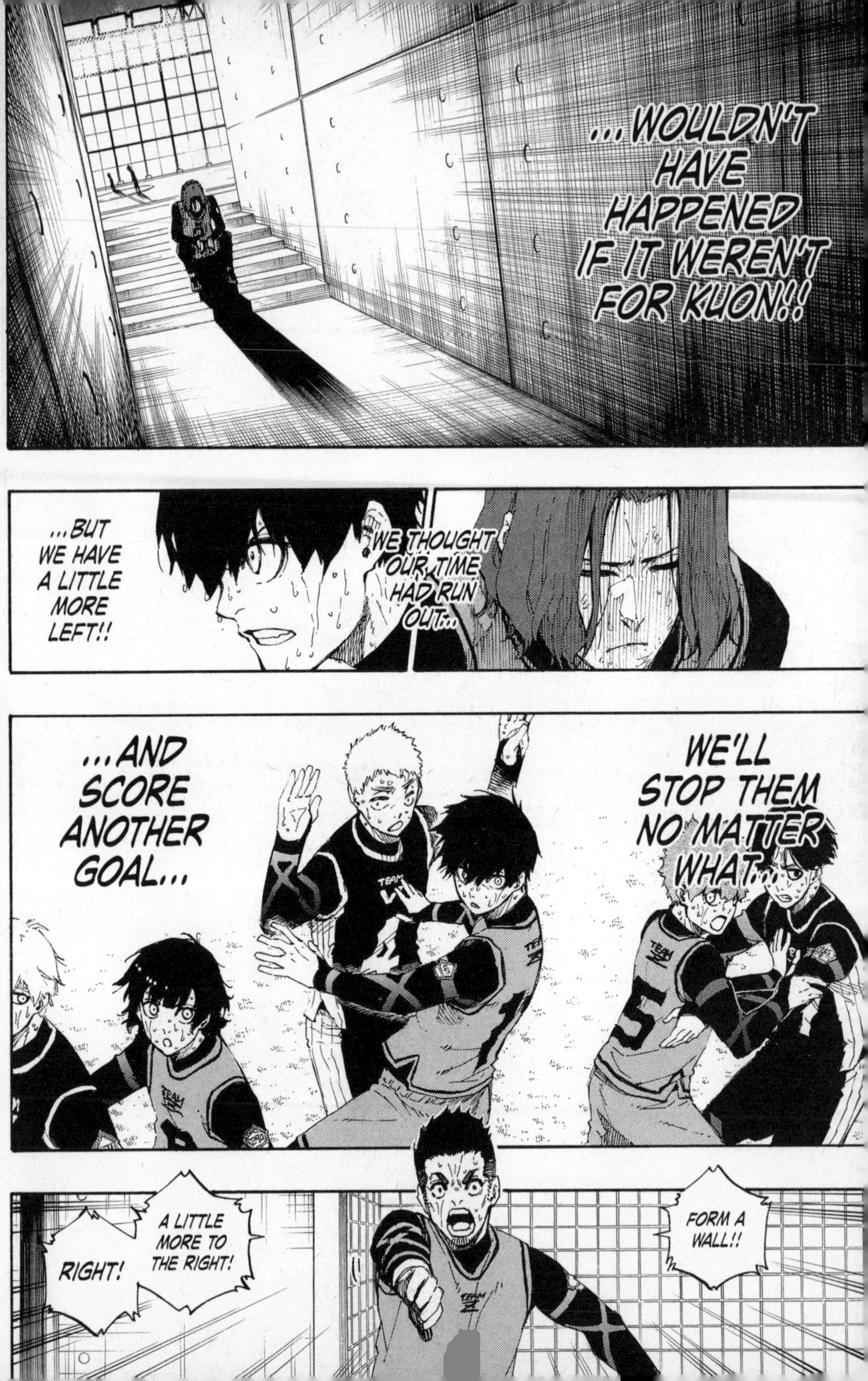
...WOULDN'T HAVE HAPPENED IF IT WEREN'T FOR KUON!!
WE THOUGHT OUR TIME HAD RUN OUT...
...BUT WE HAVE A LITTLE MORE LEFT!!
WE'LL STOP THEM NO MATTER WHAT...
...AND SCORE ANOTHER GOAL...
FORM A WALL!!
A LITTLE MORE TO THE RIGHT!
RIGHT!

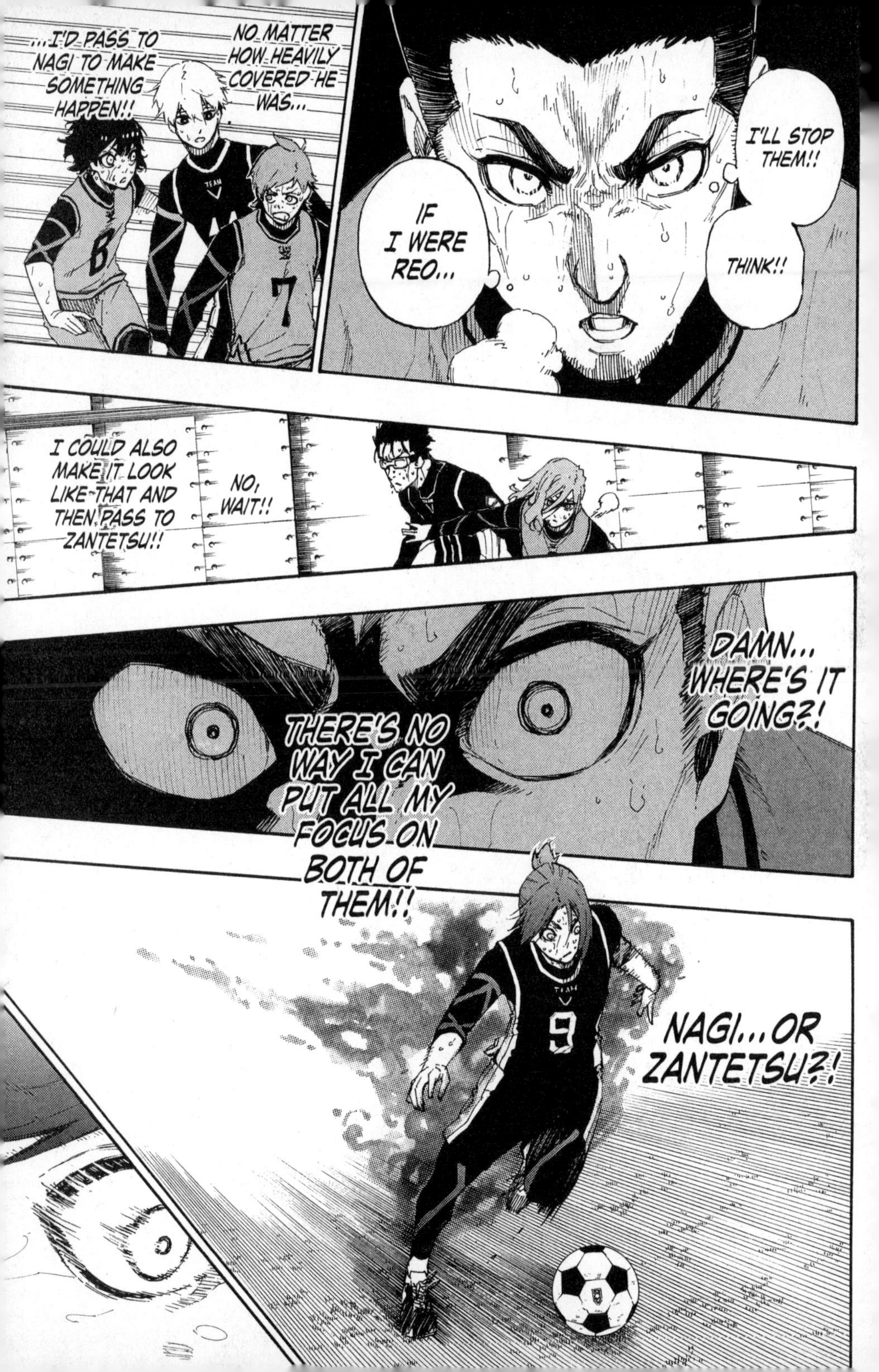
I'LL STOP THEM!!
THINK!!
IF I WERE REO...
NO MATTER HOW HEAVILY COVERED HE WAS...
...I'D PASS TO NAGI TO MAKE SOMETHING HAPPEN!!
NO, WAIT!!
I COULD ALSO MAKE IT LOOK LIKE THAT AND THEN PASS TO ZANTETSU!!
DAMN... WHERE'S IT GOING?!
THERE'S NO WAY I CAN PUT ALL MY FOCUS ON BOTH OF THEM!!
NAGI...OR ZANTETSU?!

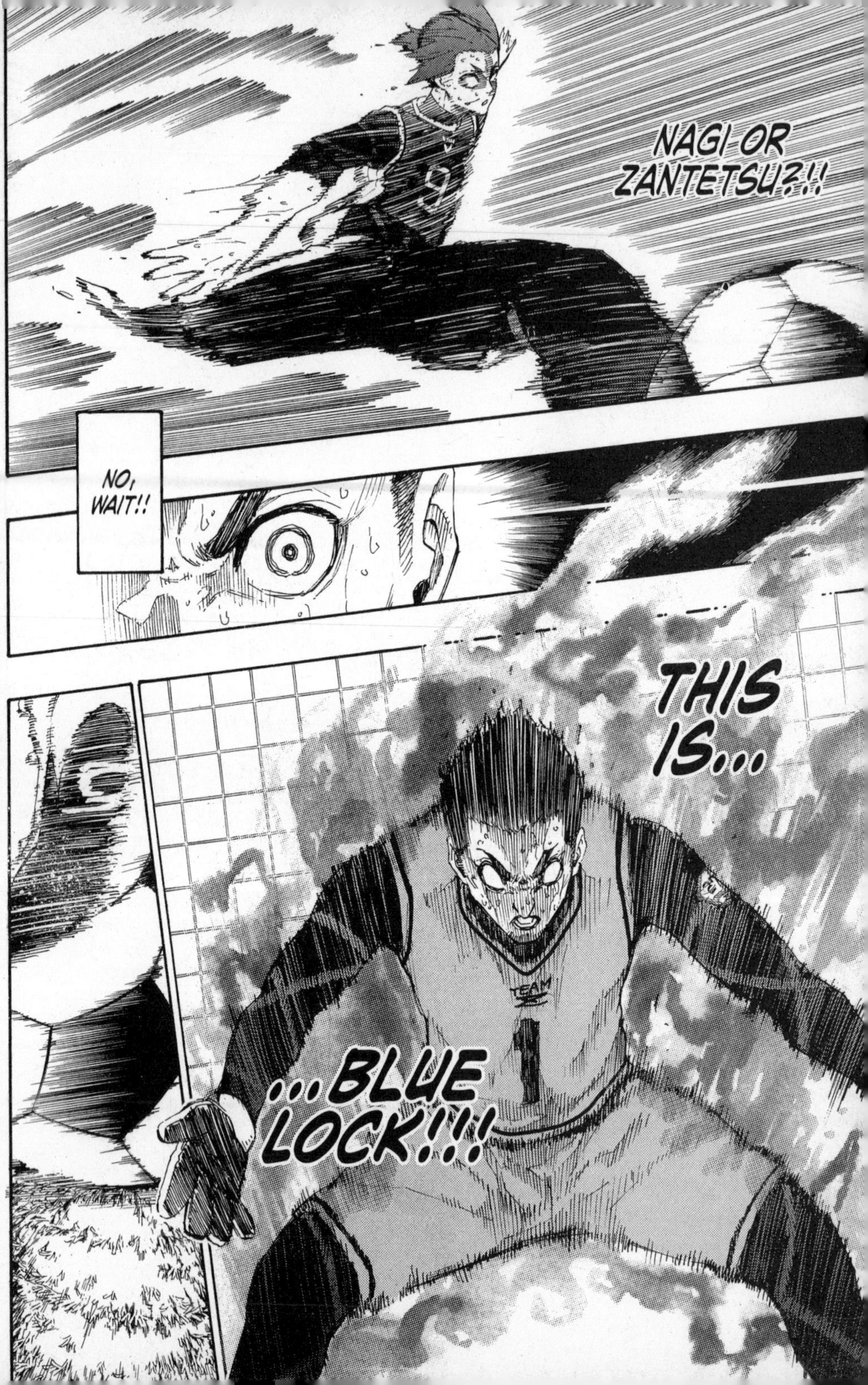
NAGI OR ZANTETSU?!!
NO, WAIT!!
THIS IS...
...BLUE LOCK!!!

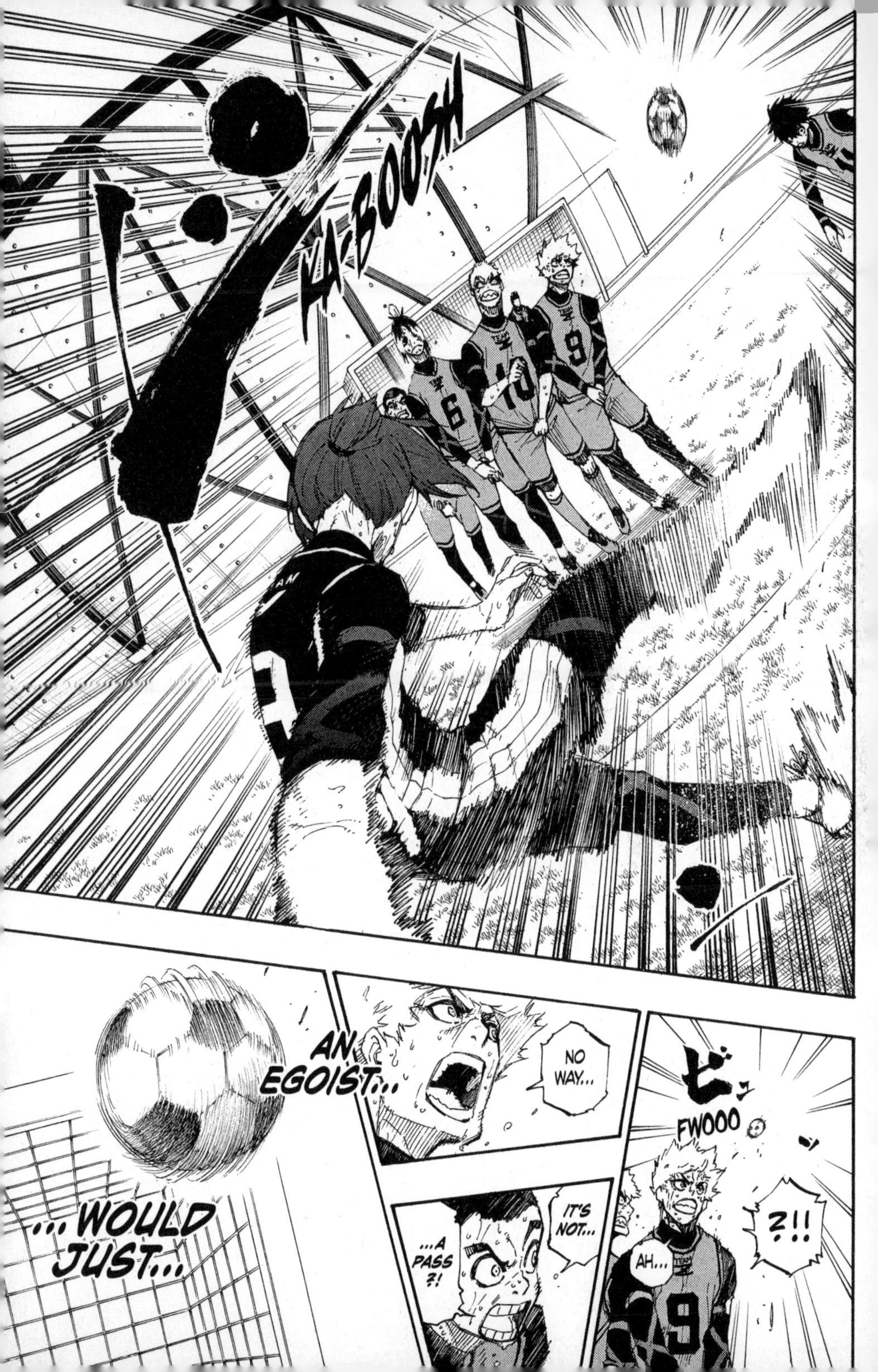
KA-BOOSH
ビュ
FWOOO
?!!
AH...
AN EGOIST...
NO WAY...
IT'S NOT...
...A PASS ?!
...WOULD JUST...

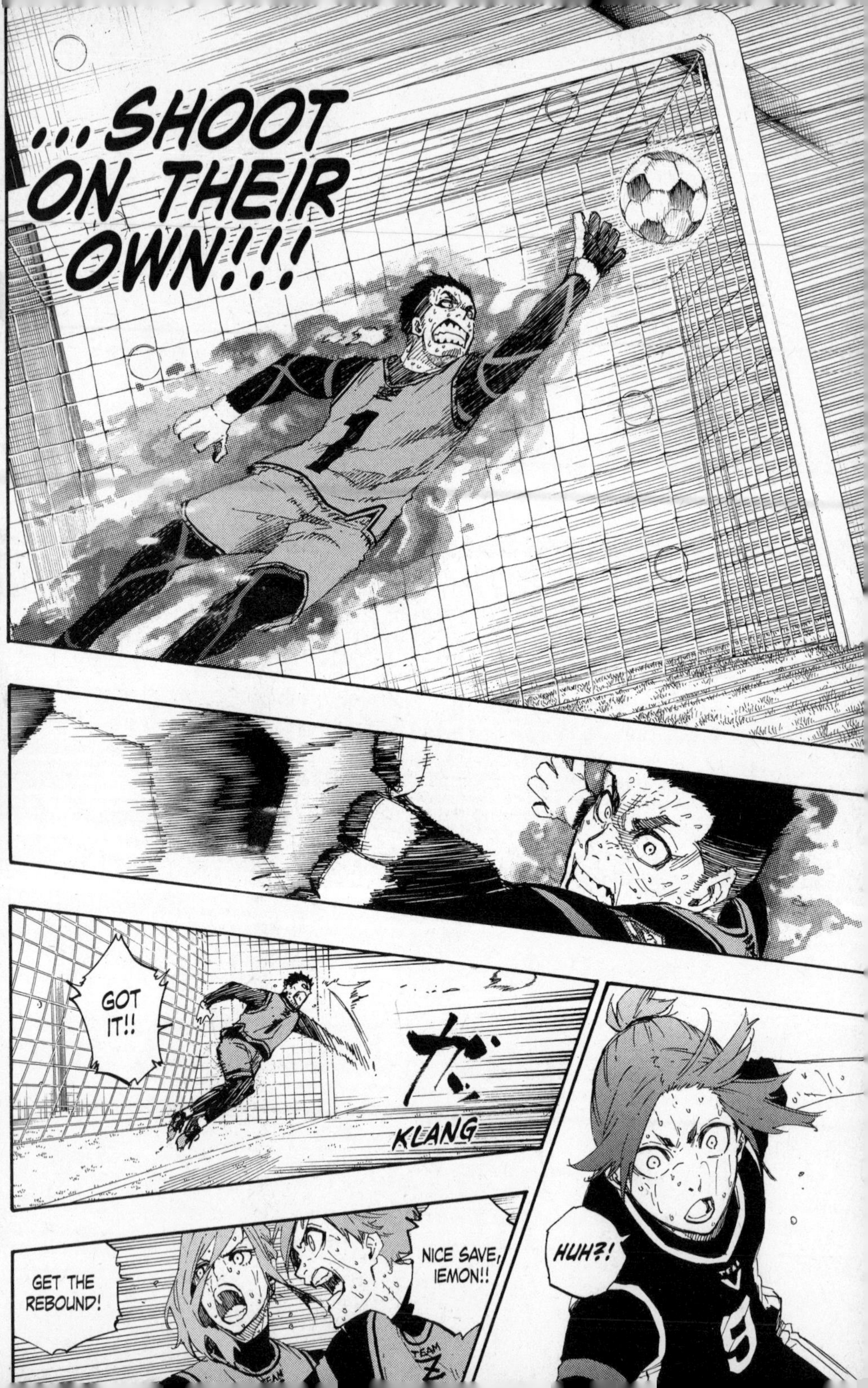
...SHOOT ON THEIR OWN!!!
HUH?!
GOT IT!!
KLANG
NICE SAVE, IEMON!!
GET THE REBOUND!

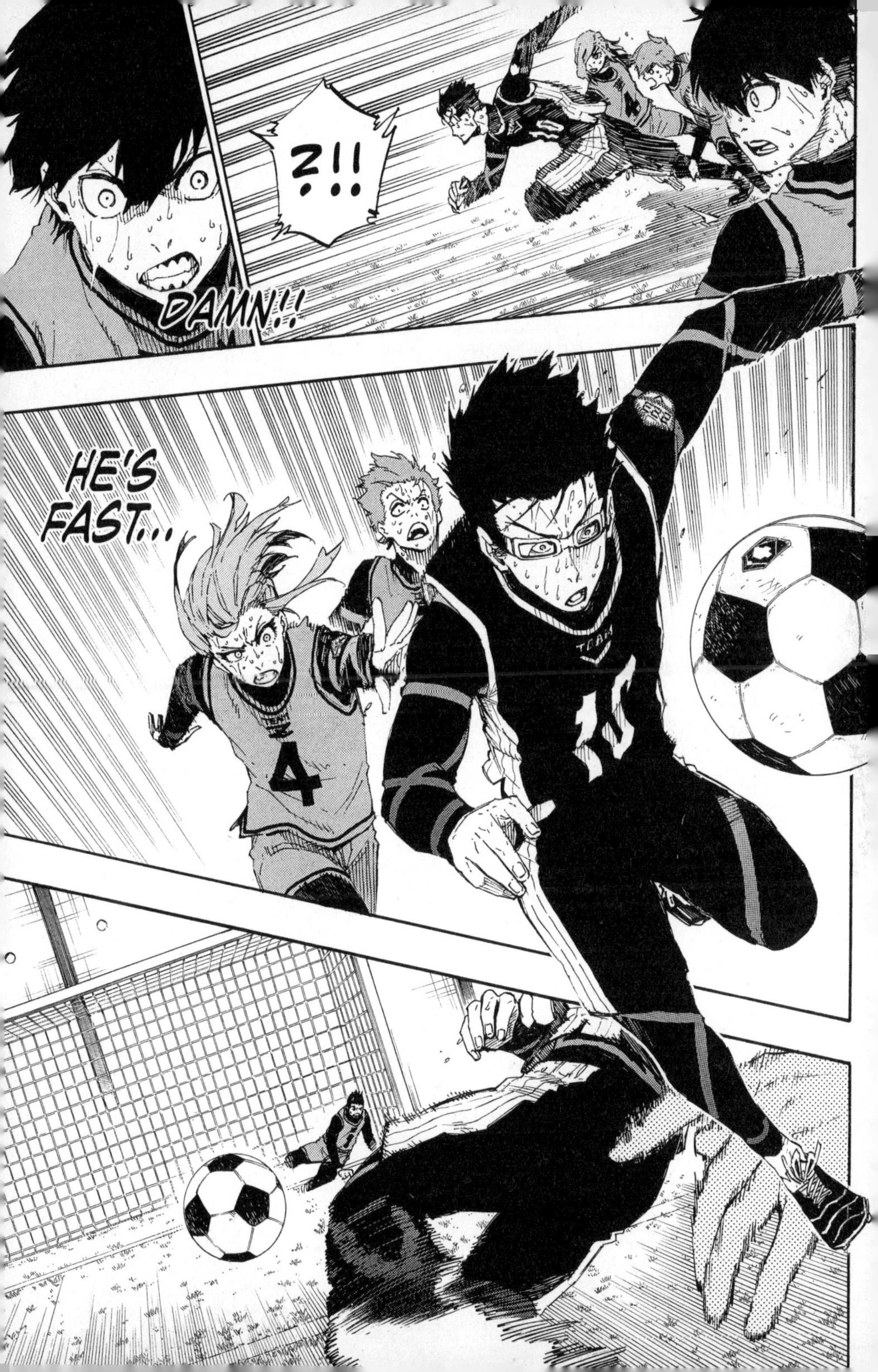
?!!
DAMN!!
HE'S FAST...

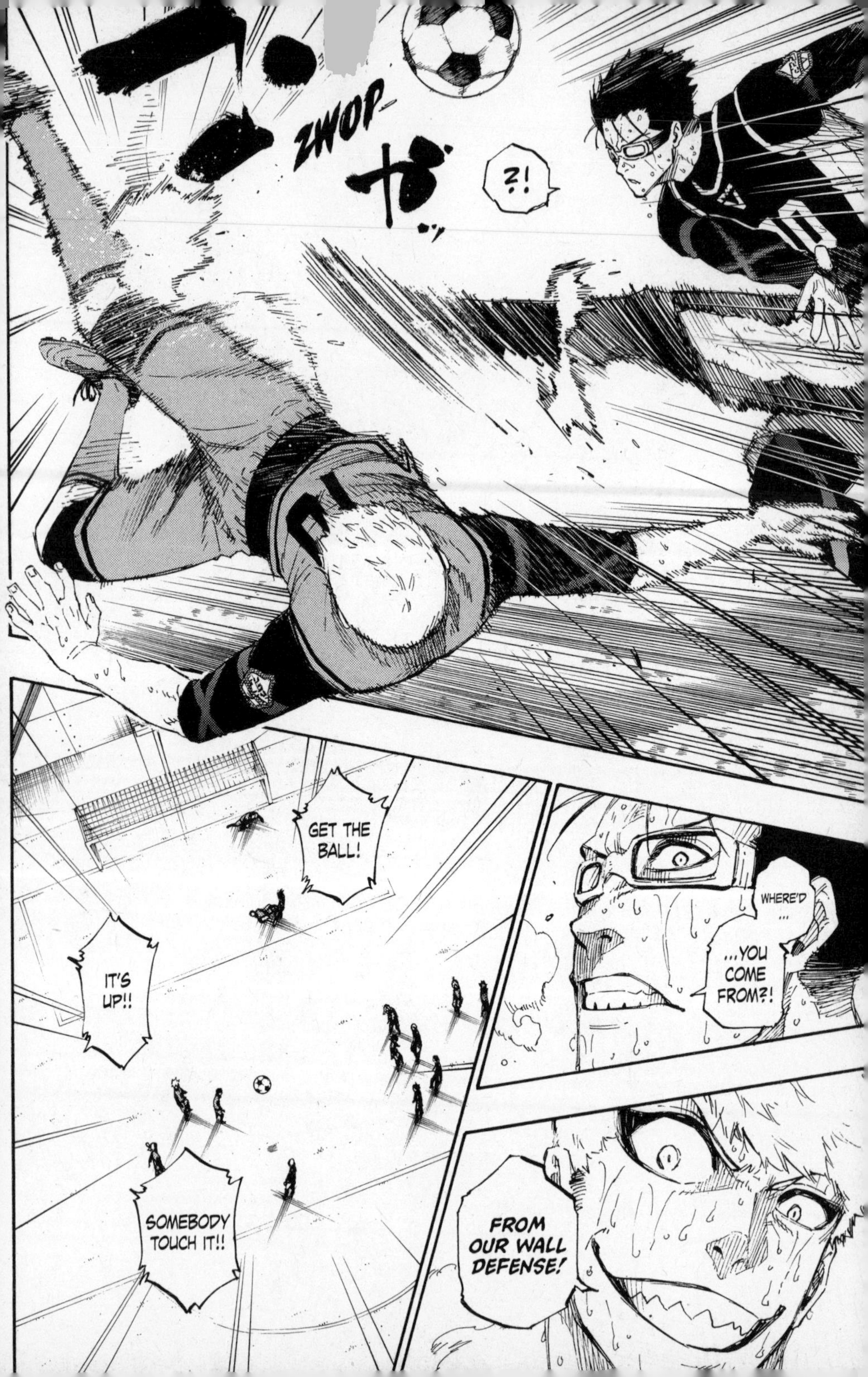
ZWOP
?!
WHERE'D ...
...YOU COME FROM?!
FROM OUR WALL DEFENSE!
GET THE BALL!
IT'S UP!!
SOMEBODY TOUCH IT!!

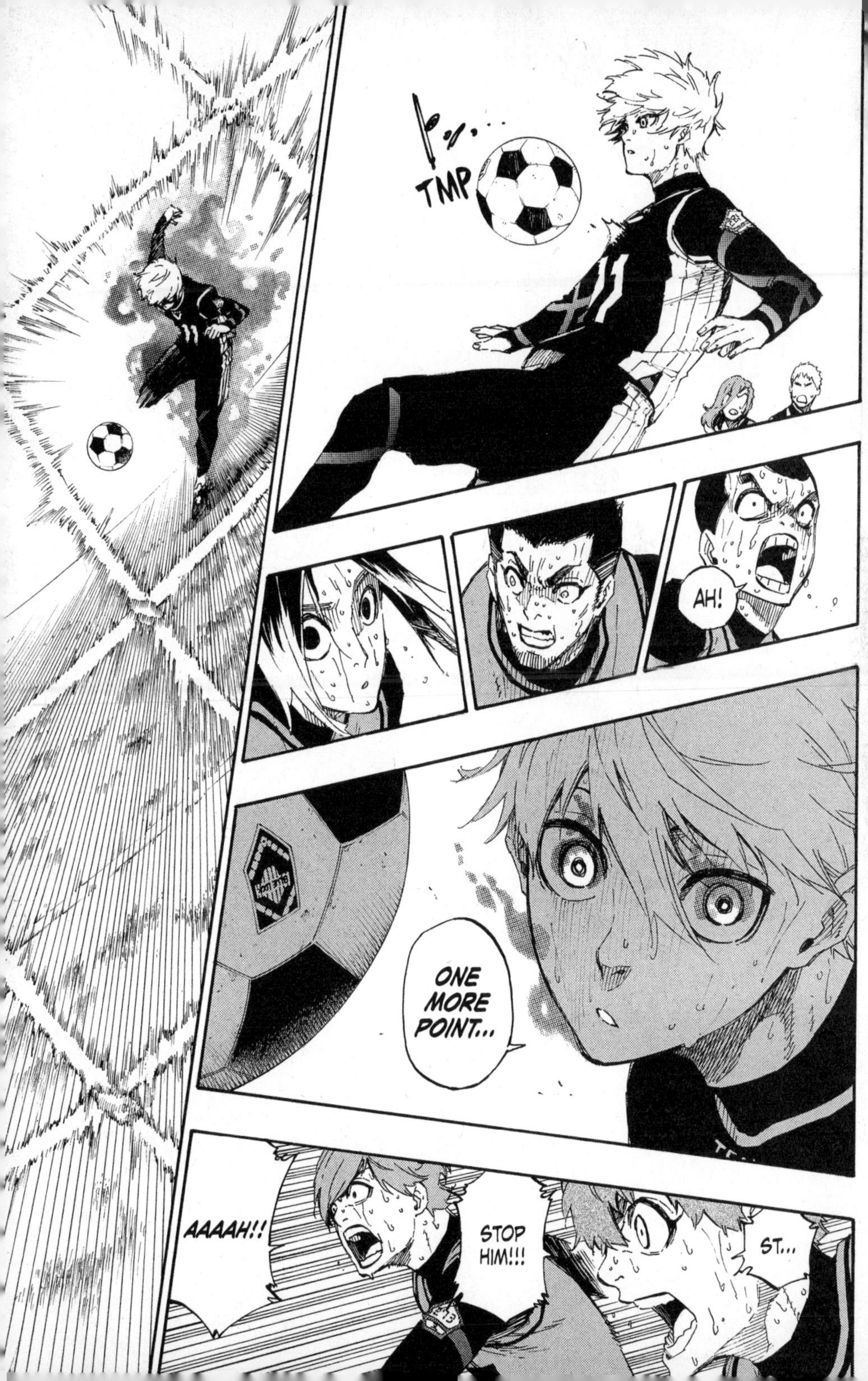
TMP
AH!
ONE MORE POINT...
ST...
STOP HIM!!!
AAAAH!!

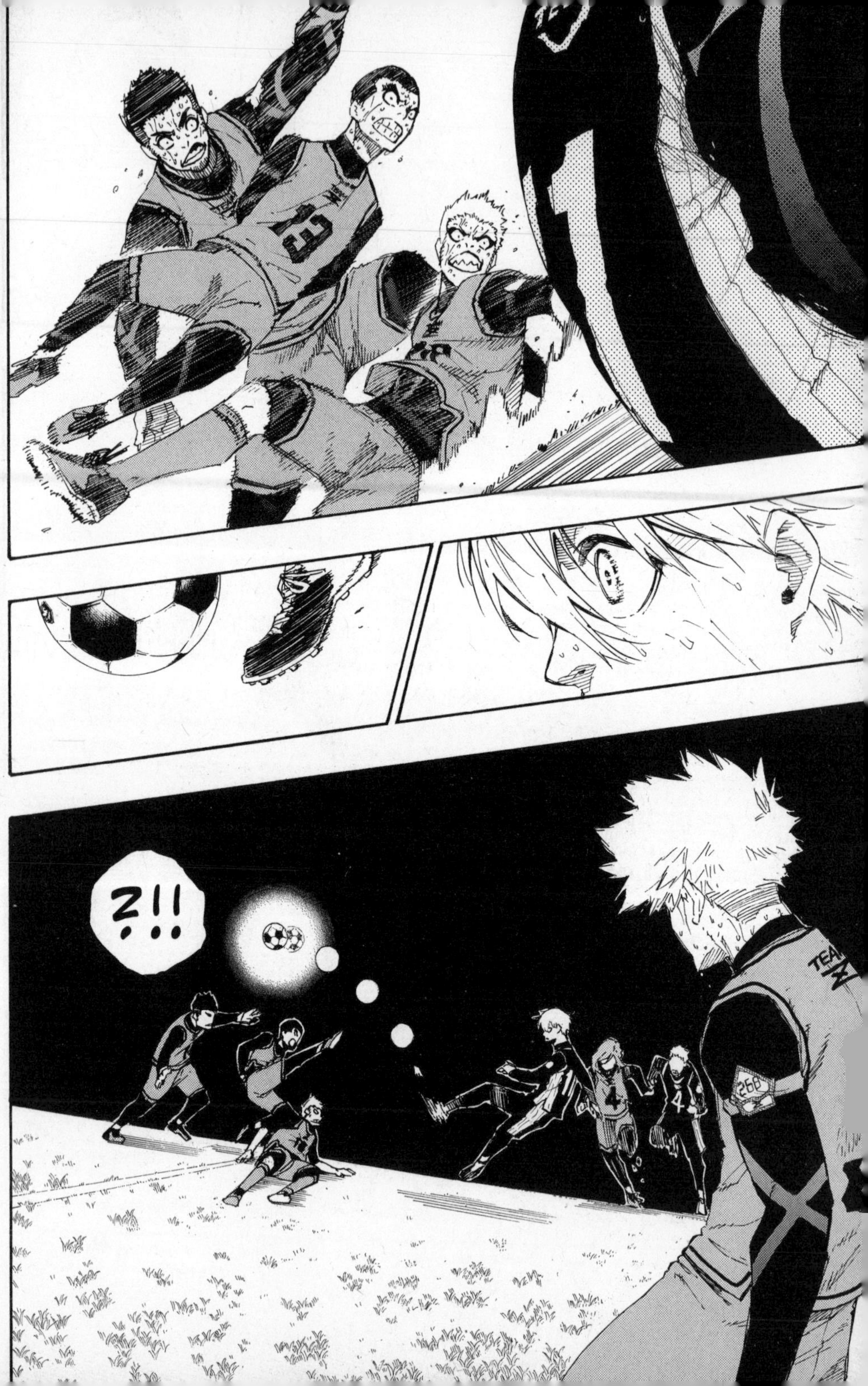
?!!

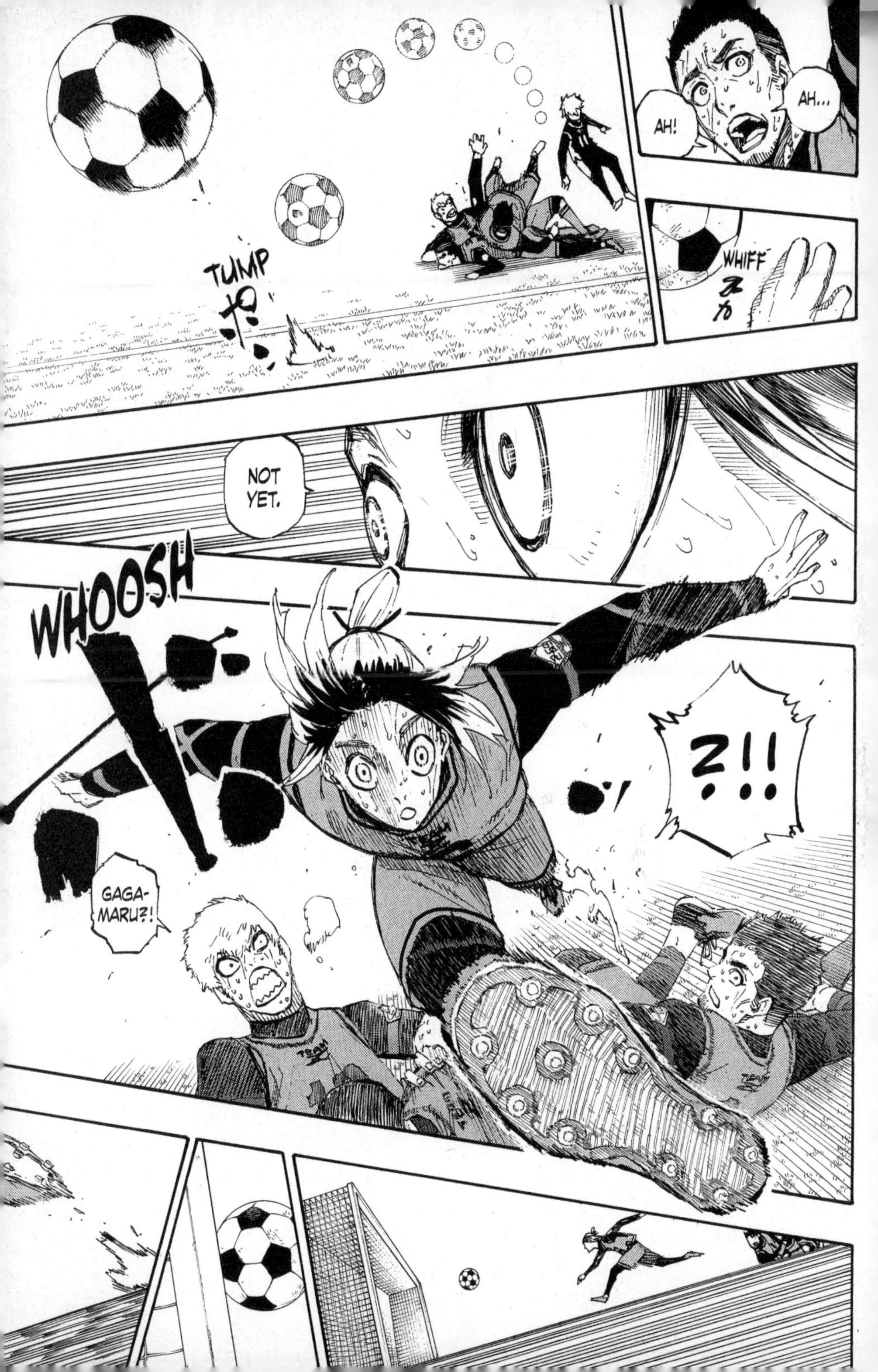
AH...
AH!
WHIFF
TUMP
NOT YET.
?!!
WHOOSH
GAGA-MARU?!

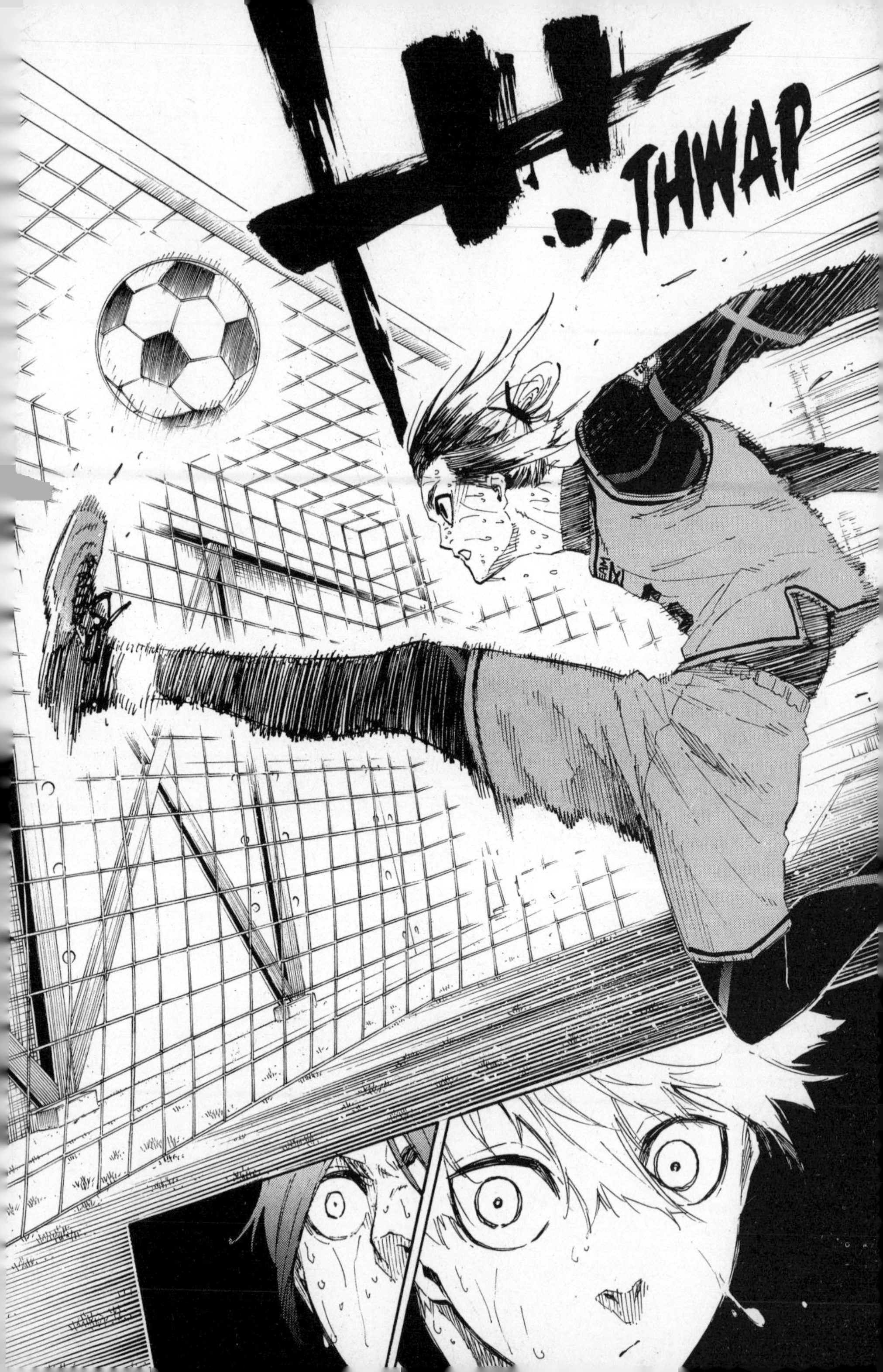
THWAP

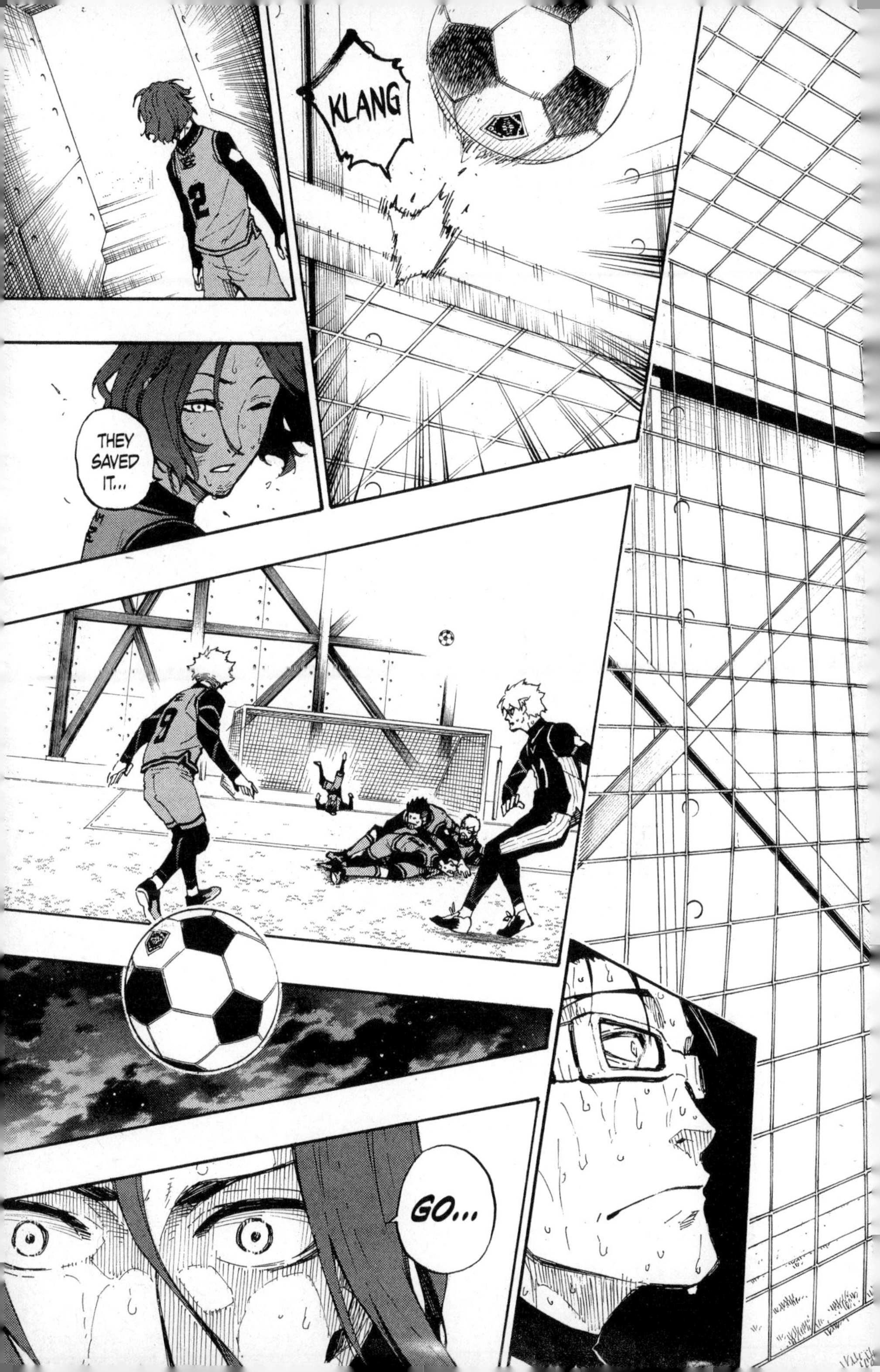
KLANG
THEY SAVED IT...
GO...

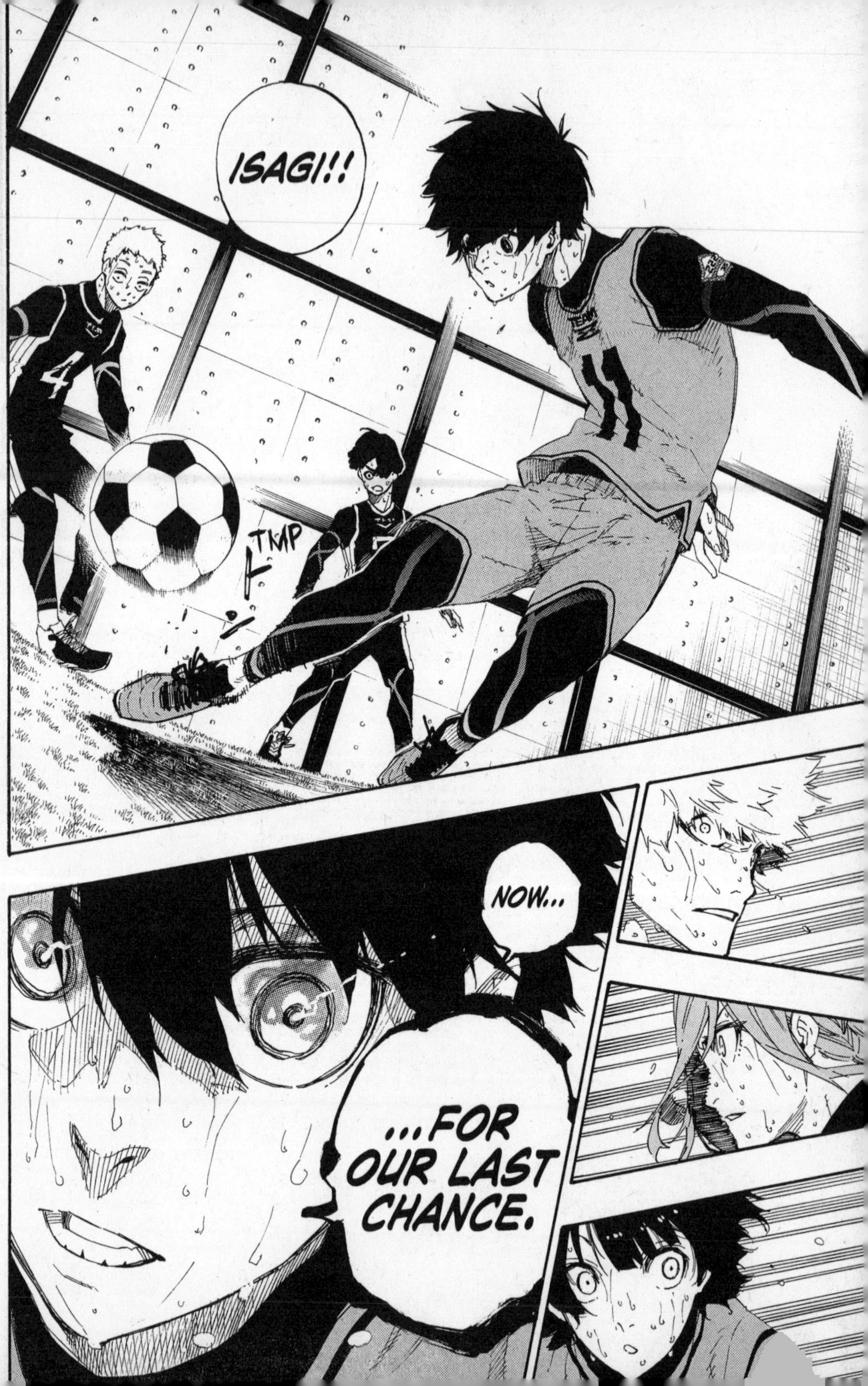
ISAGI!!
TMP
NOW...
...FOR OUR LAST CHANCE.

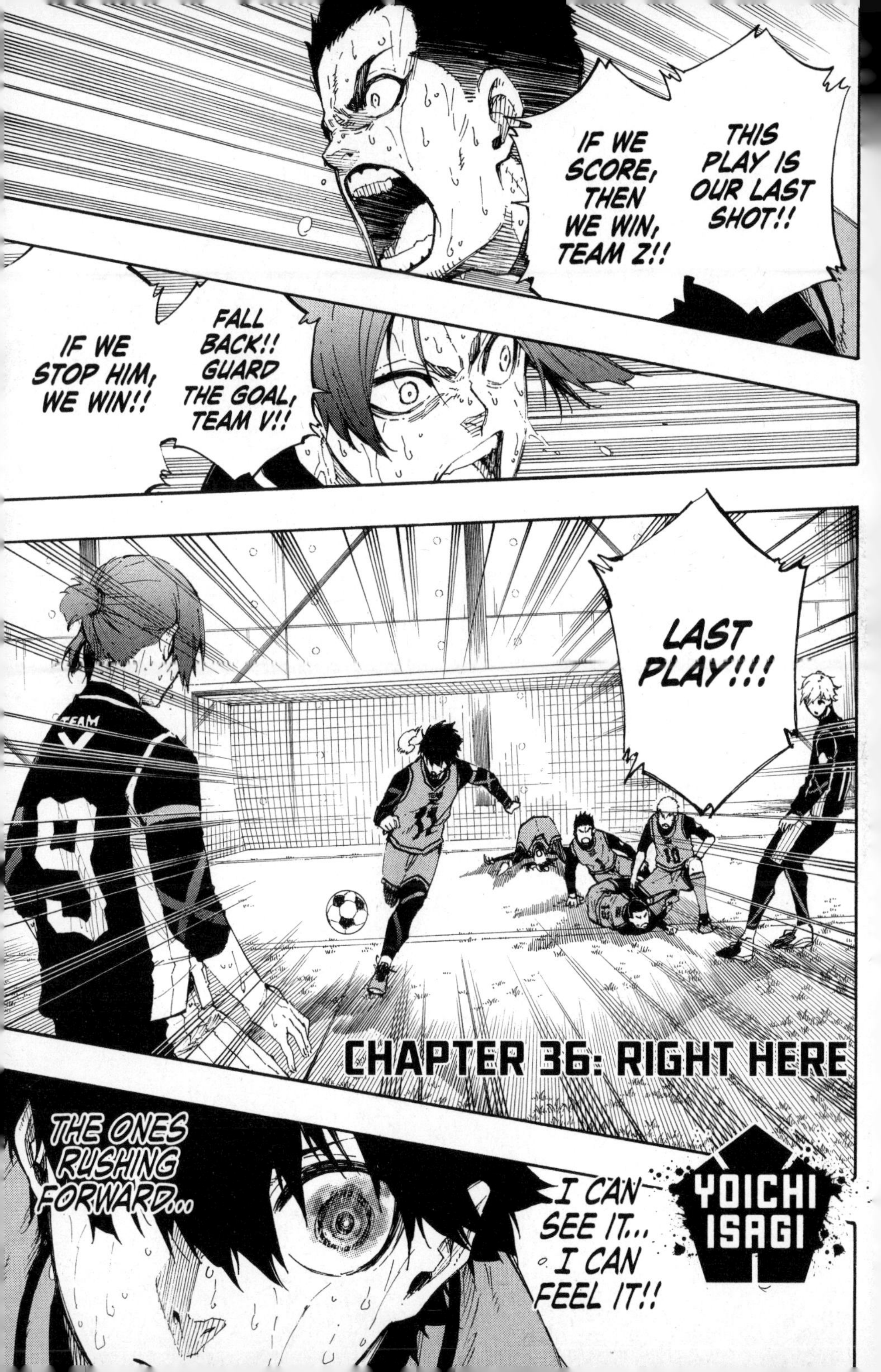
THIS PLAY IS OUR LAST SHOT!!
IF WE SCORE, THEN WE WIN, TEAM Z!!
FALL BACK!! GUARD THE GOAL, TEAM V!!
IF WE STOP HIM, WE WIN!!
LAST PLAY!!!
TEAM
CHAPTER 36: RIGHT HERE
YOICHI ISAGI
I CAN SEE IT... I CAN FEEL IT!!
THE ONES RUSHING FORWARD...

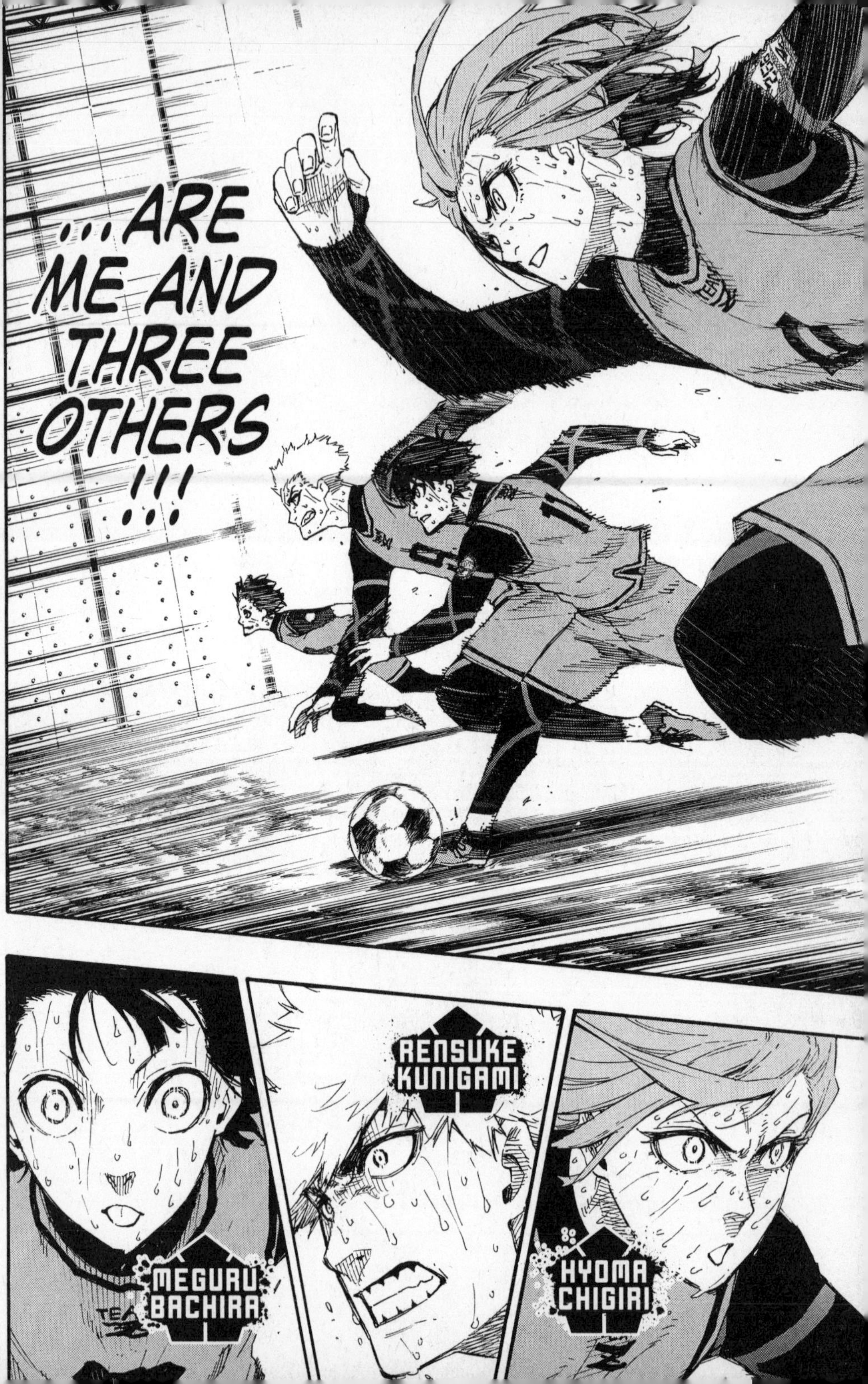
...ARE ME AND THREE OTHERS!!!
HYOMA CHIGIRI
RENSUKE KUNIGAMI
MEGURU BACHIRA

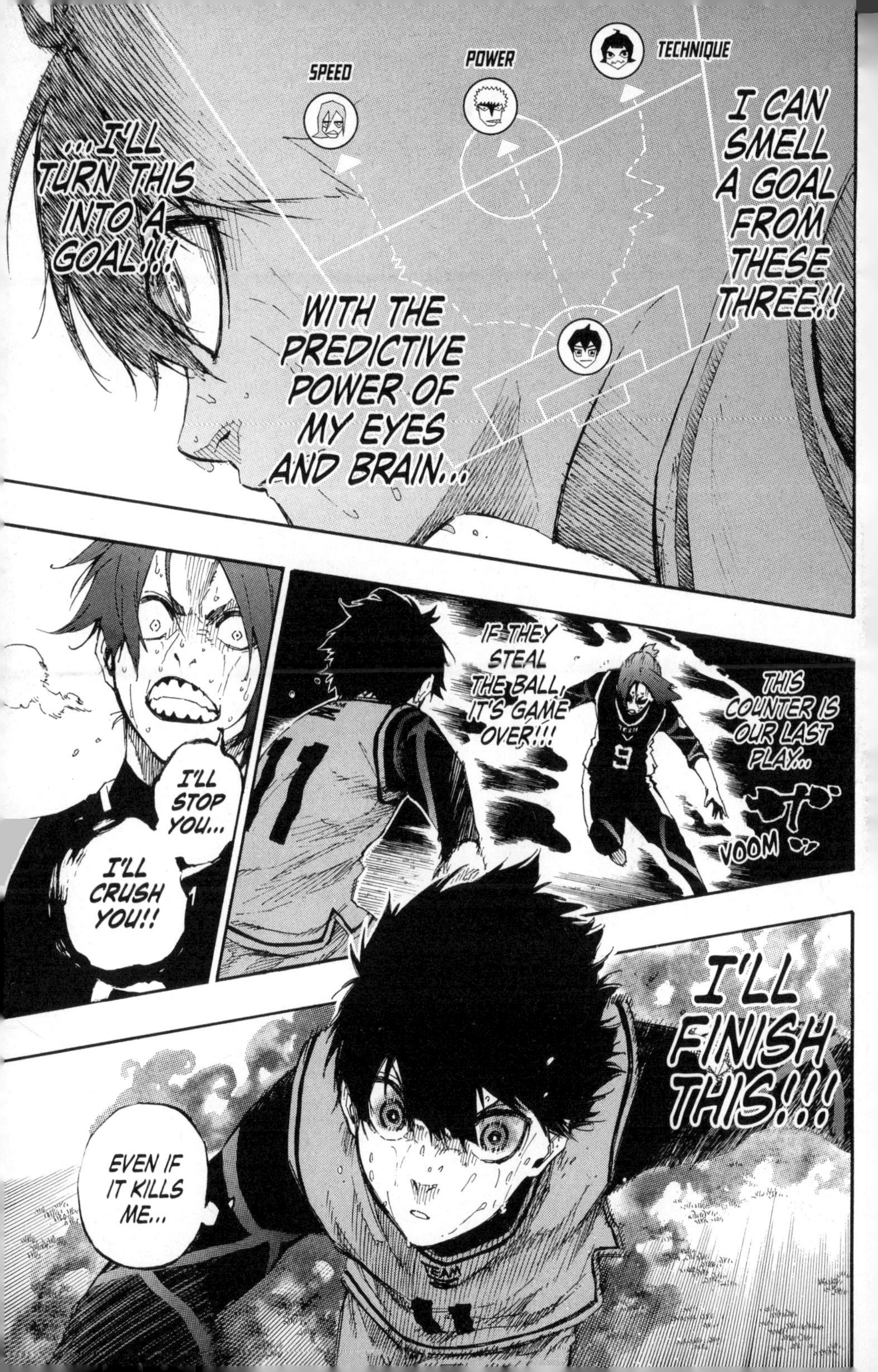
I CAN SMELL A GOAL FROM THESE THREE!!
TECHNIQUE
POWER
SPEED
WITH THE PREDICTIVE POWER OF MY EYES AND BRAIN...
...I'LL TURN THIS INTO A GOAL!!!
THIS COUNTER IS OUR LAST PLAY...
VOOM
IF THEY STEAL THE BALL, IT'S GAME OVER!!!
I'LL STOP YOU...
I'LL CRUSH YOU!!
I'LL FINISH THIS!!!
EVEN IF IT KILLS ME...

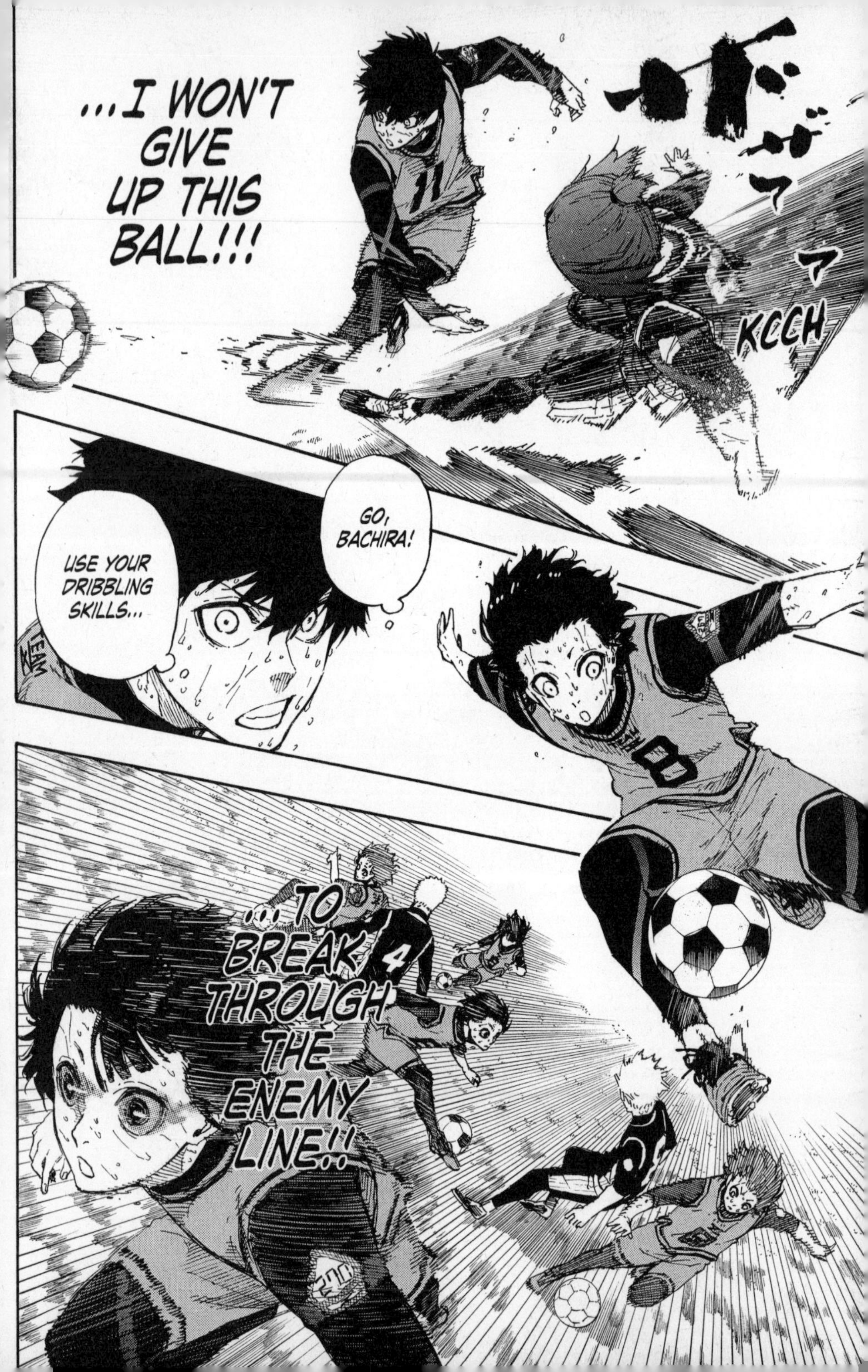
...I WON'T GIVE UP THIS BALL!!!
KCCH
GO, BACHIRA!
USE YOUR DRIBBLING SKILLS...
...TO BREAK THROUGH THE ENEMY LINE!!

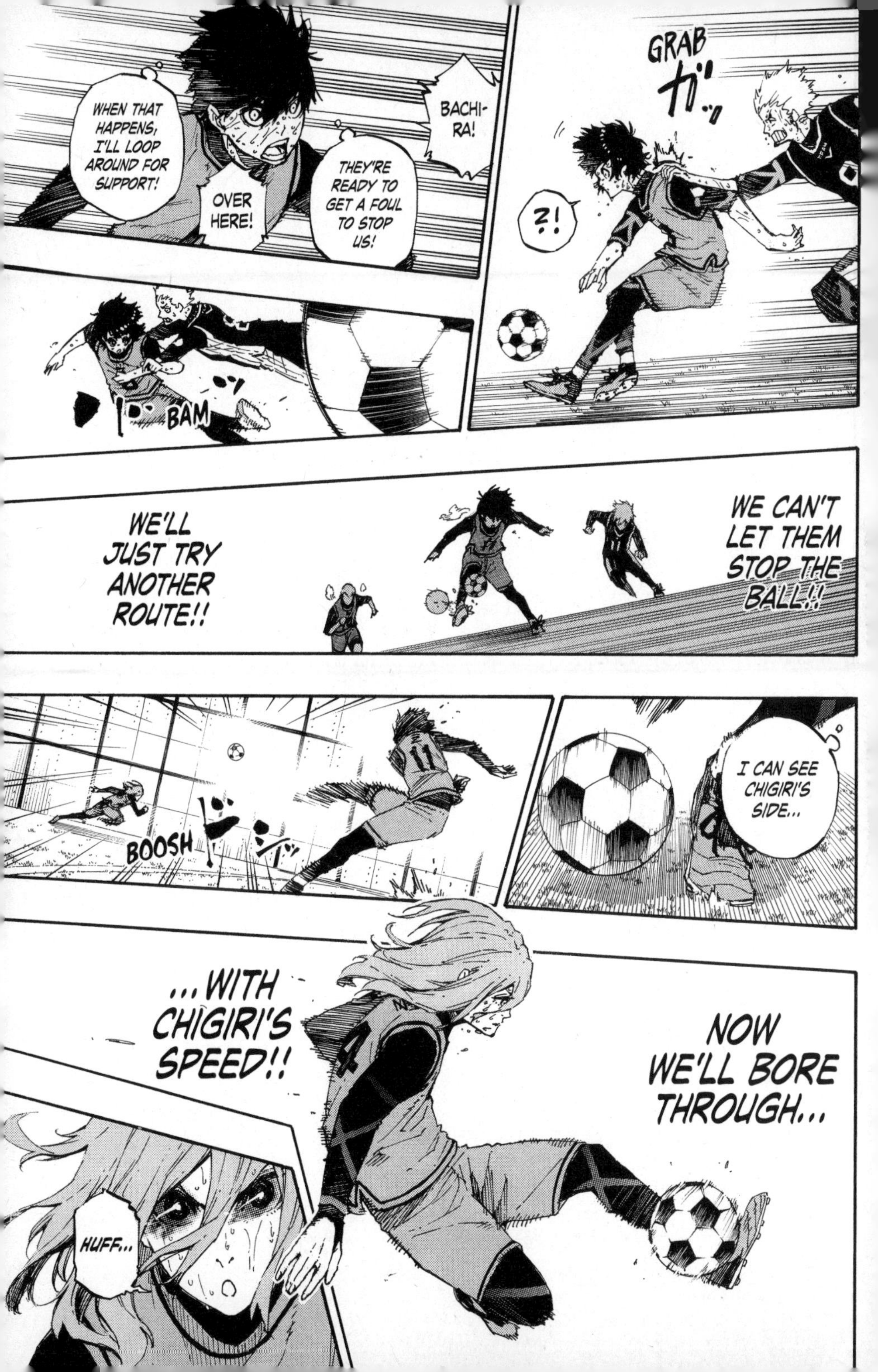
GRAB
?!
BACHI-RA!
THEY'RE READY TO GET A FOUL TO STOP US!
WHEN THAT HAPPENS, I'LL LOOP AROUND FOR SUPPORT!
OVER HERE!
BAM
WE CAN'T LET THEM STOP THE BALL!!
WE'LL JUST TRY ANOTHER ROUTE!!
I CAN SEE CHIGIRI'S SIDE...
BOOSH
NOW WE'LL BORE THROUGH...
...WITH CHIGIRI'S SPEED!!
HUFF...

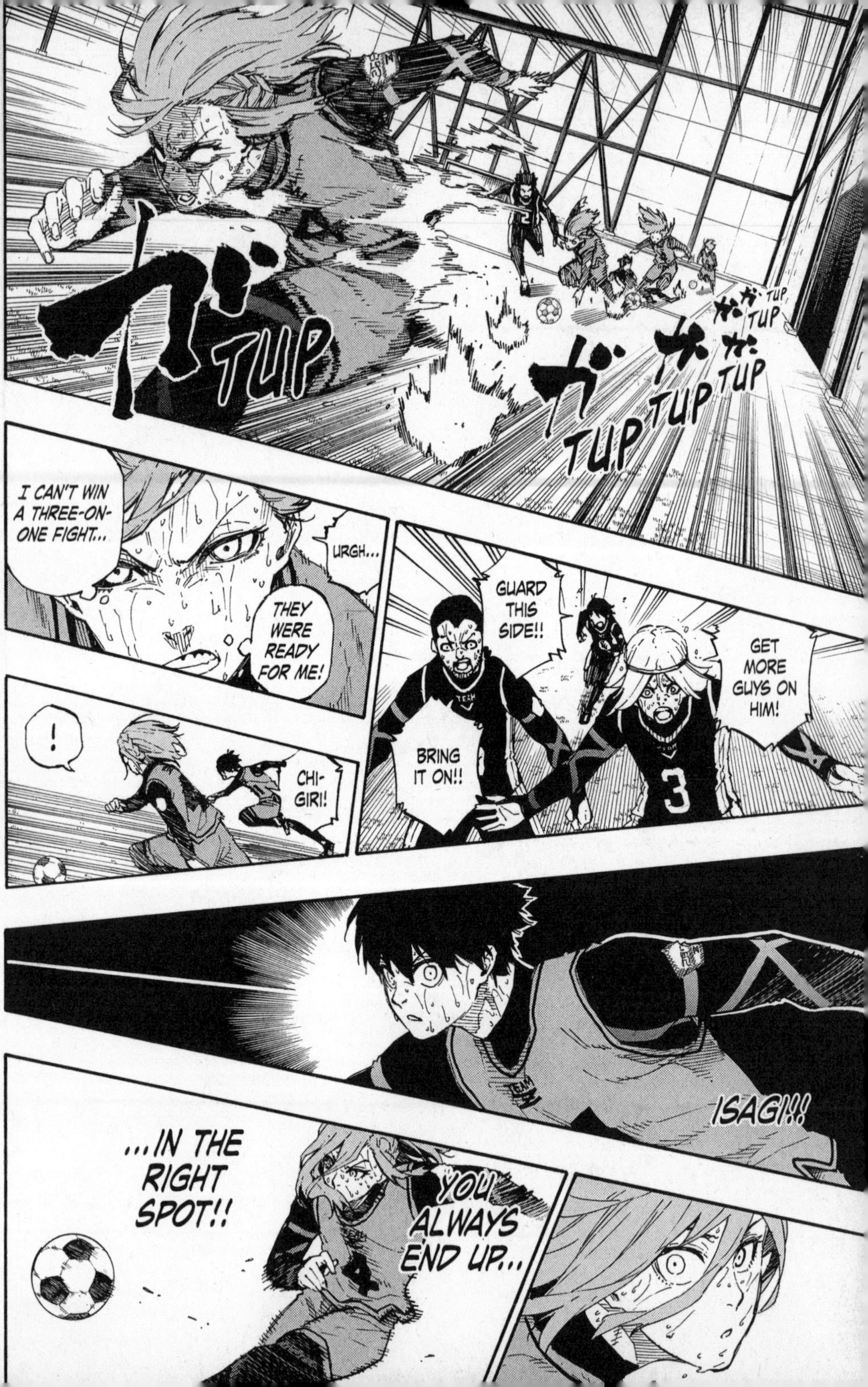
TUP
TUP TUP TUP TUP TUP
GET MORE GUYS ON HIM!
GUARD THIS SIDE!!
BRING IT ON!!
URGH...
I CAN'T WIN A THREE-ON-ONE FIGHT...
THEY WERE READY FOR ME!
CHI-GIRI!
!
ISAGI!!
YOU ALWAYS END UP...
...IN THE RIGHT SPOT!!

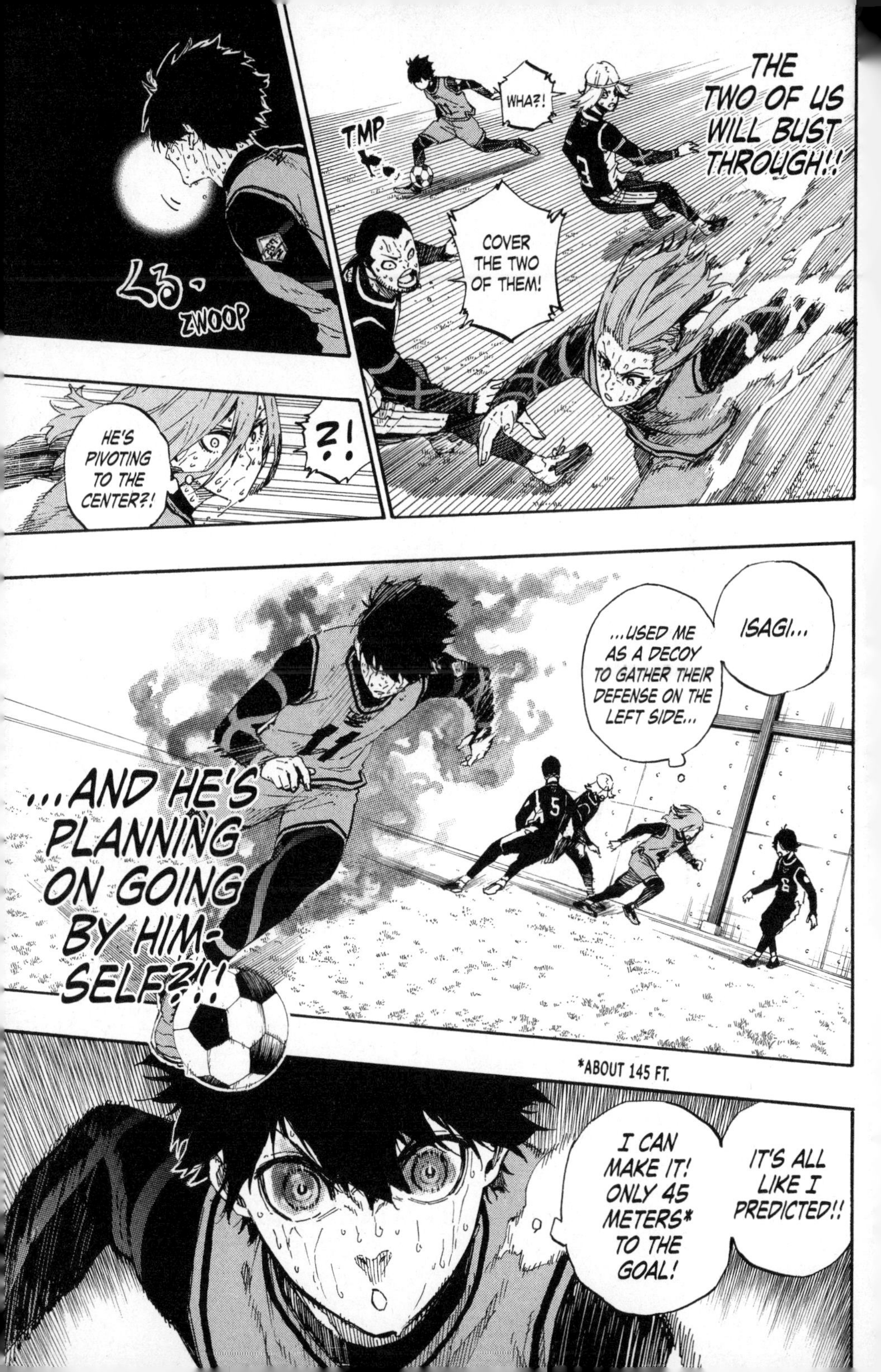
THE TWO OF US WILL BUST THROUGH!!
WHA?!
TMP
COVER THE TWO OF THEM!
ZWOOP
?!
HE'S PIVOTING TO THE CENTER?!
ISAGI...
...USED ME AS A DECOY TO GATHER THEIR DEFENSE ON THE LEFT SIDE...
...AND HE'S PLANNING ON GOING BY HIM-SELF?!!
IT'S ALL LIKE I PREDICTED!!
I CAN MAKE IT! ONLY 45 METERS* TO THE GOAL!
*ABOUT 145 FT.

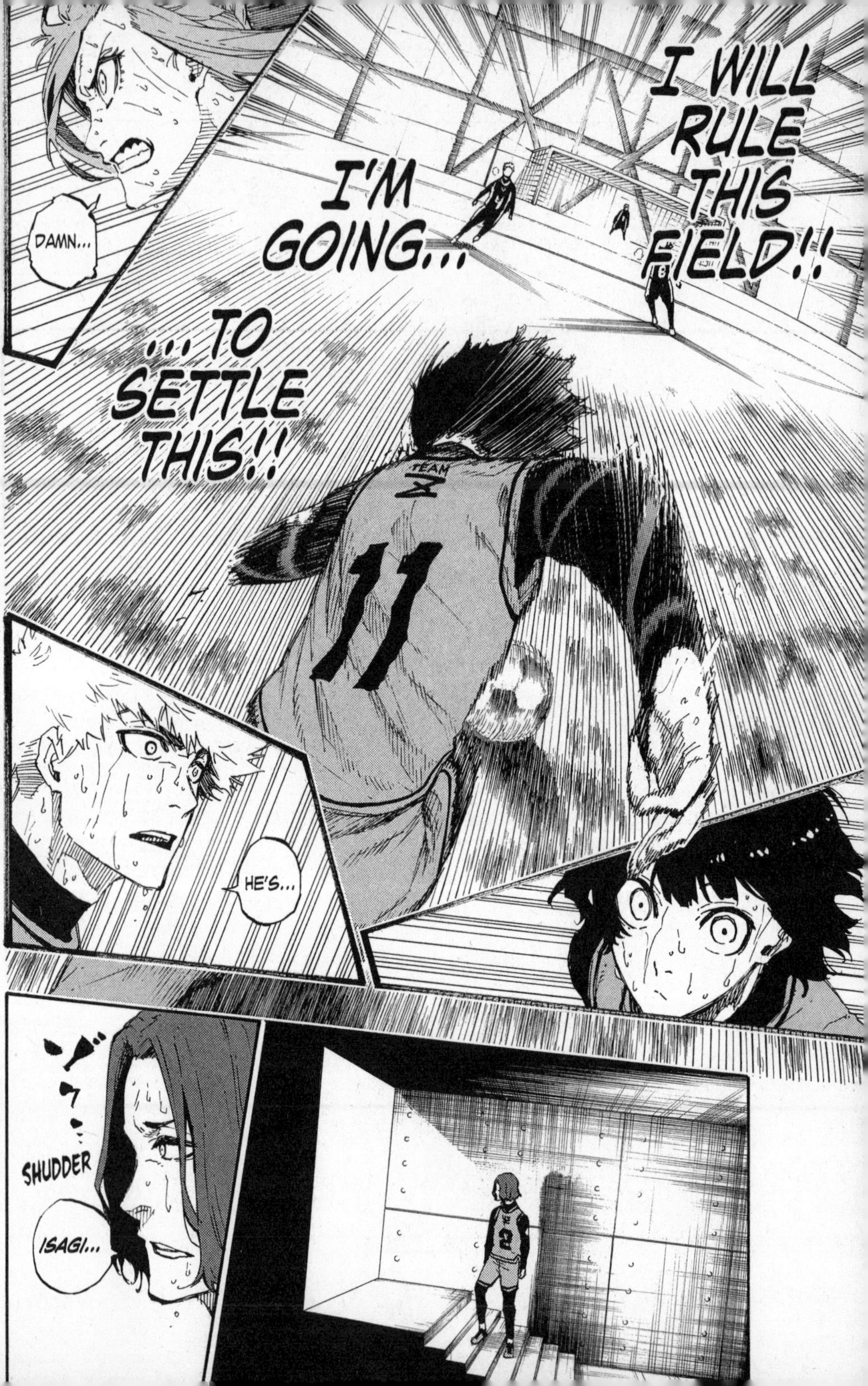
I WILL RULE THIS FIELD!!
I'M GOING...
...TO SETTLE THIS!!
DAMN...
HE'S...
SHUDDER
ISAGI...

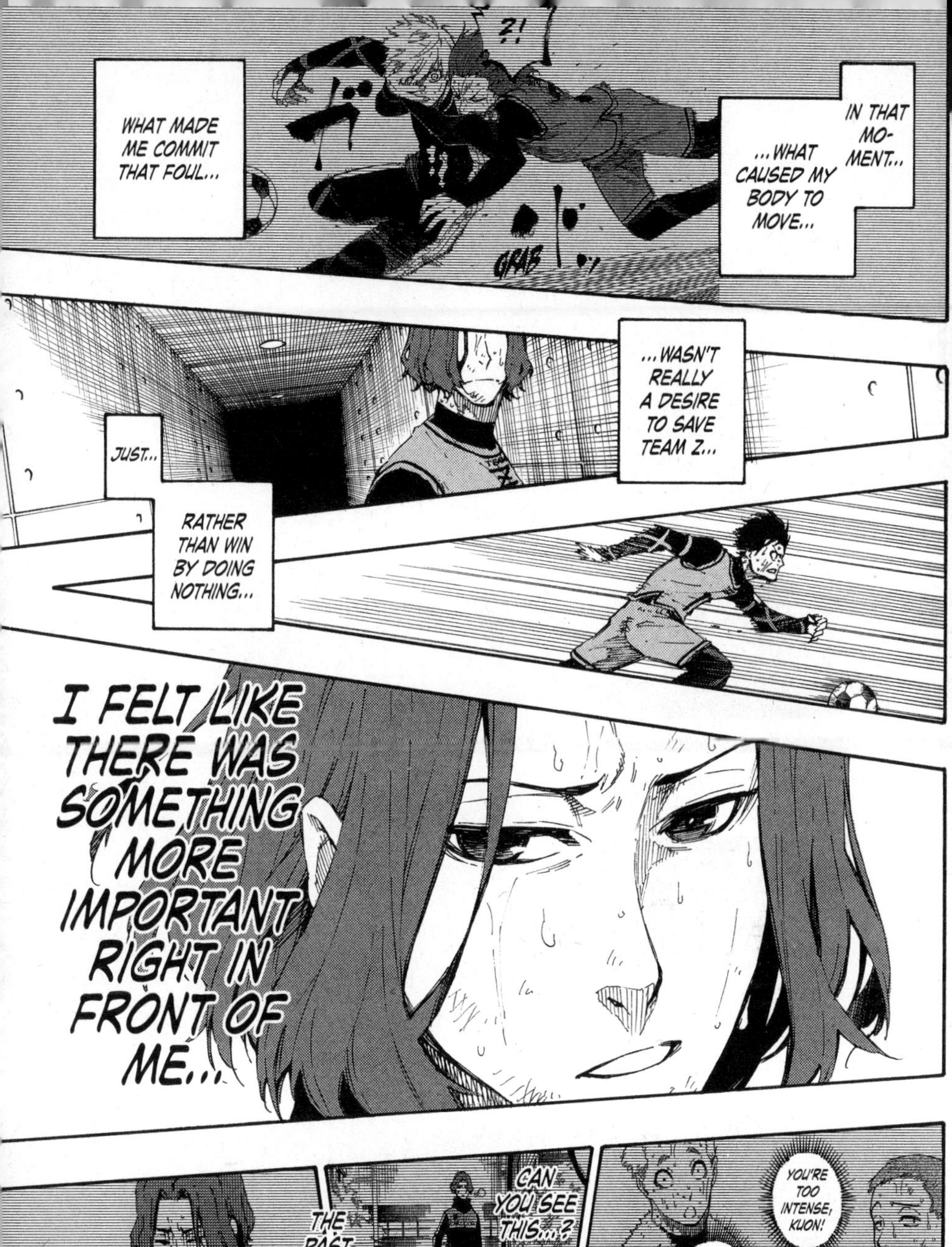
Z!
IN THAT MOMENT...
...WHAT CAUSED MY BODY TO MOVE...
WHAT MADE ME COMMIT THAT FOUL...
GRAB
...WASN'T REALLY A DESIRE TO SAVE TEAM Z...
JUST...
RATHER THAN WIN BY DOING NOTHING...
I FELT LIKE THERE WAS SOMETHING MORE IMPORTANT RIGHT IN FRONT OF ME...
YOU'RE TOO INTENSE, KUON!
ISN'T THAT ENOUGH?
CAN YOU SEE THIS...?
THE PAST ME...

THE KIND OF SOCCER YOU WANTED TO BELIEVE IN BACK THEN...

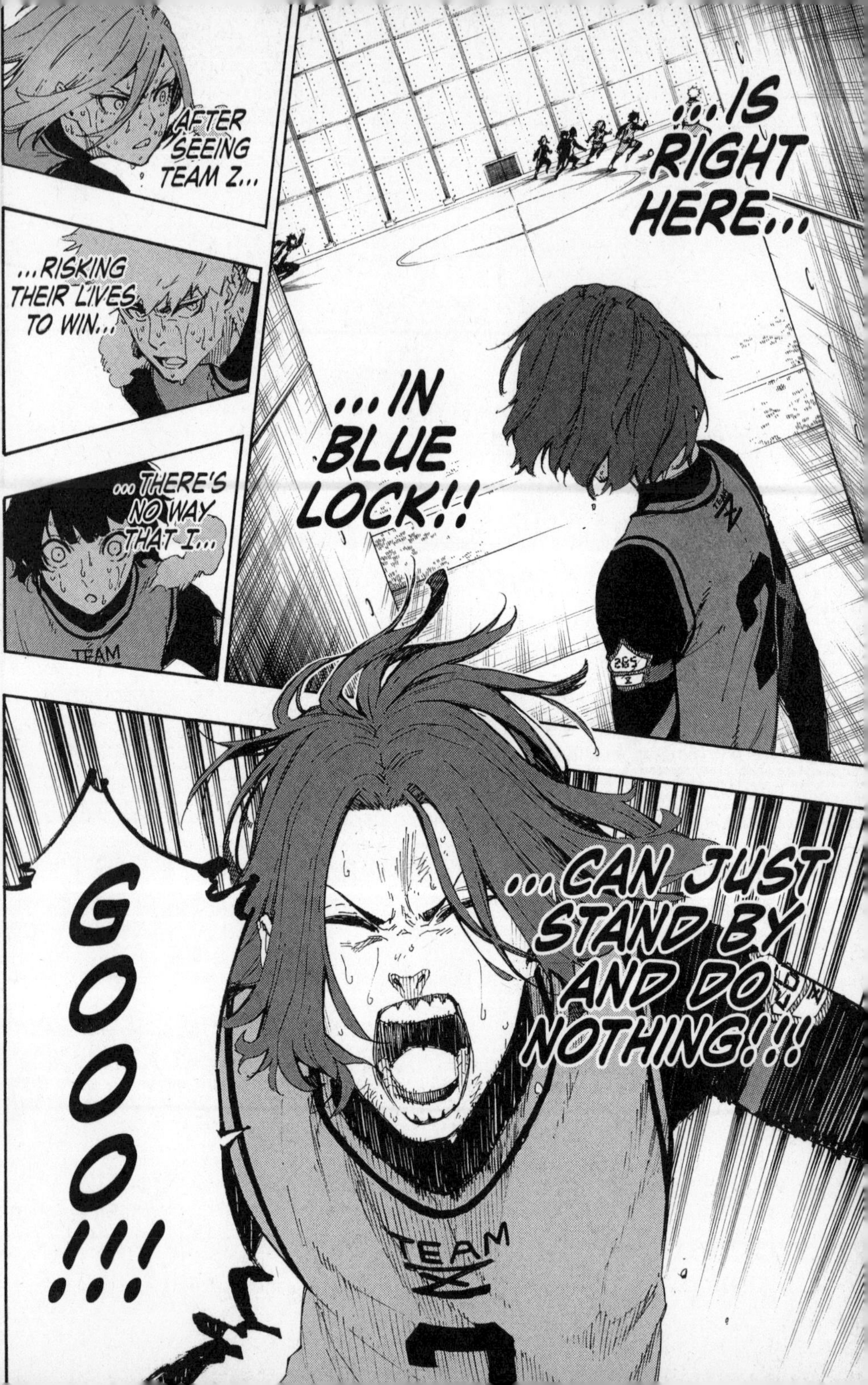
...IS RIGHT HERE...
...IN BLUE LOCK!!
AFTER SEEING TEAM Z...
...RISKING THEIR LIVES TO WIN...
...THERE'S NO WAY THAT I...
...CAN JUST STAND BY AND DO NOTHING!!!
GOOOO!!!

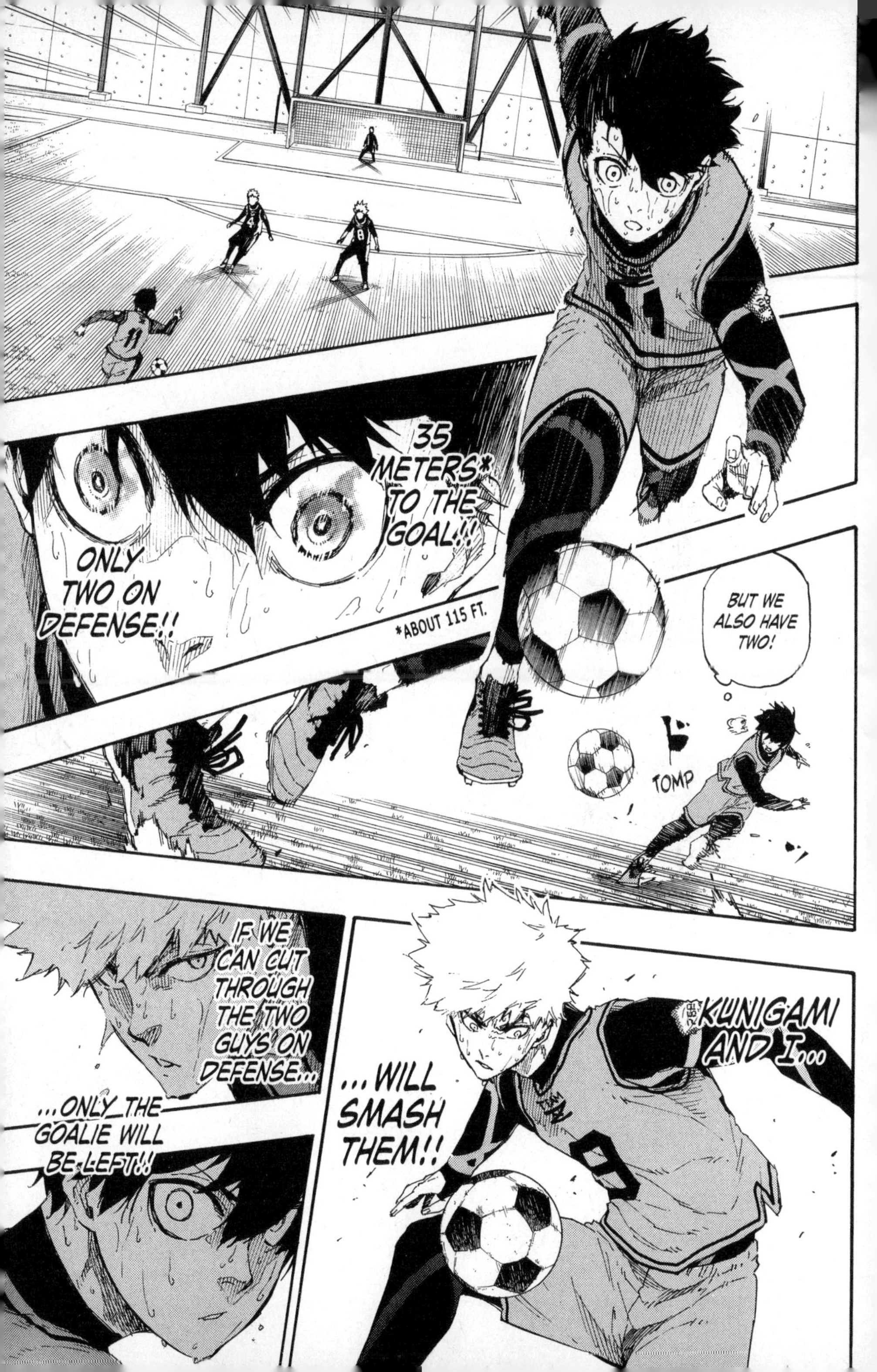
35 METERS* TO THE GOAL!!
ONLY TWO ON DEFENSE!!
*ABOUT 115 FT.
BUT WE ALSO HAVE TWO!
TOMP
KUNIGAMI AND I...
...WILL SMASH THEM!!
IF WE CAN CUT THROUGH THE TWO GUYS ON DEFENSE...
...ONLY THE GOALIE WILL BE LEFT!!

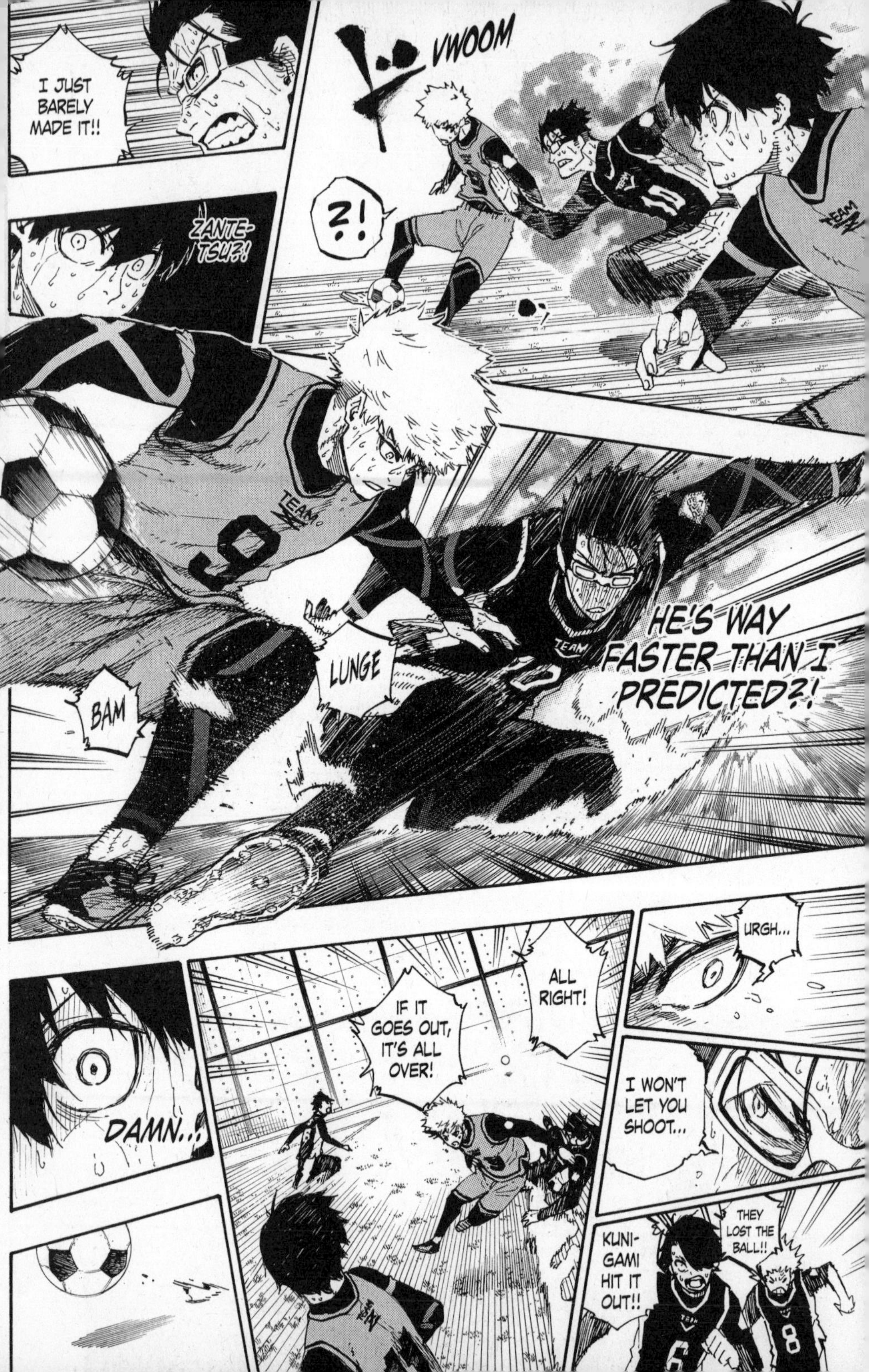
VWOOM
?!
I JUST BARELY MADE IT!!
ZANTE-TSU?!
HE'S WAY FASTER THAN I PREDICTED?!
LUNGE
BAM
URGH...
I WON'T LET YOU SHOOT...
THEY LOST THE BALL!!
KUNI-GAMI HIT IT OUT!!
ALL RIGHT!
IF IT GOES OUT, IT'S ALL OVER!
DAMN...

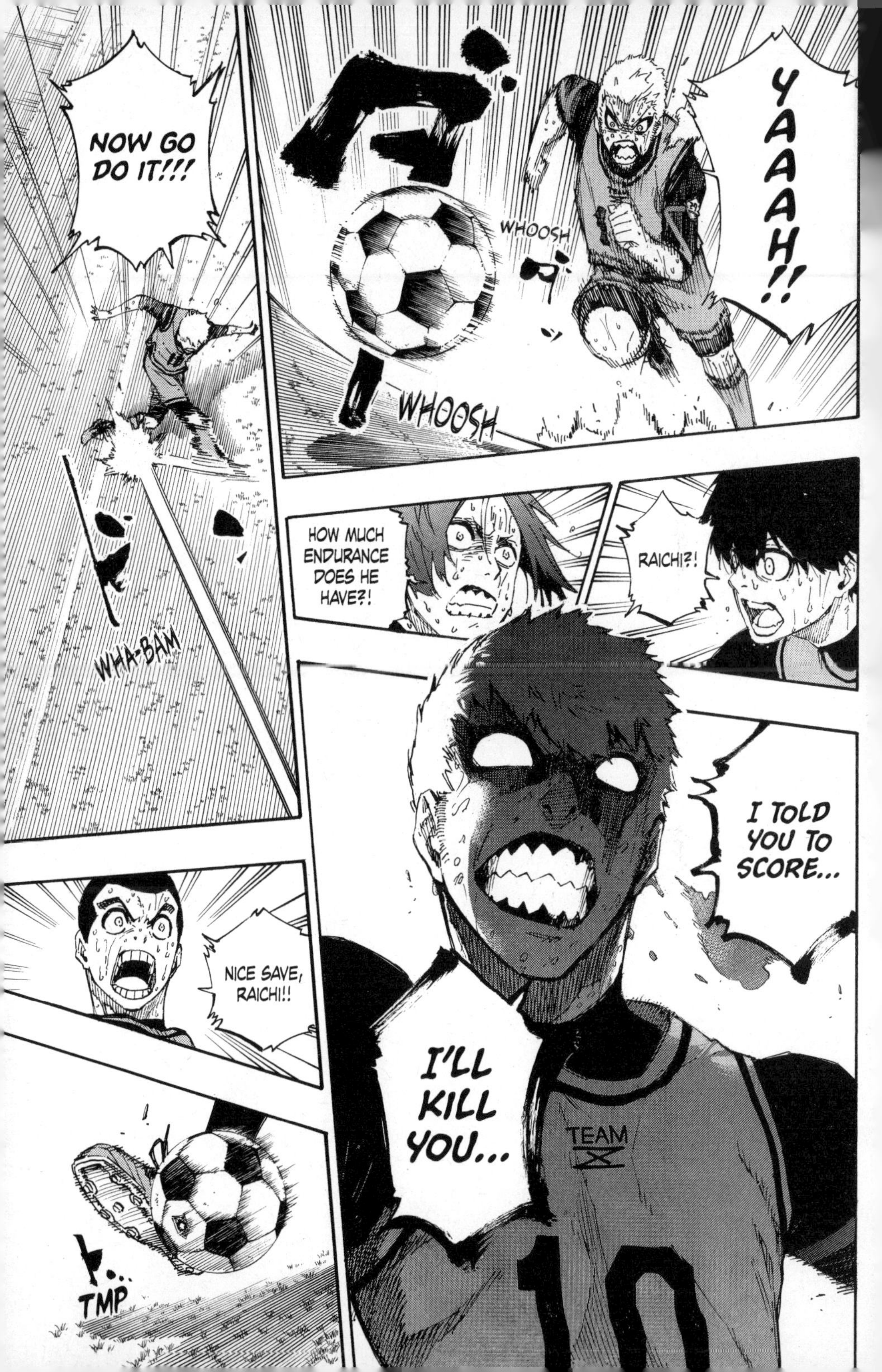
YAAAAH!!
WHOOSH
WHOOSH
NOW GO DO IT!!!
WHA-BAM
RAICHI?!
HOW MUCH ENDURANCE DOES HE HAVE?!
I TOLD YOU TO SCORE...
I'LL KILL YOU...
TEAM X
NICE SAVE, RAICHI!!
TMP

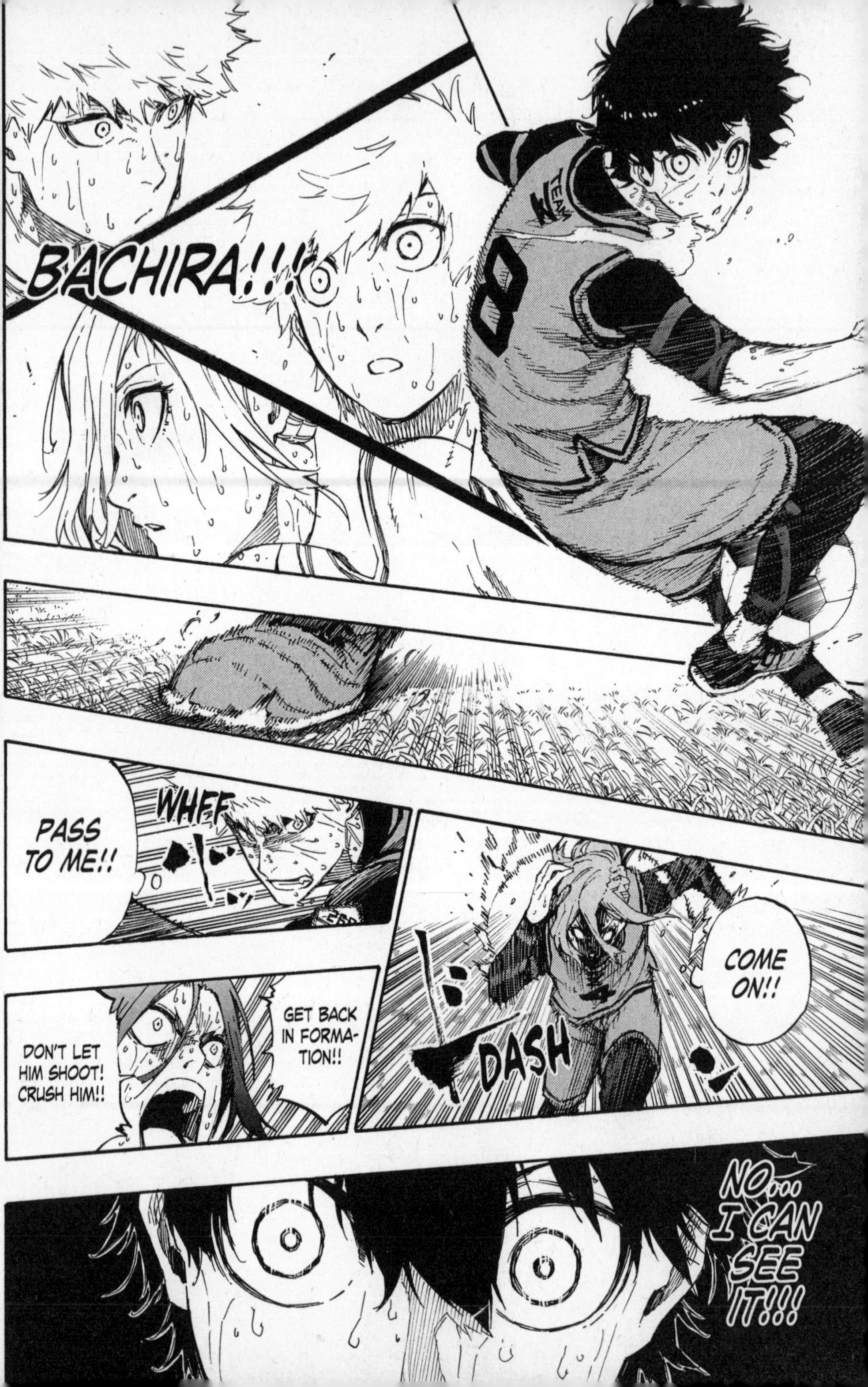
BACHIRA!!!
COME ON!!
DASH
WHFF
PASS TO ME!!
GET BACK IN FORMATION!!
DON'T LET HIM SHOOT! CRUSH HIM!!
NO... I CAN SEE IT!!!

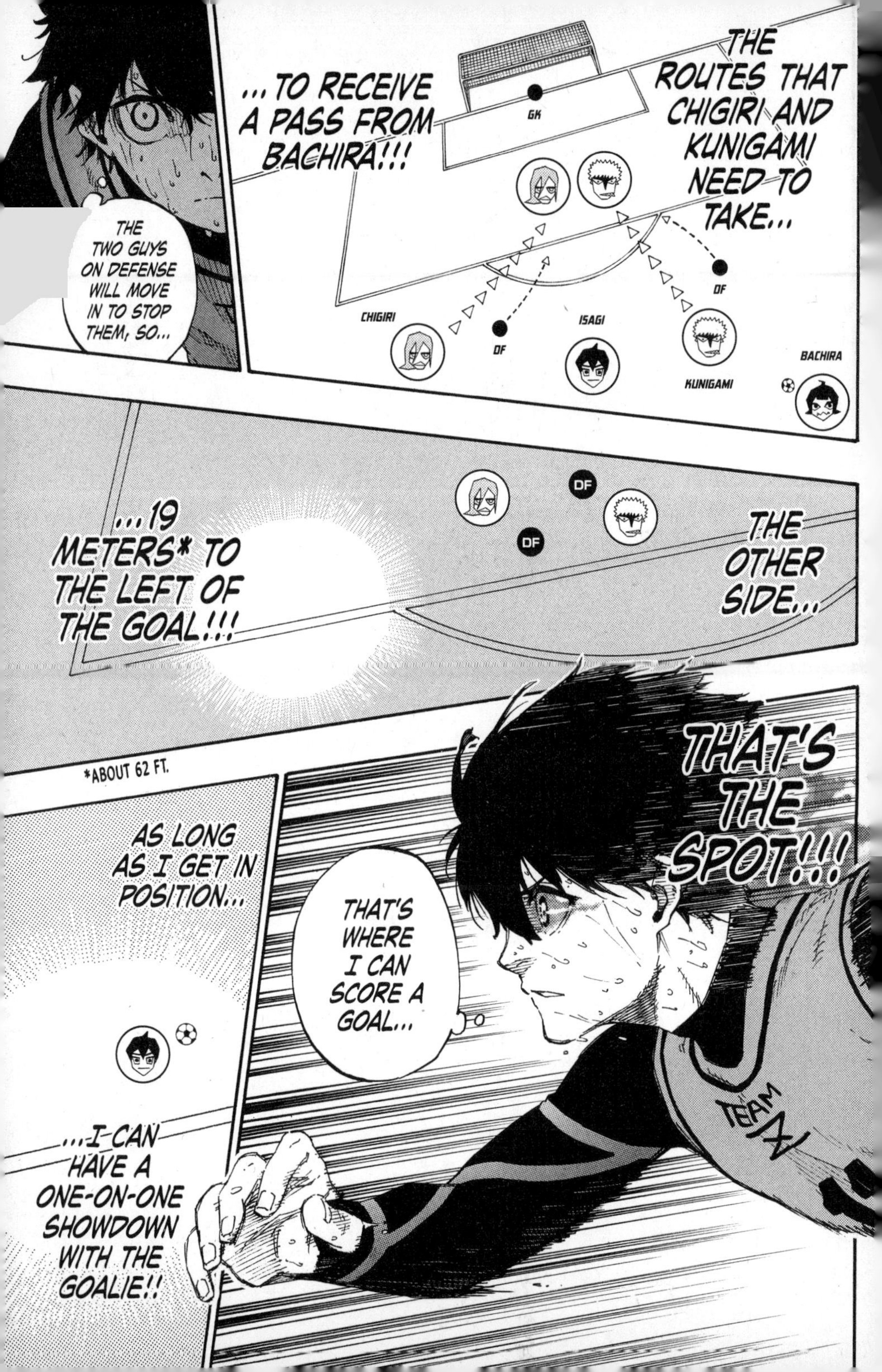

THE ROUTES THAT CHIGIRI AND KUNIGAMI NEED TO TAKE...
...TO RECEIVE A PASS FROM BACHIRA!!!
GK
DF
DF
CHIGIRI
ISAGI
KUNIGAMI
BACHIRA
THE TWO GUYS ON DEFENSE WILL MOVE IN TO STOP THEM, SO...
DF
DF
THE OTHER SIDE...
...19 METERS* TO THE LEFT OF THE GOAL!!!
*ABOUT 62 FT.
THAT'S THE SPOT!!!
THAT'S WHERE I CAN SCORE A GOAL...
TEAM Z
AS LONG AS I GET IN POSITION...
...I CAN HAVE A ONE-ON-ONE SHOWDOWN WITH THE GOALIE!!

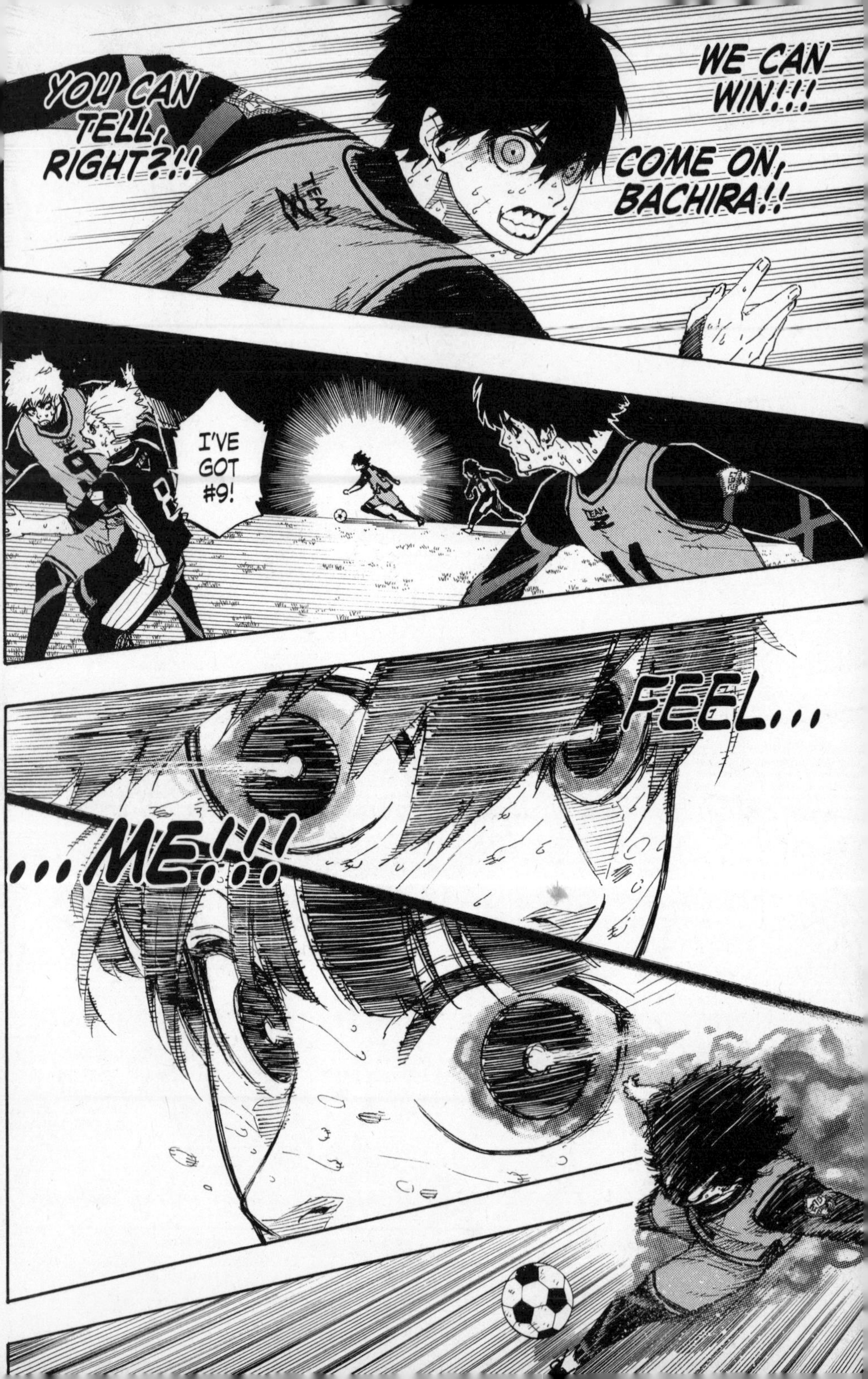
WE CAN WIN!!!
COME ON, BACHIRA!!
YOU CAN TELL, RIGHT?!!
I'VE GOT #9!
FEEL...
...ME!!!

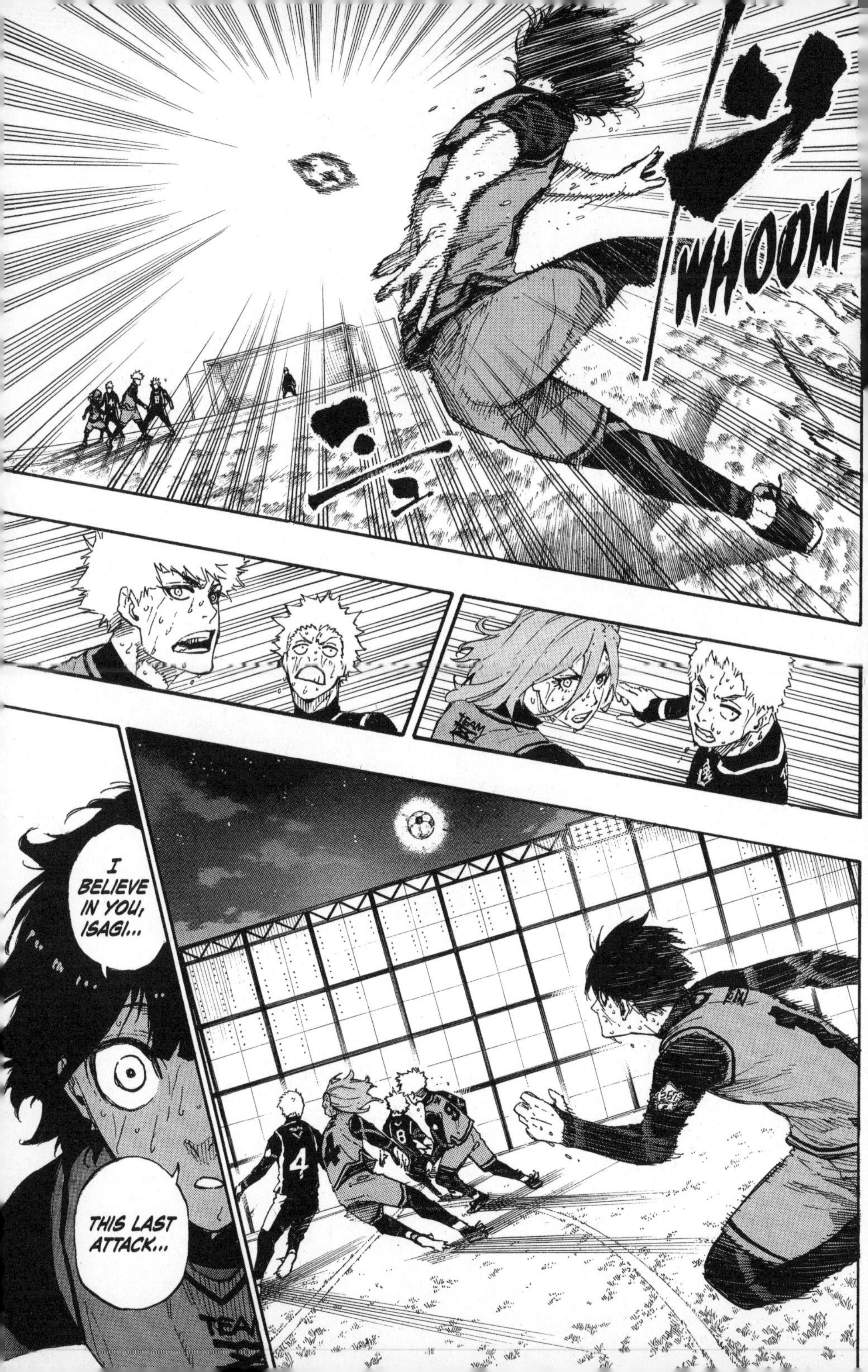
WHOOM
I BELIEVE IN YOU, ISAGI...
THIS LAST ATTACK...

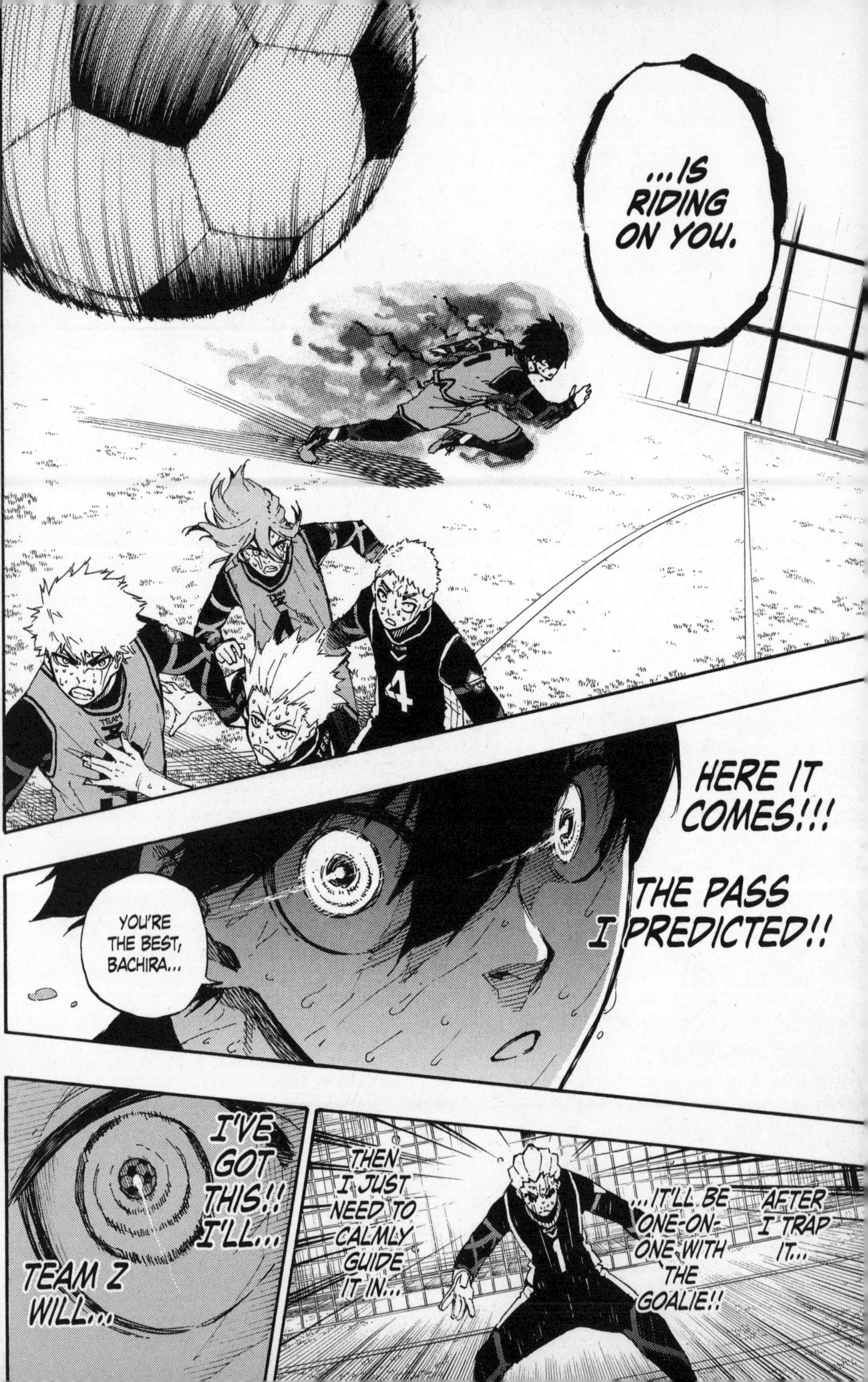
...IS RIDING ON YOU.
HERE IT COMES!!!
THE PASS I PREDICTED!!
YOU'RE THE BEST, BACHIRA...
AFTER I TRAP IT...
...IT'LL BE ONE-ON-ONE WITH THE GOALIE!!
THEN I JUST NEED TO CALMLY GUIDE IT IN...
I'VE GOT THIS!! I'LL...
TEAM Z WILL...

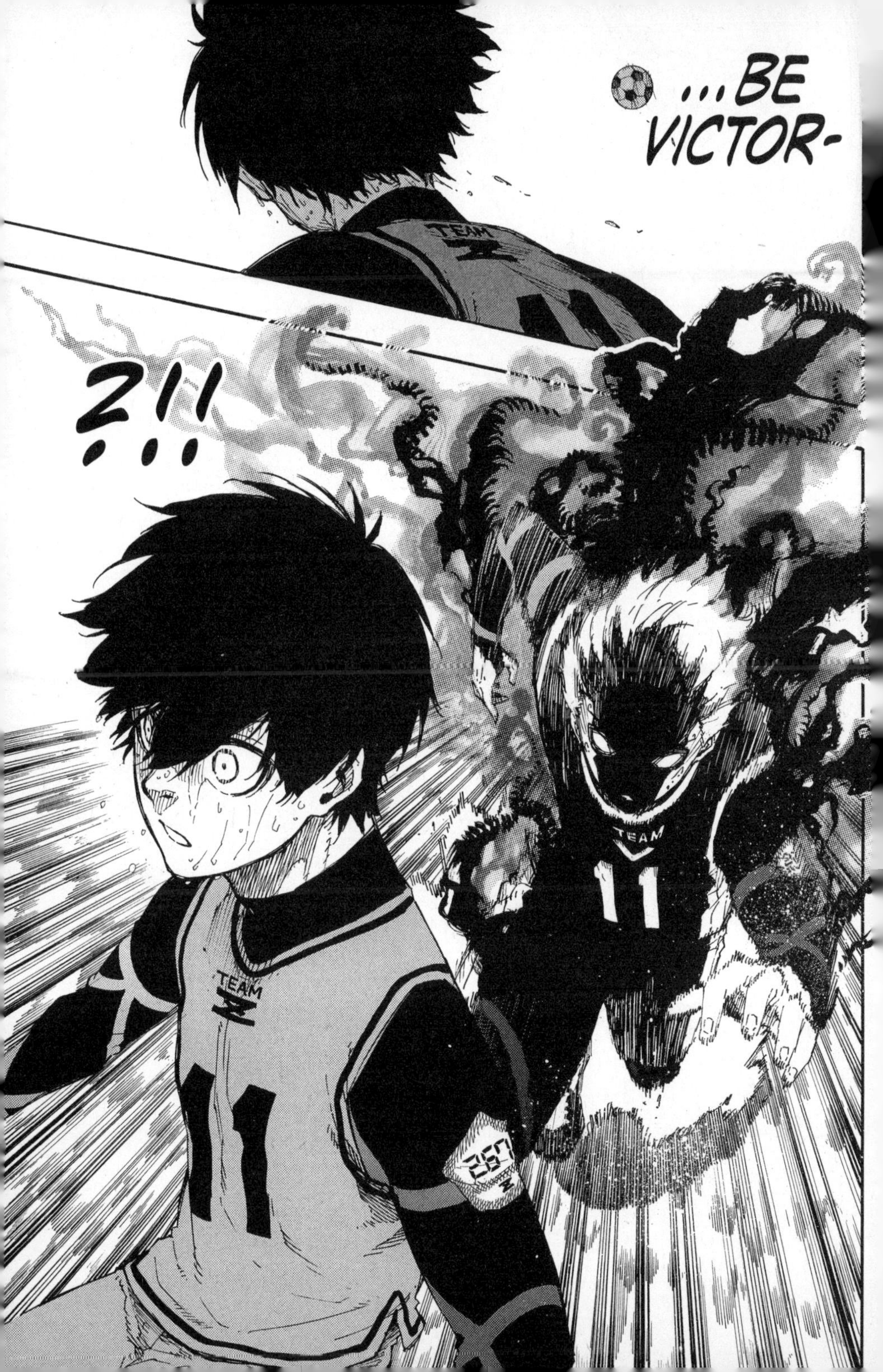
...BE VICTOR-
?!!

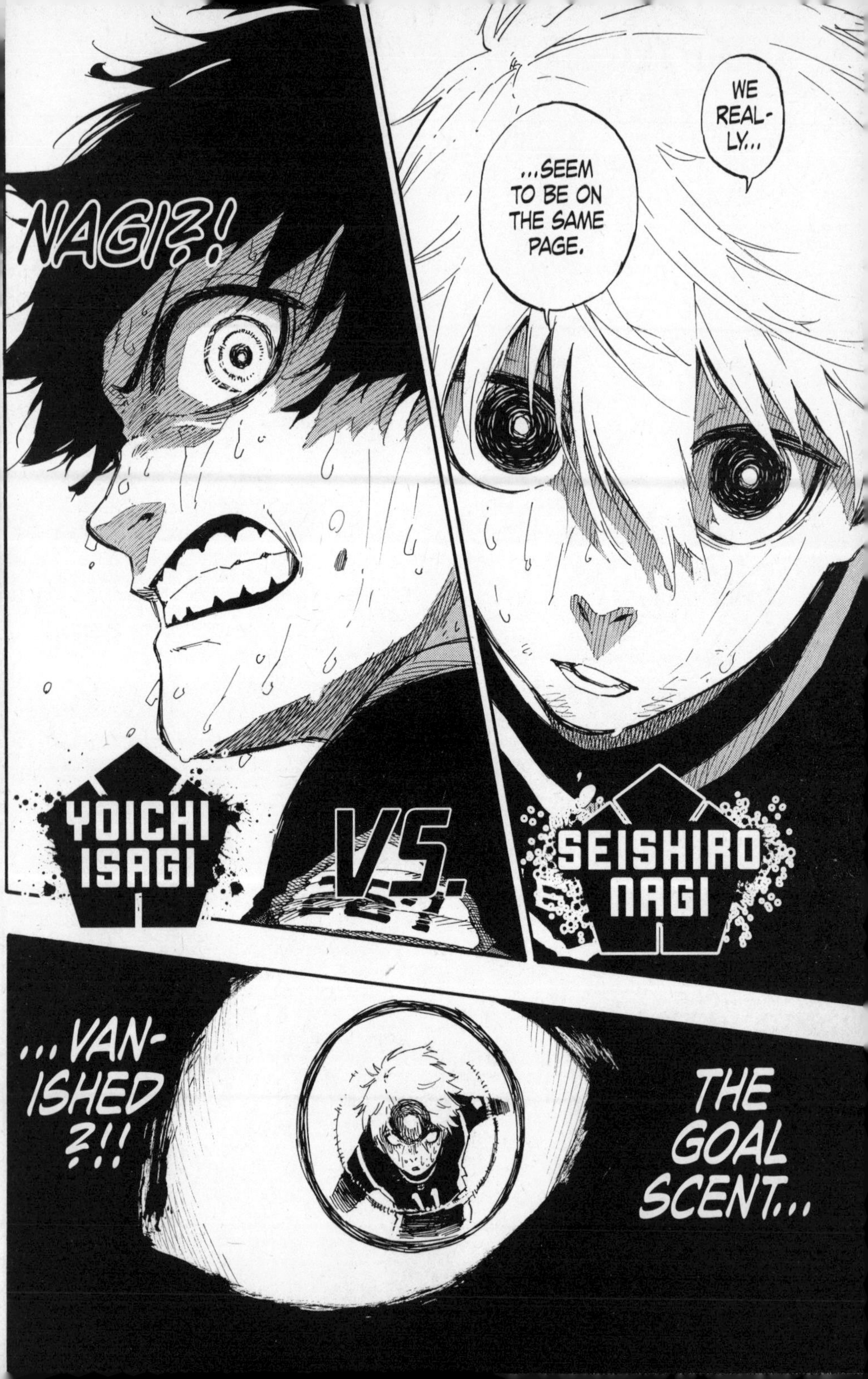
WE REAL-LY...
...SEEM TO BE ON THE SAME PAGE.
NAGI?!
YOICHI ISAGI
V.S.
SEISHIRO NAGI
THE GOAL SCENT...
...VAN-ISHED?!!

# CHAPTER 37: THE LAST PIECE

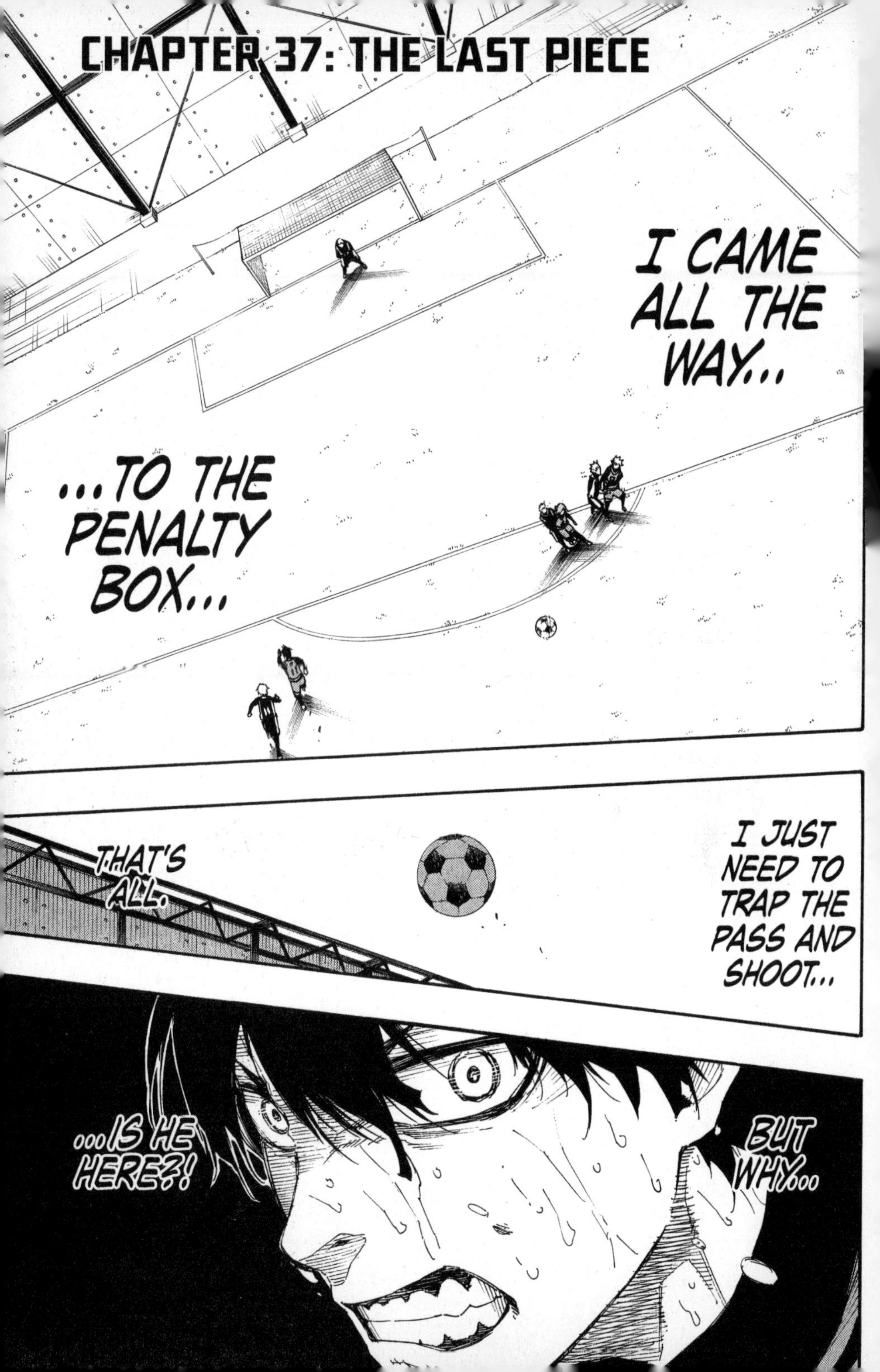
I CAME ALL THE WAY...
...TO THE PENALTY BOX...
I JUST NEED TO TRAP THE PASS AND SHOOT...
THAT'S ALL.
BUT WHY...
...IS HE HERE?!

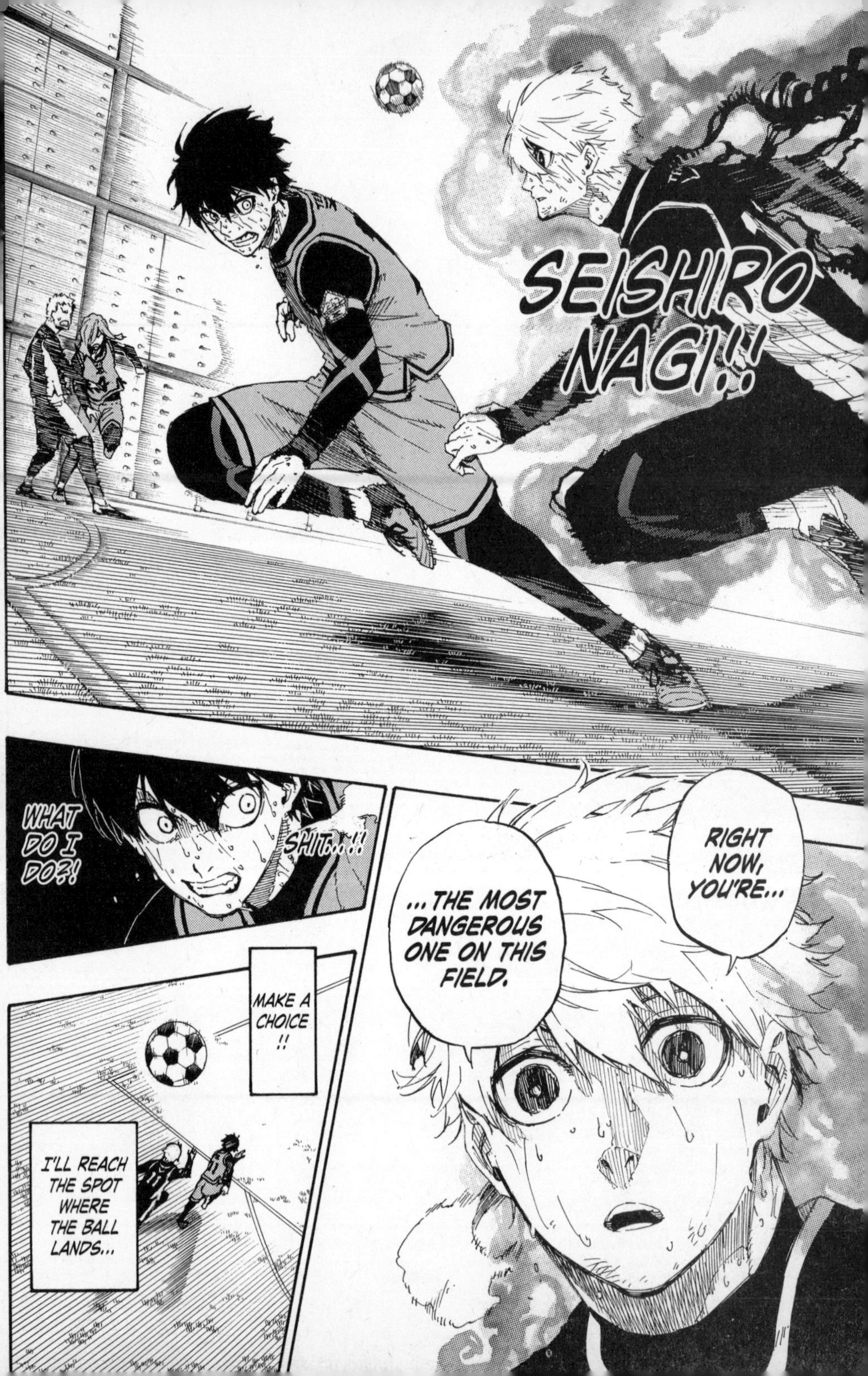
SEISHIRO NAGI!!
RIGHT NOW, YOU'RE...
...THE MOST DANGEROUS ONE ON THIS FIELD.
SHIT...!!
WHAT DO I DO?!
MAKE A CHOICE!!
I'LL REACH THE SPOT WHERE THE BALL LANDS...

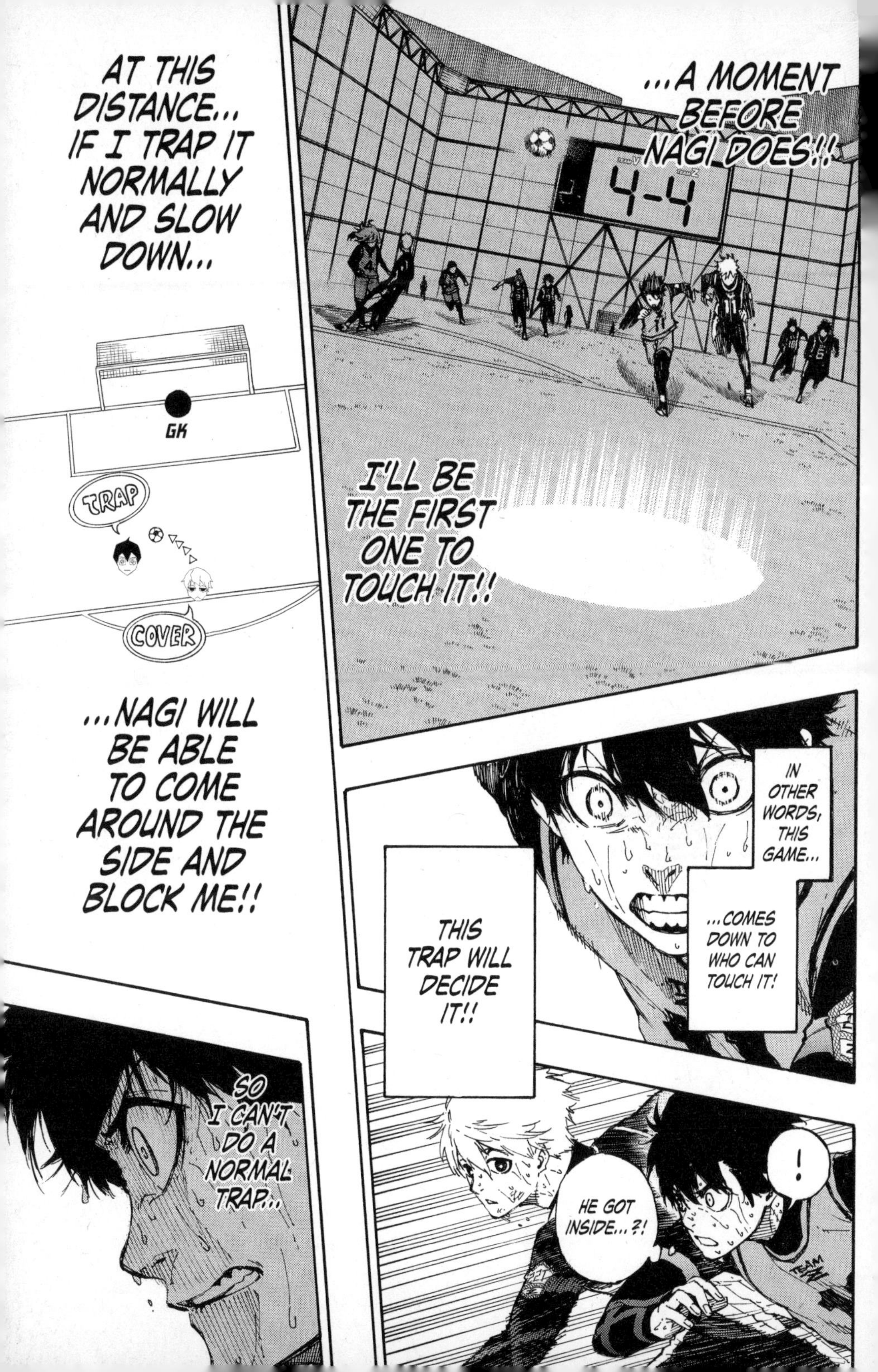
...A MOMENT BEFORE NAGI DOES!!
TEAM V TEAM Z
4-4
I'LL BE THE FIRST ONE TO TOUCH IT!!
AT THIS DISTANCE... IF I TRAP IT NORMALLY AND SLOW DOWN...
GK
TRAP
COVER
...NAGI WILL BE ABLE TO COME AROUND THE SIDE AND BLOCK ME!!
IN OTHER WORDS, THIS GAME...
...COMES DOWN TO WHO CAN TOUCH IT!
THIS TRAP WILL DECIDE IT!!
!
HE GOT INSIDE...?!
SO I CAN'T DO A NORMAL TRAP...

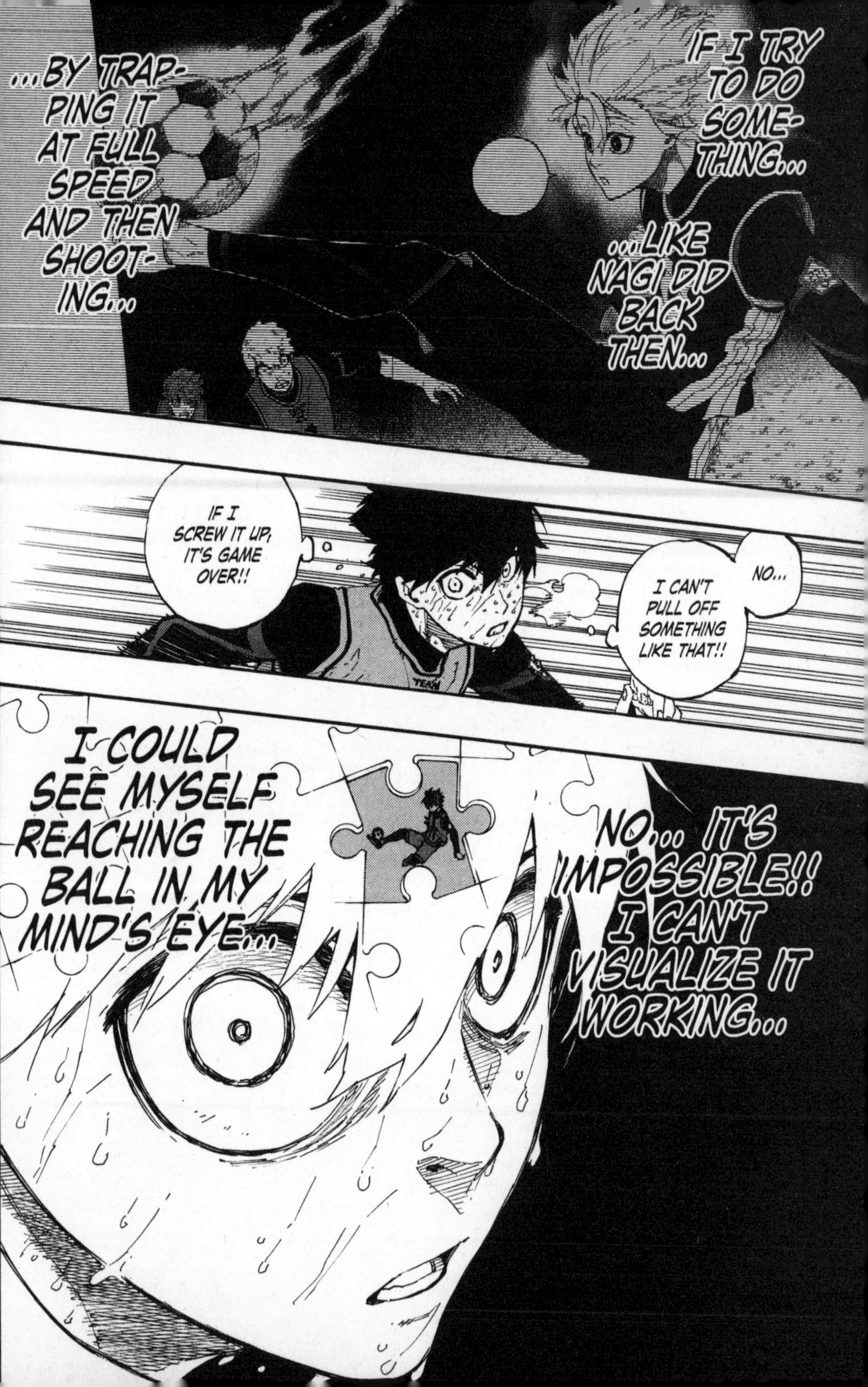
IF I TRY TO DO SOMETHING...
...LIKE NAGI DID BACK THEN...
...BY TRAPPING IT AT FULL SPEED AND THEN SHOOTING...
NO...
I CAN'T PULL OFF SOMETHING LIKE THAT!!
IF I SCREW IT UP, IT'S GAME OVER!!
I COULD SEE MYSELF REACHING THE BALL IN MY MIND'S EYE...
NO... IT'S IMPOSSIBLE!! I CAN'T VISUALIZE IT WORKING...

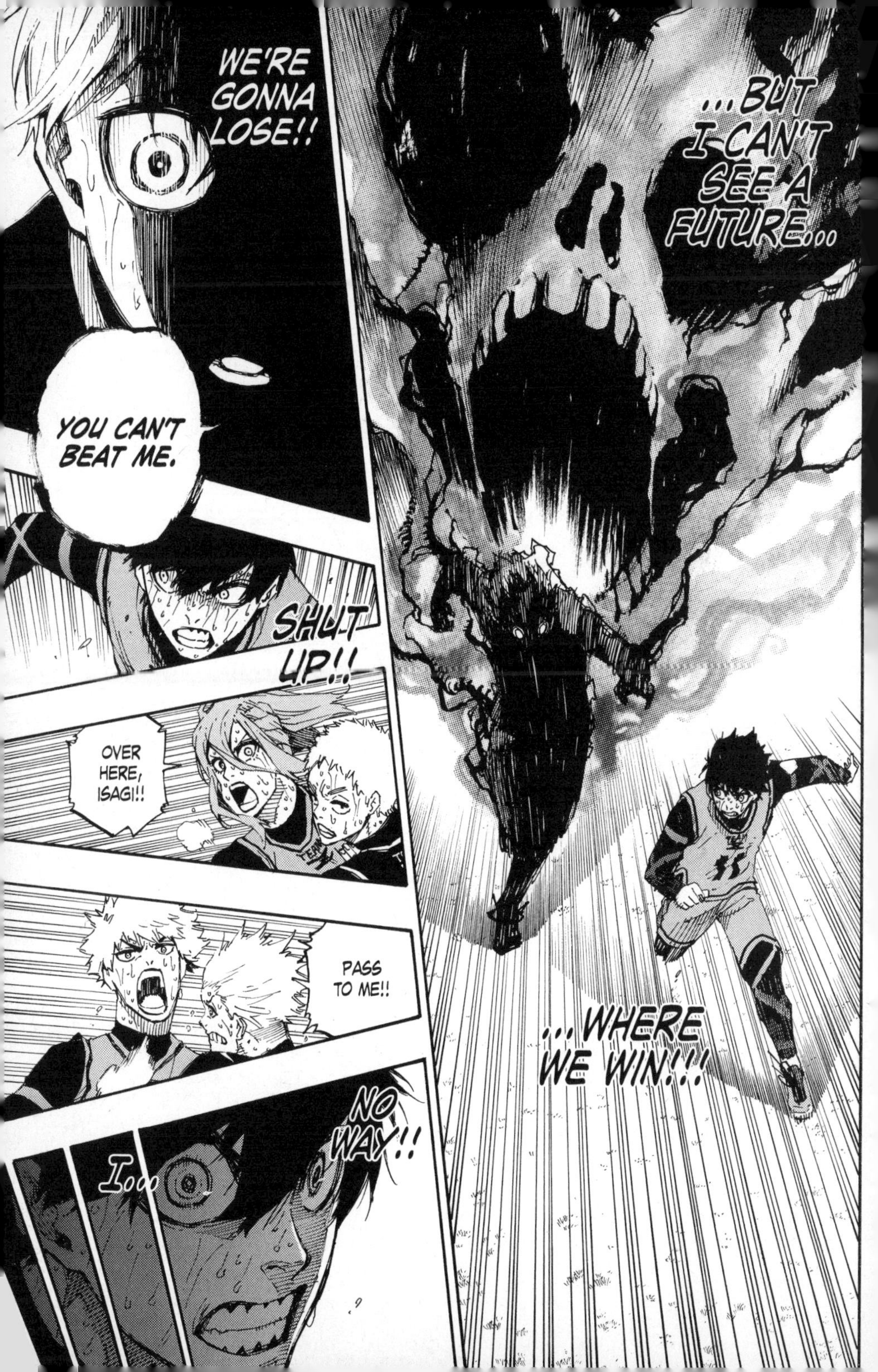
...BUT I CAN'T SEE A FUTURE...
...WHERE WE WIN!!!
WE'RE GONNA LOSE!!
YOU CAN'T BEAT ME.
SHUT UP!!
OVER HERE, ISAGI!!
PASS TO ME!!
NO WAY!!
I...

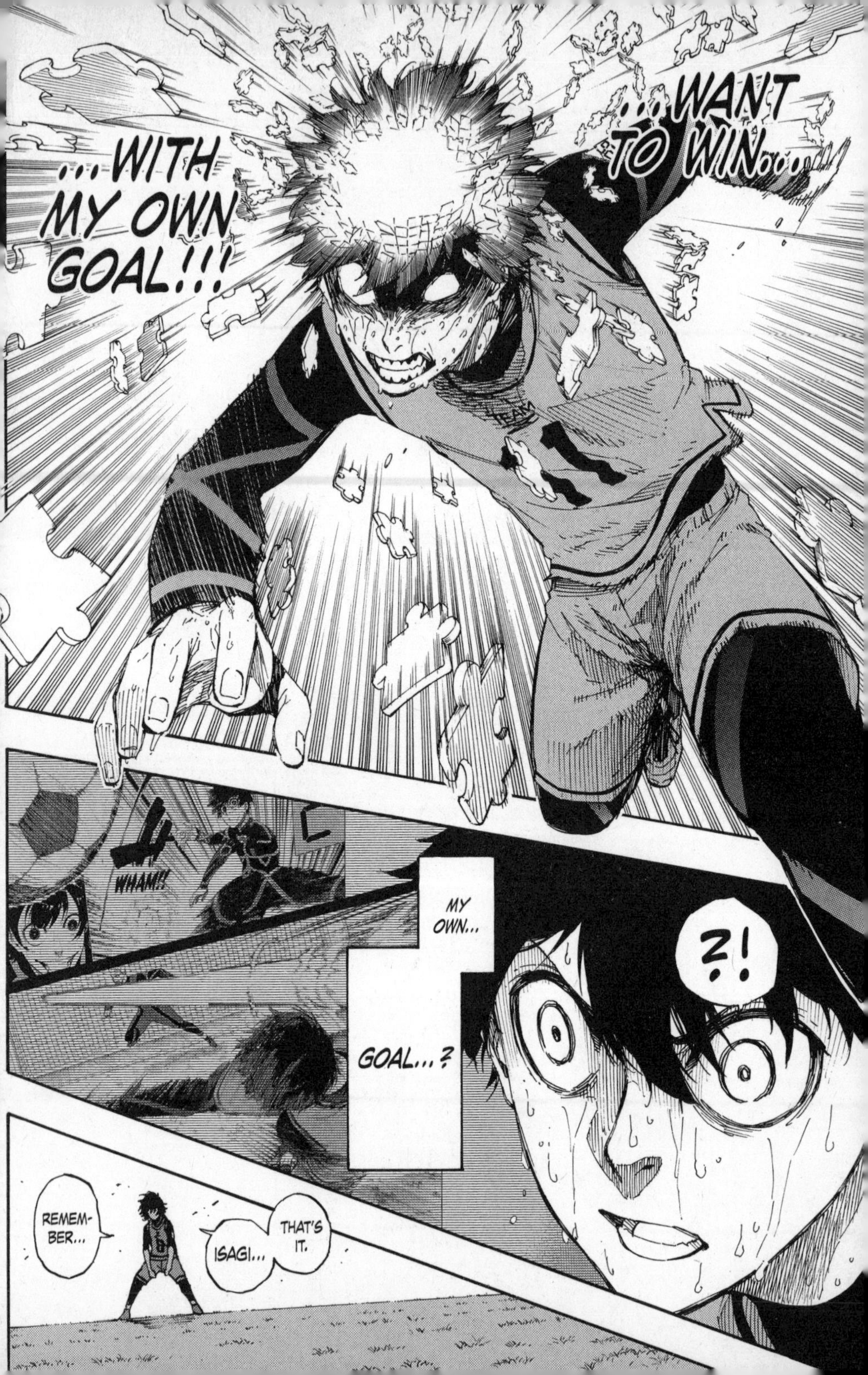

...WANT TO WIN...
...WITH MY OWN GOAL!!!
?!
MY OWN...
GOAL...?
WHAM!!
THAT'S IT.
ISAGI...
REMEMBER...

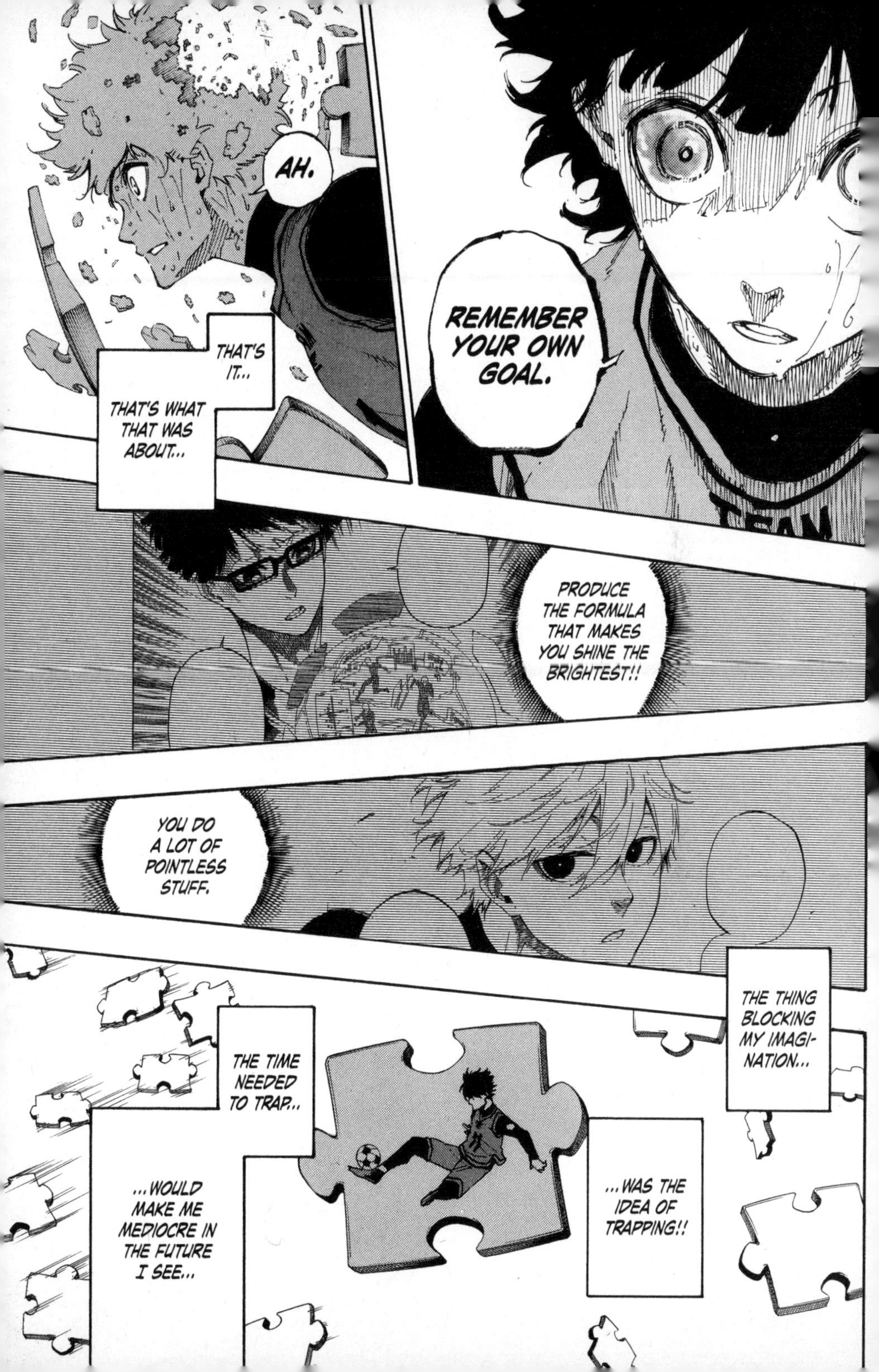
REMEMBER YOUR OWN GOAL.
AH.
THAT'S IT...
THAT'S WHAT THAT WAS ABOUT...
PRODUCE THE FORMULA THAT MAKES YOU SHINE THE BRIGHTEST!!
YOU DO A LOT OF POINTLESS STUFF.
THE THING BLOCKING MY IMAGI-NATION...
...WAS THE IDEA OF TRAPPING!!
THE TIME NEEDED TO TRAP...
...WOULD MAKE ME MEDIOCRE IN THE FUTURE I SEE...

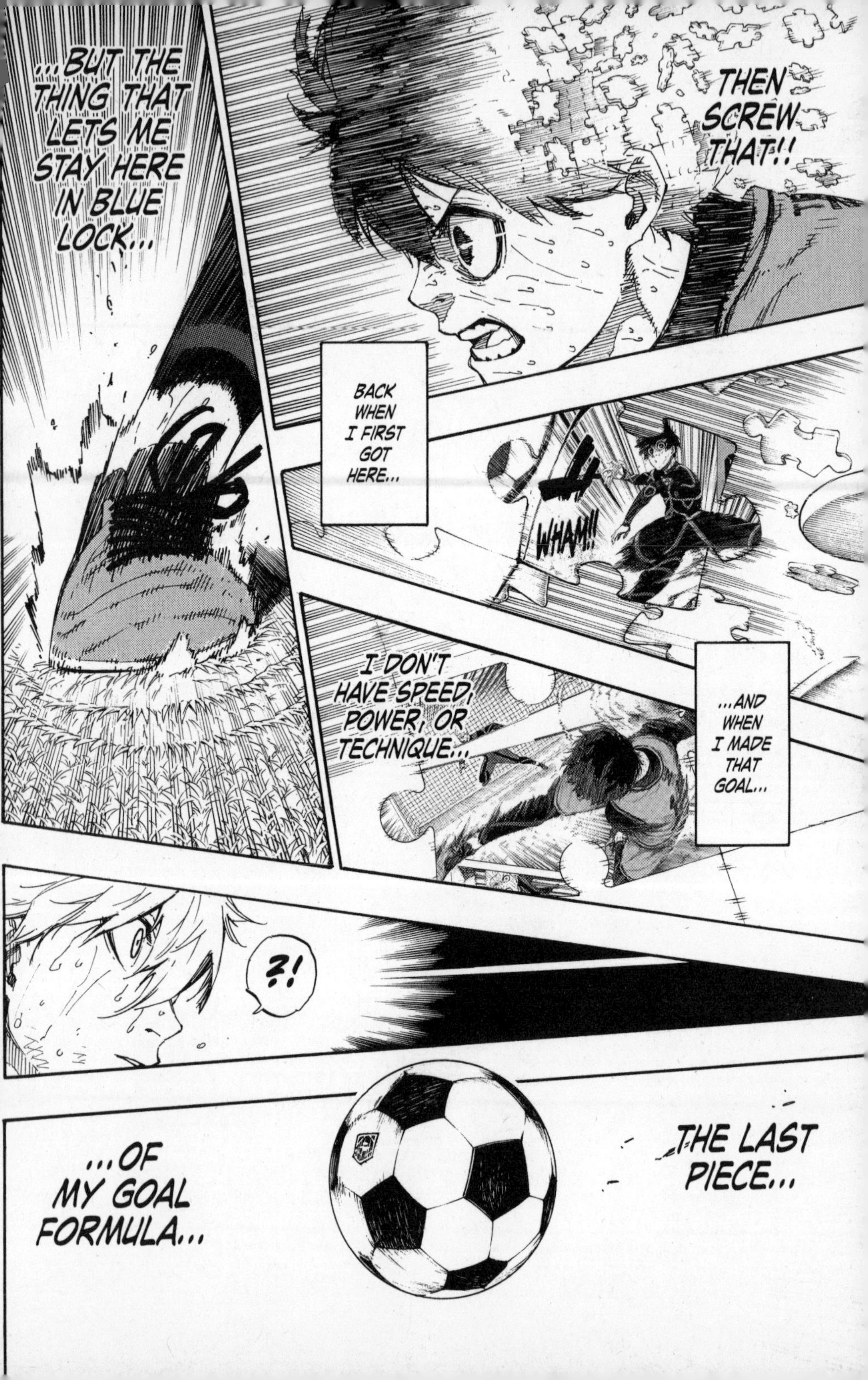
THEN SCREW THAT!!
BACK WHEN I FIRST GOT HERE...
WHAM!!
...AND WHEN I MADE THAT GOAL...
I DON'T HAVE SPEED, POWER, OR TECHNIQUE...
...BUT THE THING THAT LETS ME STAY HERE IN BLUE LOCK...
?!
THE LAST PIECE...
...OF MY GOAL FORMULA...

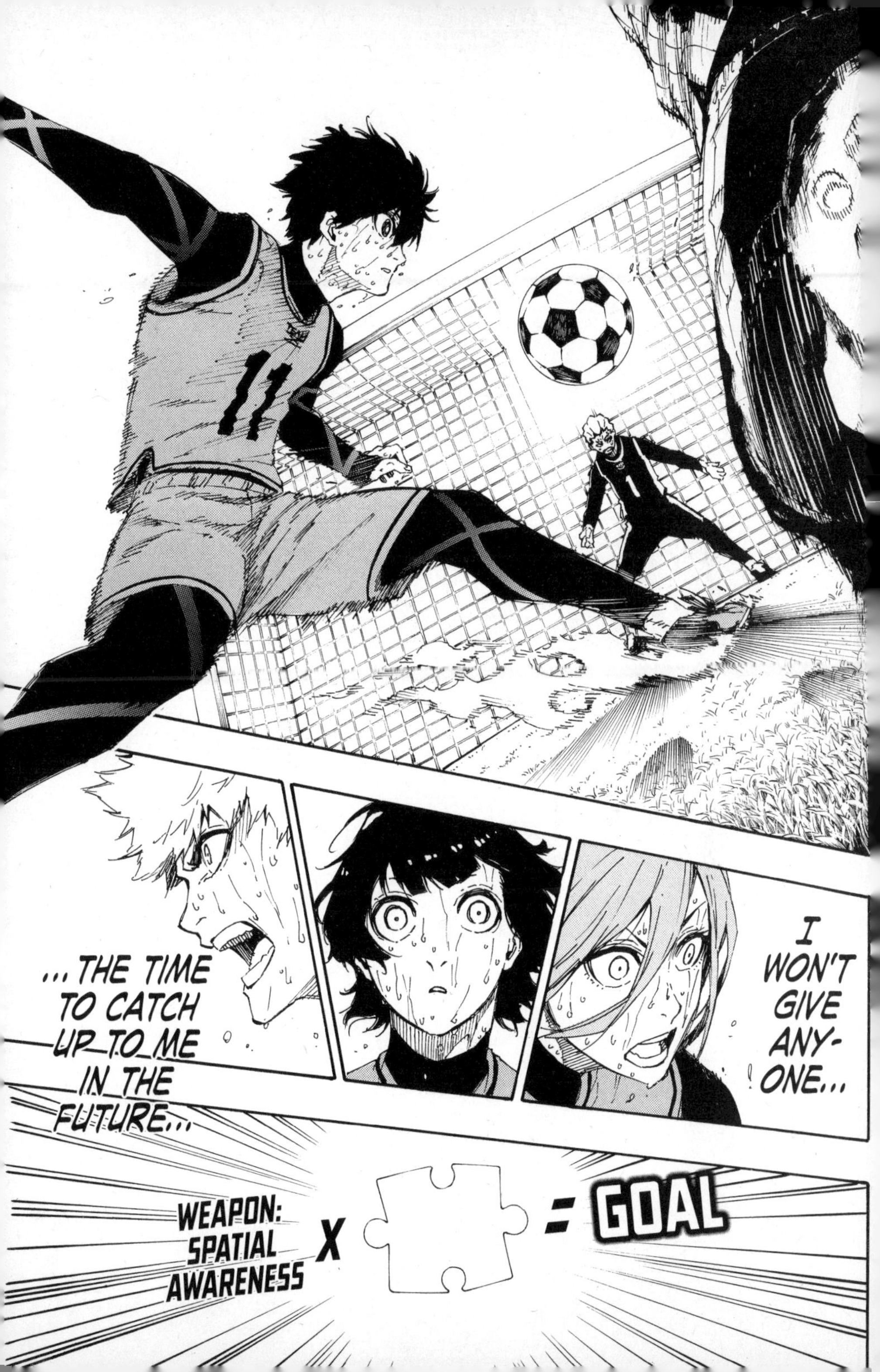
I WON'T GIVE ANYONE...
...THE TIME TO CATCH UP TO ME IN THE FUTURE...
WEAPON: SPATIAL AWARENESS
X
= GOAL

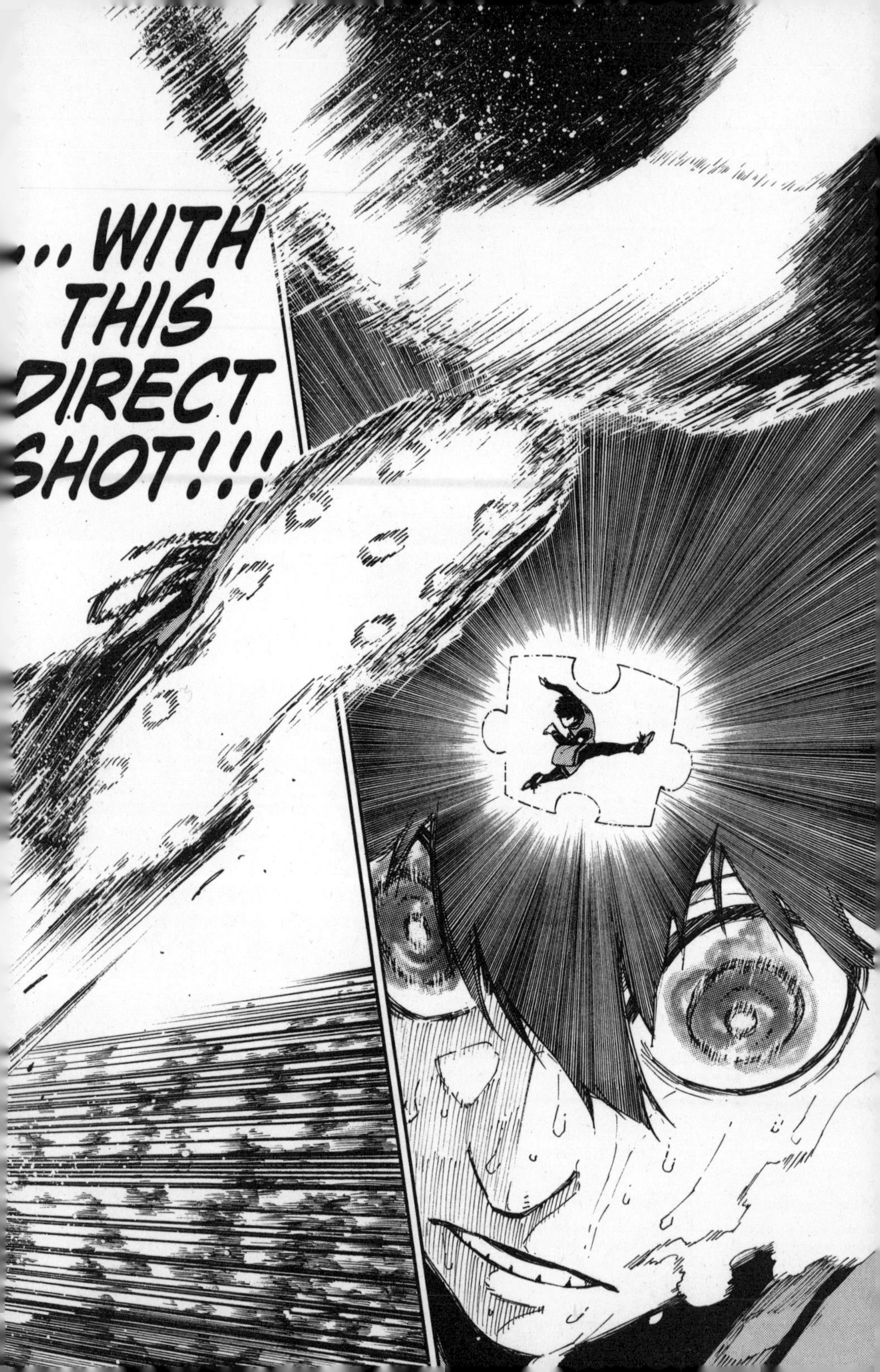
...WITH THIS DIRECT SHOT!!!

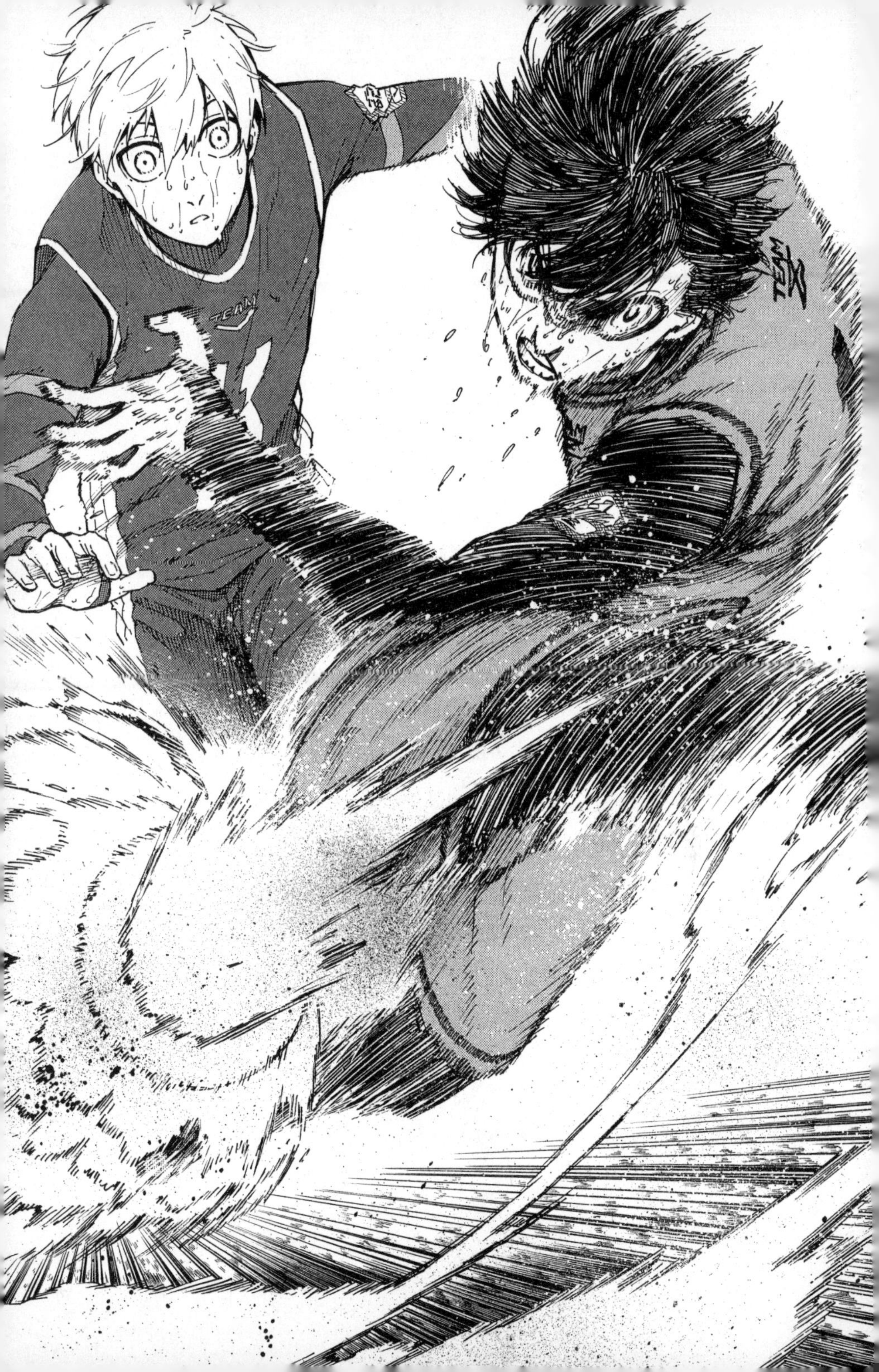
TEAM

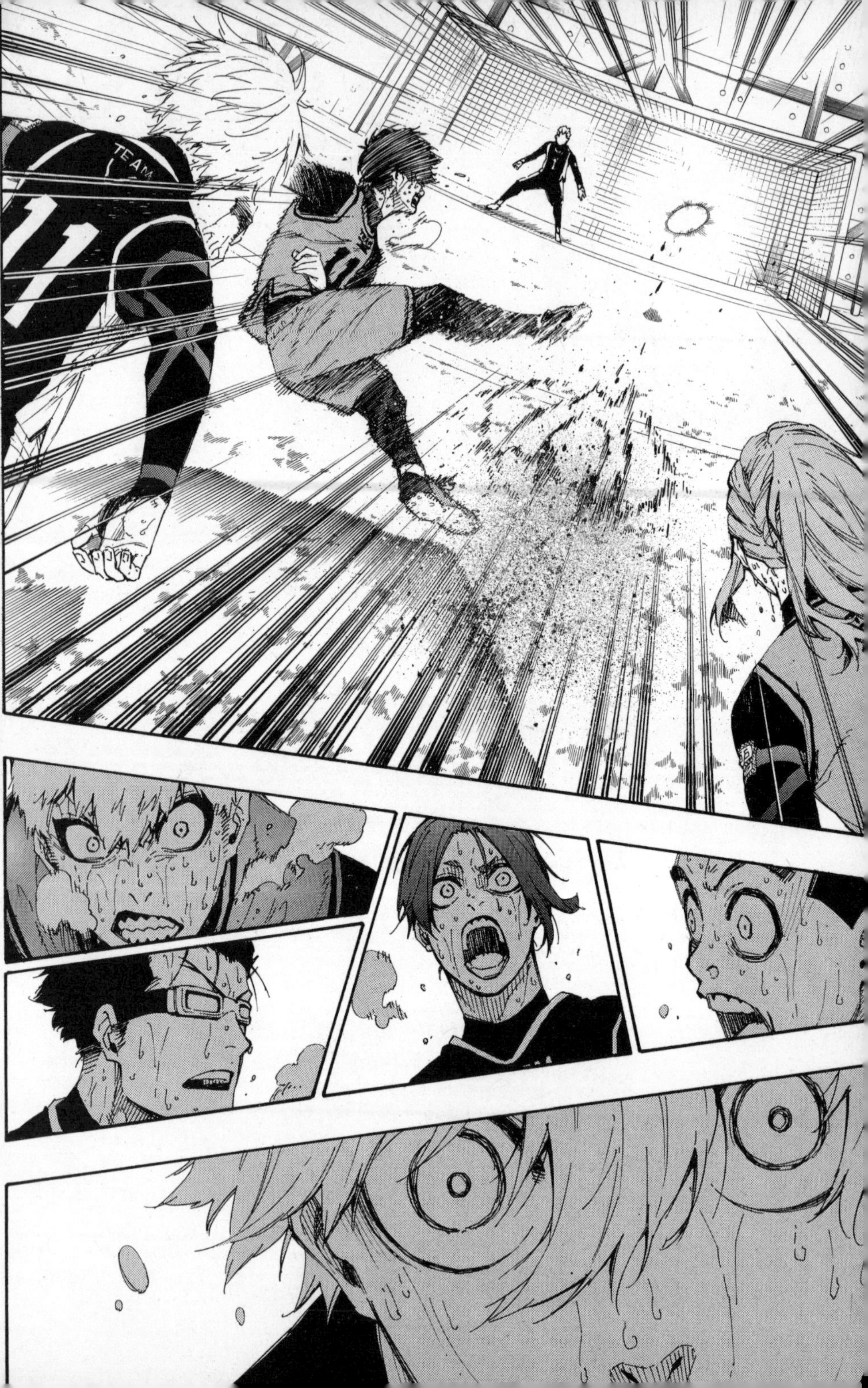
TEAM

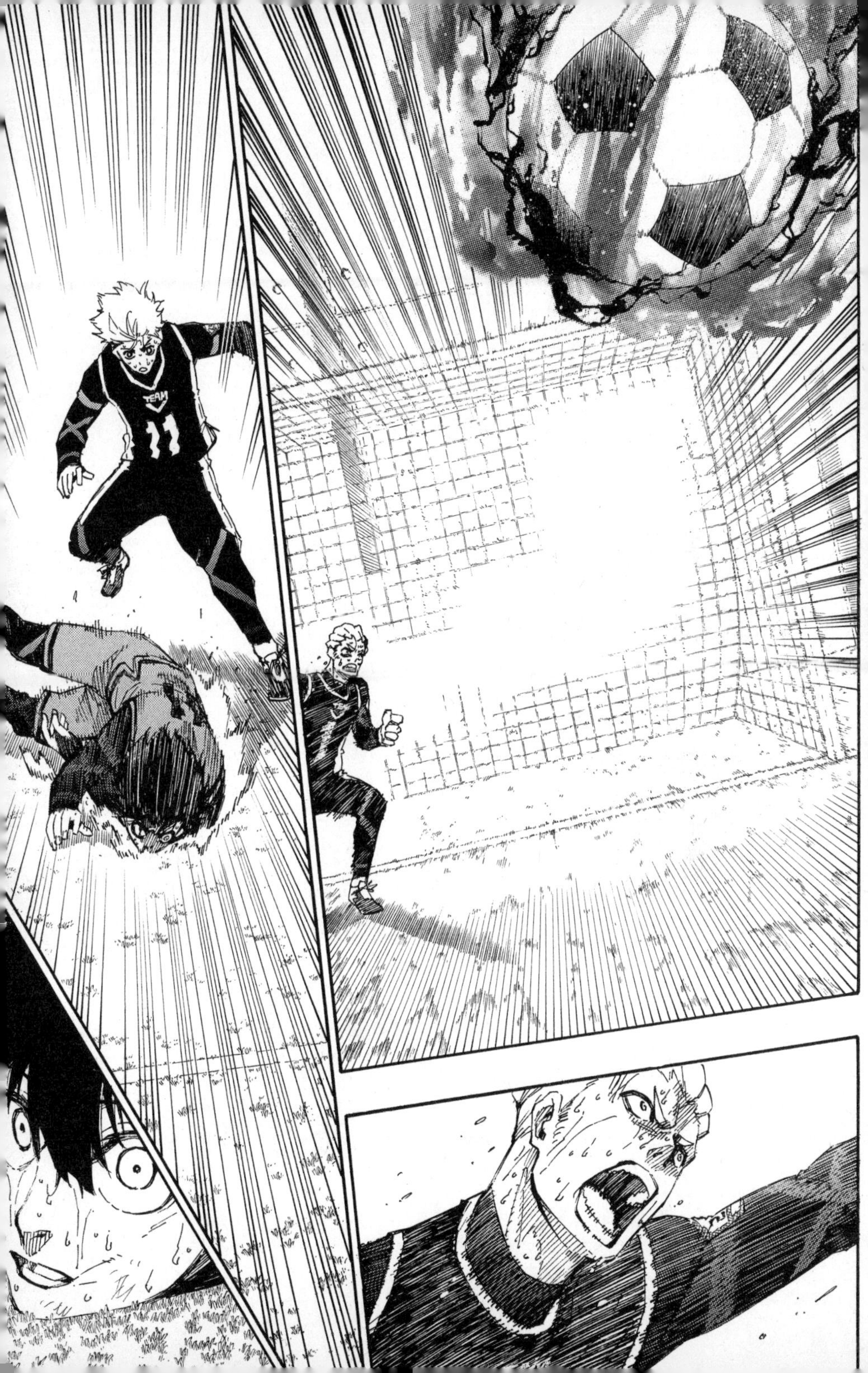

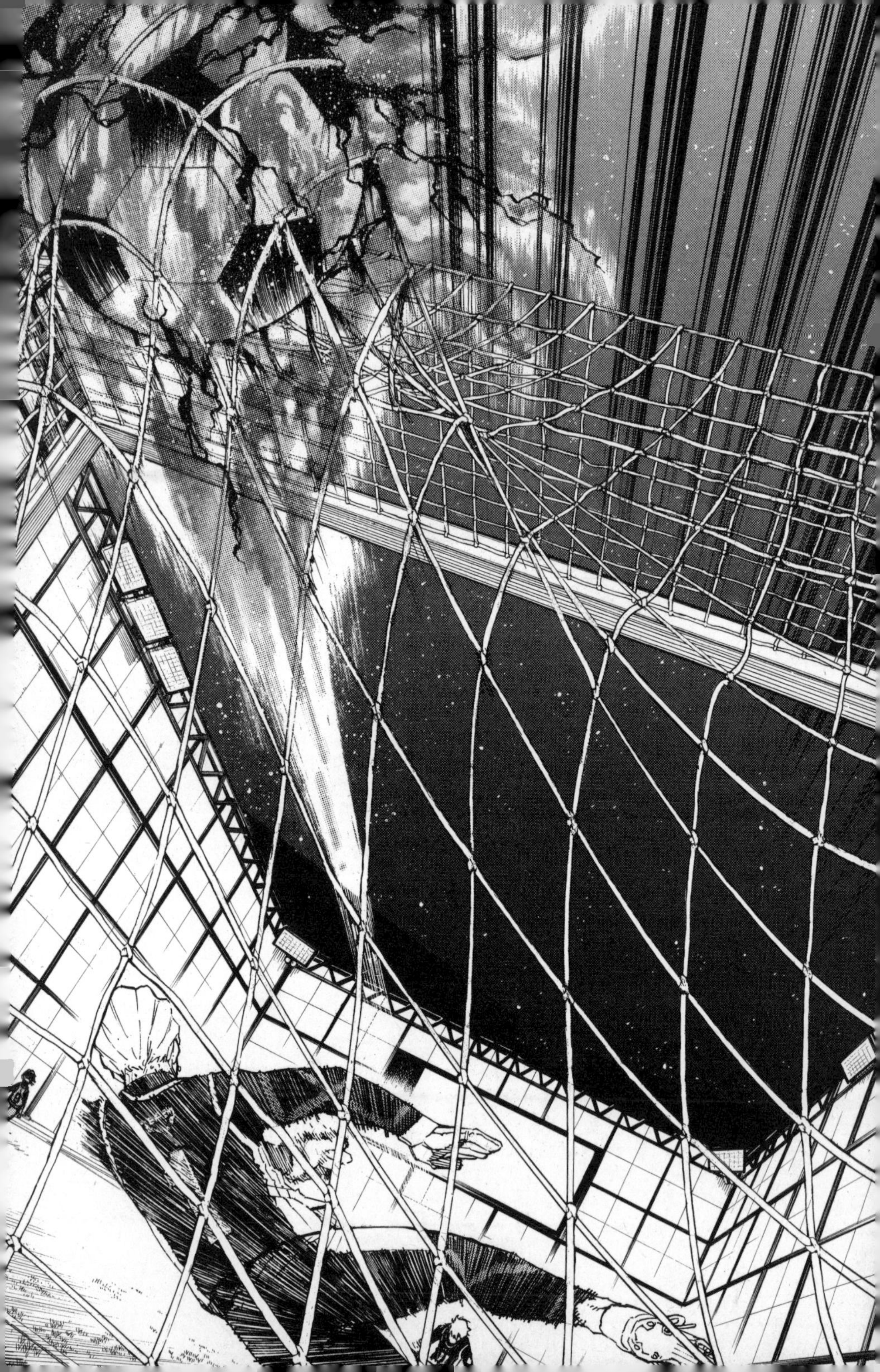

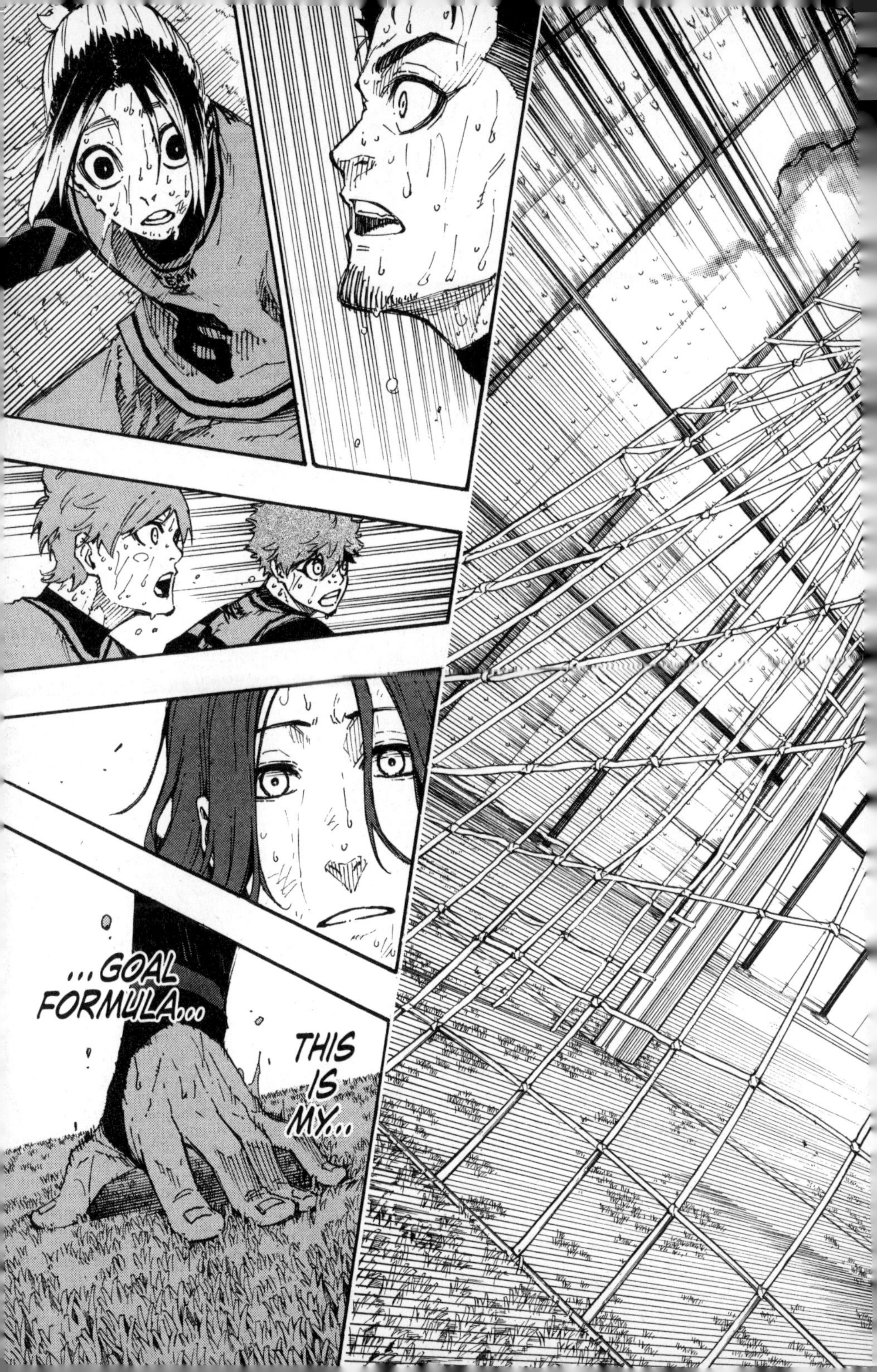
...GOAL FORMULA...
THIS IS MY...

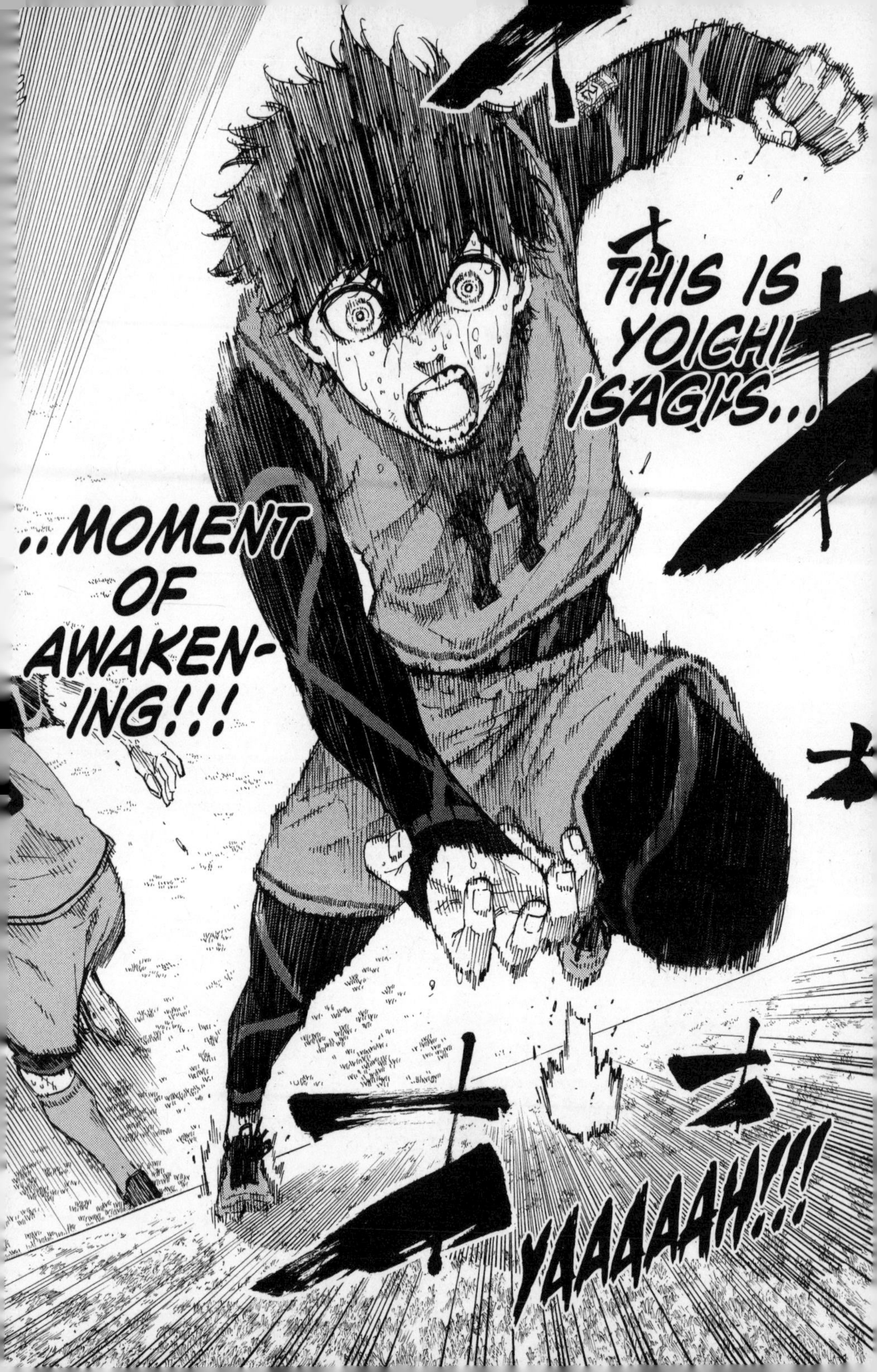
THIS IS YOICHI ISAGI'S...
...MOMENT OF AWAKEN-ING!!!
YAAAAAH!!!

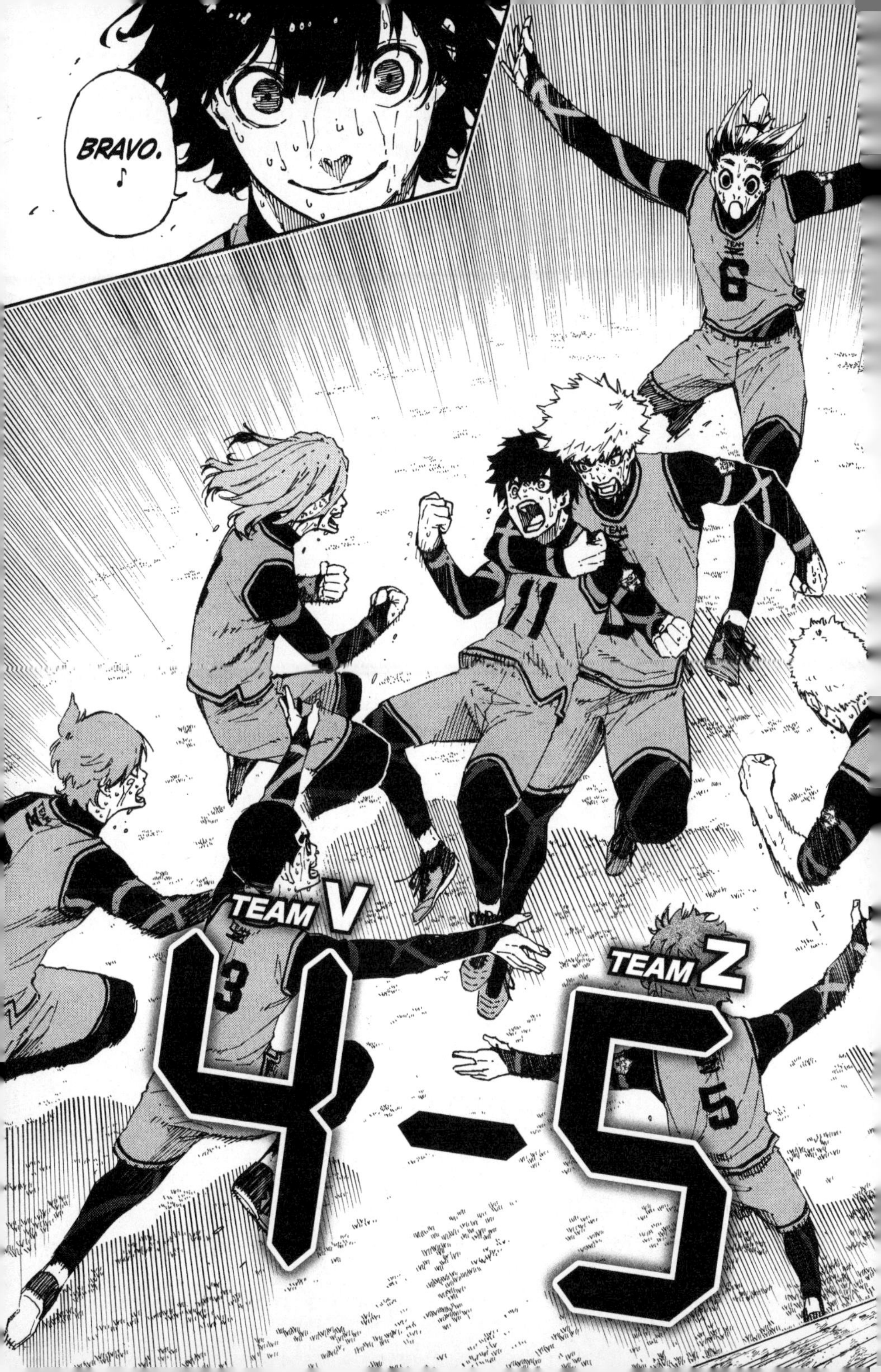
BRAVO. ♪
TEAM V
TEAM Z
4-5

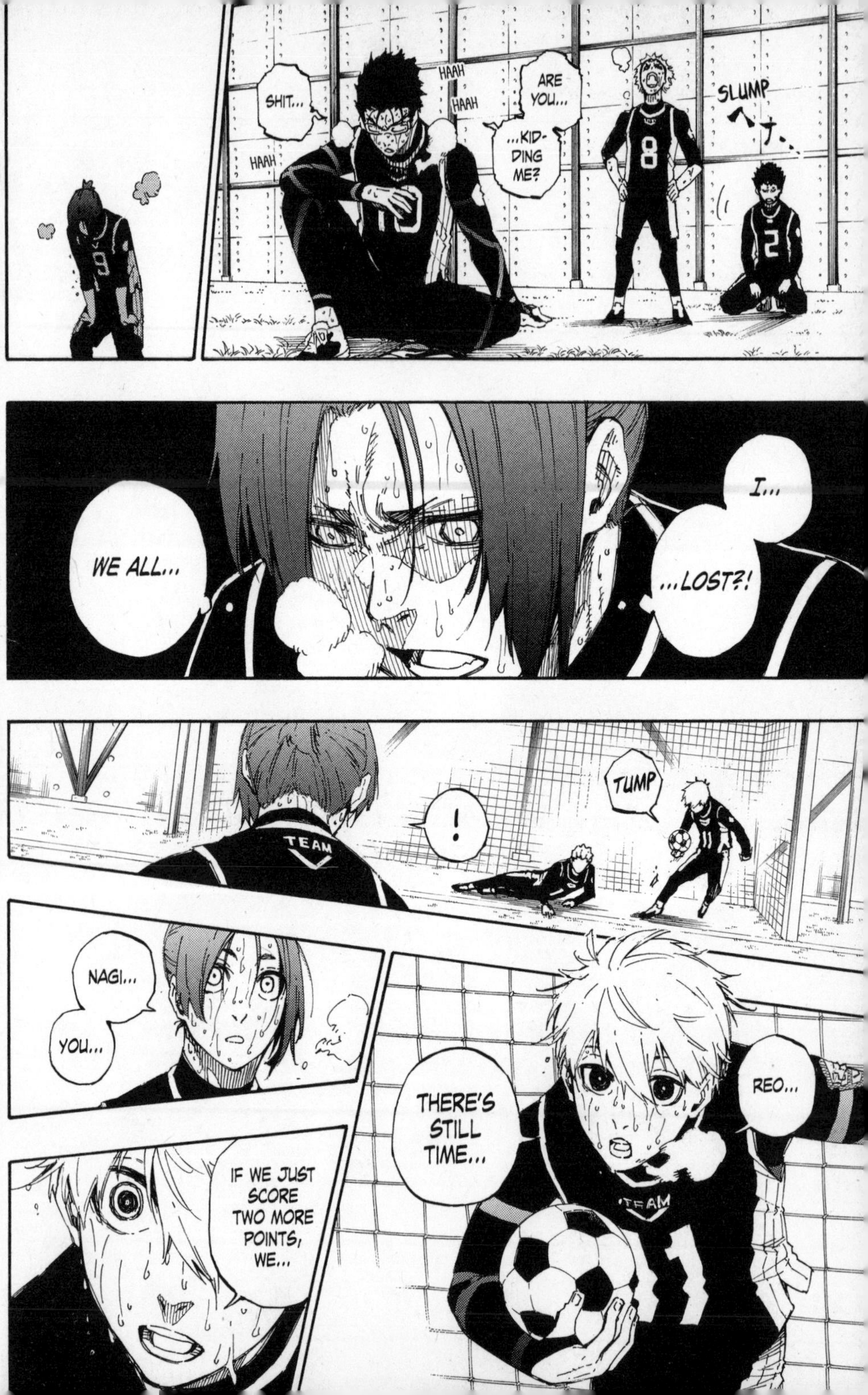
SLUMP
へナ…
ARE YOU...
...KIDDING ME?
HAAH
HAAH
SHIT...
HAAH
I...
...LOST?!
WE ALL...
TUMP
!
REO...
THERE'S STILL TIME...
NAGI...
YOU...
IF WE JUST SCORE TWO MORE POINTS, WE...

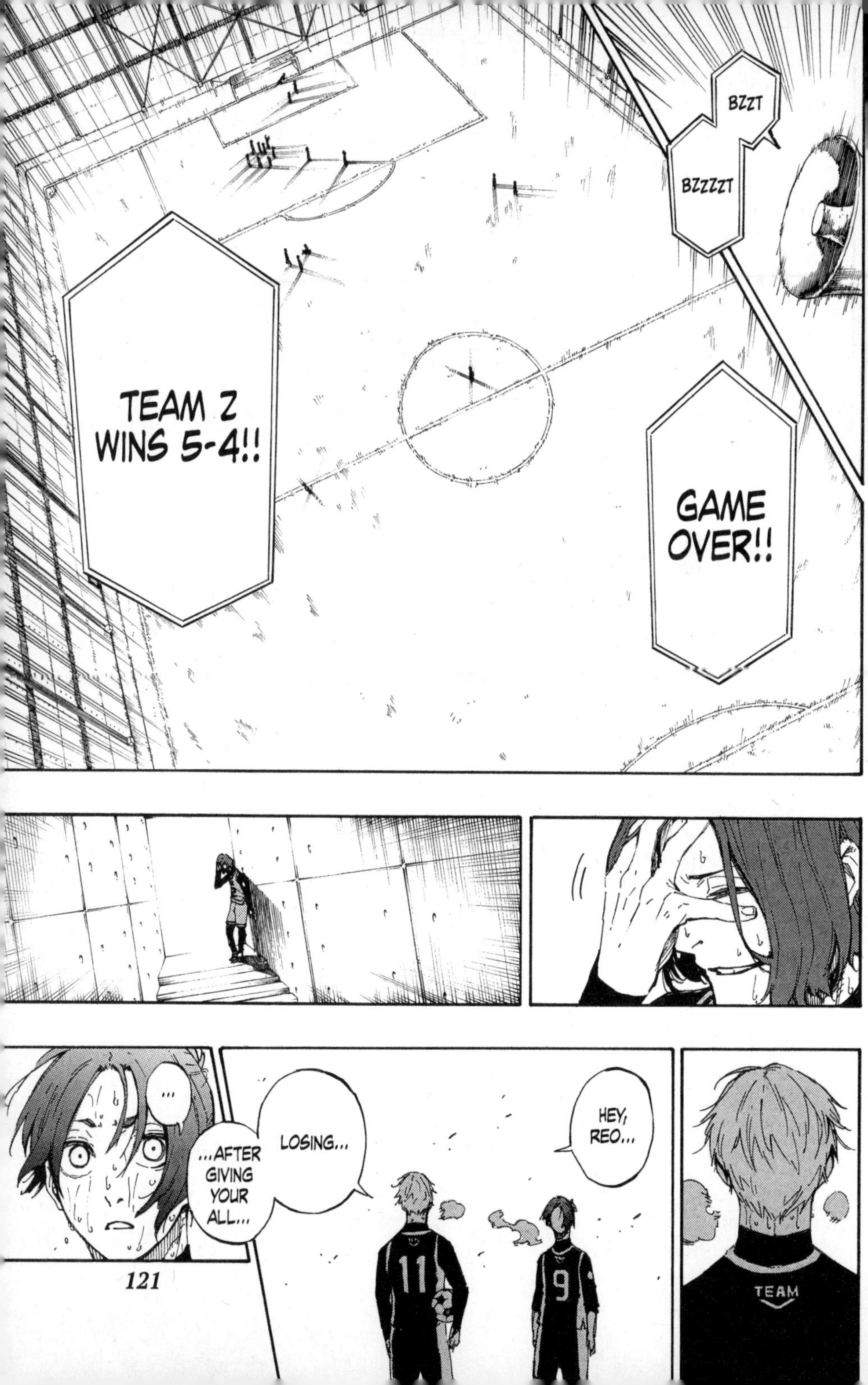
BZZT
BZZZZT
GAME OVER!!
TEAM Z WINS 5-4!!
HEY, REO...
LOSING...
...
...AFTER GIVING YOUR ALL...
TEAM

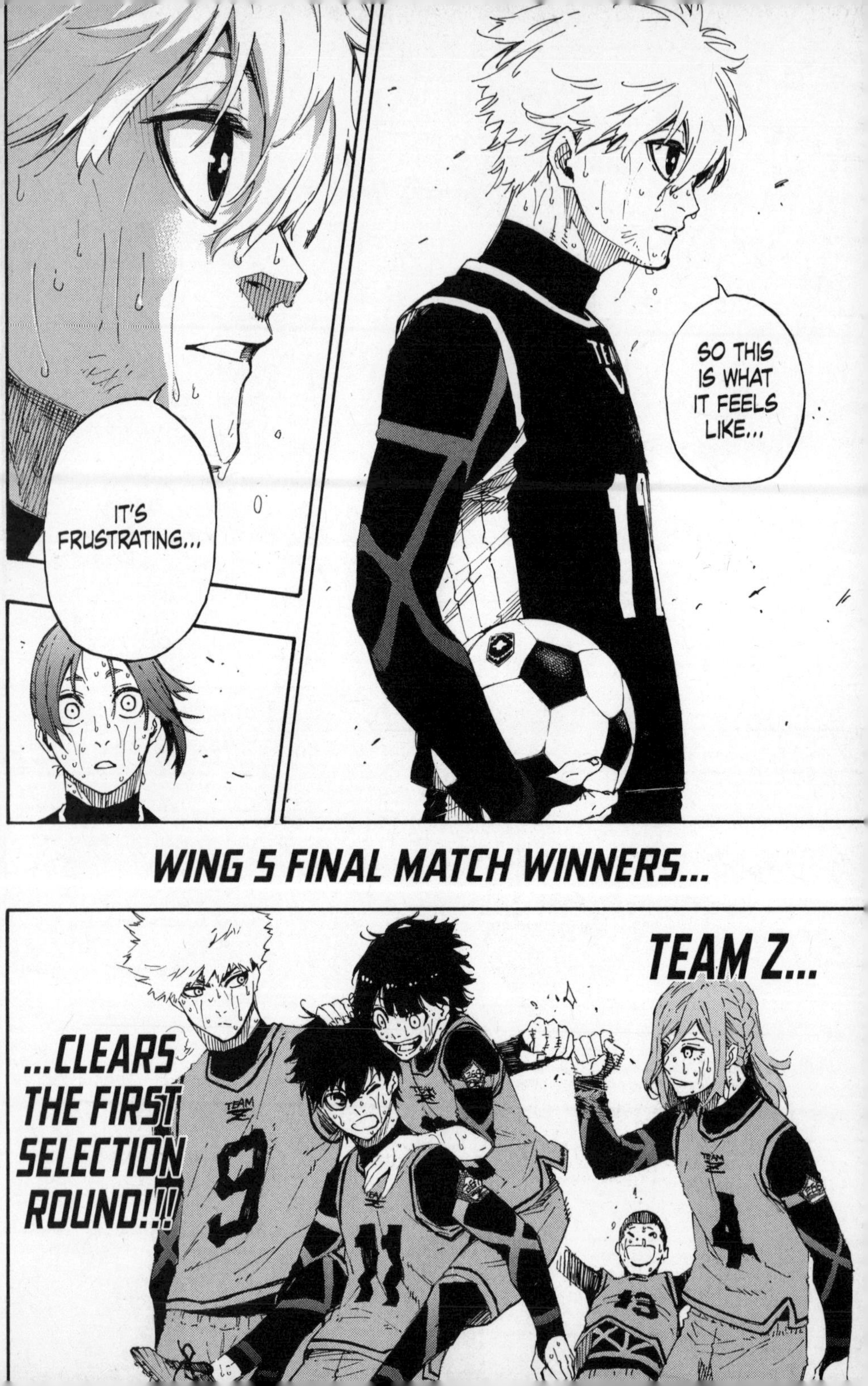
SO THIS IS WHAT IT FEELS LIKE...
IT'S FRUSTRATING...
WING 5 FINAL MATCH WINNERS...
TEAM Z...
...CLEARS THE FIRST SELECTION ROUND!!!

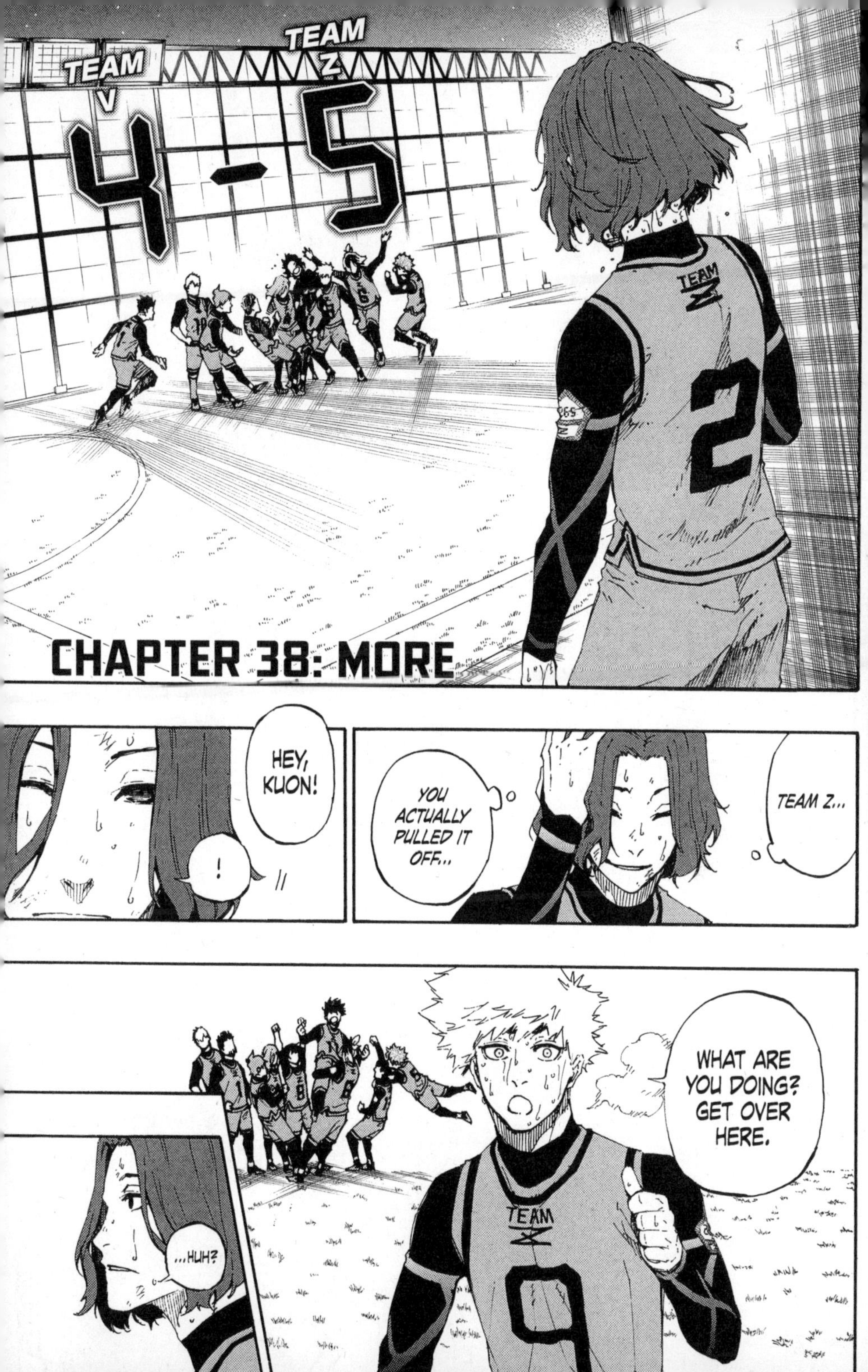
TEAM V
TEAM Z
4 - 5
CHAPTER 38: MORE
TEAM Z...
YOU ACTUALLY PULLED IT OFF...
HEY, KUON!
!
WHAT ARE YOU DOING? GET OVER HERE.
...HUH?

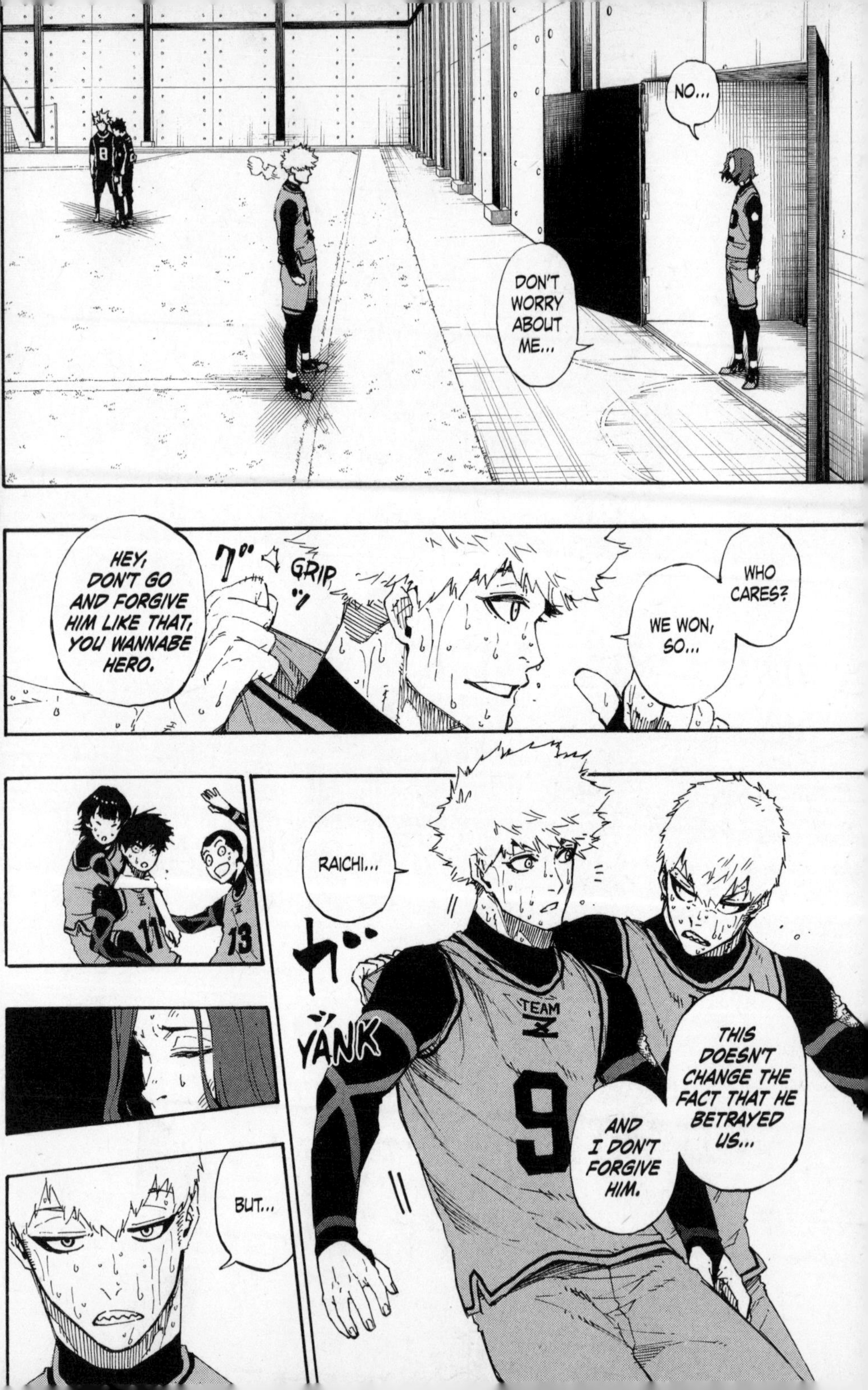
NO...
DON'T WORRY ABOUT ME...
WHO CARES?
WE WON, SO...
GRIP
HEY, DON'T GO AND FORGIVE HIM LIKE THAT, YOU WANNABE HERO.
RAICHI...
YANK
THIS DOESN'T CHANGE THE FACT THAT HE BETRAYED US...
AND I DON'T FORGIVE HIM.
BUT...

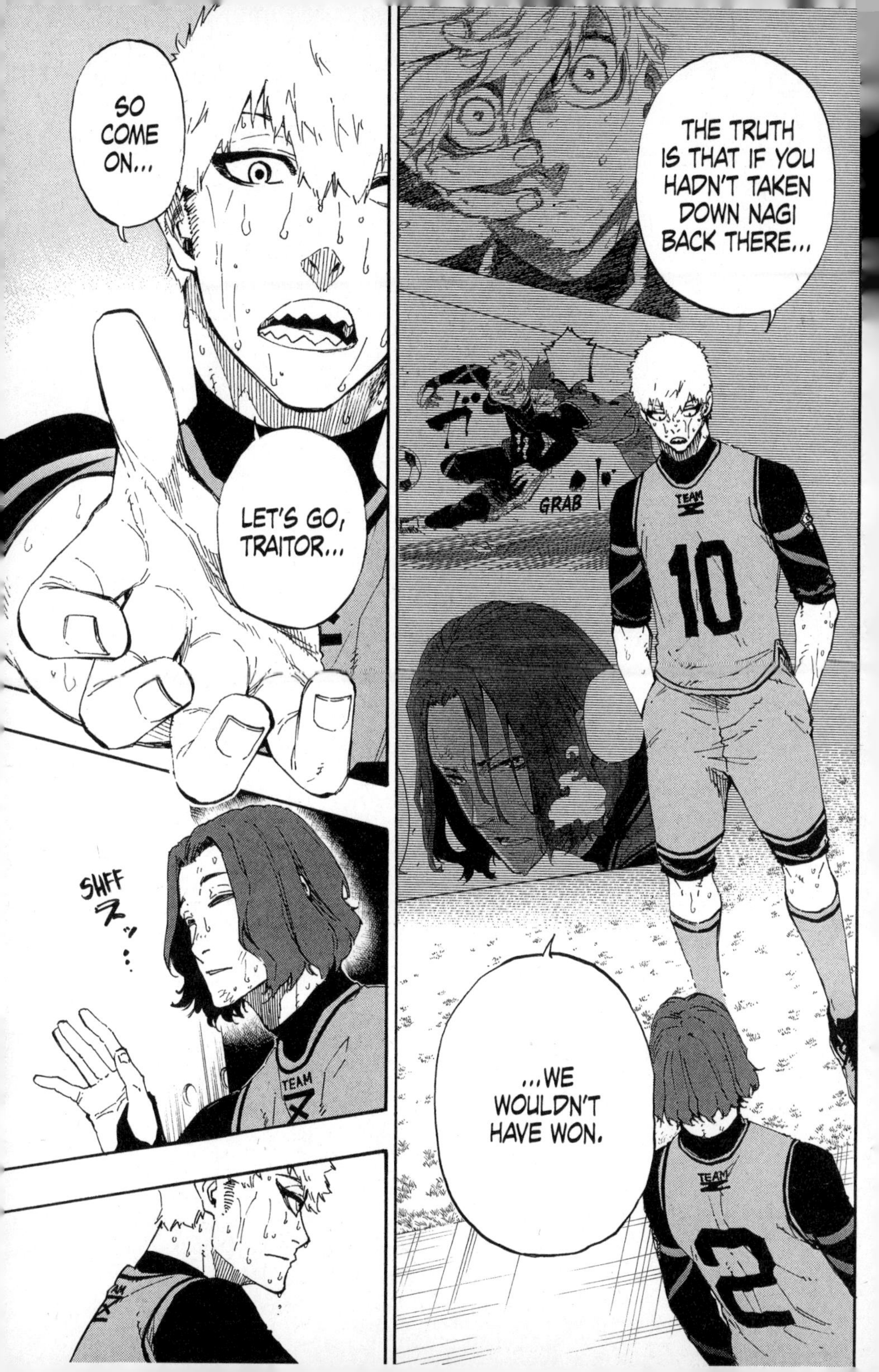
THE TRUTH IS THAT IF YOU HADN'T TAKEN DOWN NAGI BACK THERE...
GRAB
...WE WOULDN'T HAVE WON.
SO COME ON...
LET'S GO, TRAITOR...
SHFF

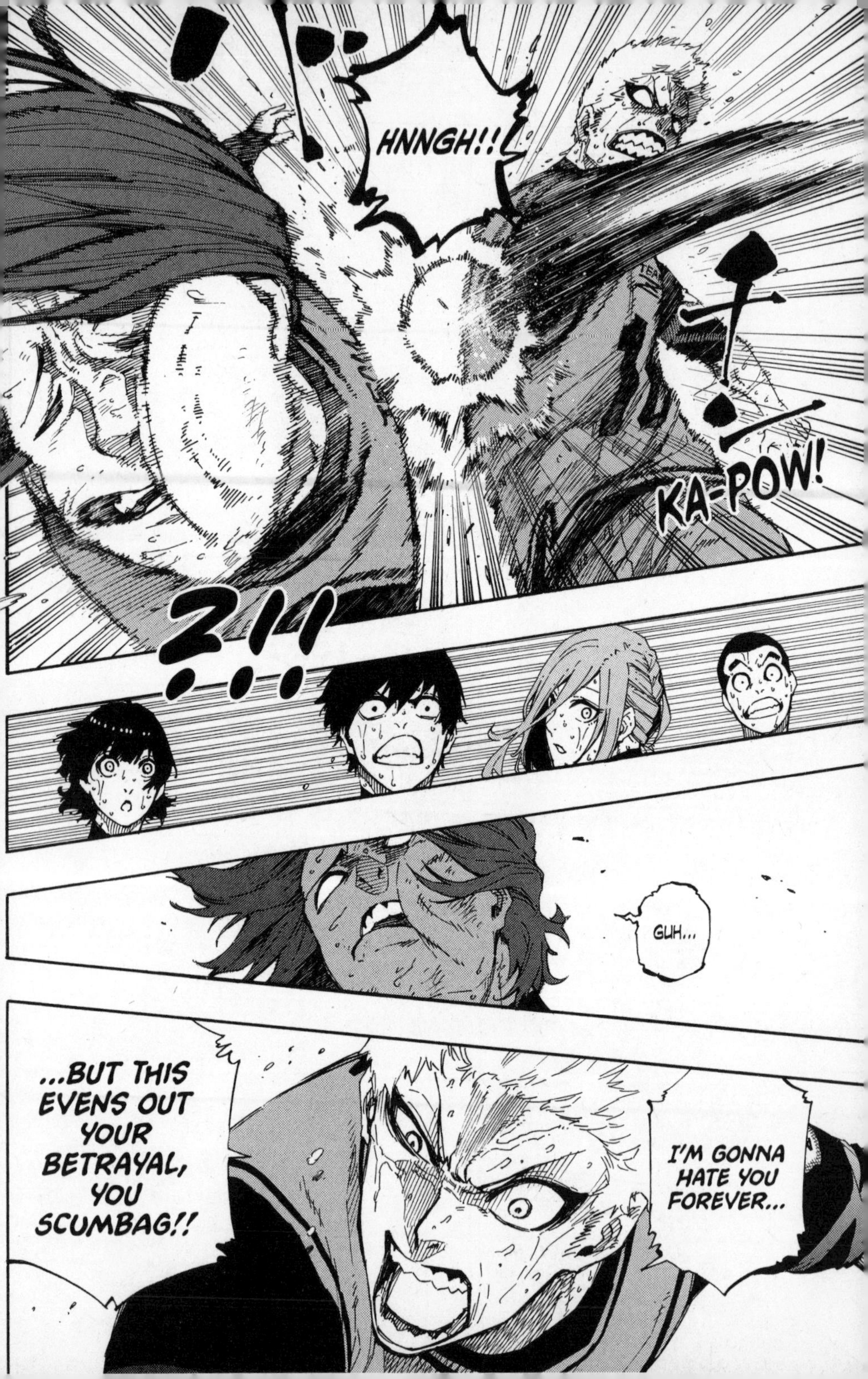
HNNGH!!
KA-POW!
GUH...
I'M GONNA HATE YOU FOREVER...
...BUT THIS EVENS OUT YOUR BETRAYAL, YOU SCUMBAG!!

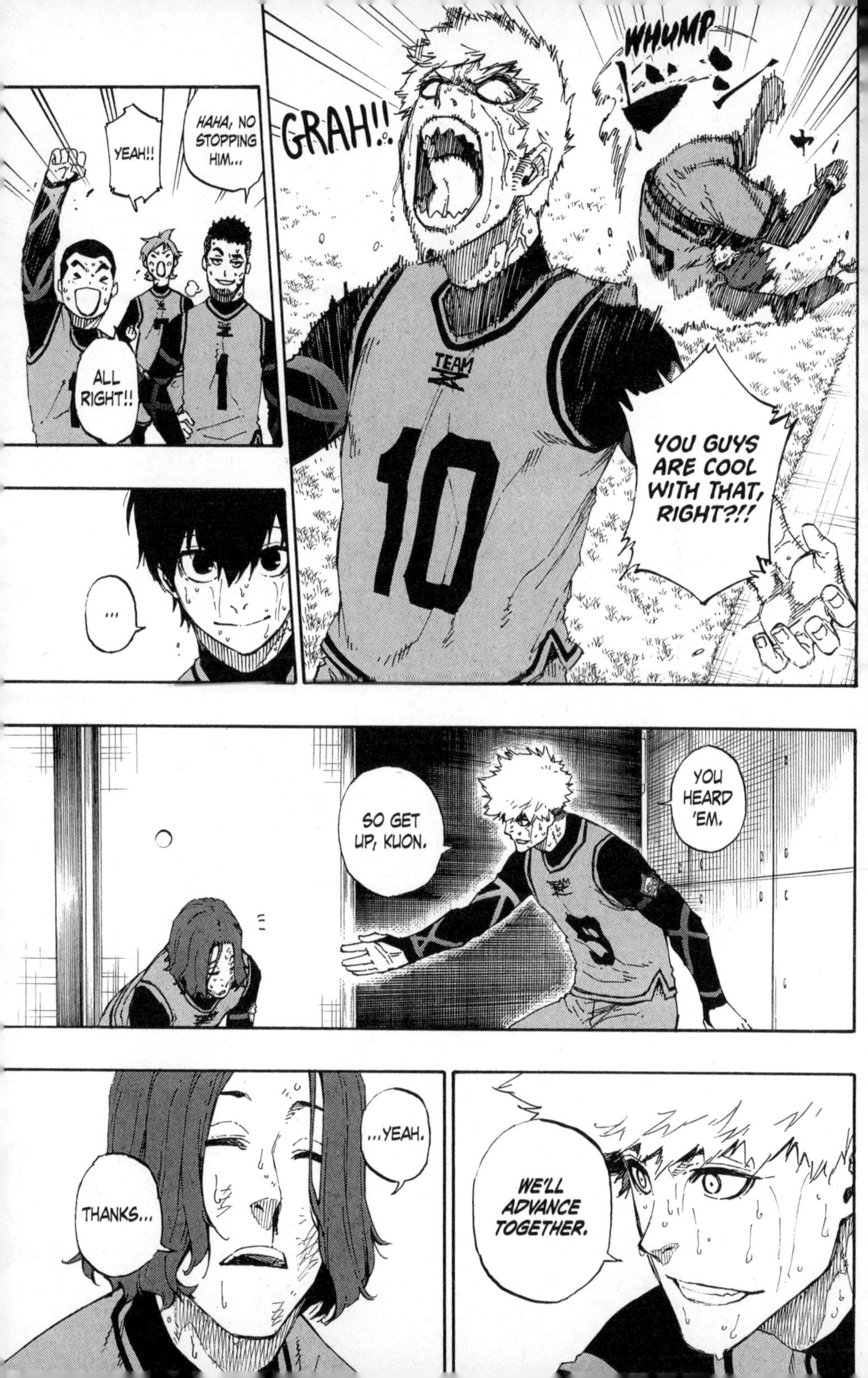
WHUMP
GRAH!!
YOU GUYS ARE COOL WITH THAT, RIGHT?!!
HAHA, NO STOPPING HIM...
YEAH!!
ALL RIGHT!!
...
YOU HEARD 'EM.
SO GET UP, KUON.
WE'LL ADVANCE TOGETHER.
...YEAH.
THANKS...

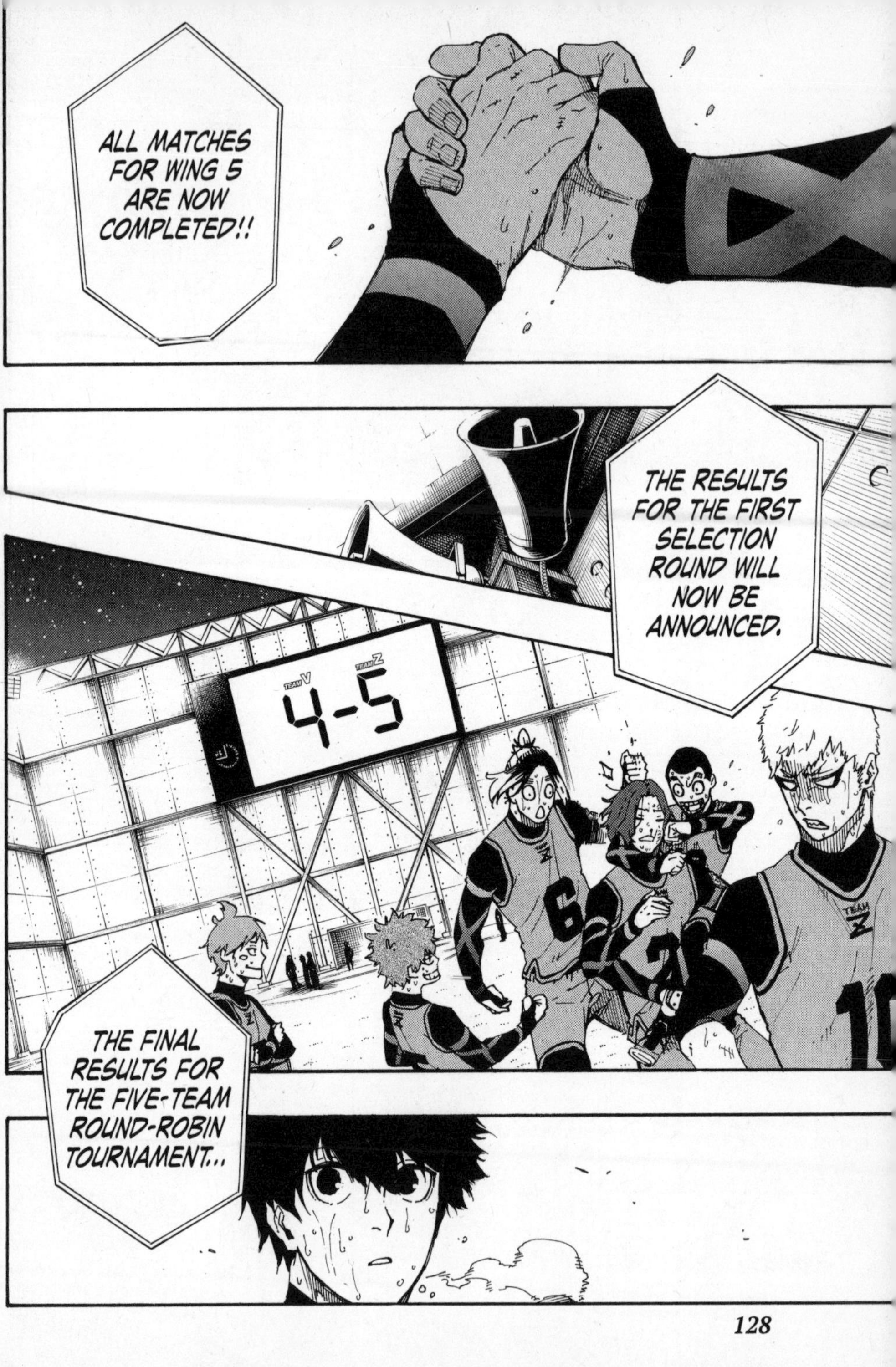
ALL MATCHES FOR WING 5 ARE NOW COMPLETED!!
THE RESULTS FOR THE FIRST SELECTION ROUND WILL NOW BE ANNOUNCED.
TEAM V
TEAM Z
4-5
THE FINAL RESULTS FOR THE FIVE-TEAM ROUND-ROBIN TOURNAMENT...

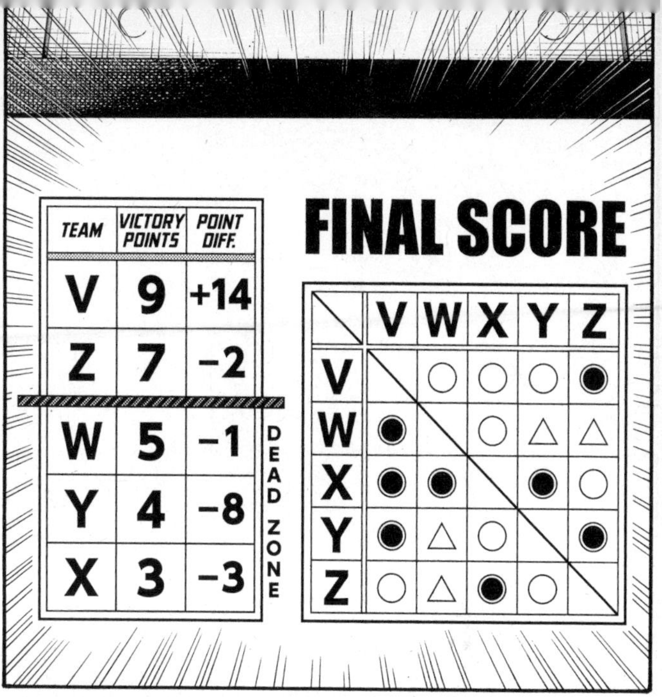
FINAL SCORE
TEAM | VICTORY POINTS | POINT DIFF.
V | 9 | +14
Z | 7 | −2
W | 5 | −1
Y | 4 | −8
X | 3 | −3
DEAD ZONE
V W X Y Z

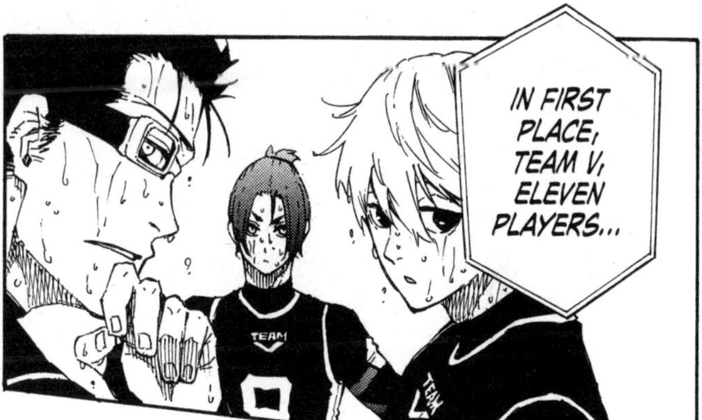
IN FIRST PLACE, TEAM V, ELEVEN PLAYERS...

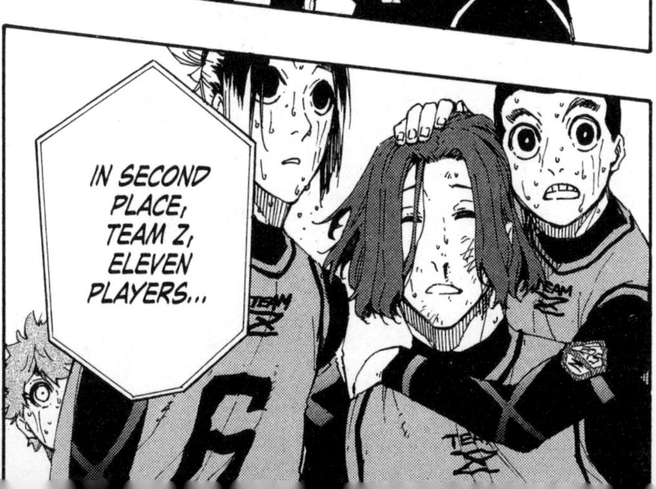
IN SECOND PLACE, TEAM Z, ELEVEN PLAYERS...

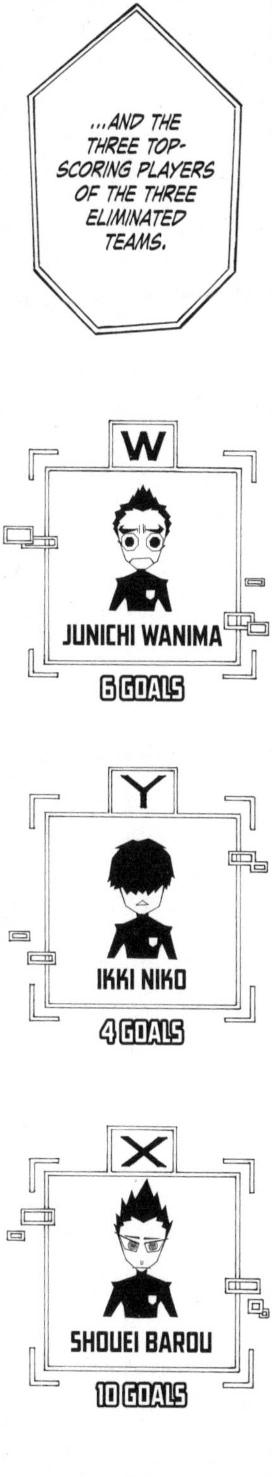
...AND THE THREE TOP-SCORING PLAYERS OF THE THREE ELIMINATED TEAMS.
W
JUNICHI WANIMA
6 GOALS
Y
IKKI NIKO
4 GOALS
X
SHOUEI BAROU
10 GOALS

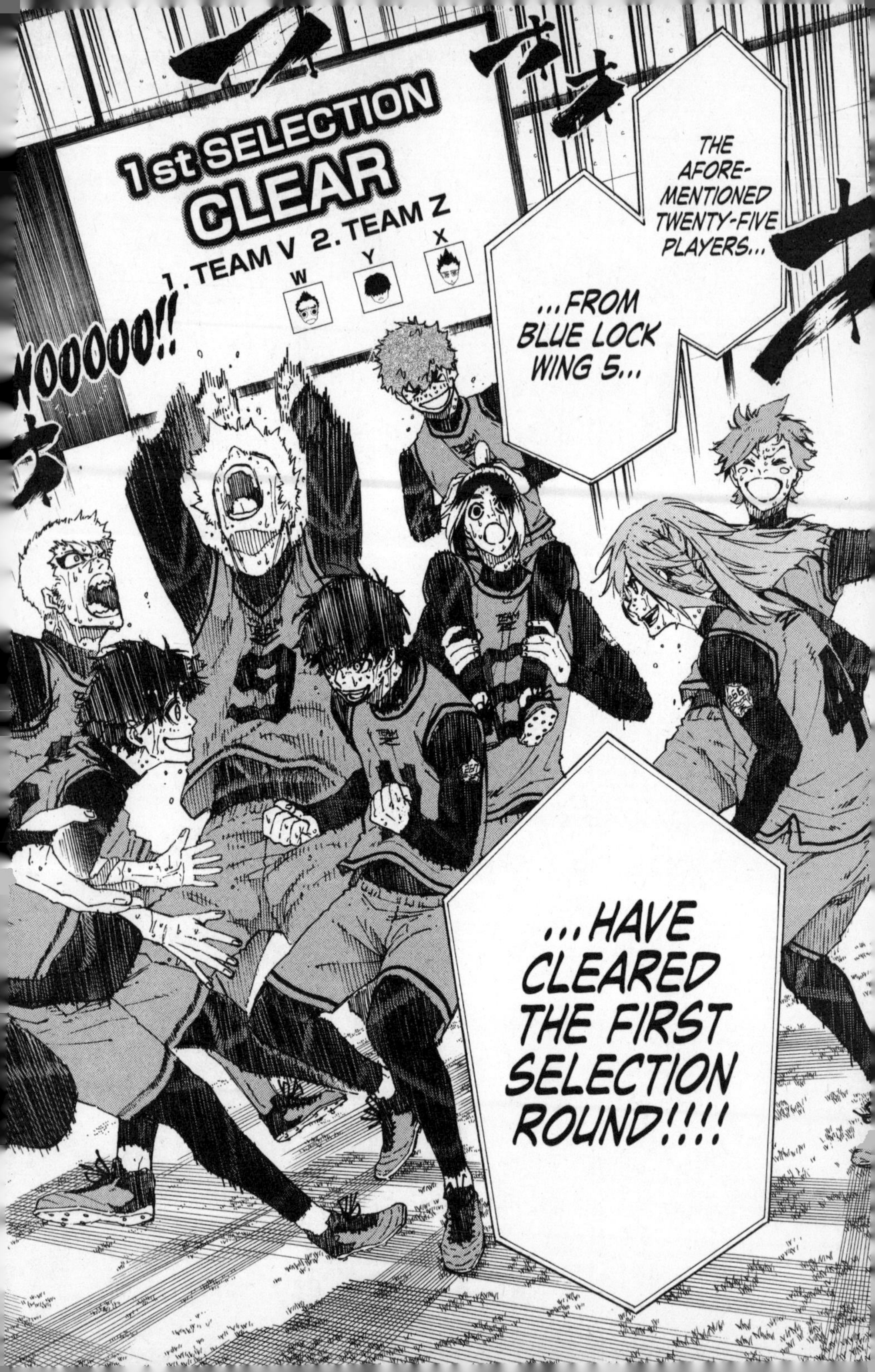
THE AFORE-MENTIONED TWENTY-FIVE PLAYERS...
...FROM BLUE LOCK WING 5...
1st SELECTION CLEAR
1. TEAM V 2. TEAM Z
W
Y
X
OOOOO!!
...HAVE CLEARED THE FIRST SELECTION ROUND!!!!

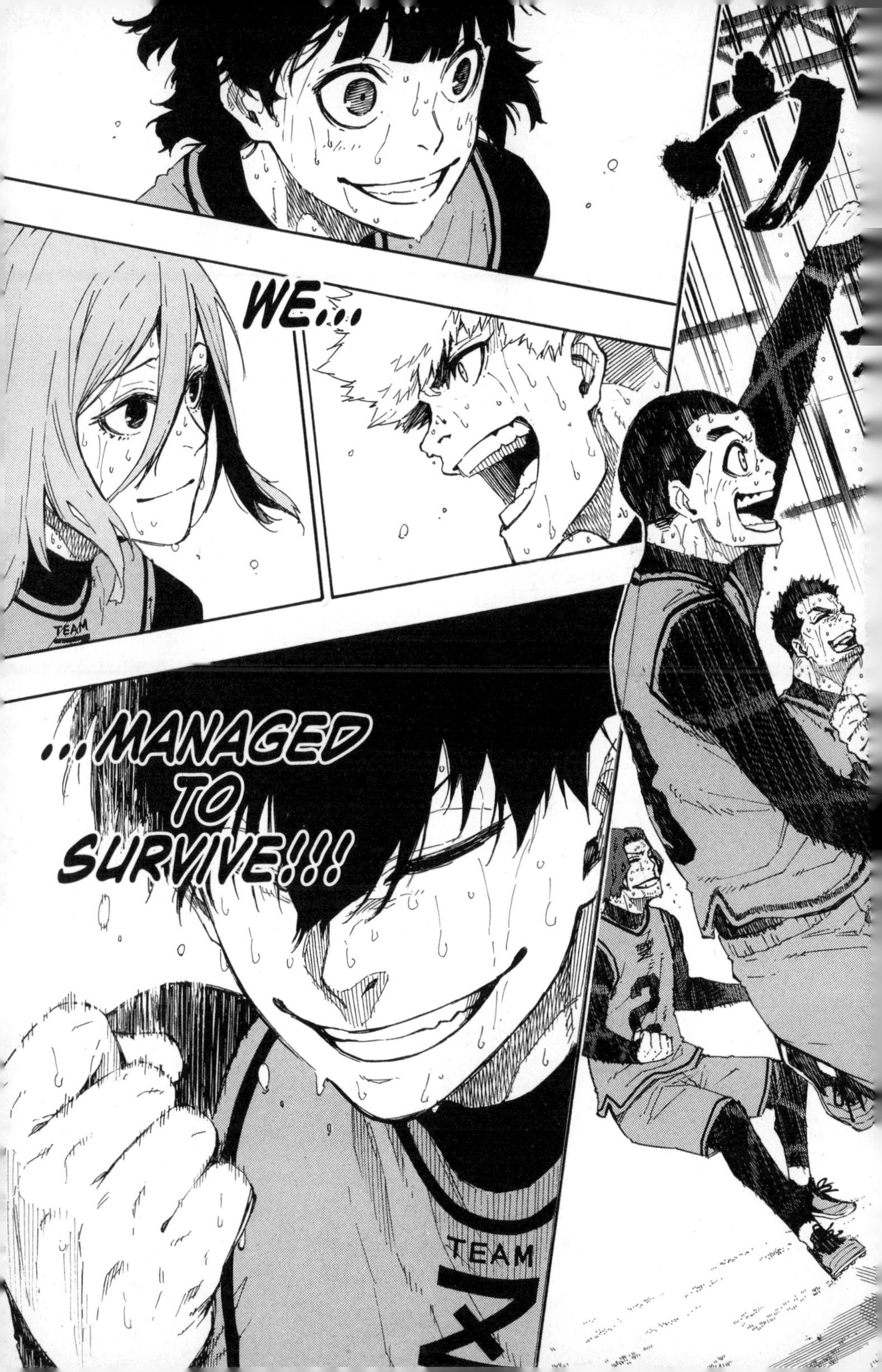
WE...
...MANAGED TO SURVIVE!!!
TEAM
TEAM

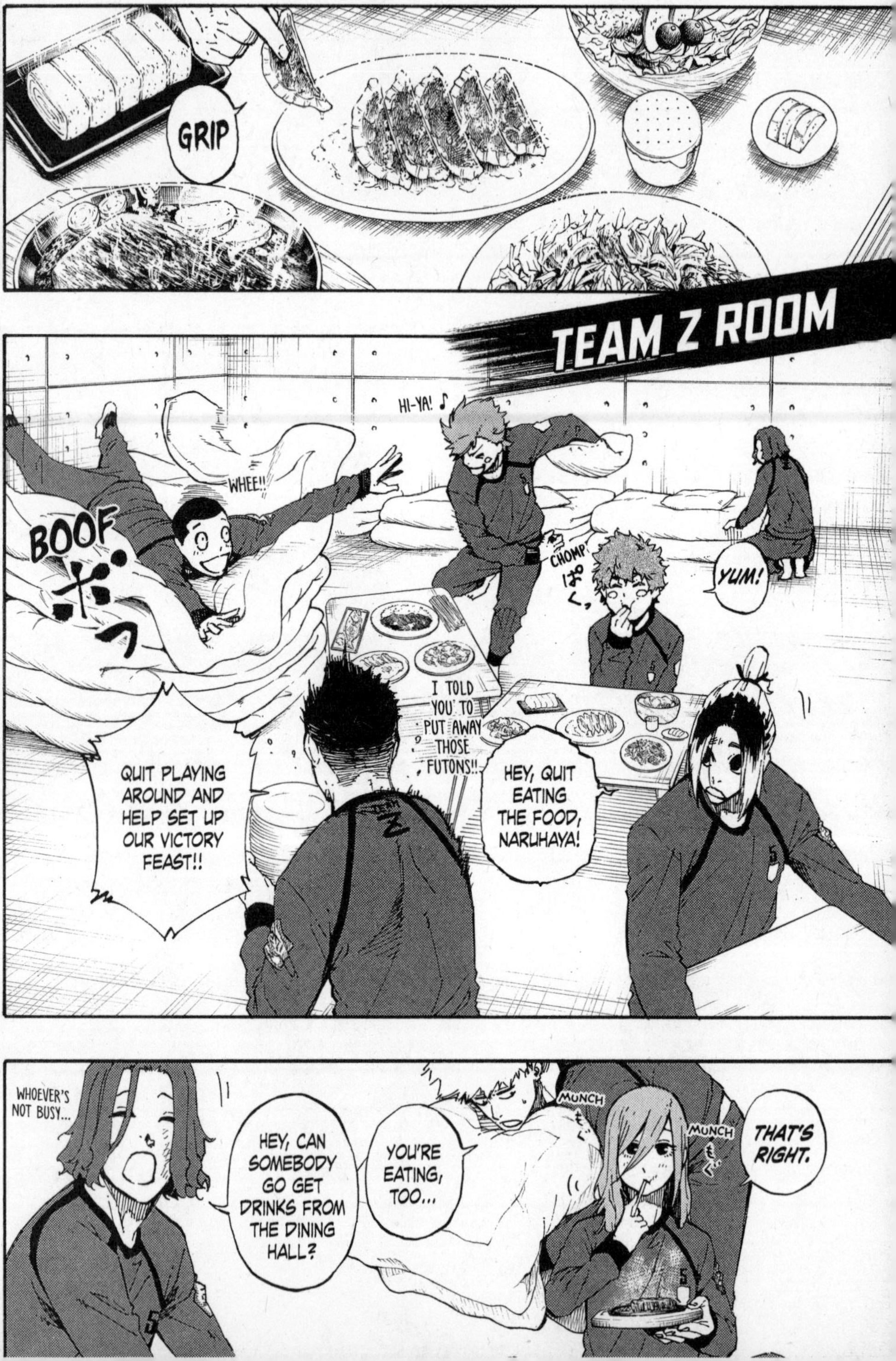
GRIP
TEAM Z ROOM
YUM!
CHOMP
HI-YA! ♪
WHEE!!
BOOF
HEY, QUIT EATING THE FOOD, NARUHAYA!
I TOLD YOU TO PUT AWAY THOSE FUTONS!!
QUIT PLAYING AROUND AND HELP SET UP OUR VICTORY FEAST!!
THAT'S RIGHT.
MUNCH
MUNCH
YOU'RE EATING, TOO...
HEY, CAN SOMEBODY GO GET DRINKS FROM THE DINING HALL?
WHOEVER'S NOT BUSY...

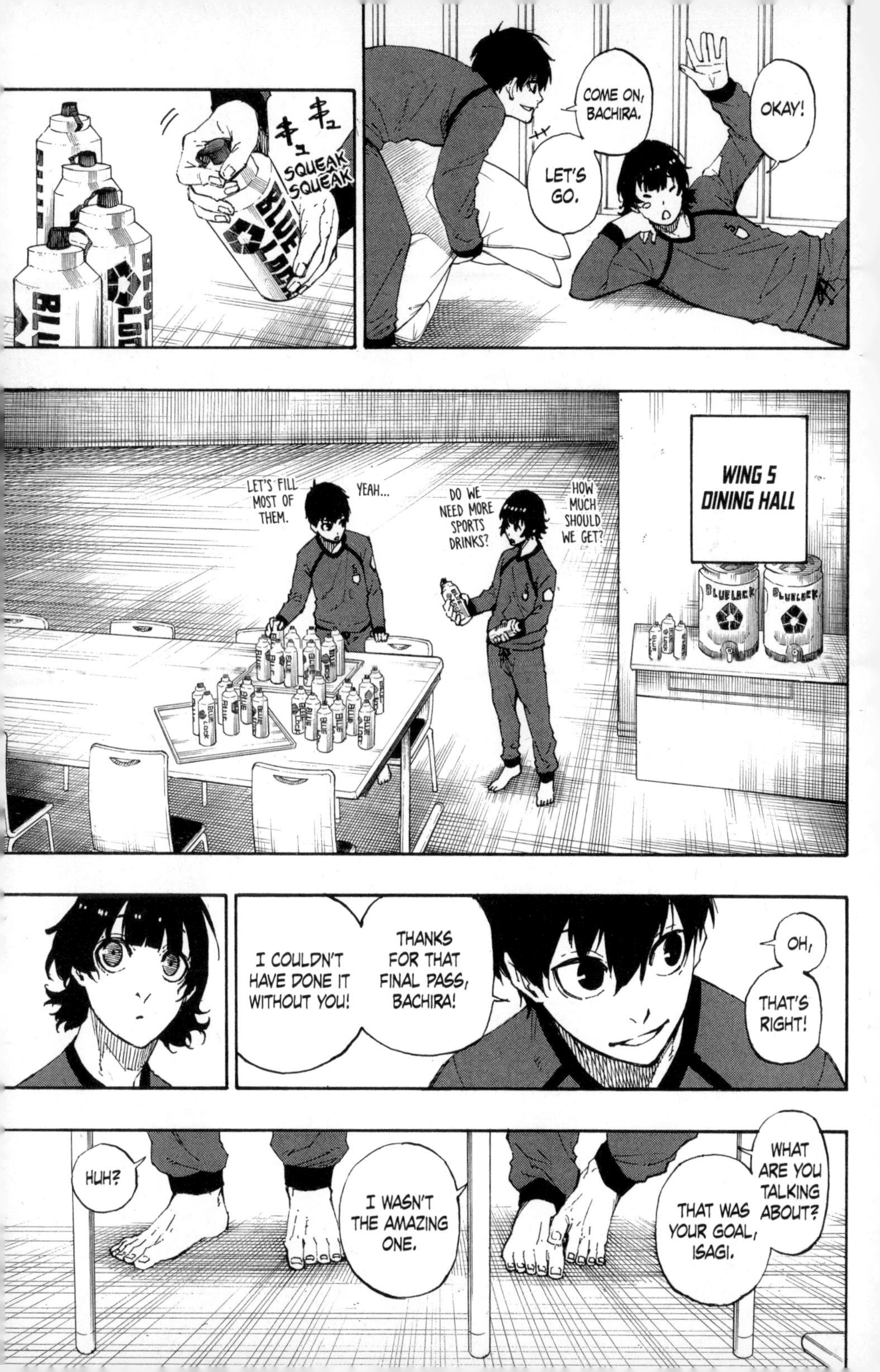
COME ON, BACHIRA.
LET'S GO.
OKAY!
キュ キュ
SQUEAK SQUEAK
WING 5 DINING HALL
HOW MUCH SHOULD WE GET?
DO WE NEED MORE SPORTS DRINKS?
YEAH...
LET'S FILL MOST OF THEM.
OH, THAT'S RIGHT!
THANKS FOR THAT FINAL PASS, BACHIRA!
I COULDN'T HAVE DONE IT WITHOUT YOU!
WHAT ARE YOU TALKING ABOUT?
THAT WAS YOUR GOAL, ISAGI.
I WASN'T THE AMAZING ONE.
HUH?

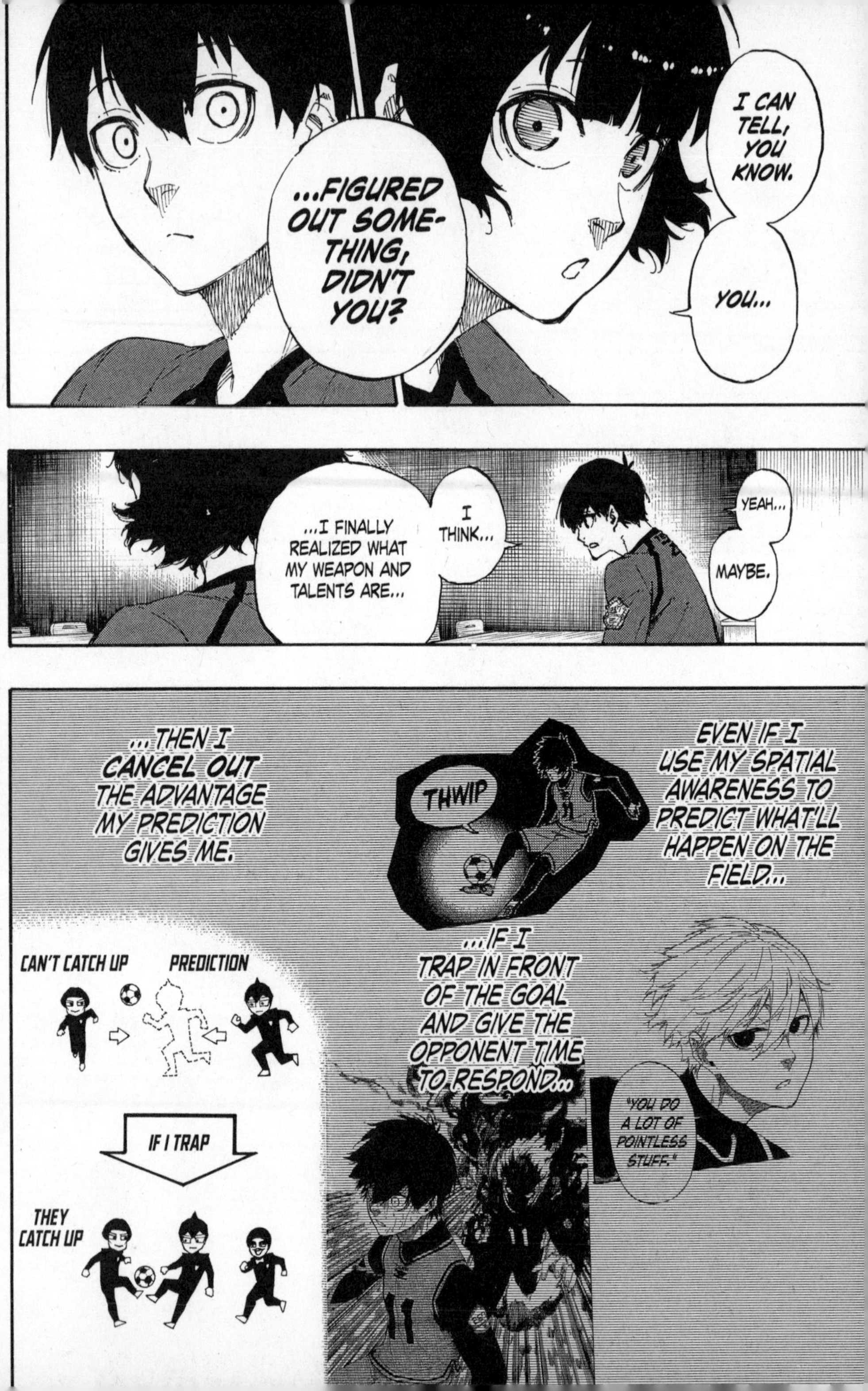
I CAN TELL, YOU KNOW.
YOU...
...FIGURED OUT SOMETHING, DIDN'T YOU?
YEAH... MAYBE.
I THINK...
...I FINALLY REALIZED WHAT MY WEAPON AND TALENTS ARE...
EVEN IF I USE MY SPATIAL AWARENESS TO PREDICT WHAT'LL HAPPEN ON THE FIELD...
THWIP
...THEN I CANCEL OUT THE ADVANTAGE MY PREDICTION GIVES ME.
"YOU DO A LOT OF POINTLESS STUFF."
...IF I TRAP IN FRONT OF THE GOAL AND GIVE THE OPPONENT TIME TO RESPOND...
PREDICTION
CAN'T CATCH UP
IF I TRAP
THEY CATCH UP

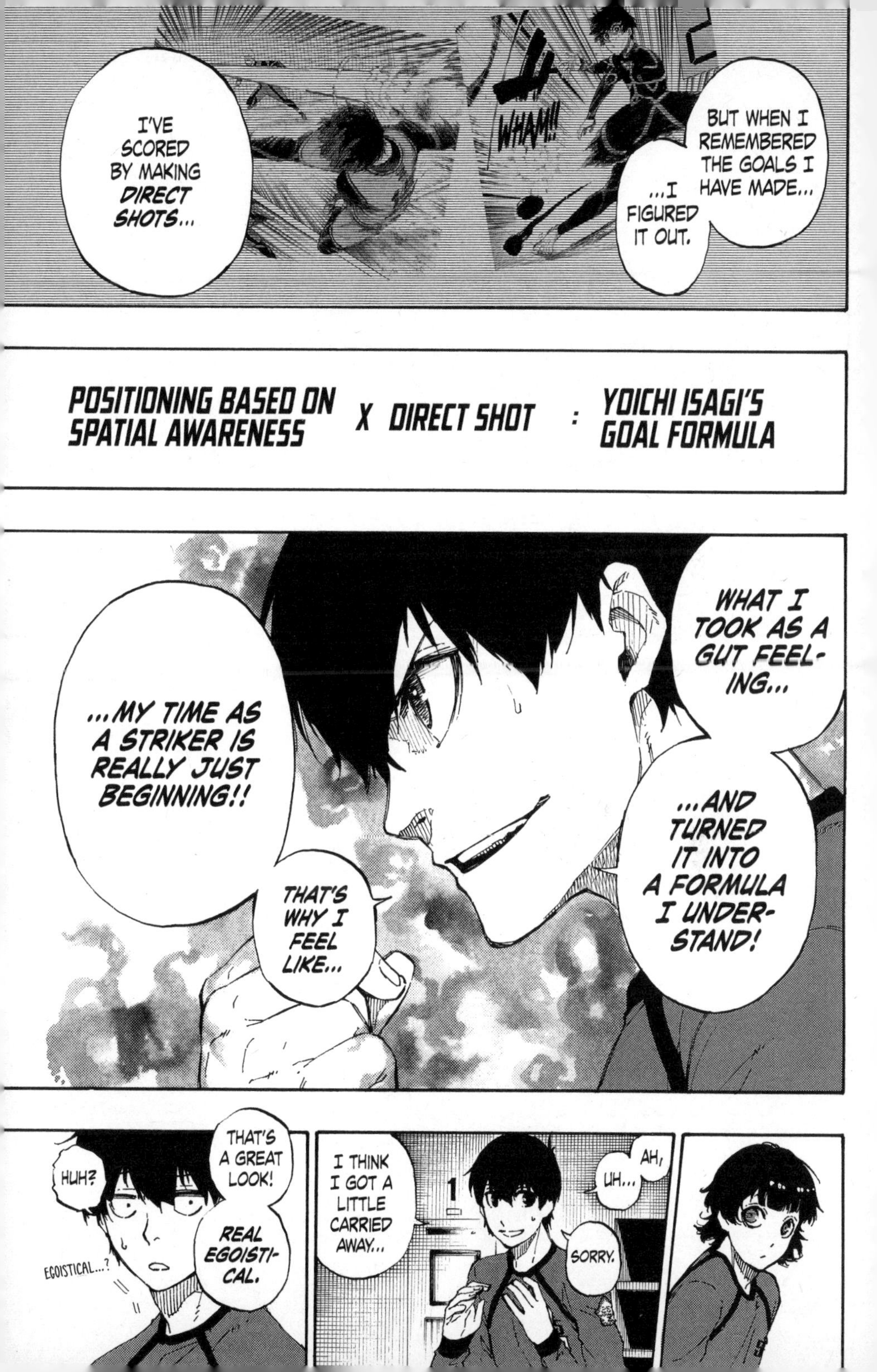
BUT WHEN I REMEMBERED THE GOALS I HAVE MADE...
...I FIGURED IT OUT.
WHAM!!
I'VE SCORED BY MAKING DIRECT SHOTS...
POSITIONING BASED ON SPATIAL AWARENESS X DIRECT SHOT : YOICHI ISAGI'S GOAL FORMULA
WHAT I TOOK AS A GUT FEELING...
...AND TURNED IT INTO A FORMULA I UNDERSTAND!
THAT'S WHY I FEEL LIKE...
...MY TIME AS A STRIKER IS REALLY JUST BEGINNING!!
AH, UH...
I THINK I GOT A LITTLE CARRIED AWAY...
SORRY.
THAT'S A GREAT LOOK!
HUH?
REAL EGOISTICAL.
EGOISTICAL...?

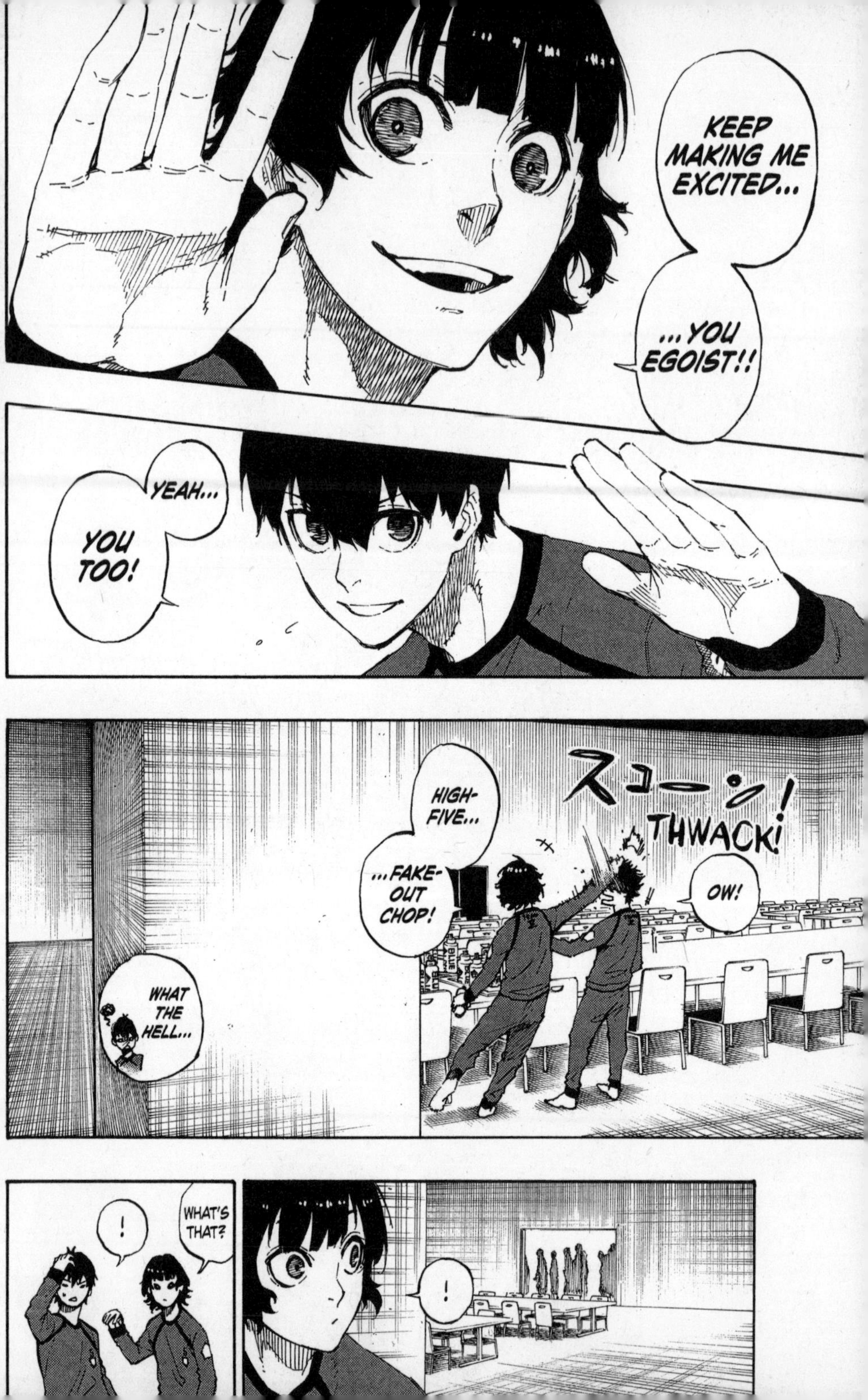
KEEP MAKING ME EXCITED...
...YOU EGOIST!!
YEAH...
YOU TOO!
HIGH-FIVE...
...FAKE-OUT CHOP!
スコーン! THWACK!
OW!
WHAT THE HELL...
!
WHAT'S THAT?
!

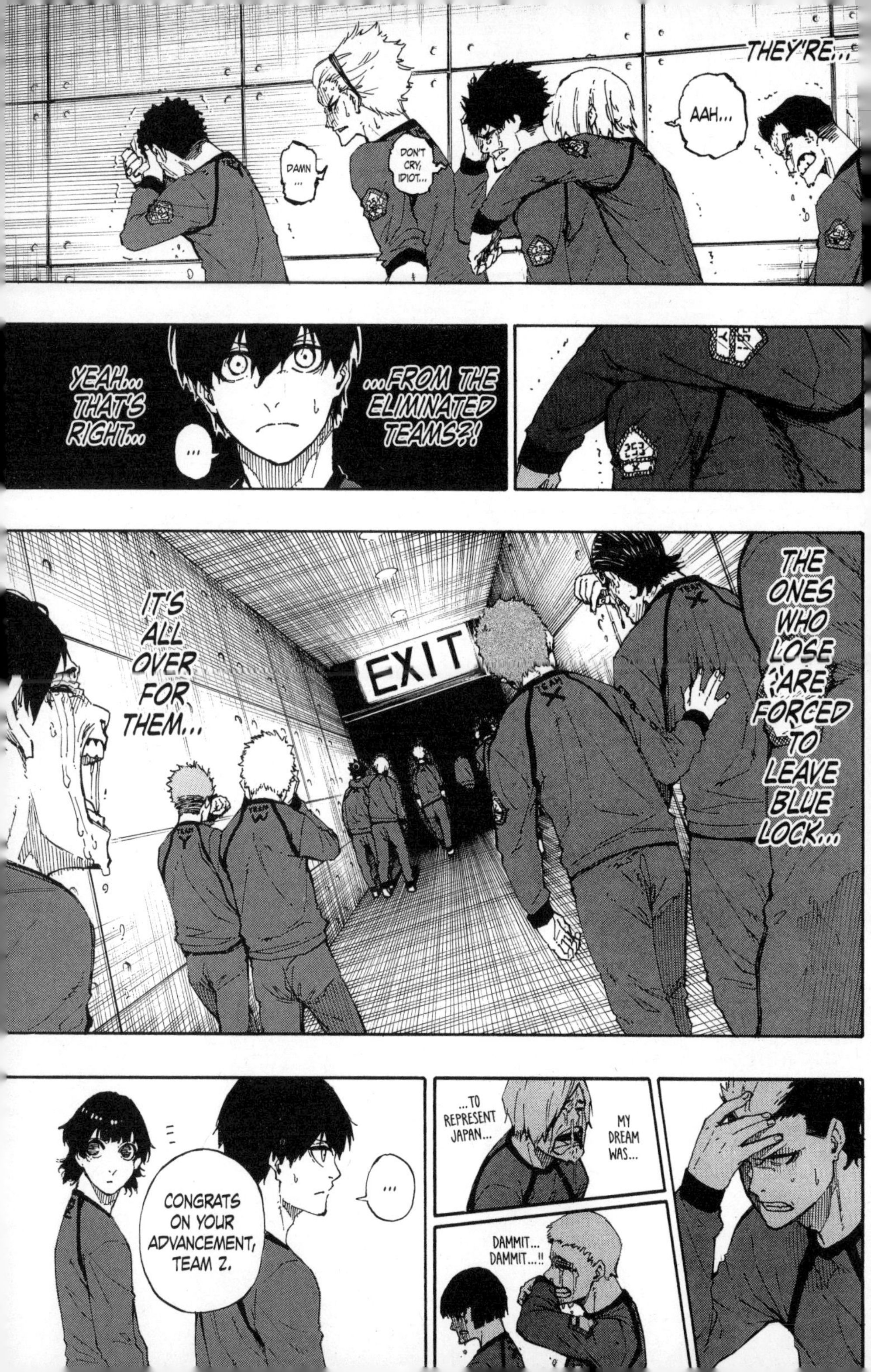
THEY'RE...
AAH...
DON'T CRY, IDIOT...
DAMN...
...FROM THE ELIMINATED TEAMS?!
...
YEAH... THAT'S RIGHT...
THE ONES WHO LOSE ARE FORCED TO LEAVE BLUE LOCK...
EXIT
IT'S ALL OVER FOR THEM...
MY DREAM WAS...
...TO REPRESENT JAPAN...
DAMMIT... DAMMIT...!!
...
CONGRATS ON YOUR ADVANCEMENT, TEAM Z.

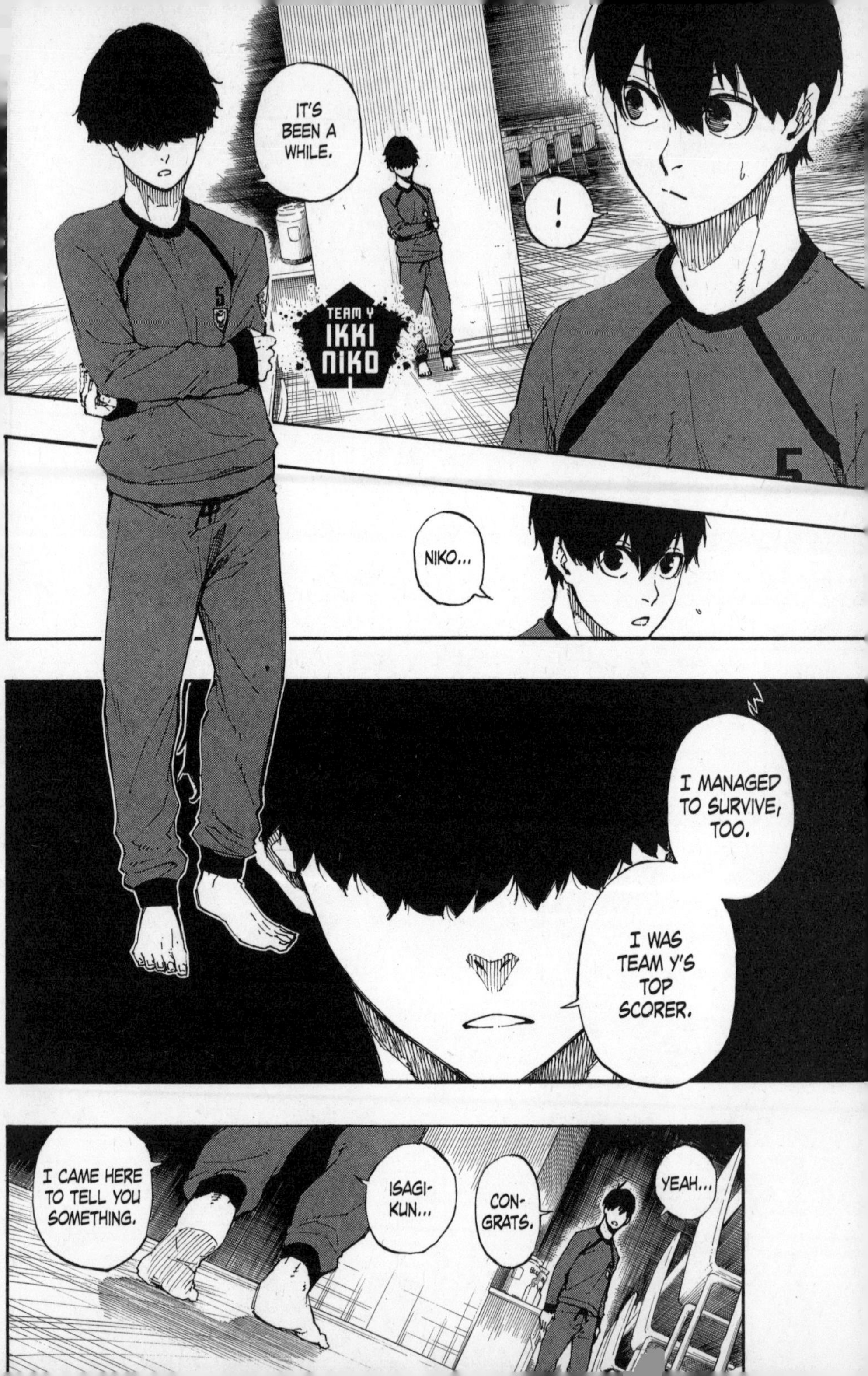
IT'S BEEN A WHILE.
!
TEAM Y IKKI NIKO
NIKO...
I MANAGED TO SURVIVE, TOO.
I WAS TEAM Y'S TOP SCORER.
YEAH...
CON-GRATS.
ISAGI-KUN...
I CAME HERE TO TELL YOU SOMETHING.

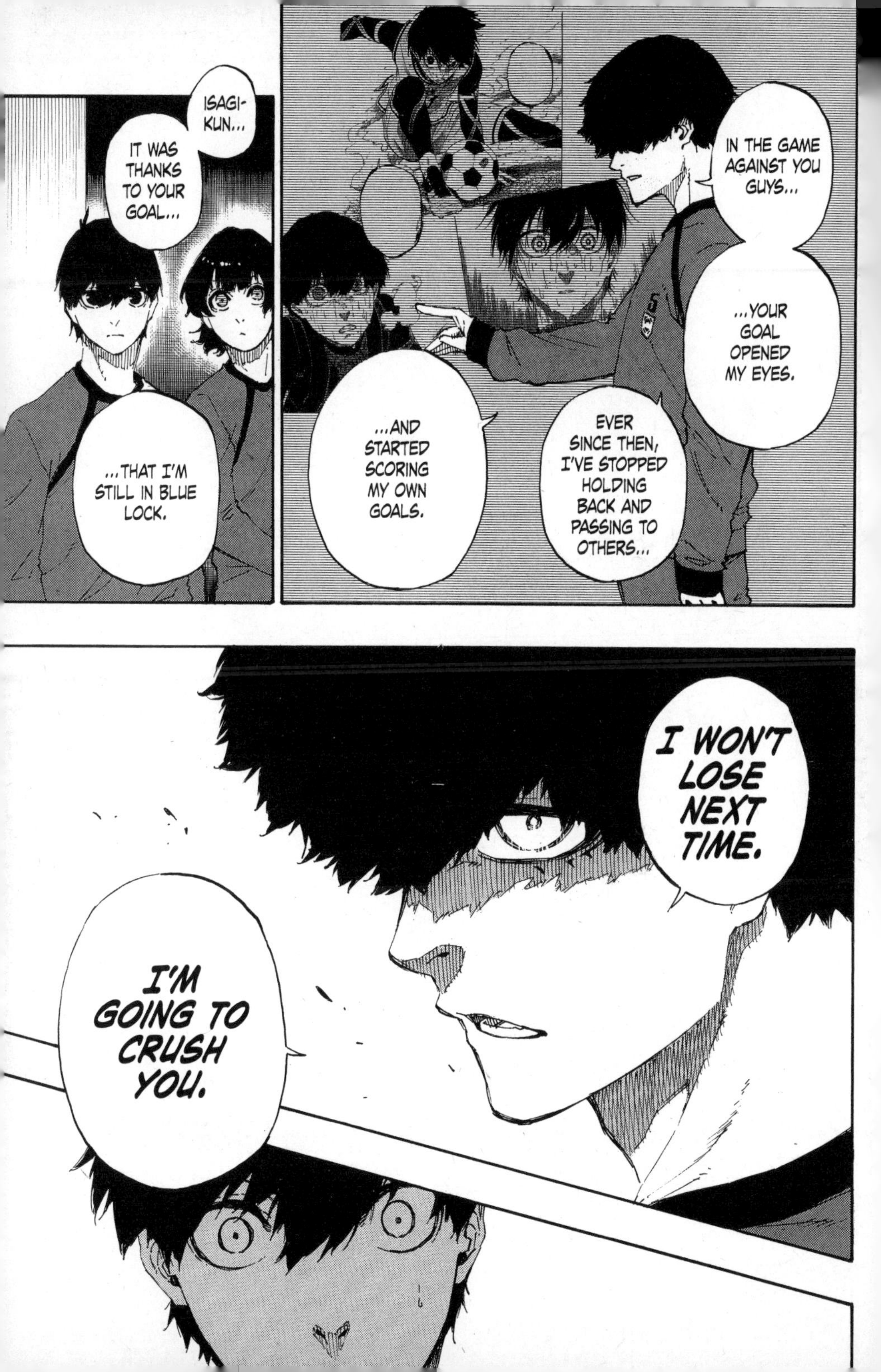
IN THE GAME AGAINST YOU GUYS...
...YOUR GOAL OPENED MY EYES.
EVER SINCE THEN, I'VE STOPPED HOLDING BACK AND PASSING TO OTHERS...
...AND STARTED SCORING MY OWN GOALS.
ISAGI-KUN...
IT WAS THANKS TO YOUR GOAL...
...THAT I'M STILL IN BLUE LOCK.
I WON'T LOSE NEXT TIME.
I'M GOING TO CRUSH YOU.

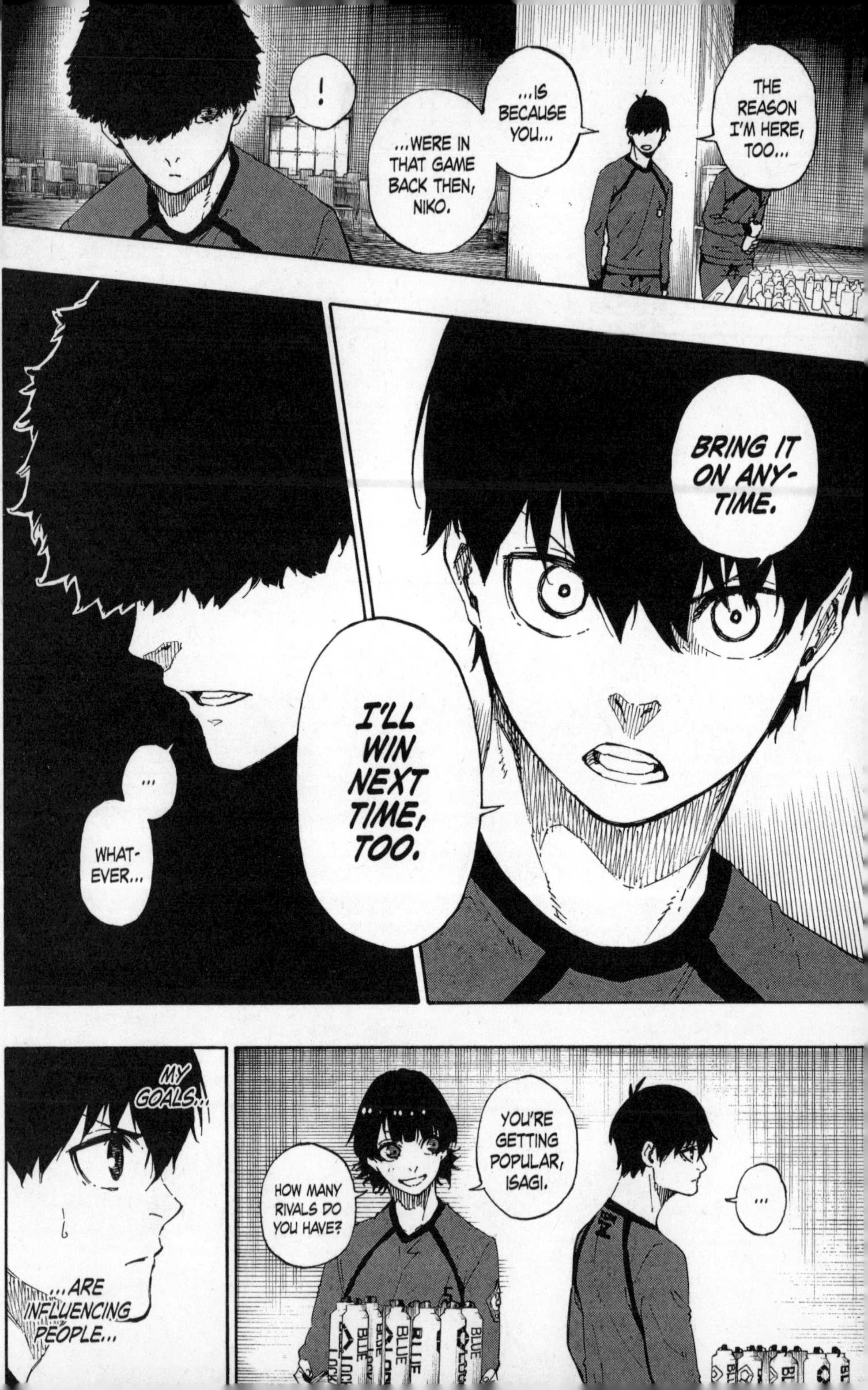
THE REASON I'M HERE, TOO...
...IS BECAUSE YOU...
...WERE IN THAT GAME BACK THEN, NIKO.
!
BRING IT ON ANY-TIME.
I'LL WIN NEXT TIME, TOO.
...
WHAT-EVER...
...
YOU'RE GETTING POPULAR, ISAGI.
HOW MANY RIVALS DO YOU HAVE?
MY GOALS...
...ARE INFLUENCING PEOPLE...

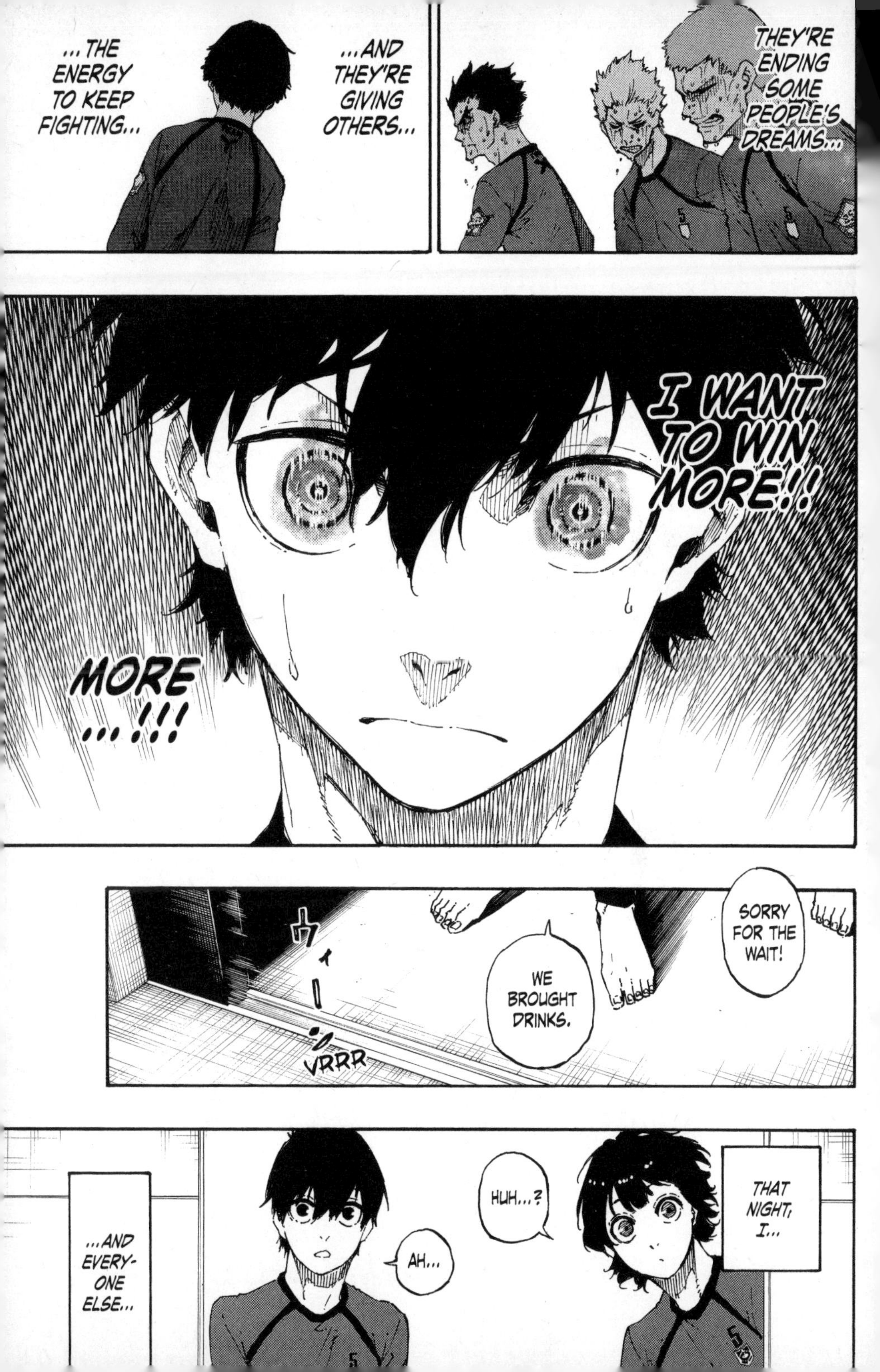

THEY'RE ENDING SOME PEOPLE'S DREAMS...
...AND THEY'RE GIVING OTHERS...
...THE ENERGY TO KEEP FIGHTING...
I WANT TO WIN MORE!!
MORE ...!!!
SORRY FOR THE WAIT!
WE BROUGHT DRINKS.
ウィーン
VRRR
THAT NIGHT, I...
HUH...?
AH...
...AND EVERY-ONE ELSE...

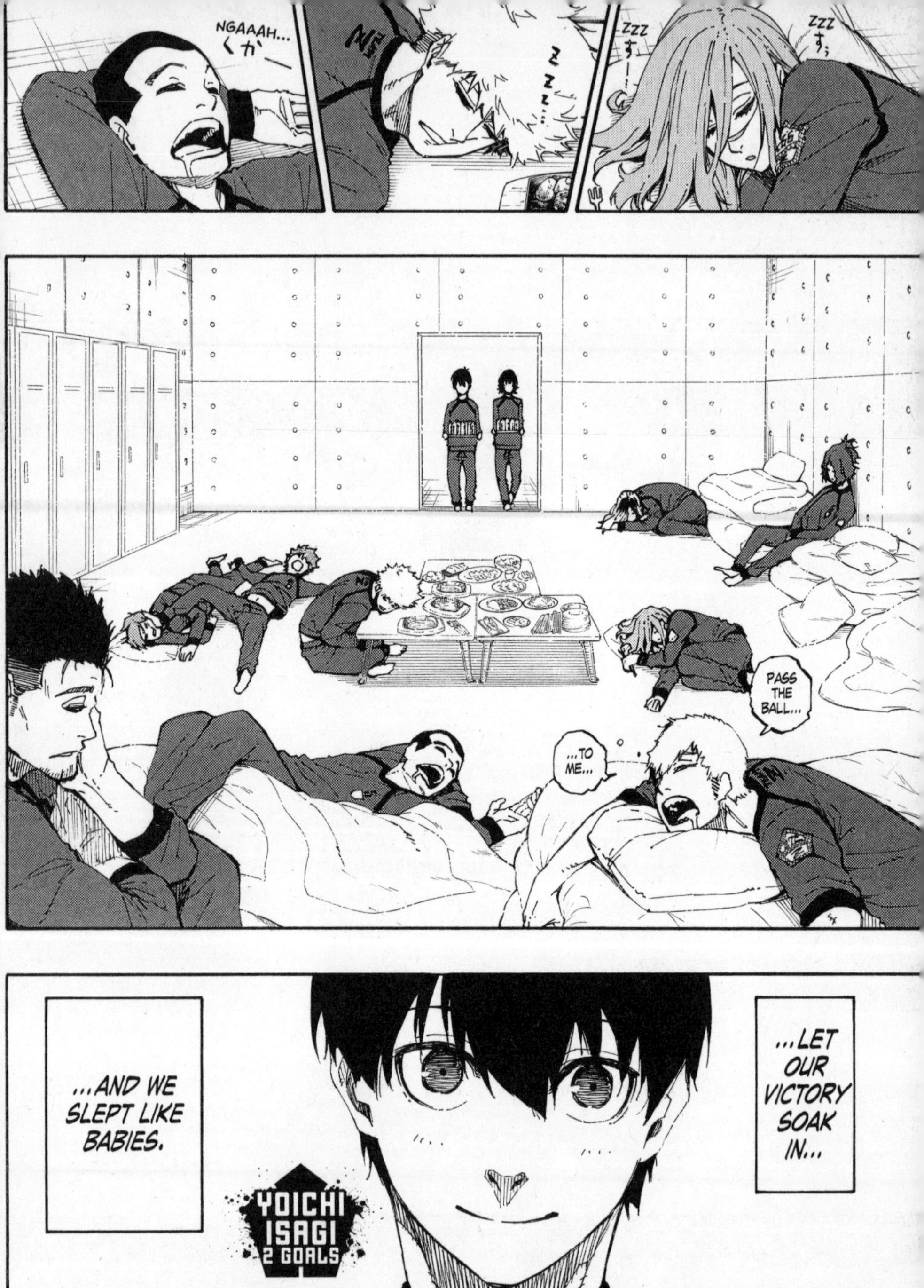
ZZZ すっ
ZZZ す…
Z Z Z...
NGAAAH... くが—
PASS THE BALL...
...TO ME...
...LET OUR VICTORY SOAK IN...
...AND WE SLEPT LIKE BABIES.
YOICHI ISAGI 2 GOALS

TEAM Z ADVANCES TO THE SECOND SELECTION ROUND

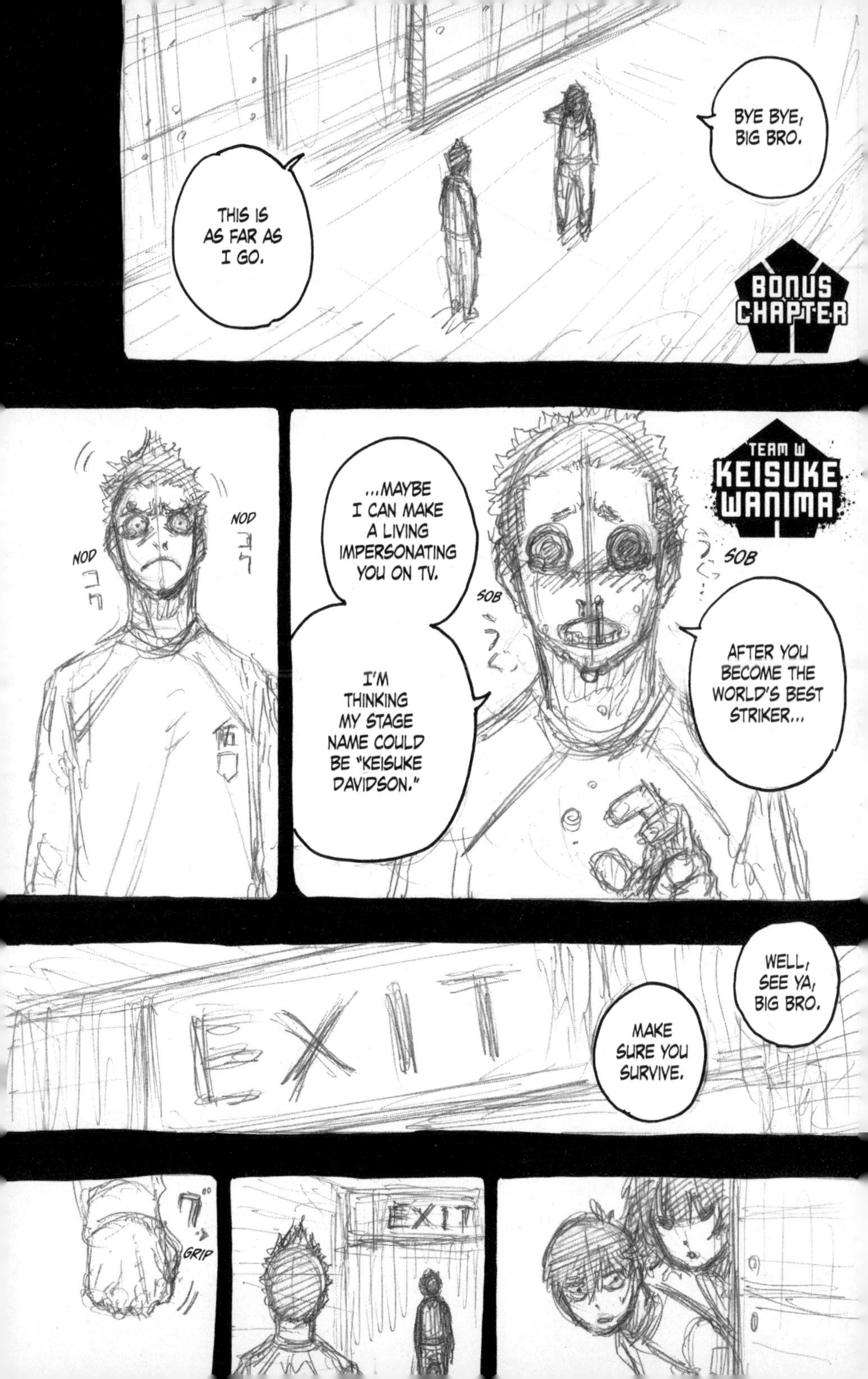
BYE BYE, BIG BRO.
THIS IS AS FAR AS I GO.
BONUS CHAPTER
TEAM W
KEISUKE WANIMA
SOB
AFTER YOU BECOME THE WORLD'S BEST STRIKER...
...MAYBE I CAN MAKE A LIVING IMPERSONATING YOU ON TV.
I'M THINKING MY STAGE NAME COULD BE "KEISUKE DAVIDSON."
SOB
NOD
NOD
WELL, SEE YA, BIG BRO.
MAKE SURE YOU SURVIVE.
EXIT
EXIT
GRIP

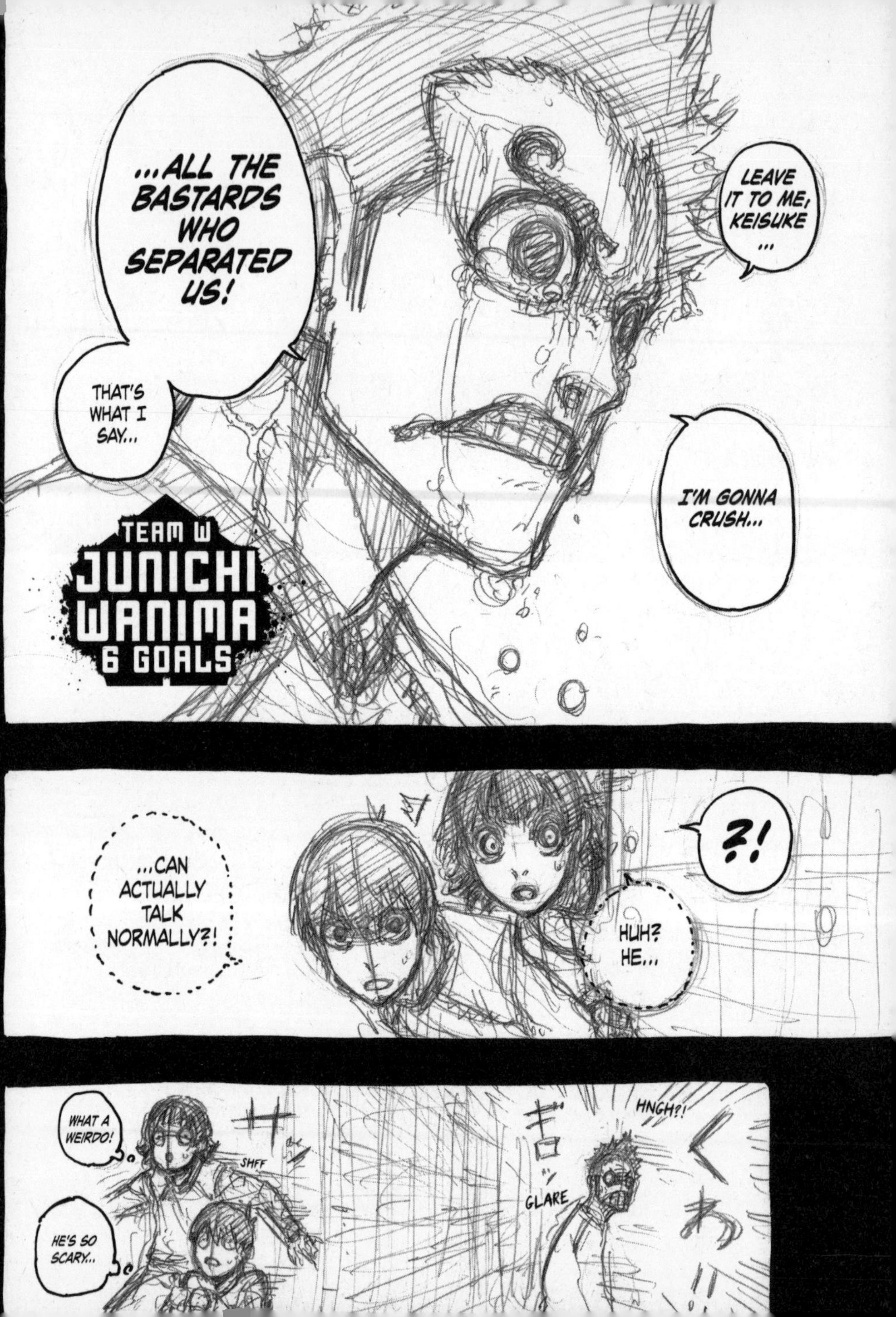
LEAVE IT TO ME, KEISUKE...
I'M GONNA CRUSH...
...ALL THE BASTARDS WHO SEPARATED US!
THAT'S WHAT I SAY...
TEAM W
JUNICHI WANIMA
6 GOALS
?!
HUH? HE...
...CAN ACTUALLY TALK NORMALLY?!
HNGH?!
GLARE
SHFF
WHAT A WEIRDO!
HE'S SO SCARY...

# CHAPTER 39: HUNGRY

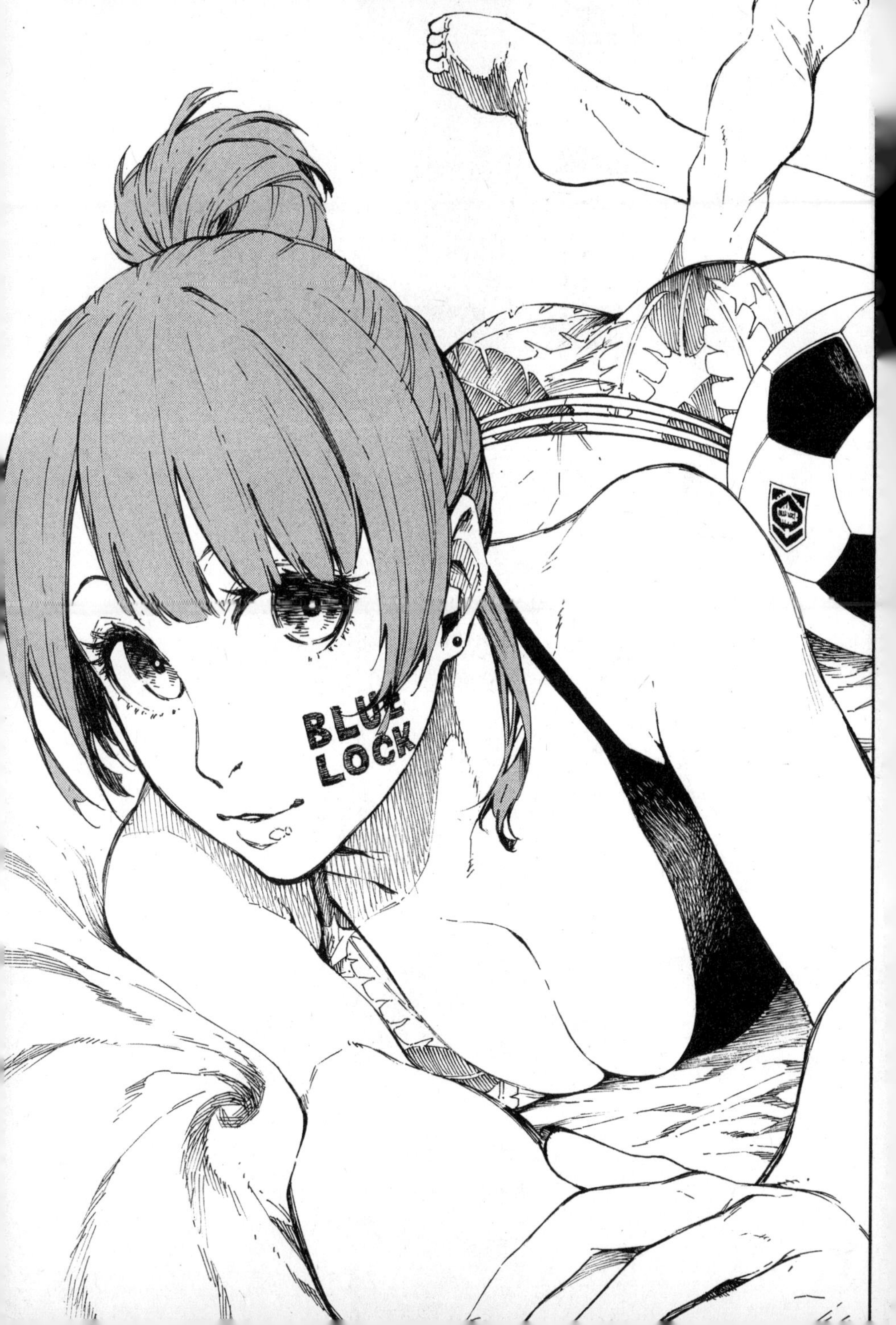
BLUE LOCK

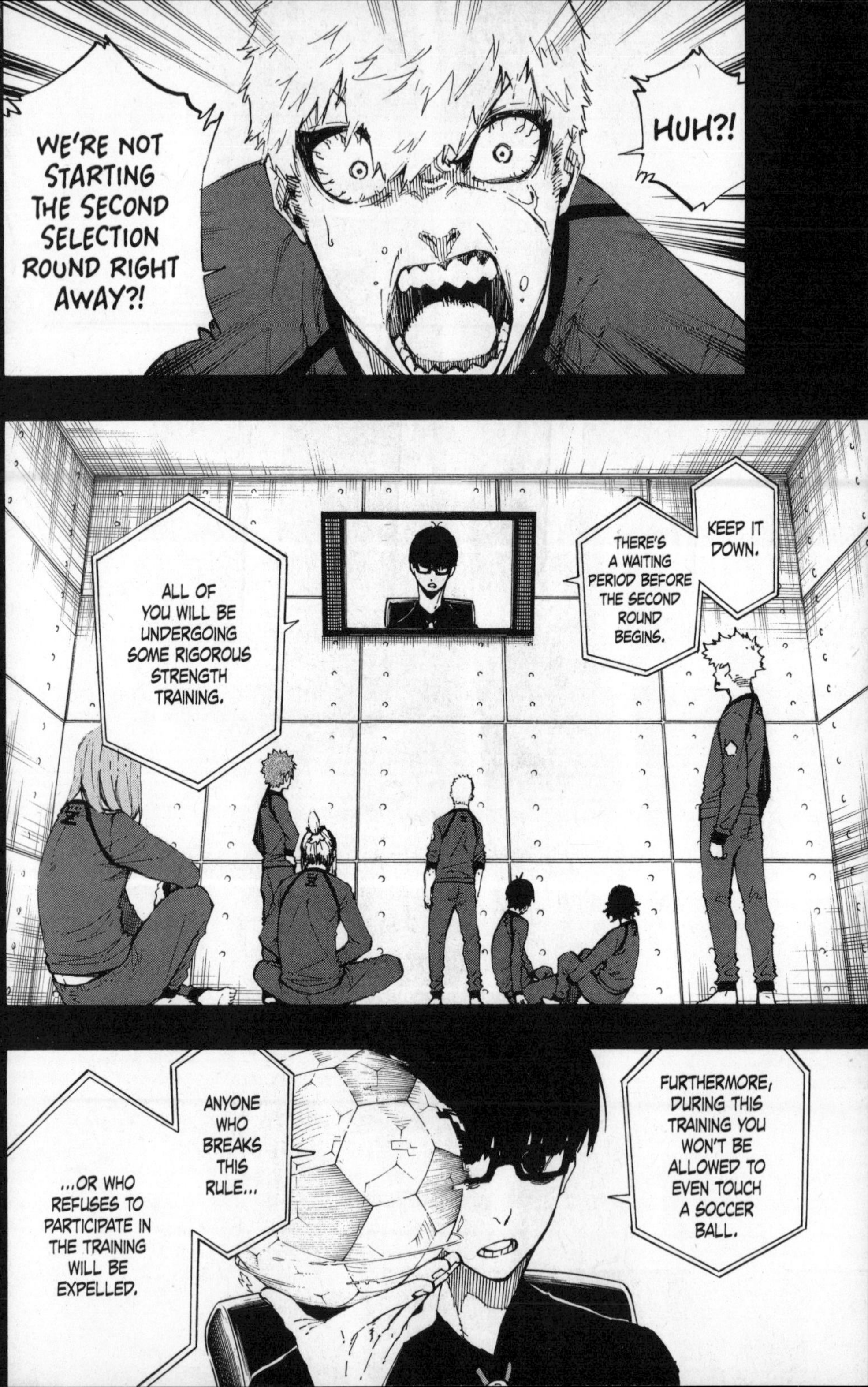
HUH?!
WE'RE NOT STARTING THE SECOND SELECTION ROUND RIGHT AWAY?!
KEEP IT DOWN.
THERE'S A WAITING PERIOD BEFORE THE SECOND ROUND BEGINS.
ALL OF YOU WILL BE UNDERGOING SOME RIGOROUS STRENGTH TRAINING.
FURTHERMORE, DURING THIS TRAINING YOU WON'T BE ALLOWED TO EVEN TOUCH A SOCCER BALL.
ANYONE WHO BREAKS THIS RULE...
...OR WHO REFUSES TO PARTICIPATE IN THE TRAINING WILL BE EXPELLED.

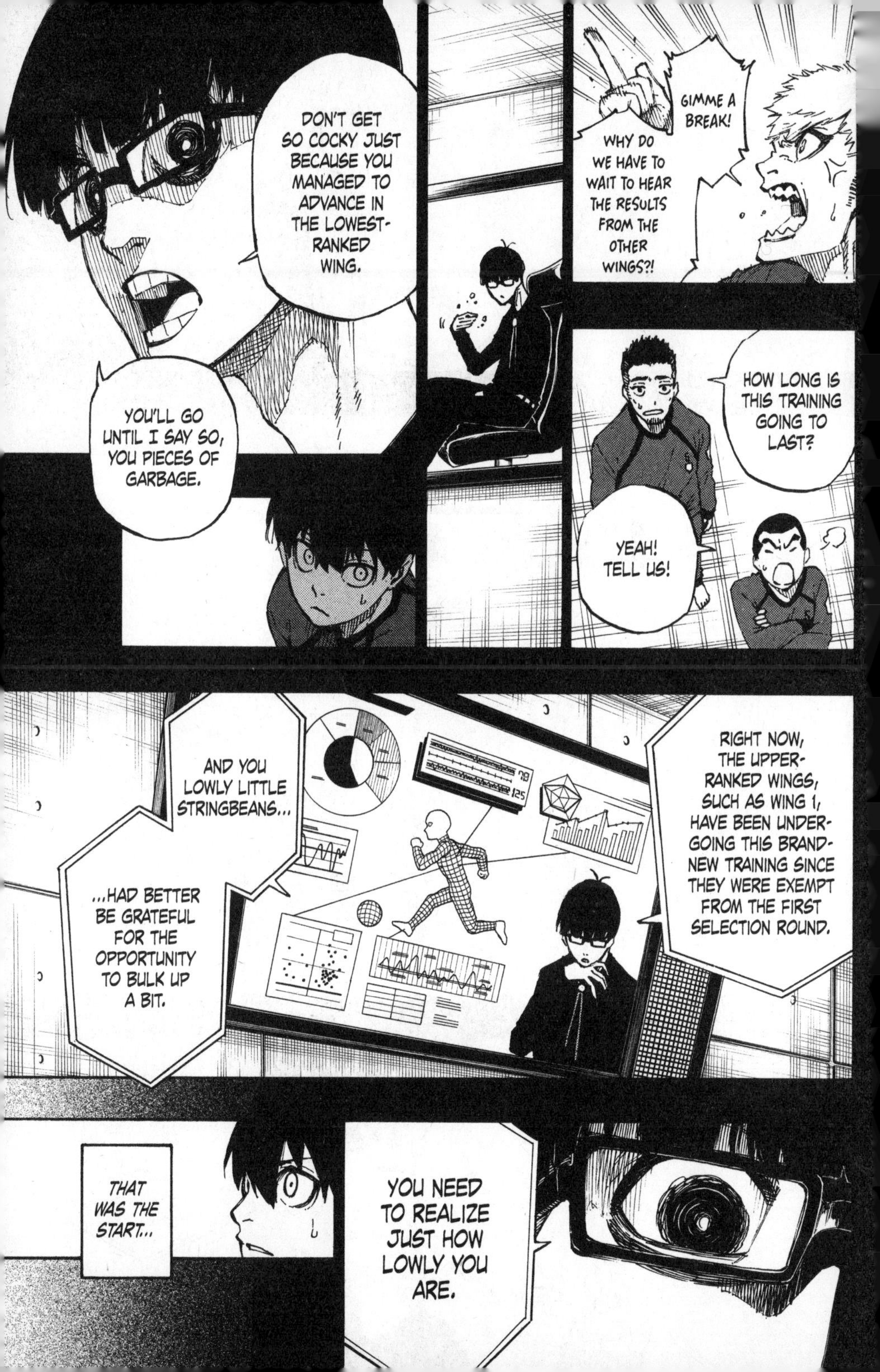
GIMME A BREAK!
WHY DO WE HAVE TO WAIT TO HEAR THE RESULTS FROM THE OTHER WINGS?!
HOW LONG IS THIS TRAINING GOING TO LAST?
YEAH! TELL US!
DON'T GET SO COCKY JUST BECAUSE YOU MANAGED TO ADVANCE IN THE LOWEST-RANKED WING.
YOU'LL GO UNTIL I SAY SO, YOU PIECES OF GARBAGE.
RIGHT NOW, THE UPPER-RANKED WINGS, SUCH AS WING 1, HAVE BEEN UNDERGOING THIS BRAND-NEW TRAINING SINCE THEY WERE EXEMPT FROM THE FIRST SELECTION ROUND.
AND YOU LOWLY LITTLE STRINGBEANS...
...HAD BETTER BE GRATEFUL FOR THE OPPORTUNITY TO BULK UP A BIT.
YOU NEED TO REALIZE JUST HOW LOWLY YOU ARE.
THAT WAS THE START...

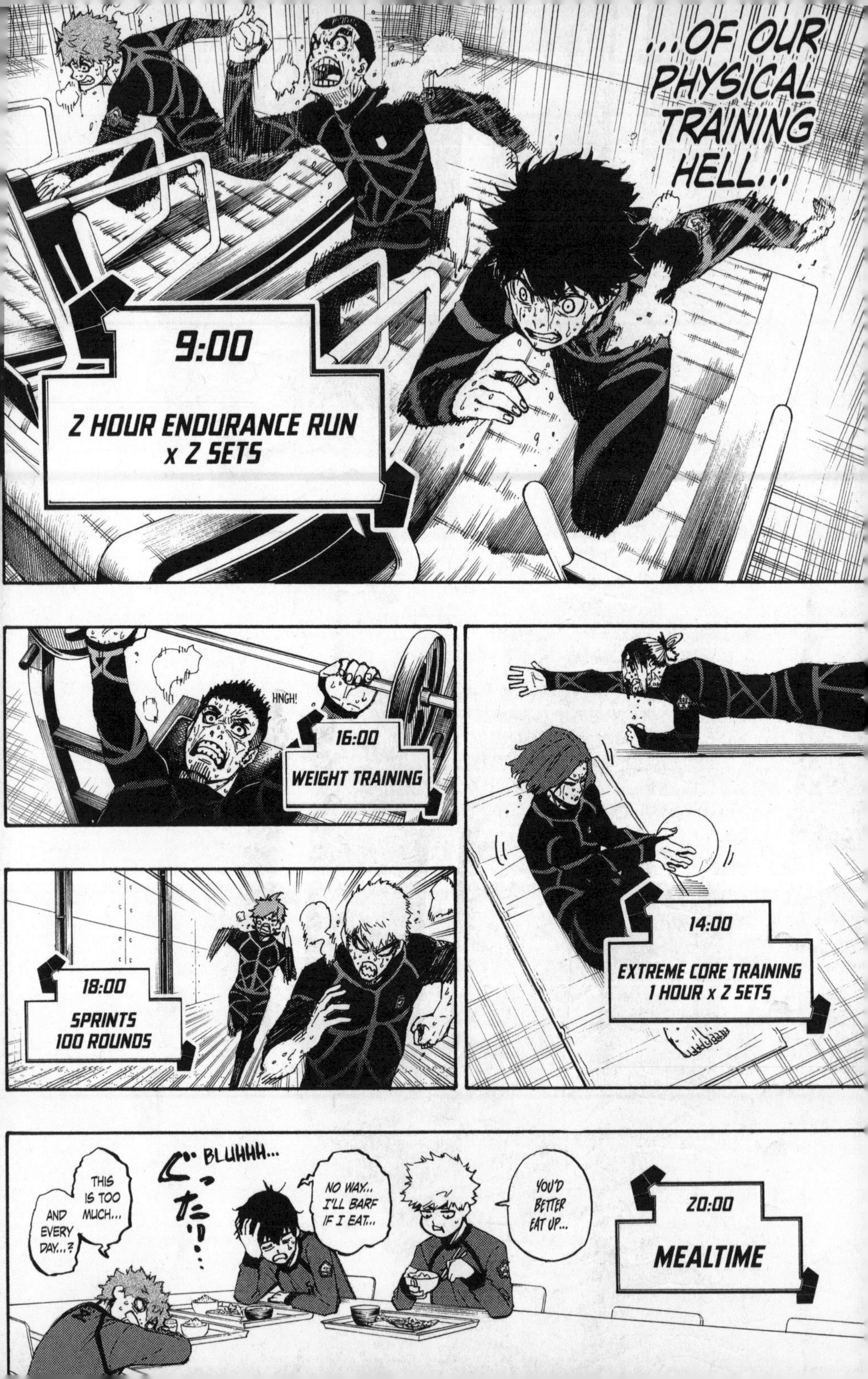
...OF OUR PHYSICAL TRAINING HELL...
9:00
2 HOUR ENDURANCE RUN x 2 SETS
14:00
EXTREME CORE TRAINING 1 HOUR x 2 SETS
HNGH!
16:00
WEIGHT TRAINING
18:00
SPRINTS 100 ROUNDS
20:00
MEALTIME
YOU'D BETTER EAT UP...
NO WAY... I'LL BARF IF I EAT...
BLUHHH...
THIS IS TOO MUCH...
AND EVERY DAY...?

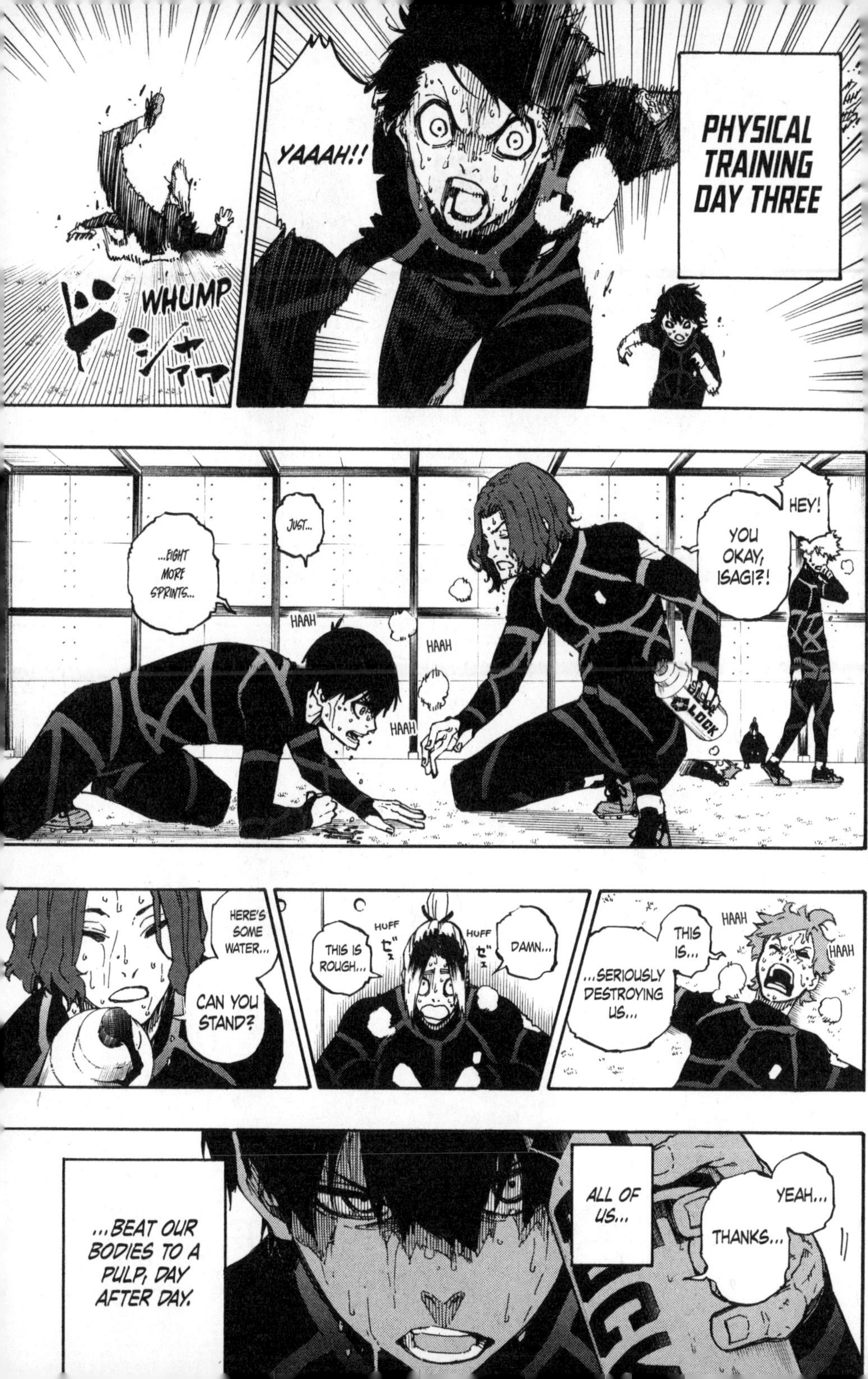

PHYSICAL TRAINING DAY THREE
YAAAH!!
WHUMP
HEY!
YOU OKAY, ISAGI?!
HAAH
HAAH
HAAH
JUST...
...FIGHT MORE SPRINTS...
HAAH
THIS IS...
...SERIOUSLY DESTROYING US...
HAAH
DAMN...
HUFF
HUFF
THIS IS ROUGH...
HERE'S SOME WATER...
CAN YOU STAND?
YEAH...
THANKS...
ALL OF US...
...BEAT OUR BODIES TO A PULP, DAY AFTER DAY.

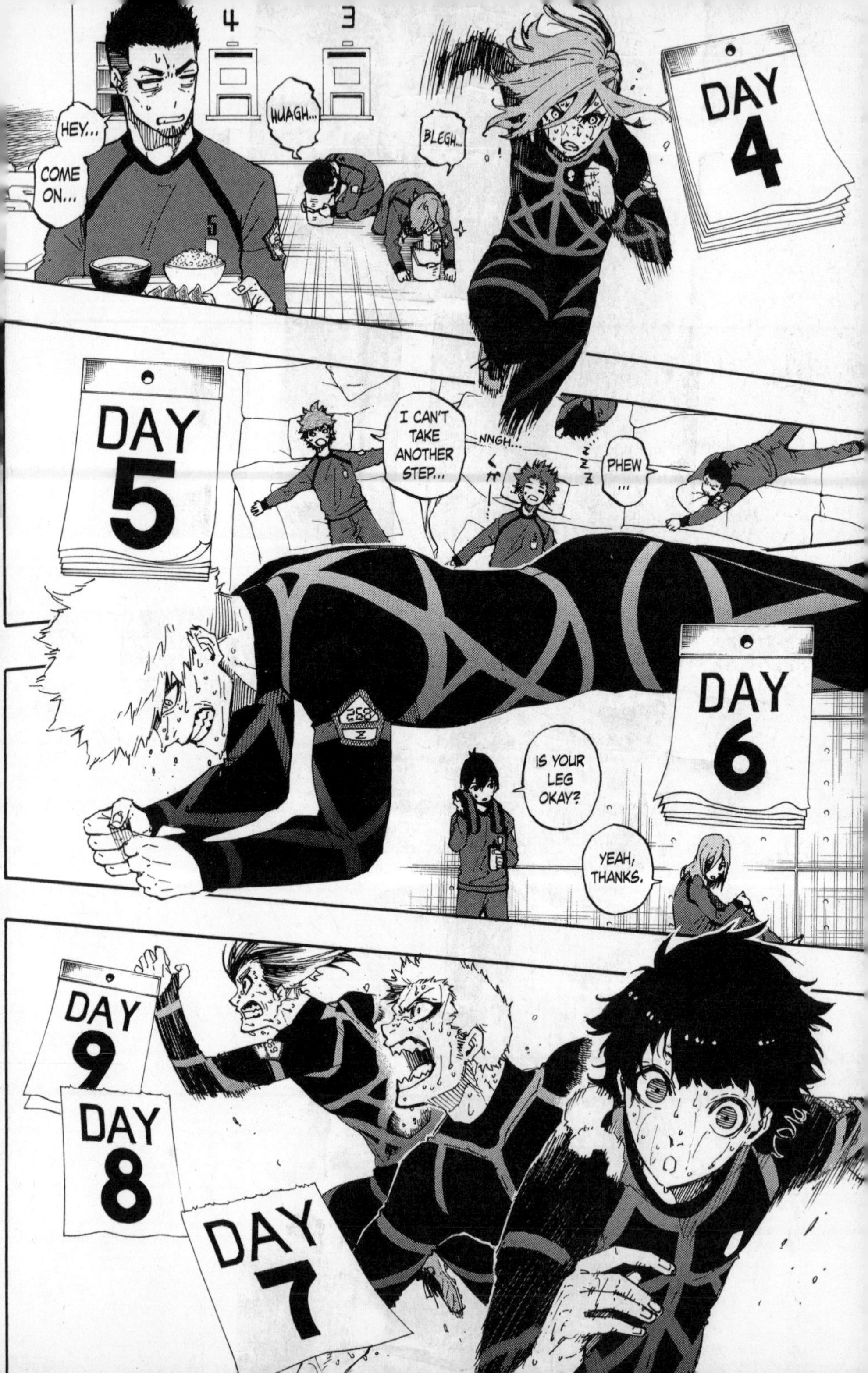
DAY 4
BLEGH...
HUAGH...
HEY...
COME ON...
PHEW ...
NNGH...
I CAN'T TAKE ANOTHER STEP...
DAY 5
DAY 6
IS YOUR LEG OKAY?
YEAH, THANKS.
DAY 9
DAY 8
DAY 7

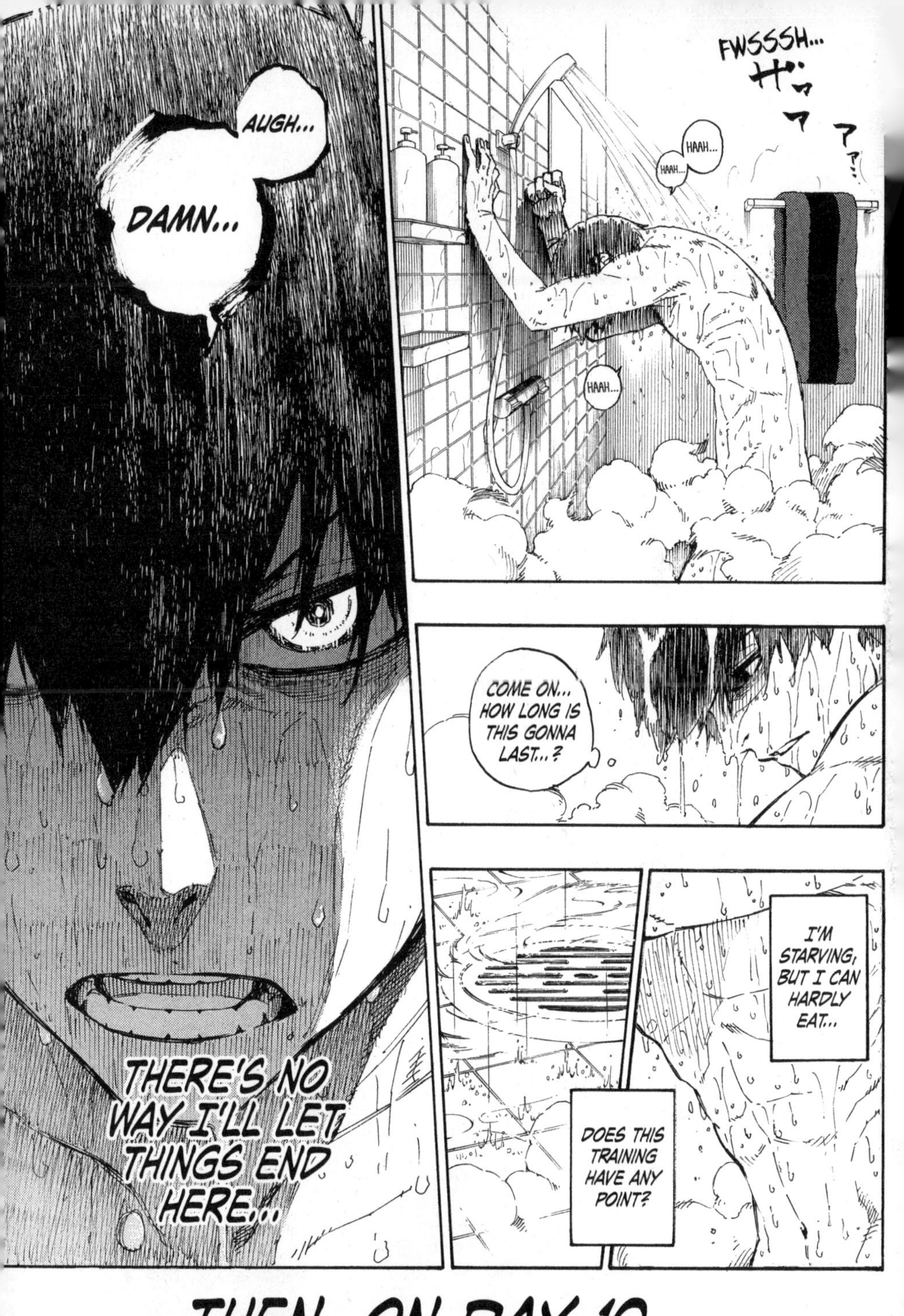
FWSSSH...
ザァァァ
HAAH...
HAAH...
HAAH...
COME ON... HOW LONG IS THIS GONNA LAST...?
I'M STARVING, BUT I CAN HARDLY EAT...
DOES THIS TRAINING HAVE ANY POINT?
AUGH...
DAMN...
THERE'S NO WAY I'LL LET THINGS END HERE...

THEN, ON DAY 10...

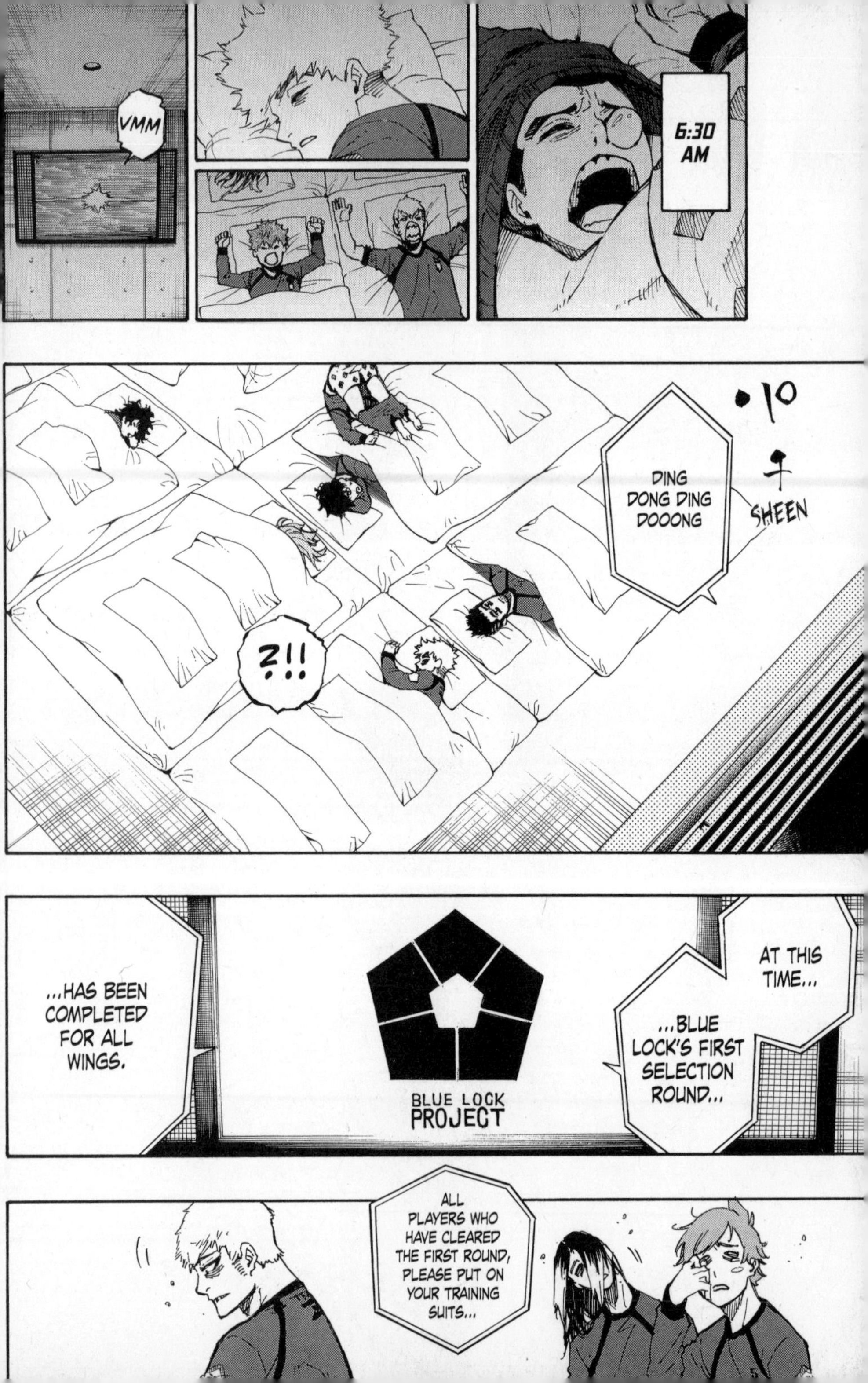
6:30 AM
VMM
SHEEN
DING DONG DING DOOONG
?!!
AT THIS TIME...
...BLUE LOCK'S FIRST SELECTION ROUND...
BLUE LOCK PROJECT
...HAS BEEN COMPLETED FOR ALL WINGS.
ALL PLAYERS WHO HAVE CLEARED THE FIRST ROUND, PLEASE PUT ON YOUR TRAINING SUITS...

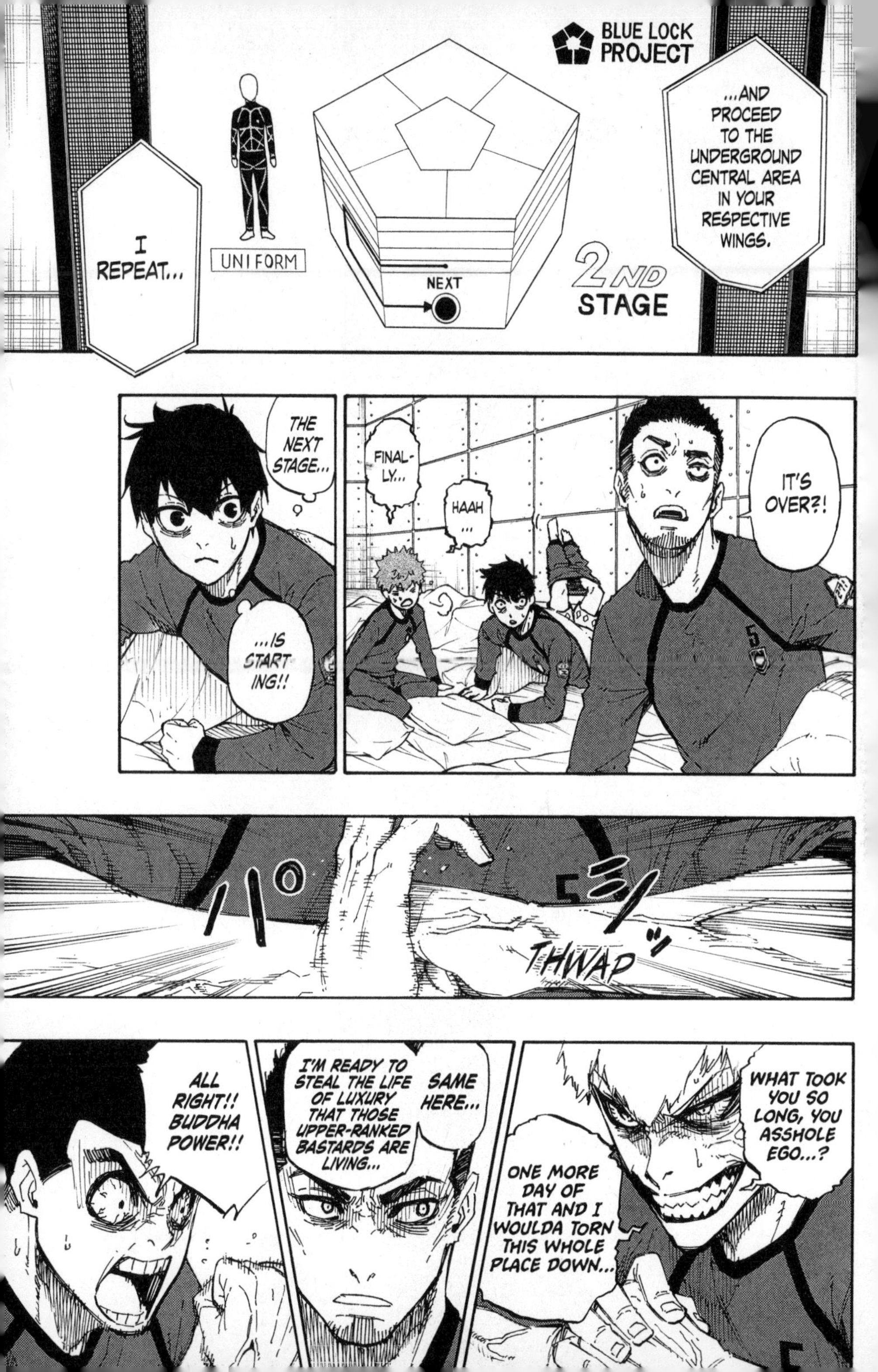
BLUE LOCK PROJECT
...AND PROCEED TO THE UNDERGROUND CENTRAL AREA IN YOUR RESPECTIVE WINGS.
2ND STAGE
NEXT
UNIFORM
I REPEAT...
IT'S OVER?!
HAAH...
FINAL-LY...
THE NEXT STAGE...
...IS START-ING!!
THWAP
WHAT TOOK YOU SO LONG, YOU ASSHOLE EGO...?
ONE MORE DAY OF THAT AND I WOULDA TORN THIS WHOLE PLACE DOWN...
SAME HERE...
I'M READY TO STEAL THE LIFE OF LUXURY THAT THOSE UPPER-RANKED BASTARDS ARE LIVING...
ALL RIGHT!! BUDDHA POWER!!

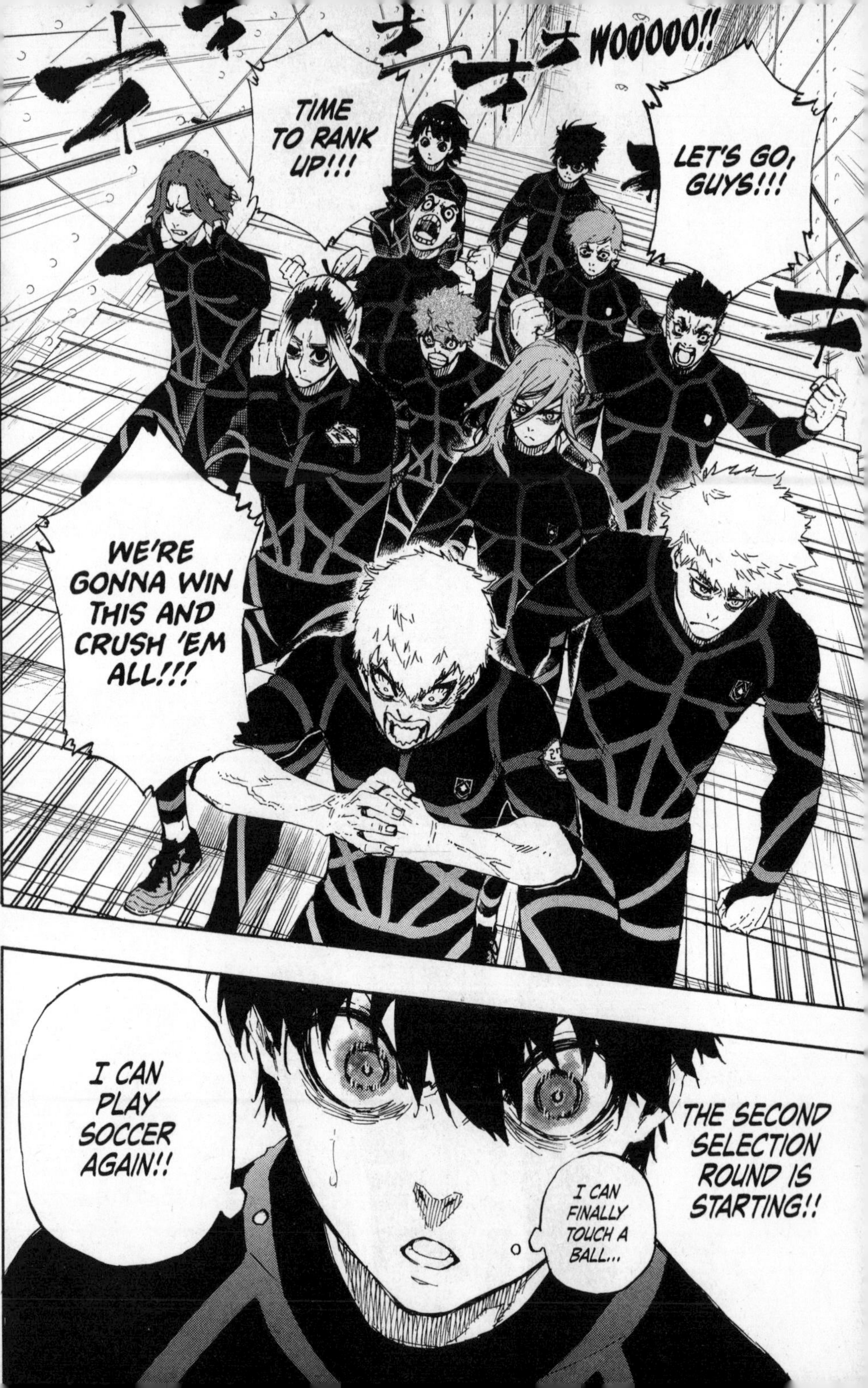
WOOOOO!!
LET'S GO, GUYS!!!
TIME TO RANK UP!!!
WE'RE GONNA WIN THIS AND CRUSH 'EM ALL!!!
THE SECOND SELECTION ROUND IS STARTING!!
I CAN FINALLY TOUCH A BALL...
I CAN PLAY SOCCER AGAIN!!

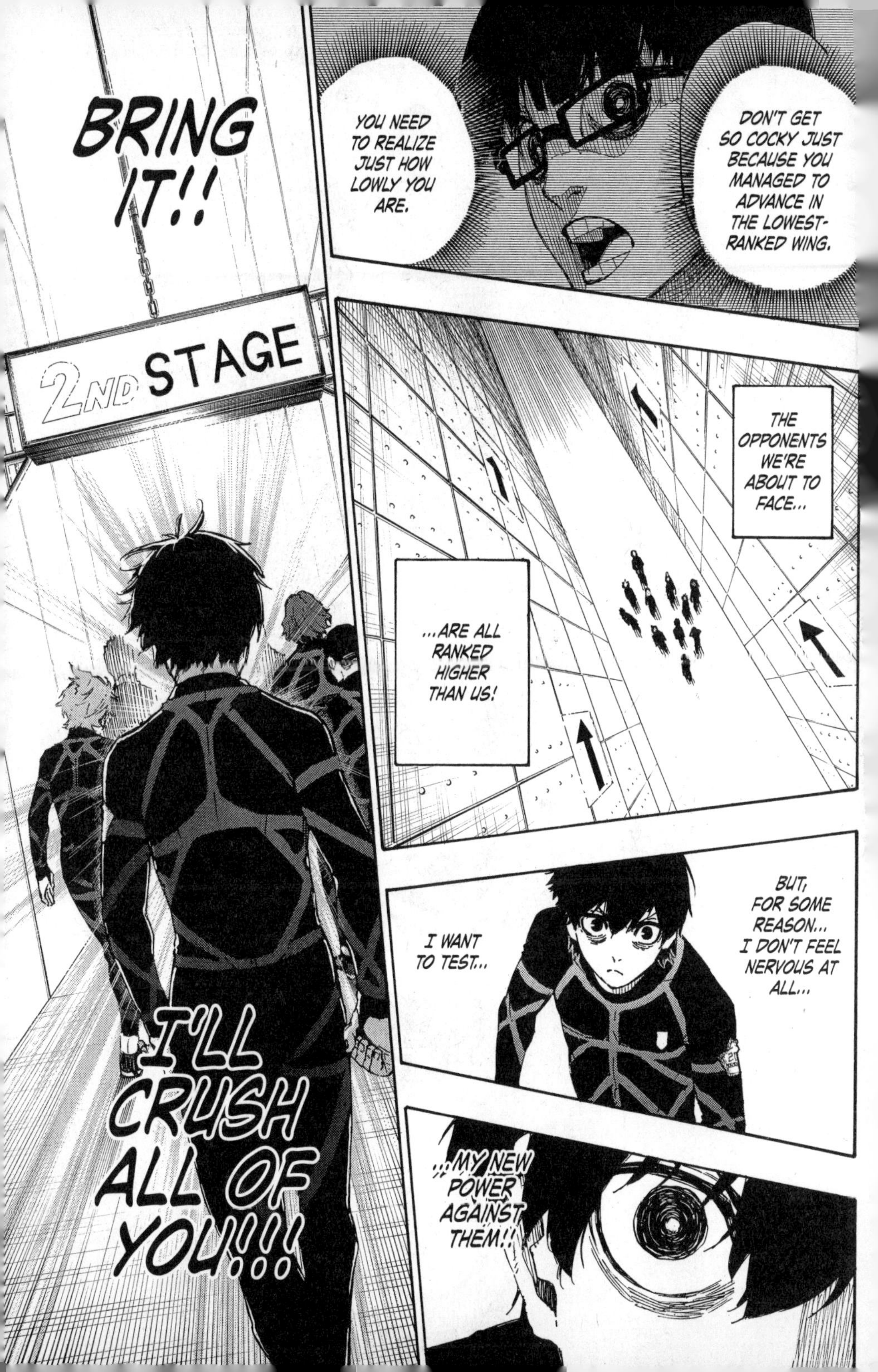
DON'T GET SO COCKY JUST BECAUSE YOU MANAGED TO ADVANCE IN THE LOWEST-RANKED WING.
YOU NEED TO REALIZE JUST HOW LOWLY YOU ARE.
THE OPPONENTS WE'RE ABOUT TO FACE...
...ARE ALL RANKED HIGHER THAN US!
BUT, FOR SOME REASON... I DON'T FEEL NERVOUS AT ALL...
I WANT TO TEST...
...MY NEW POWER AGAINST THEM!!
BRING IT!!
2ND STAGE
I'LL CRUSH ALL OF YOU!!!

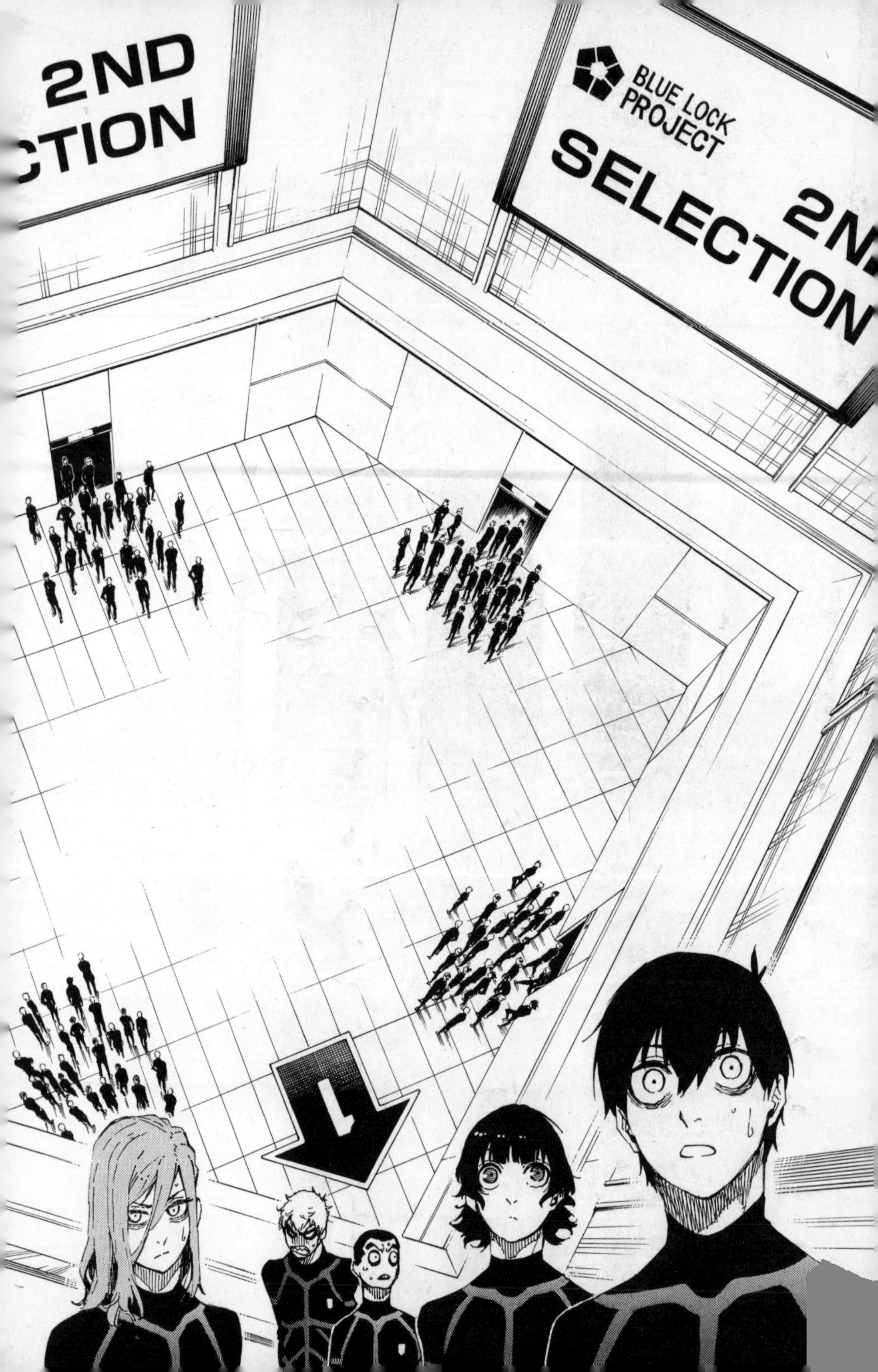

2ND
CTION
BLUE LOCK PROJECT
SELECTION
2N
SELECTION

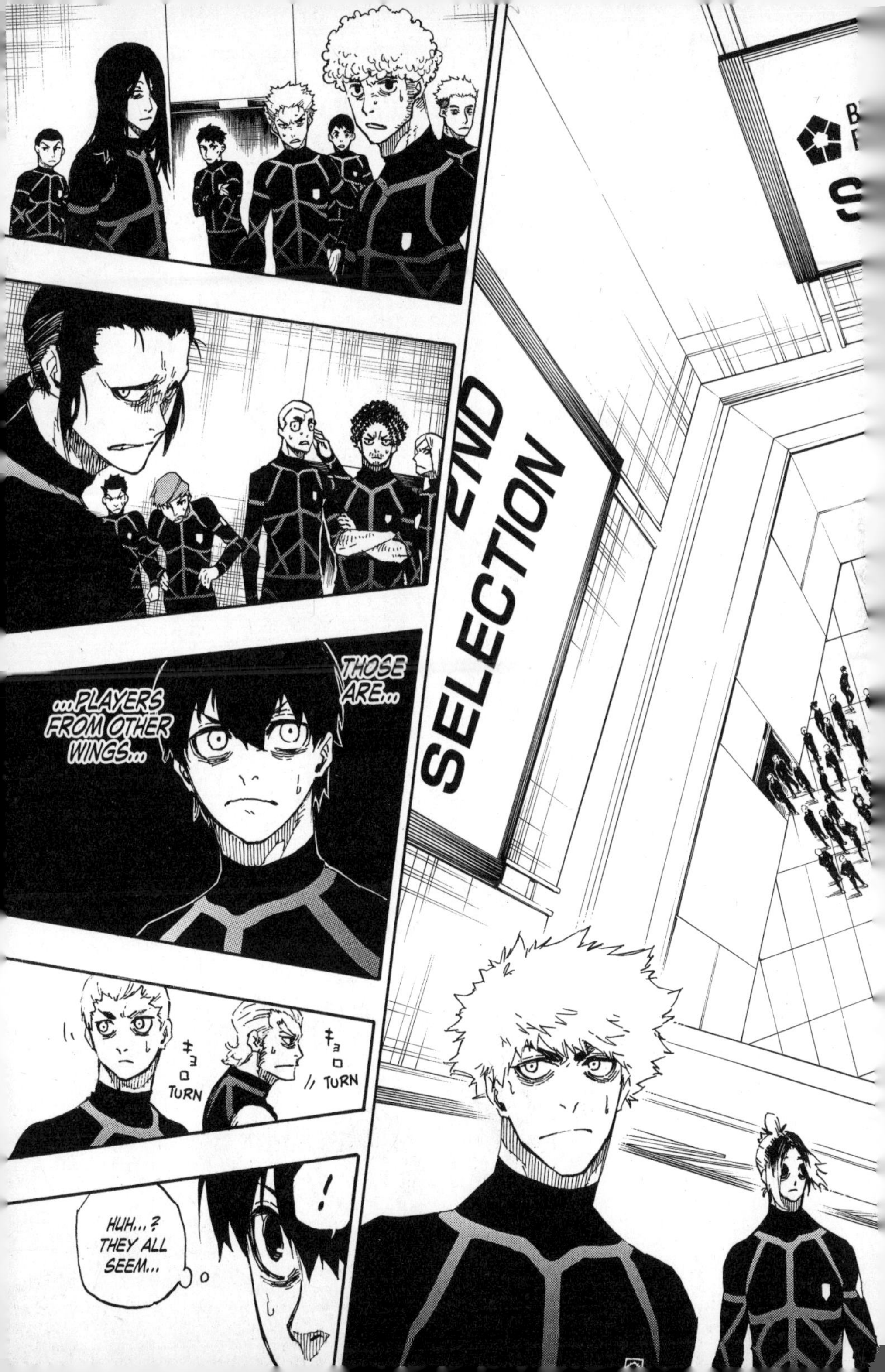
2ND SELECTION
THOSE ARE...
...PLAYERS FROM OTHER WINGS...
キョロ TURN
キョロ TURN
!
HUH...? THEY ALL SEEM...

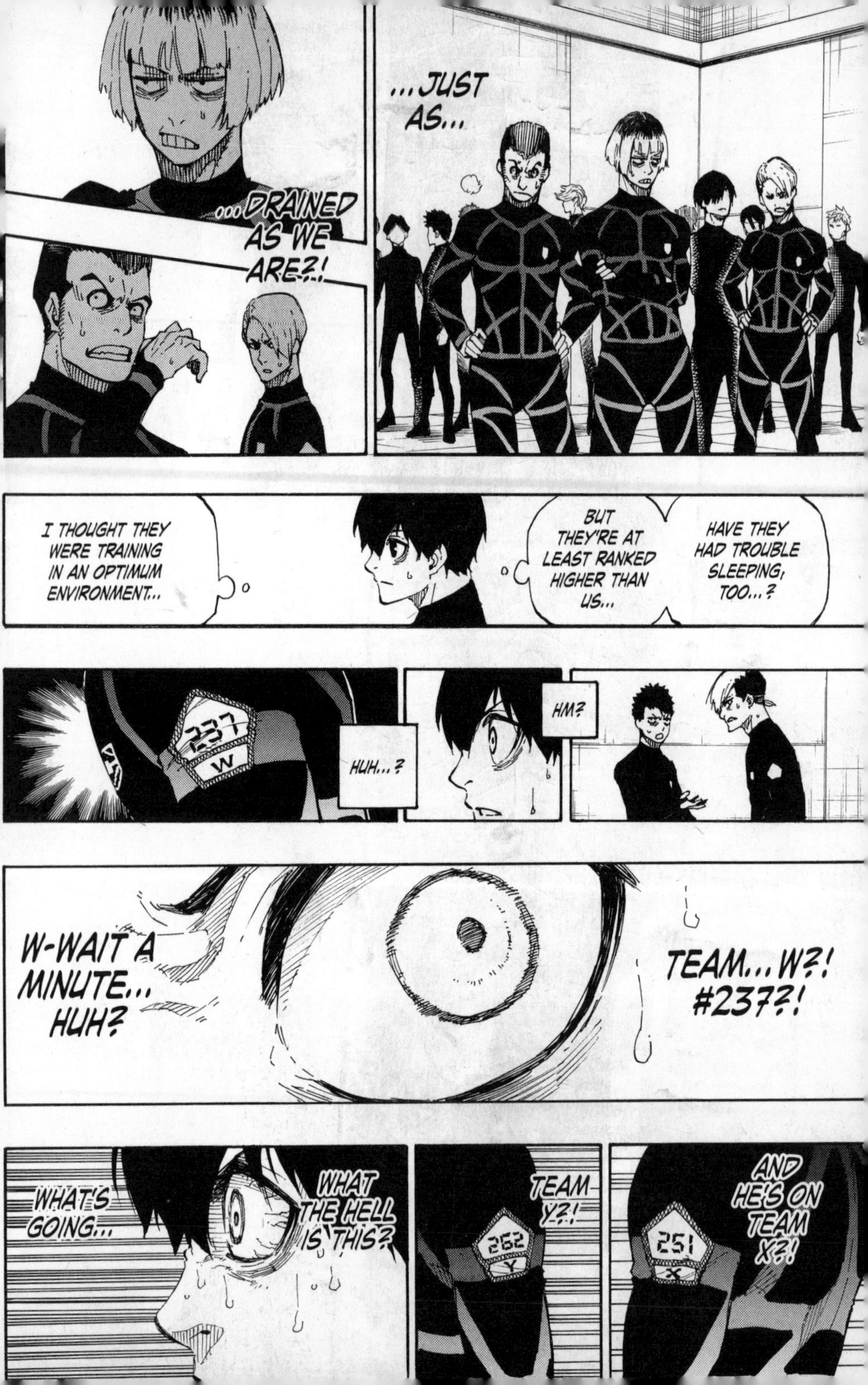
...JUST AS...
...DRAINED AS WE ARE?!
HAVE THEY HAD TROUBLE SLEEPING, TOO...?
BUT THEY'RE AT LEAST RANKED HIGHER THAN US...
I THOUGHT THEY WERE TRAINING IN AN OPTIMUM ENVIRONMENT...
HM?
HUH...?
237
W
TEAM...W?! #237?!
W-WAIT A MINUTE... HUH?
AND HE'S ON TEAM X?!
251
X
TEAM Y?!
262
Y
WHAT THE HELL IS THIS?
WHAT'S GOING...

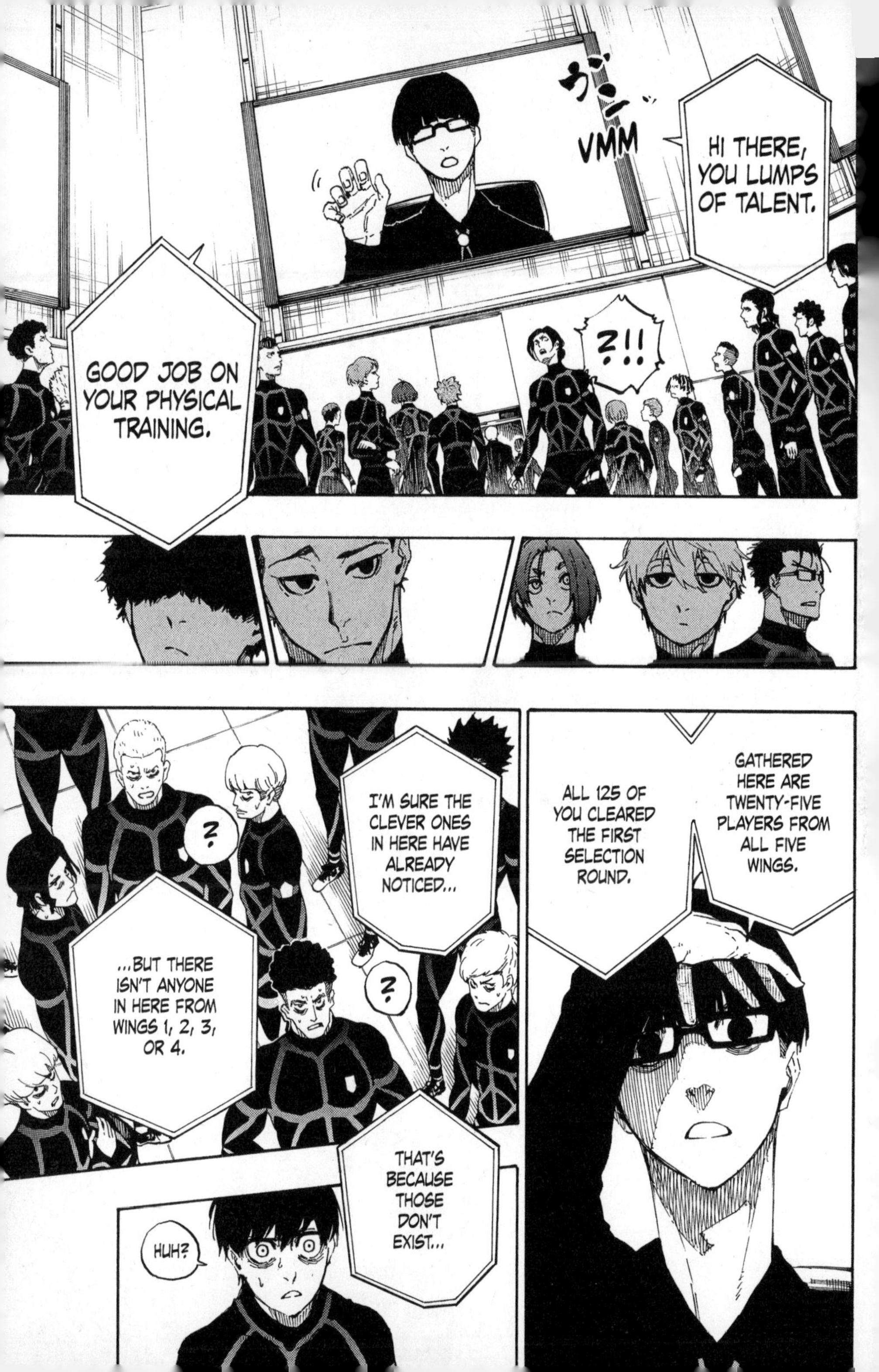
VMM
HI THERE, YOU LUMPS OF TALENT.
?!!
GOOD JOB ON YOUR PHYSICAL TRAINING.
GATHERED HERE ARE TWENTY-FIVE PLAYERS FROM ALL FIVE WINGS.
ALL 125 OF YOU CLEARED THE FIRST SELECTION ROUND.
I'M SURE THE CLEVER ONES IN HERE HAVE ALREADY NOTICED...
?
?
...BUT THERE ISN'T ANYONE IN HERE FROM WINGS 1, 2, 3, OR 4.
THAT'S BECAUSE THOSE DON'T EXIST...
HUH?

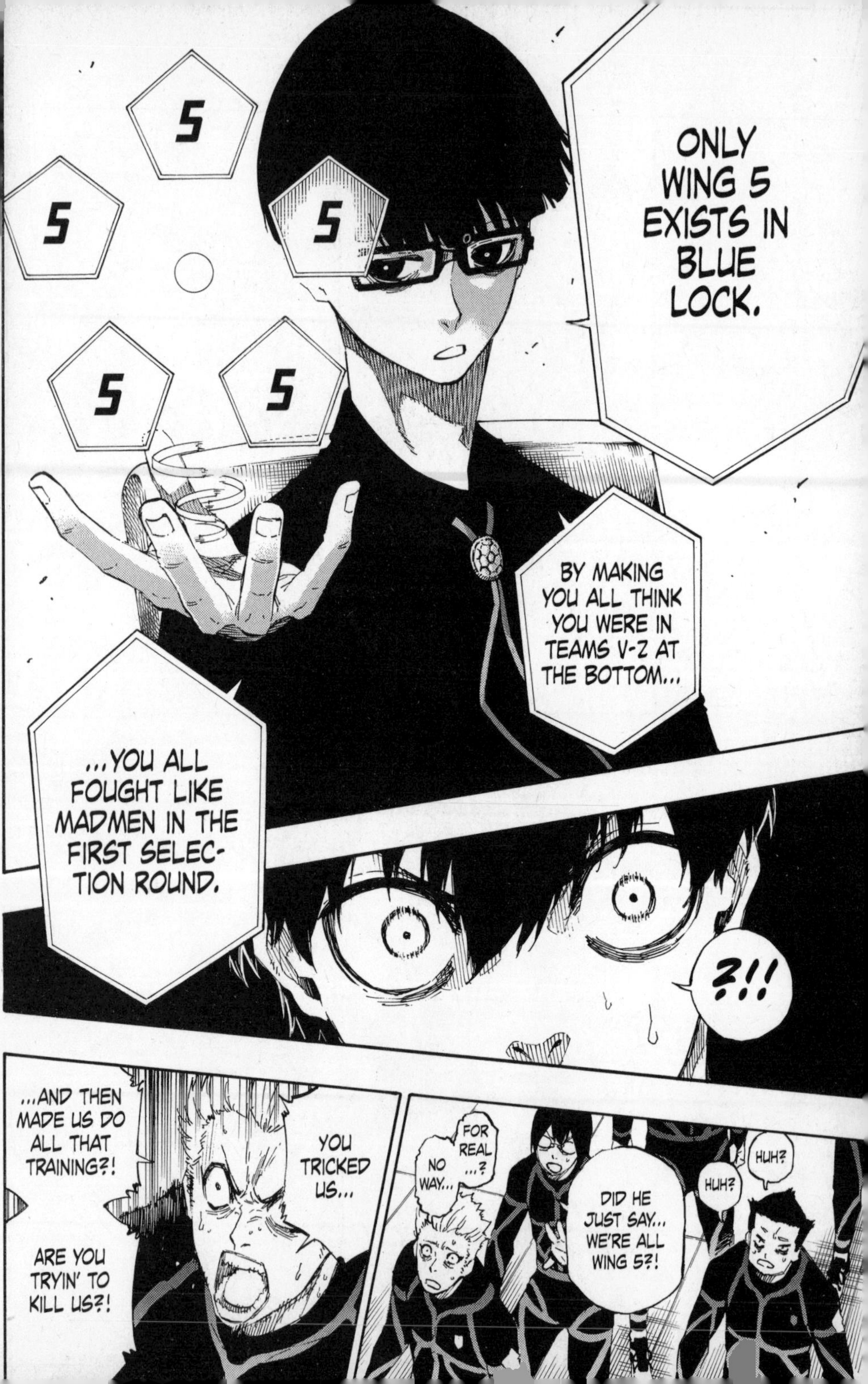
ONLY WING 5 EXISTS IN BLUE LOCK.
5
5
5
5
5
BY MAKING YOU ALL THINK YOU WERE IN TEAMS V-Z AT THE BOTTOM...
...YOU ALL FOUGHT LIKE MADMEN IN THE FIRST SELECTION ROUND.
?!!
HUH?
HUH?
DID HE JUST SAY... WE'RE ALL WING 5?!
FOR REAL...?
NO WAY...
YOU TRICKED US...
...AND THEN MADE US DO ALL THAT TRAINING?!
ARE YOU TRYIN' TO KILL US?!

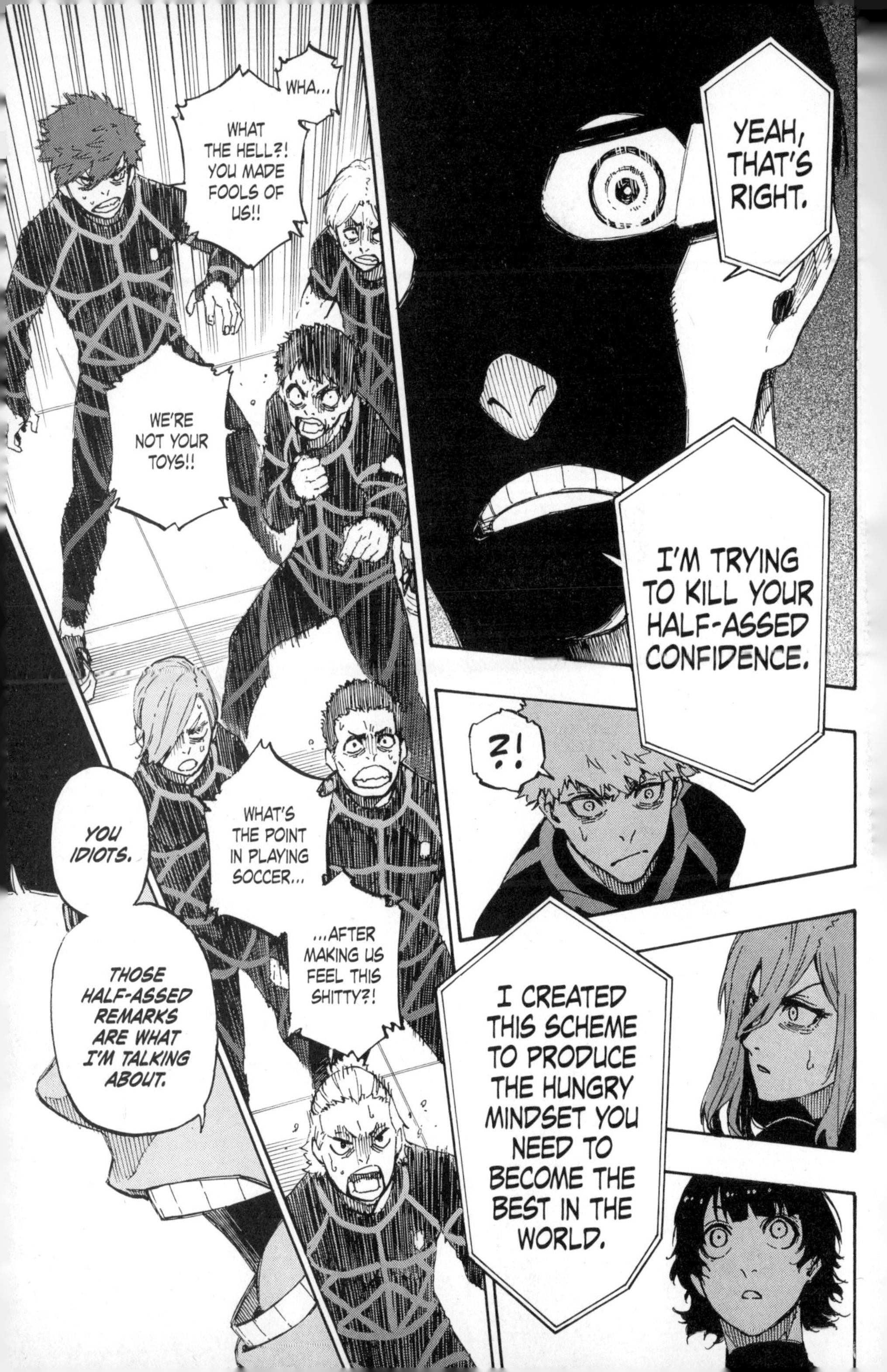

WHA...
WHAT THE HELL?! YOU MADE FOOLS OF US!!
WE'RE NOT YOUR TOYS!!
WHAT'S THE POINT IN PLAYING SOCCER...
...AFTER MAKING US FEEL THIS SHITTY?!
YOU IDIOTS.
THOSE HALF-ASSED REMARKS ARE WHAT I'M TALKING ABOUT.
YEAH, THAT'S RIGHT.
I'M TRYING TO KILL YOUR HALF-ASSED CONFIDENCE.
?!
I CREATED THIS SCHEME TO PRODUCE THE HUNGRY MINDSET YOU NEED TO BECOME THE BEST IN THE WORLD.

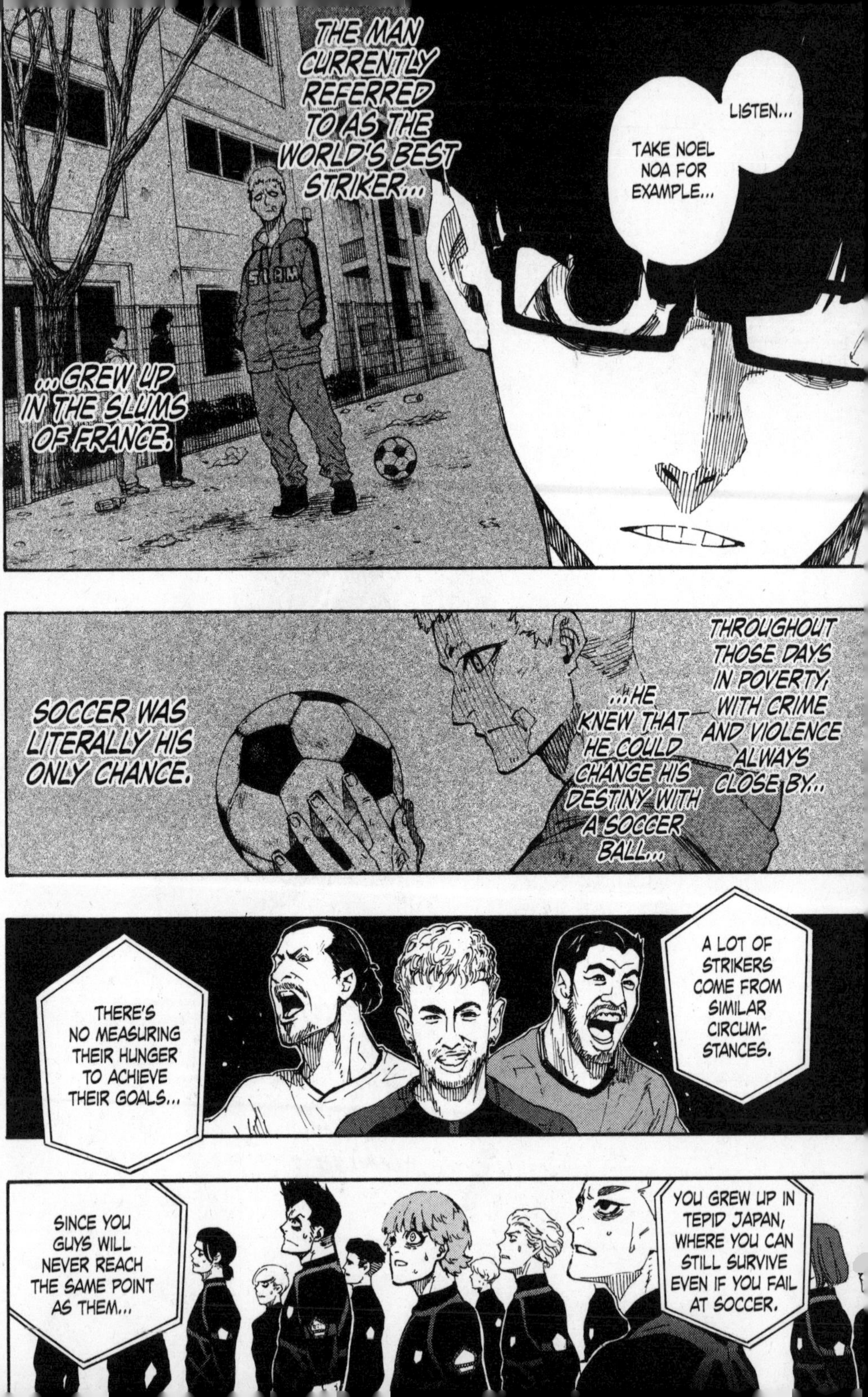
LISTEN...
TAKE NOEL NOA FOR EXAMPLE...
THE MAN CURRENTLY REFERRED TO AS THE WORLD'S BEST STRIKER...
...GREW UP IN THE SLUMS OF FRANCE.
THROUGHOUT THOSE DAYS IN POVERTY, WITH CRIME AND VIOLENCE ALWAYS CLOSE BY...
...HE KNEW THAT HE COULD CHANGE HIS DESTINY WITH A SOCCER BALL...
SOCCER WAS LITERALLY HIS ONLY CHANCE.
A LOT OF STRIKERS COME FROM SIMILAR CIRCUM-STANCES.
THERE'S NO MEASURING THEIR HUNGER TO ACHIEVE THEIR GOALS...
YOU GREW UP IN TEPID JAPAN, WHERE YOU CAN STILL SURVIVE EVEN IF YOU FAIL AT SOCCER.
SINCE YOU GUYS WILL NEVER REACH THE SAME POINT AS THEM...

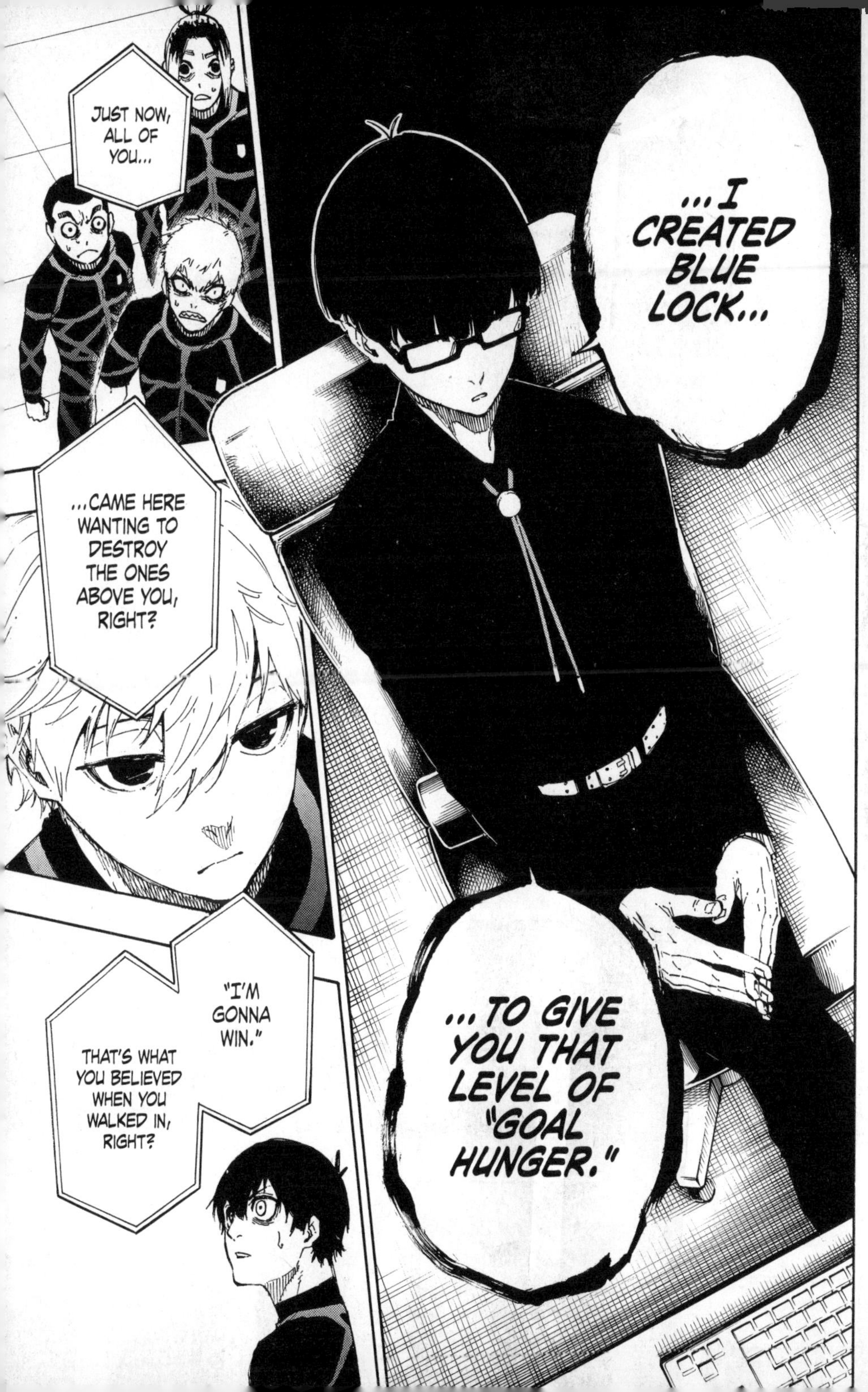
...I CREATED BLUE LOCK...
...TO GIVE YOU THAT LEVEL OF "GOAL HUNGER."
JUST NOW, ALL OF YOU...
...CAME HERE WANTING TO DESTROY THE ONES ABOVE YOU, RIGHT?
"I'M GONNA WIN."
THAT'S WHAT YOU BELIEVED WHEN YOU WALKED IN, RIGHT?

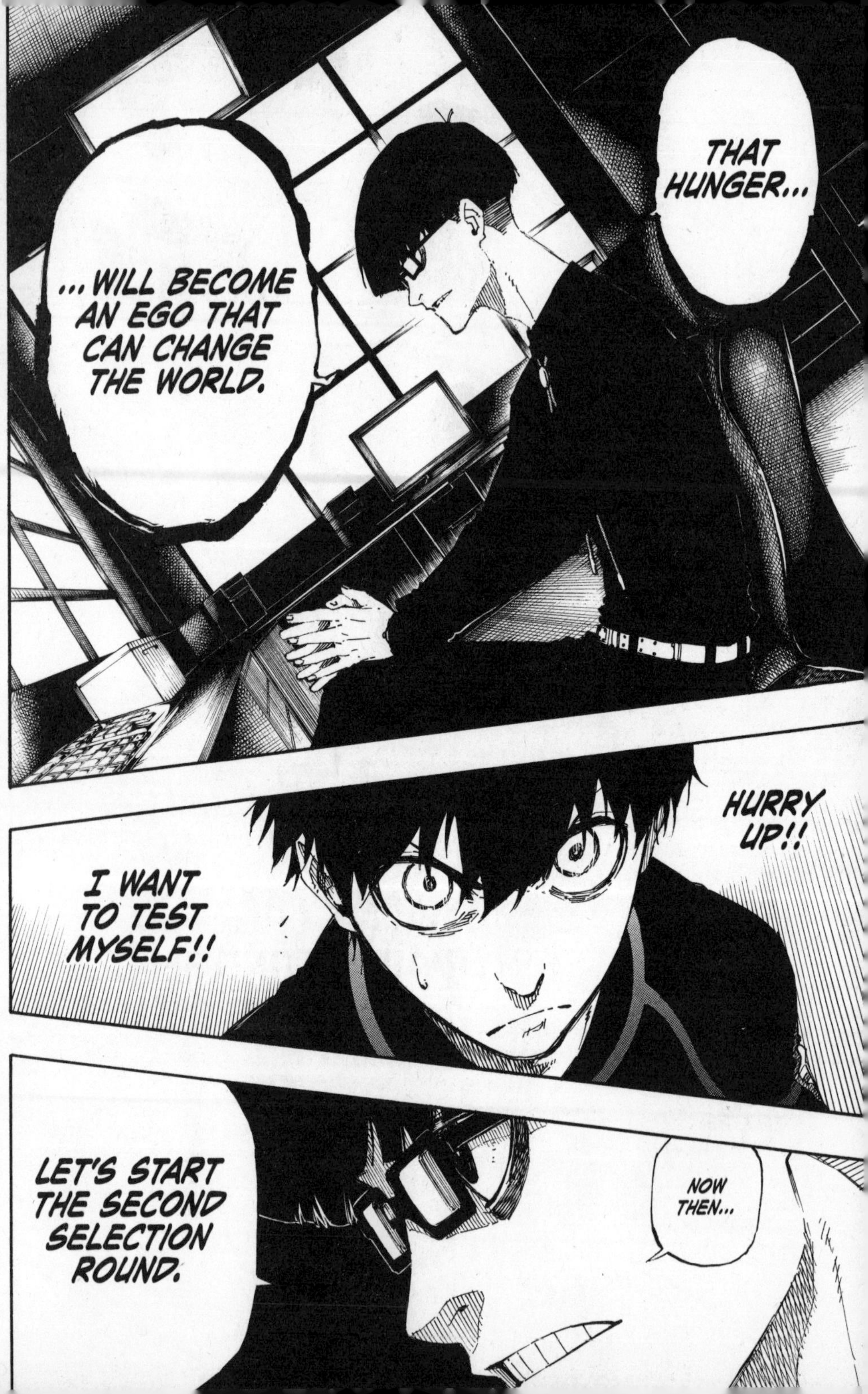
THAT HUNGER...
...WILL BECOME AN EGO THAT CAN CHANGE THE WORLD.
HURRY UP!!
I WANT TO TEST MYSELF!!
NOW THEN...
LET'S START THE SECOND SELECTION ROUND.

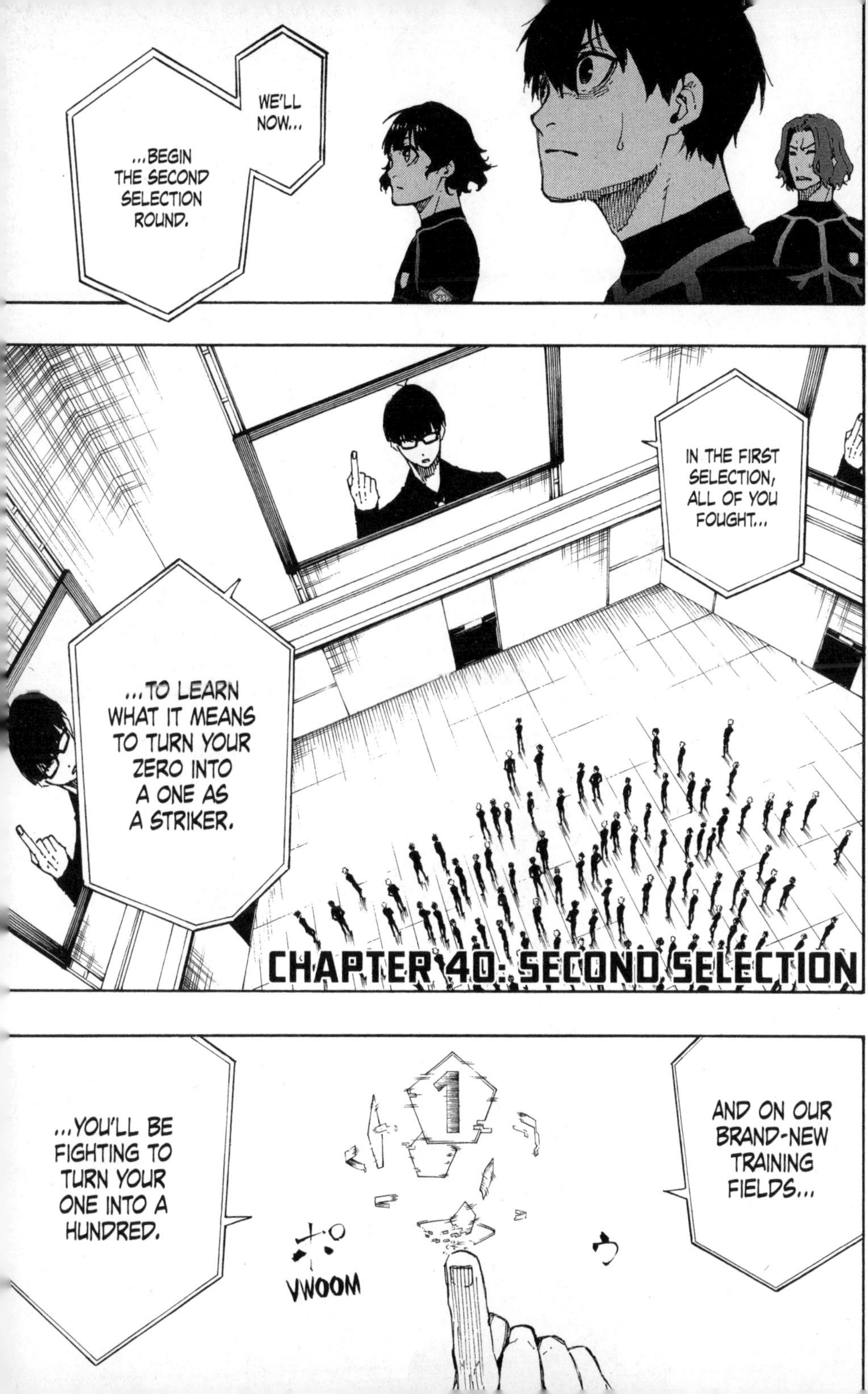
WE'LL NOW...
...BEGIN THE SECOND SELECTION ROUND.
IN THE FIRST SELECTION, ALL OF YOU FOUGHT...
...TO LEARN WHAT IT MEANS TO TURN YOUR ZERO INTO A ONE AS A STRIKER.
CHAPTER 40: SECOND SELECTION
AND ON OUR BRAND-NEW TRAINING FIELDS...
...YOU'LL BE FIGHTING TO TURN YOUR ONE INTO A HUNDRED.
1
VWOOM

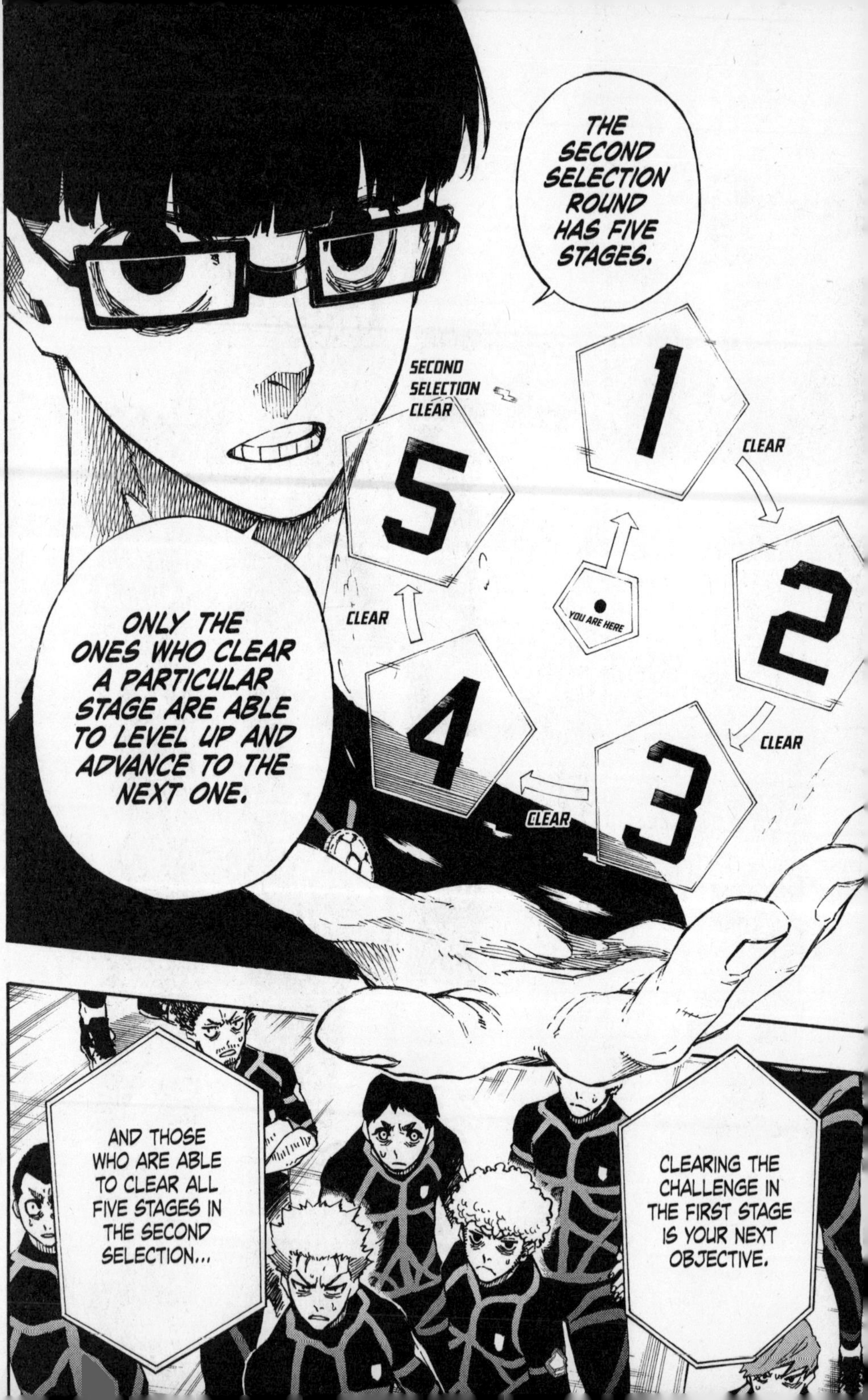
THE SECOND SELECTION ROUND HAS FIVE STAGES.
1
CLEAR
2
CLEAR
3
CLEAR
4
CLEAR
5
SECOND SELECTION CLEAR
YOU ARE HERE
ONLY THE ONES WHO CLEAR A PARTICULAR STAGE ARE ABLE TO LEVEL UP AND ADVANCE TO THE NEXT ONE.
CLEARING THE CHALLENGE IN THE FIRST STAGE IS YOUR NEXT OBJECTIVE.
AND THOSE WHO ARE ABLE TO CLEAR ALL FIVE STAGES IN THE SECOND SELECTION...

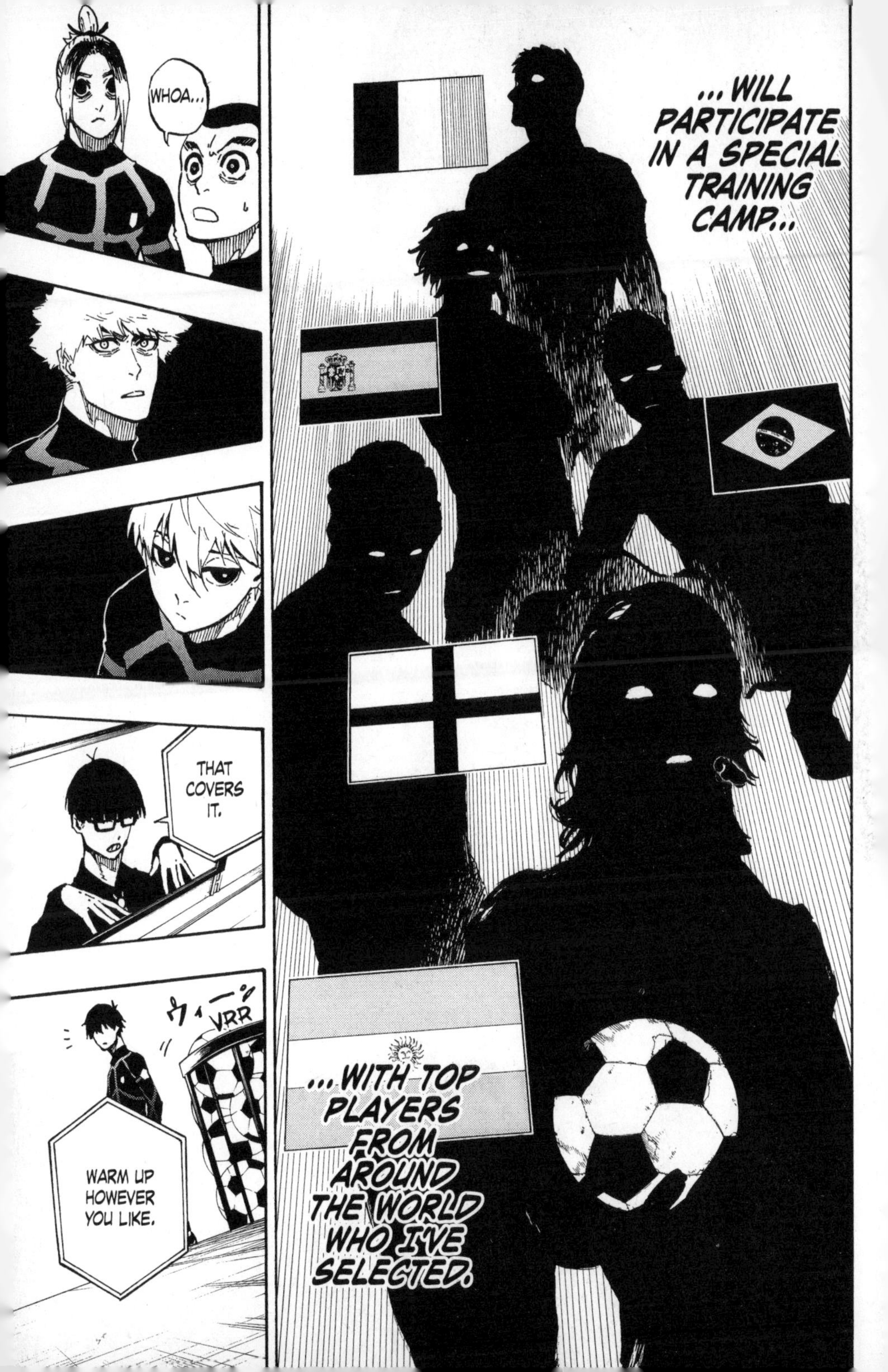
...WILL PARTICIPATE IN A SPECIAL TRAINING CAMP...
...WITH TOP PLAYERS FROM AROUND THE WORLD WHO I'VE SELECTED.
WHOA...
THAT COVERS IT.
ウィーン
VRR
WARM UP HOWEVER YOU LIKE.

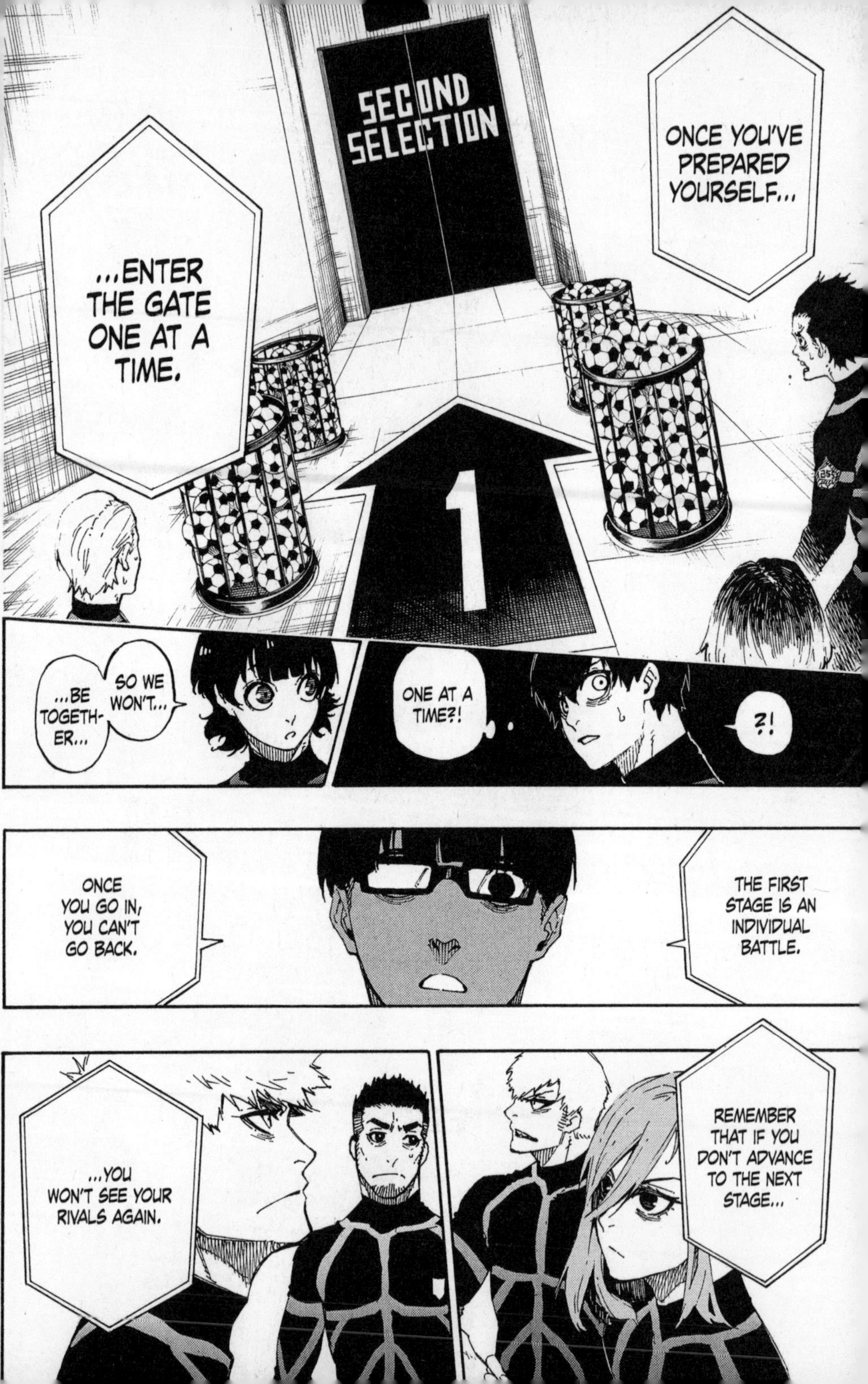
ONCE YOU'VE PREPARED YOURSELF...
SECOND SELECTION
...ENTER THE GATE ONE AT A TIME.
?!
ONE AT A TIME?!
SO WE WON'T...
...BE TOGETH-ER...
THE FIRST STAGE IS AN INDIVIDUAL BATTLE.
ONCE YOU GO IN, YOU CAN'T GO BACK.
REMEMBER THAT IF YOU DON'T ADVANCE TO THE NEXT STAGE...
...YOU WON'T SEE YOUR RIVALS AGAIN.

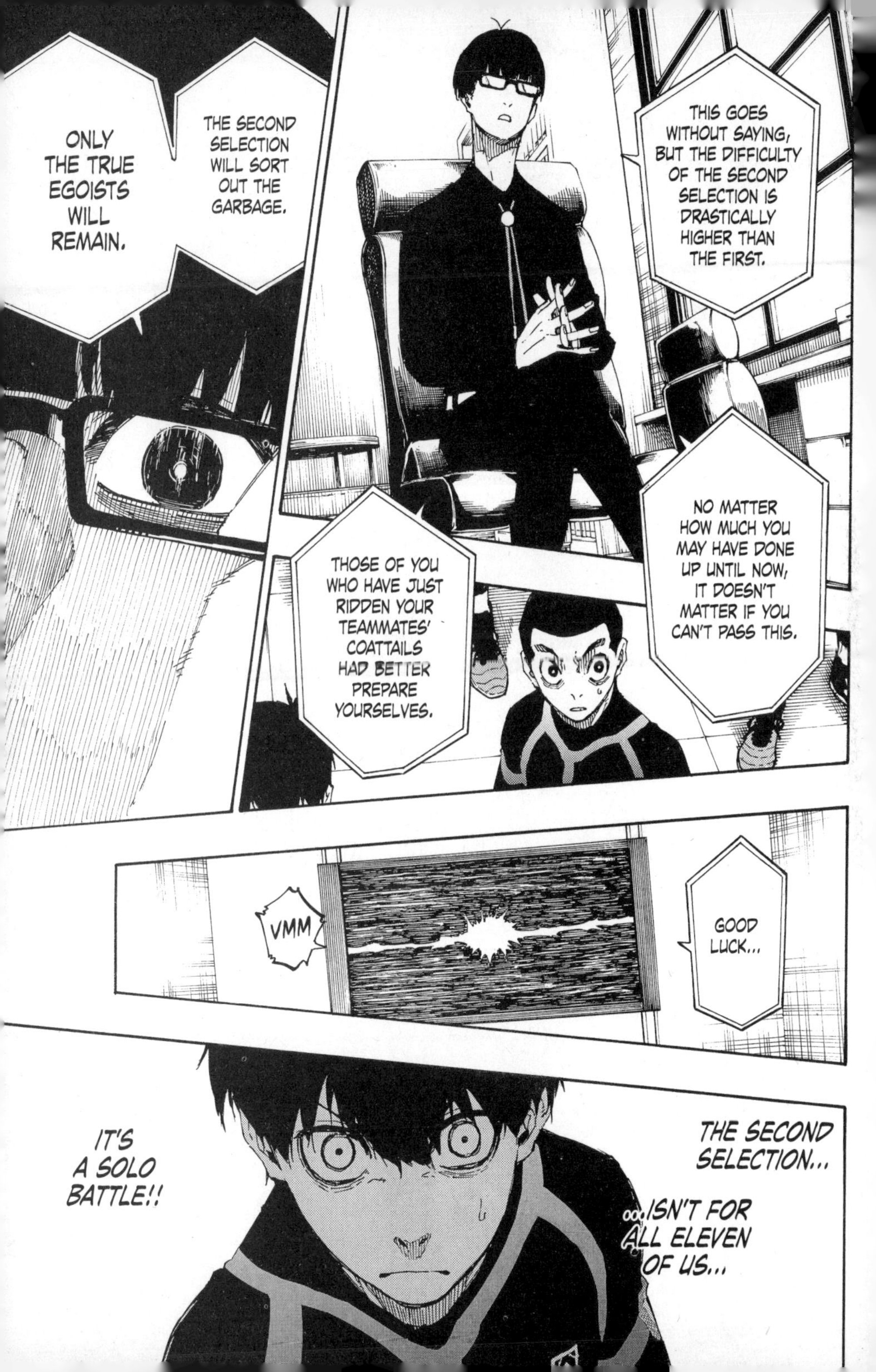

THIS GOES WITHOUT SAYING, BUT THE DIFFICULTY OF THE SECOND SELECTION IS DRASTICALLY HIGHER THAN THE FIRST.
NO MATTER HOW MUCH YOU MAY HAVE DONE UP UNTIL NOW, IT DOESN'T MATTER IF YOU CAN'T PASS THIS.
THOSE OF YOU WHO HAVE JUST RIDDEN YOUR TEAMMATES' COATTAILS HAD BETTER PREPARE YOURSELVES.
THE SECOND SELECTION WILL SORT OUT THE GARBAGE.
ONLY THE TRUE EGOISTS WILL REMAIN.
GOOD LUCK...
VMM
THE SECOND SELECTION...
...ISN'T FOR ALL ELEVEN OF US...
IT'S A SOLO BATTLE!!

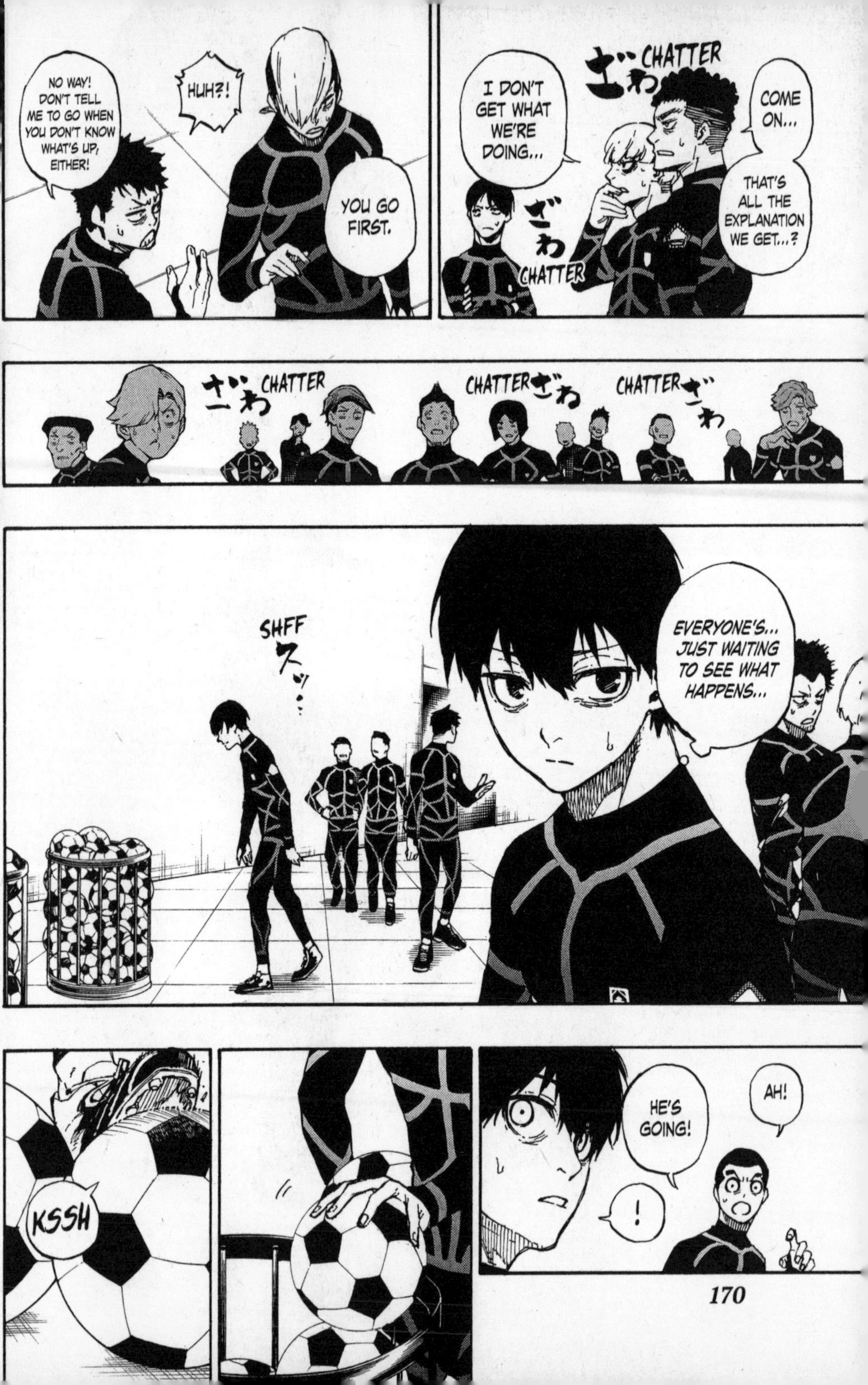
CHATTER
COME ON...
I DON'T GET WHAT WE'RE DOING...
THAT'S ALL THE EXPLANATION WE GET...?
CHATTER
YOU GO FIRST.
HUH?!
NO WAY! DON'T TELL ME TO GO WHEN YOU DON'T KNOW WHAT'S UP, EITHER!
CHATTER
CHATTER
CHATTER
EVERYONE'S... JUST WAITING TO SEE WHAT HAPPENS...
SHFF
AH!
HE'S GOING!
!
KSSH

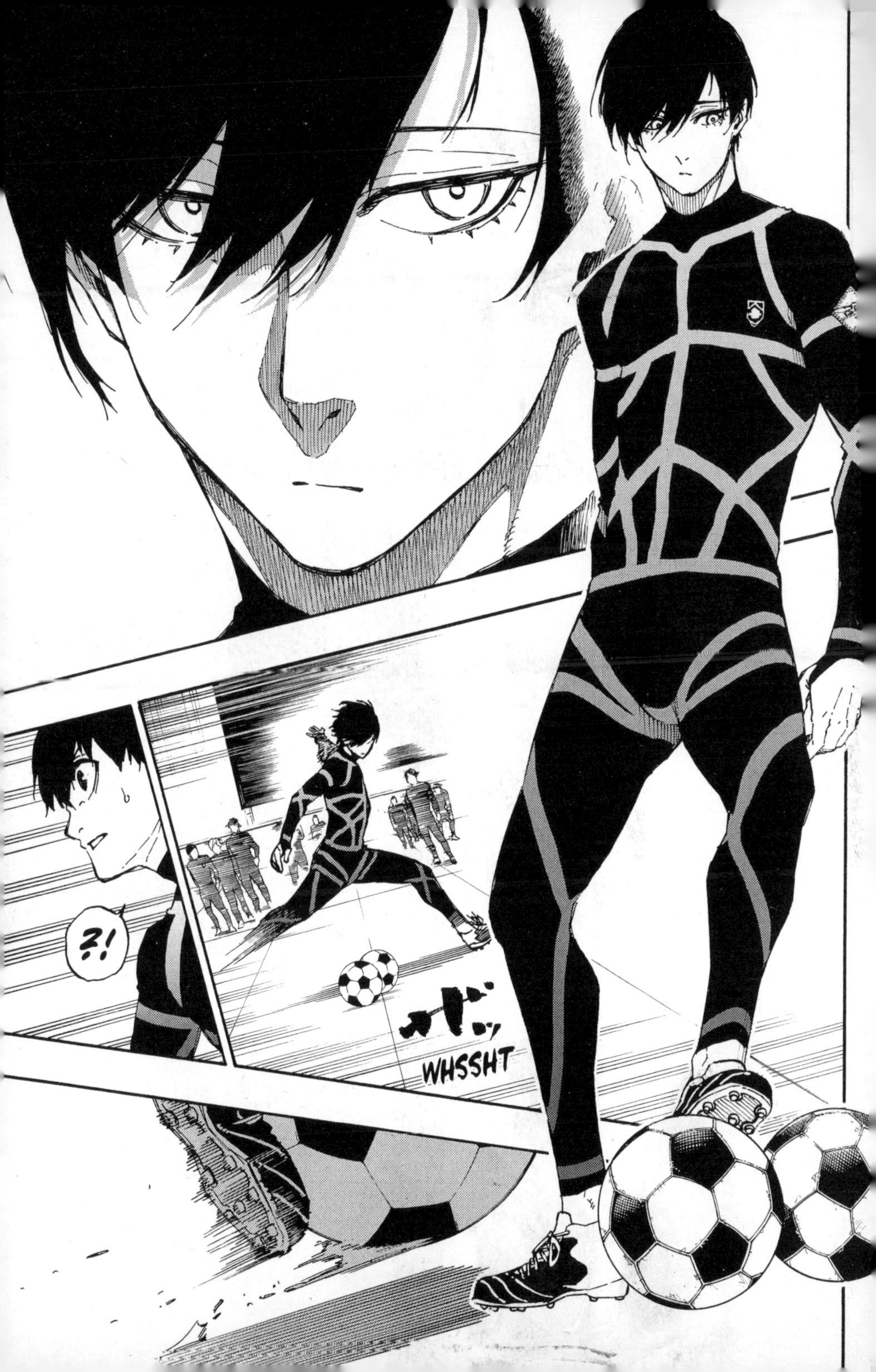
?!
WHSSHT

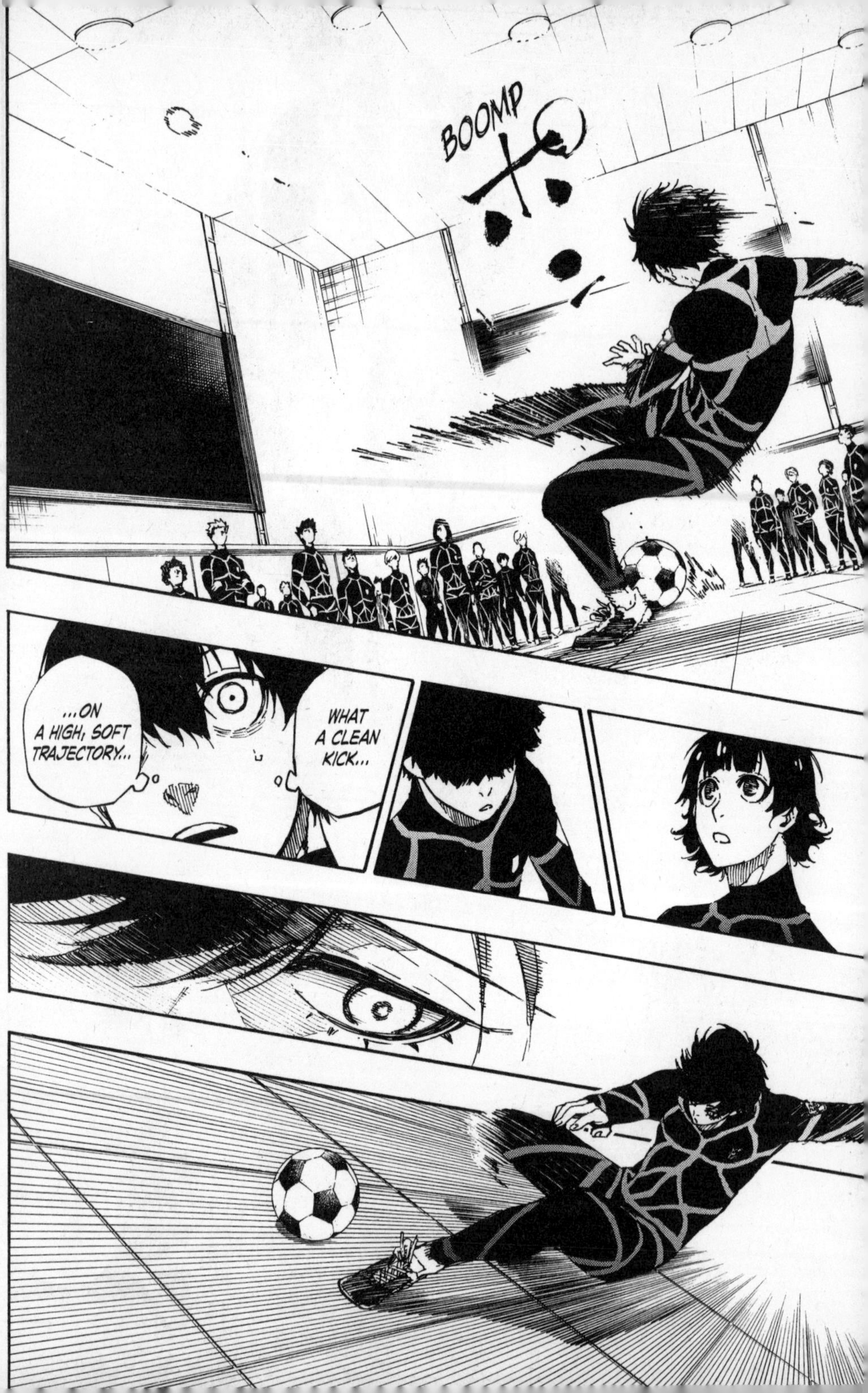
BOOMP
WHAT A CLEAN KICK...
...ON A HIGH, SOFT TRAJECTORY...

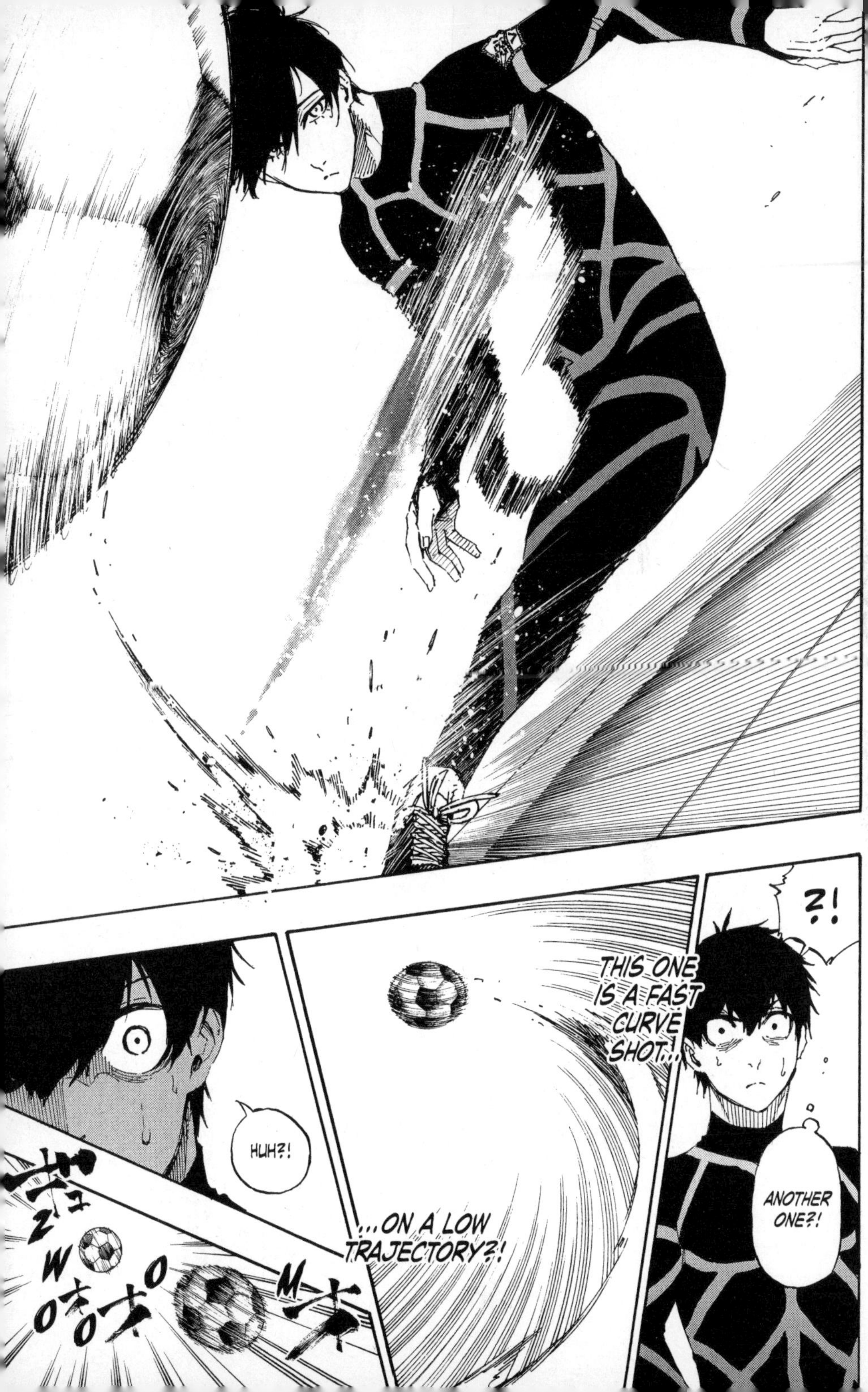
?!
THIS ONE IS A FAST CURVE SHOT...!
ANOTHER ONE?!
...ON A LOW TRAJECTORY?!
HUH?!

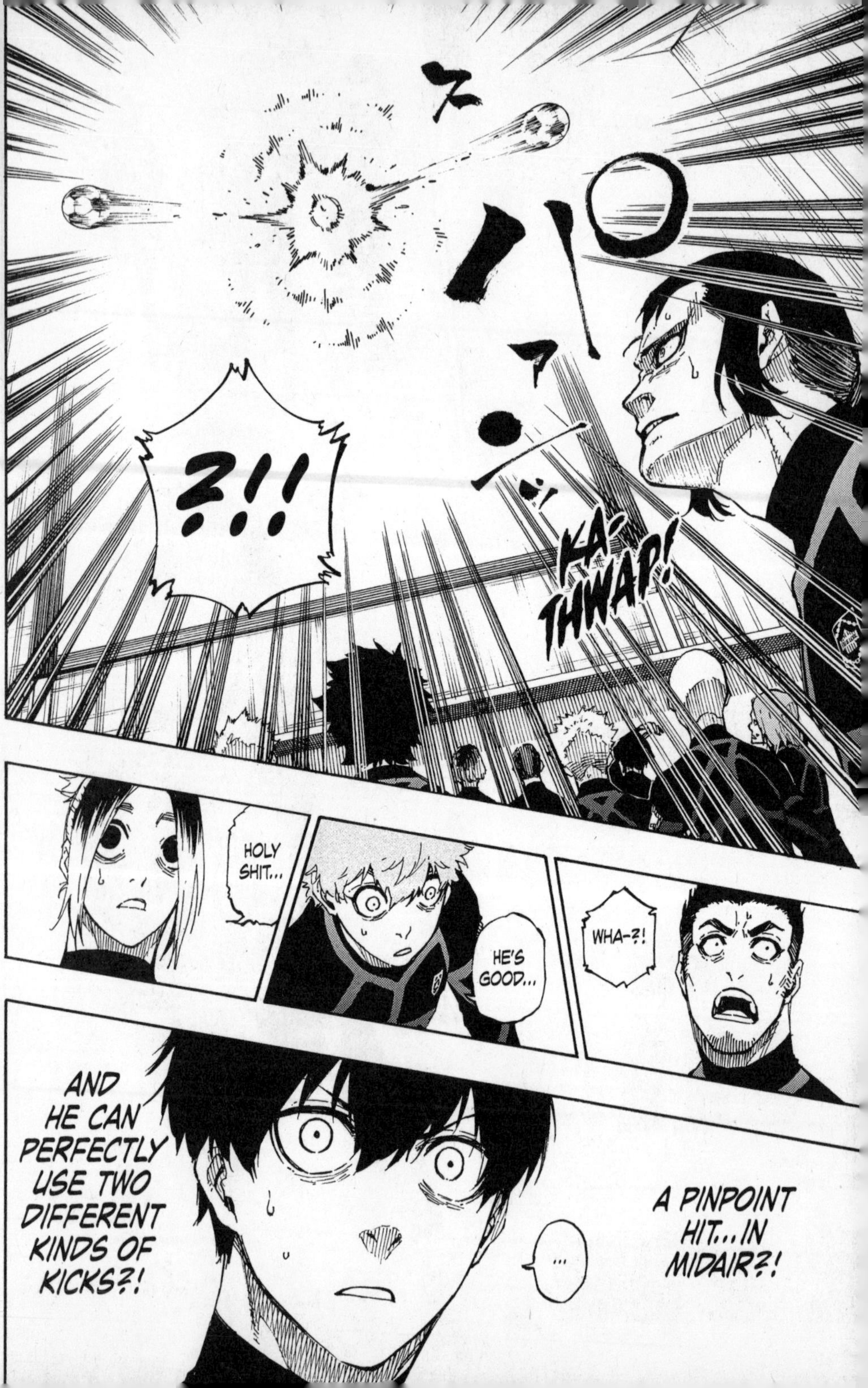
KA-THWAP!
?!!
WHA-?!
HE'S GOOD...
HOLY SHIT...
A PINPOINT HIT...IN MIDAIR?!
...
AND HE CAN PERFECTLY USE TWO DIFFERENT KINDS OF KICKS?!

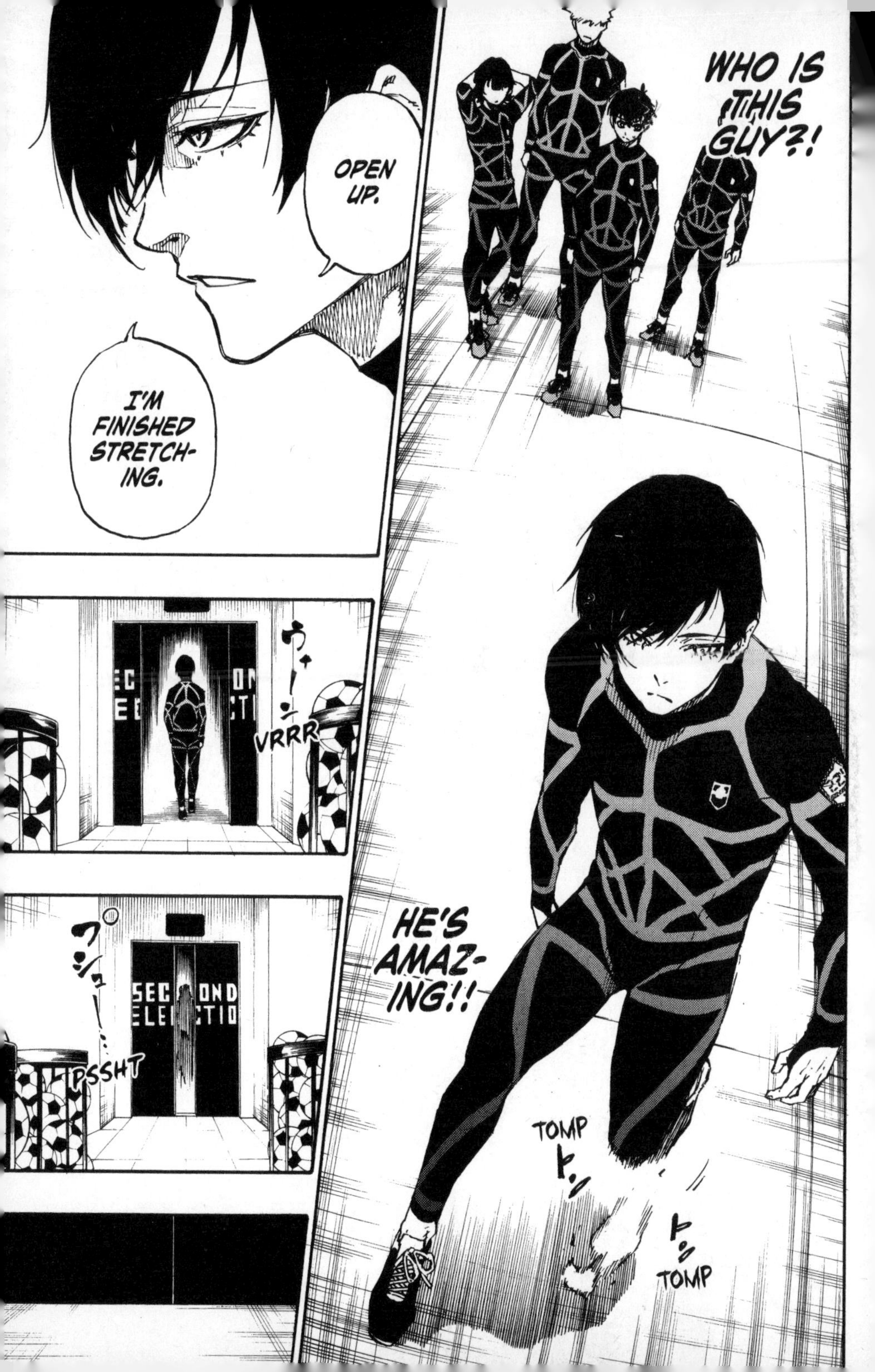
WHO IS THIS GUY?!
HE'S AMAZING!!
TOMP
トッ
トッ
TOMP
OPEN UP.
I'M FINISHED STRETCHING.
ウィーン
VRRR
プシュー…
PSSHT

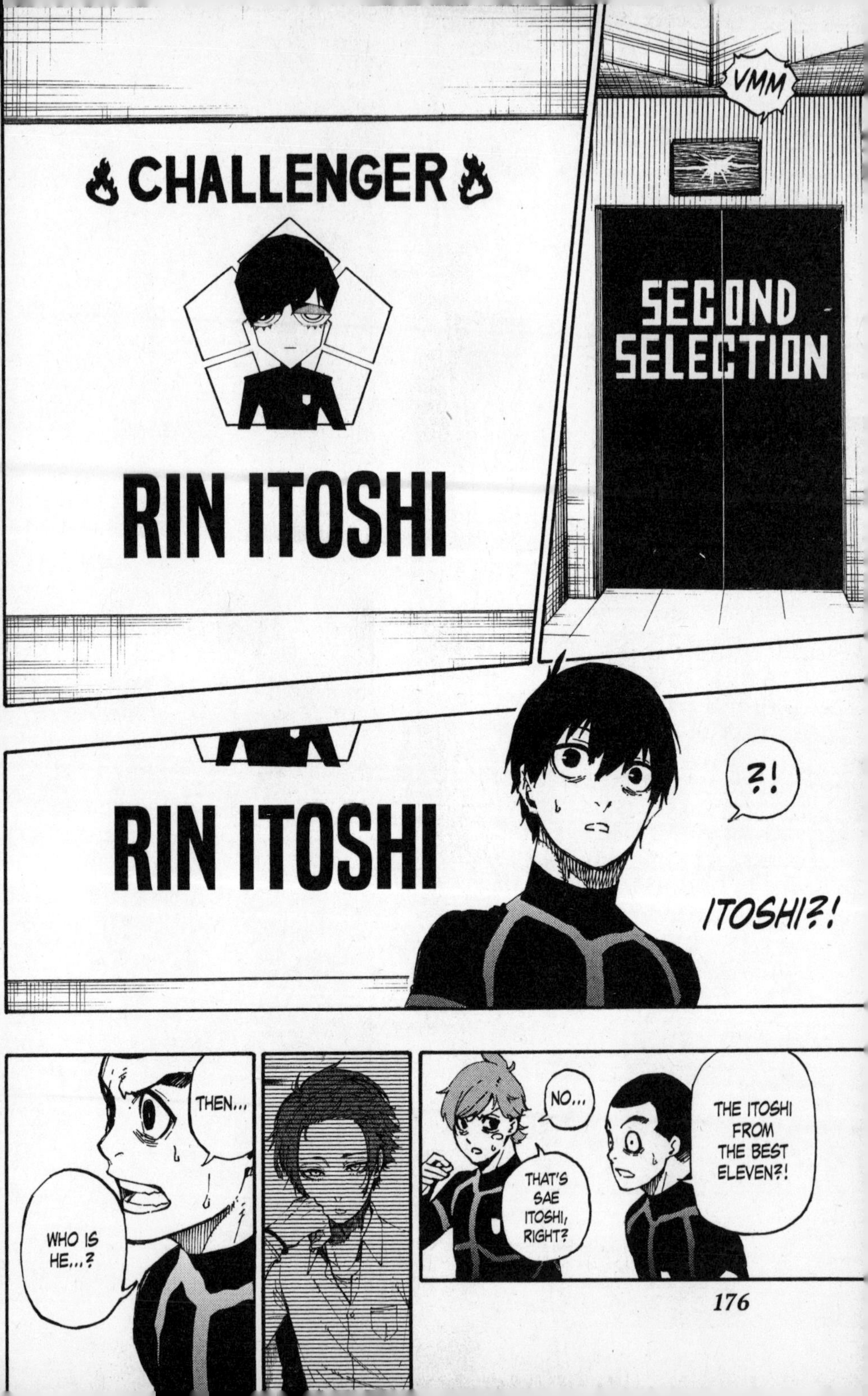
VMM
SECOND SELECTION
CHALLENGER
RIN ITOSHI
?!
ITOSHI?!
RIN ITOSHI
THE ITOSHI FROM THE BEST ELEVEN?!
NO...
THAT'S SAE ITOSHI, RIGHT?
THEN...
WHO IS HE...?

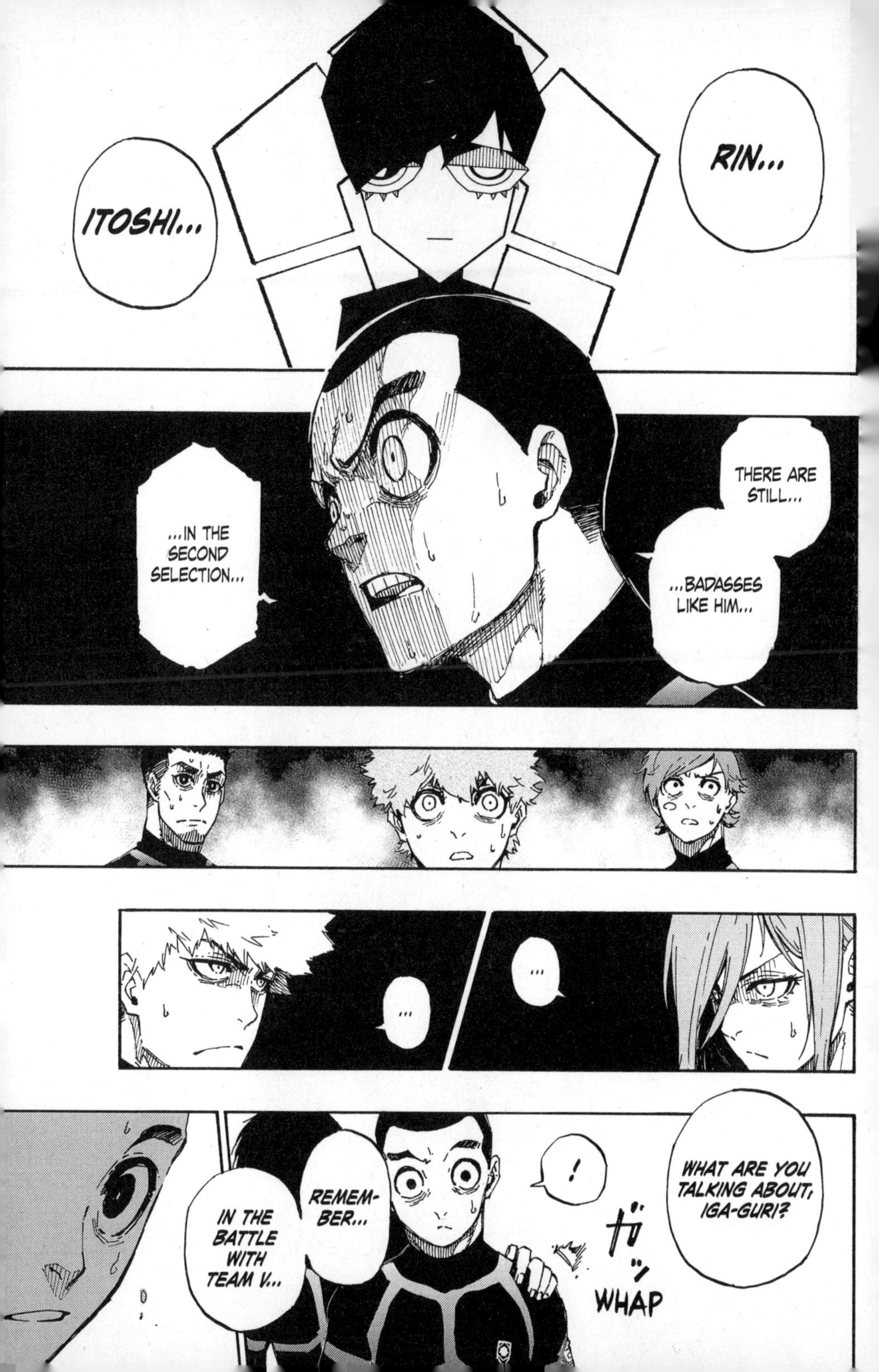
RIN...
ITOSHI...
THERE ARE STILL...
...BADASSES LIKE HIM...
...IN THE SECOND SELECTION...
...
...
WHAT ARE YOU TALKING ABOUT, IGA-GURI?
WHAP
!
REMEMBER...
IN THE BATTLE WITH TEAM V...

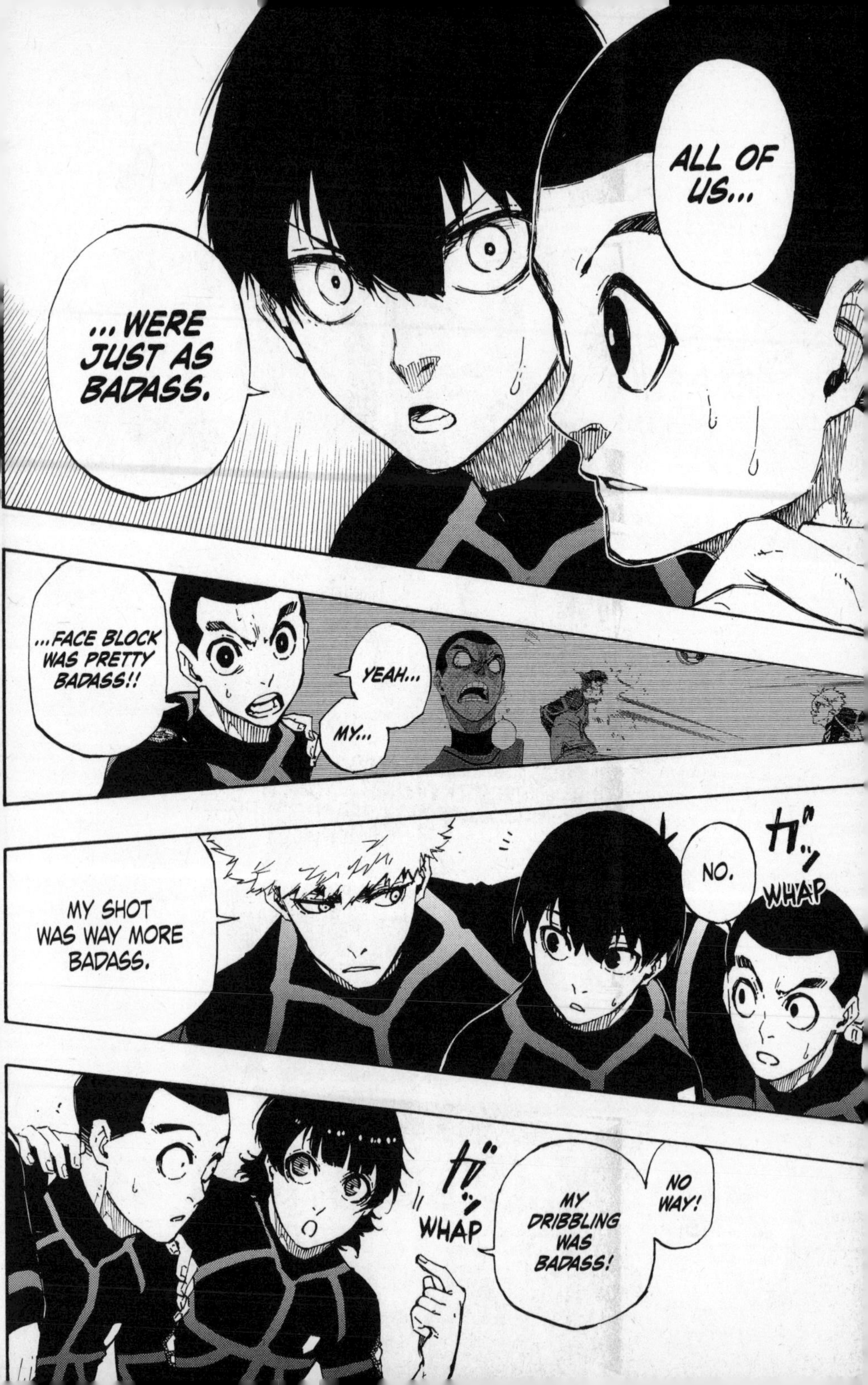
ALL OF US...
...WERE JUST AS BADASS.
YEAH...
MY...
...FACE BLOCK WAS PRETTY BADASS!!
ガッ
WHAP
NO.
MY SHOT WAS WAY MORE BADASS.
NO WAY!
MY DRIBBLING WAS BADASS!
ガッ
WHAP

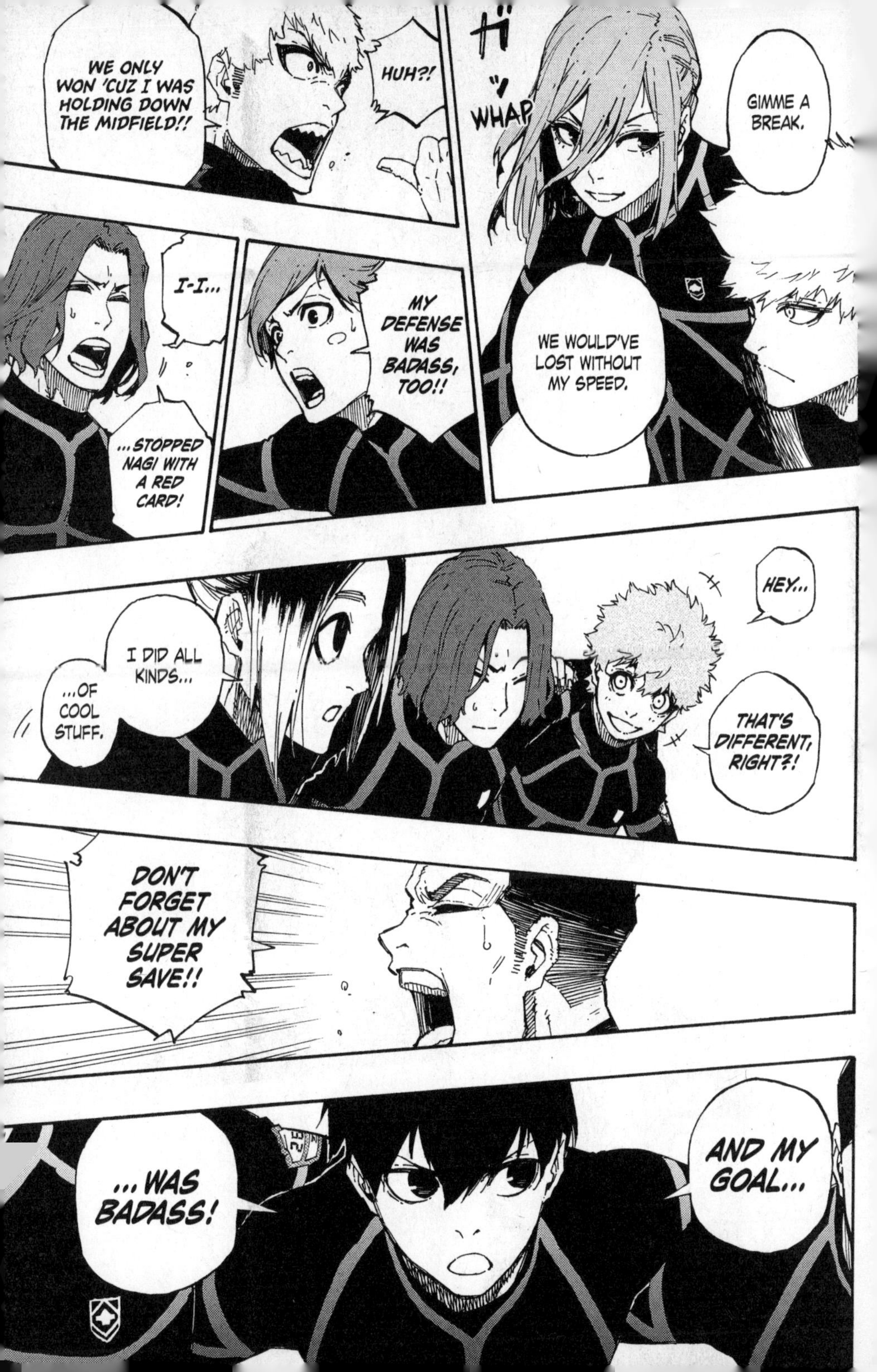
ザッ
WHAP
GIMME A BREAK.
WE WOULD'VE LOST WITHOUT MY SPEED.
HUH?!
WE ONLY WON 'CUZ I WAS HOLDING DOWN THE MIDFIELD!!
MY DEFENSE WAS BADASS, TOO!!
I-I...
...STOPPED NAGI WITH A RED CARD!
HEY...
THAT'S DIFFERENT, RIGHT?!
I DID ALL KINDS...
...OF COOL STUFF.
DON'T FORGET ABOUT MY SUPER SAVE!!
AND MY GOAL...
...WAS BADASS!

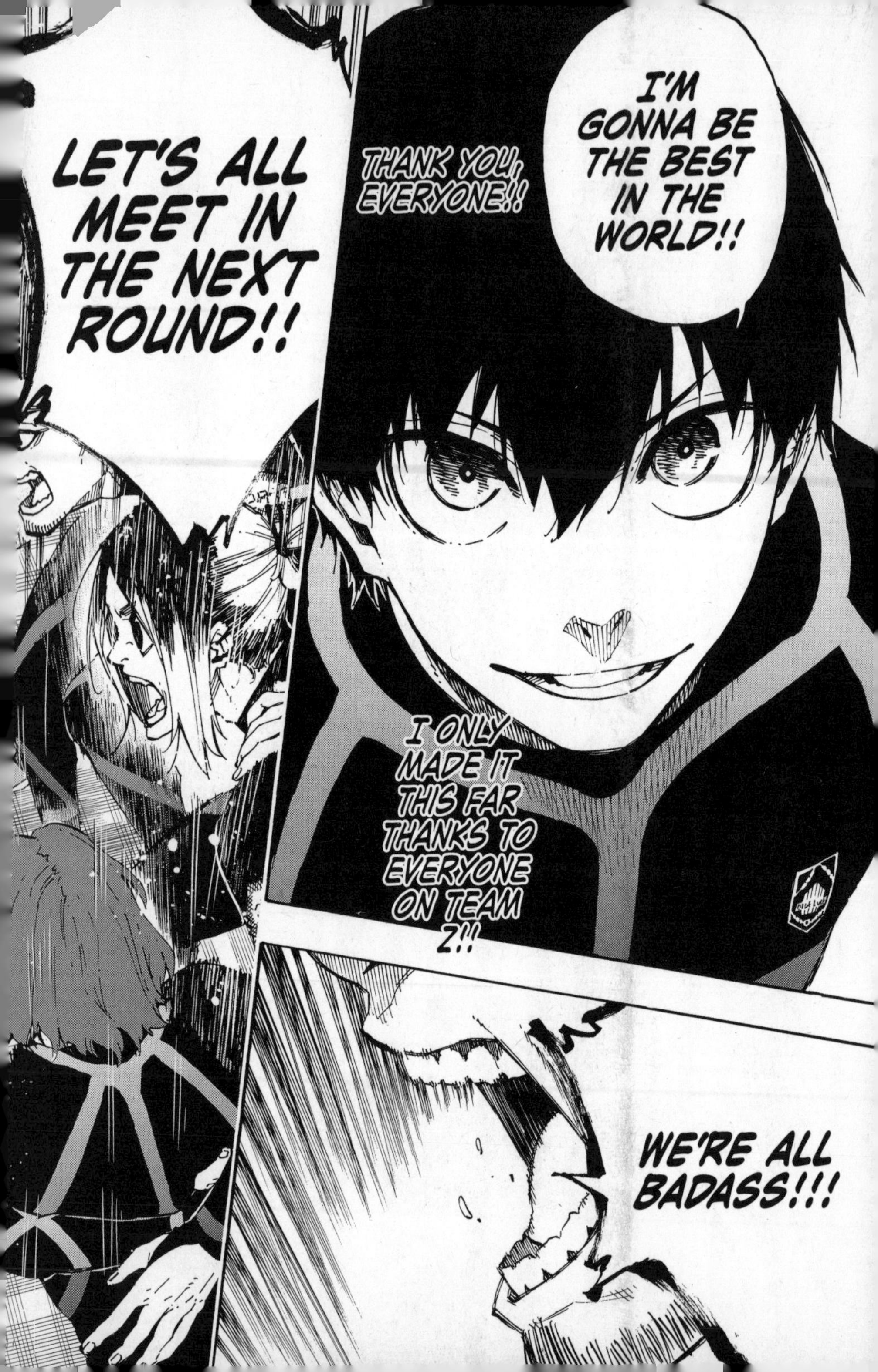
I'M GONNA BE THE BEST IN THE WORLD!!
THANK YOU, EVERYONE!!
I ONLY MADE IT THIS FAR THANKS TO EVERYONE ON TEAM Z!!
WE'RE ALL BADASS!!!
LET'S ALL MEET IN THE NEXT ROUND!!

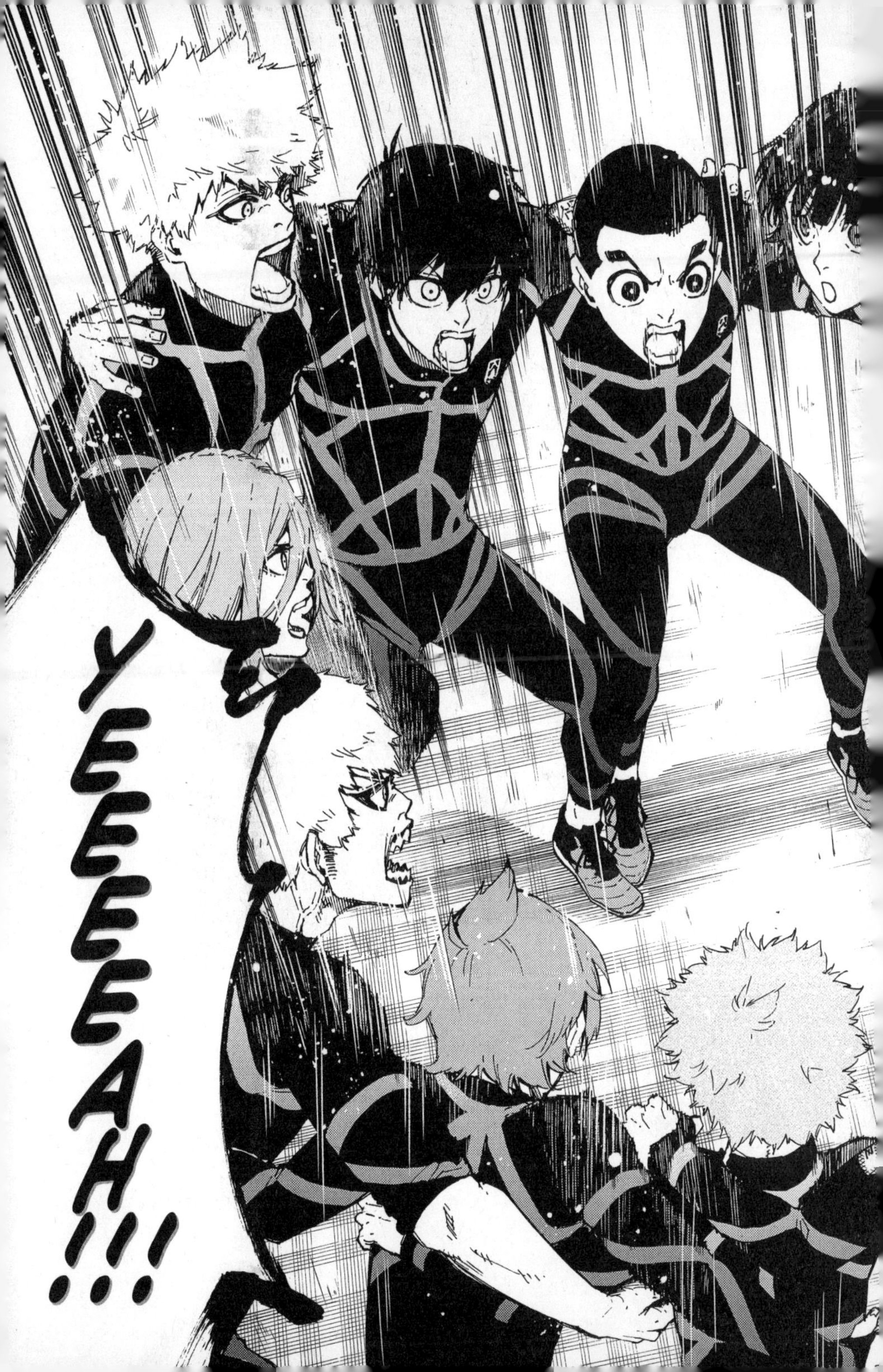
YEEEEEAH!!!

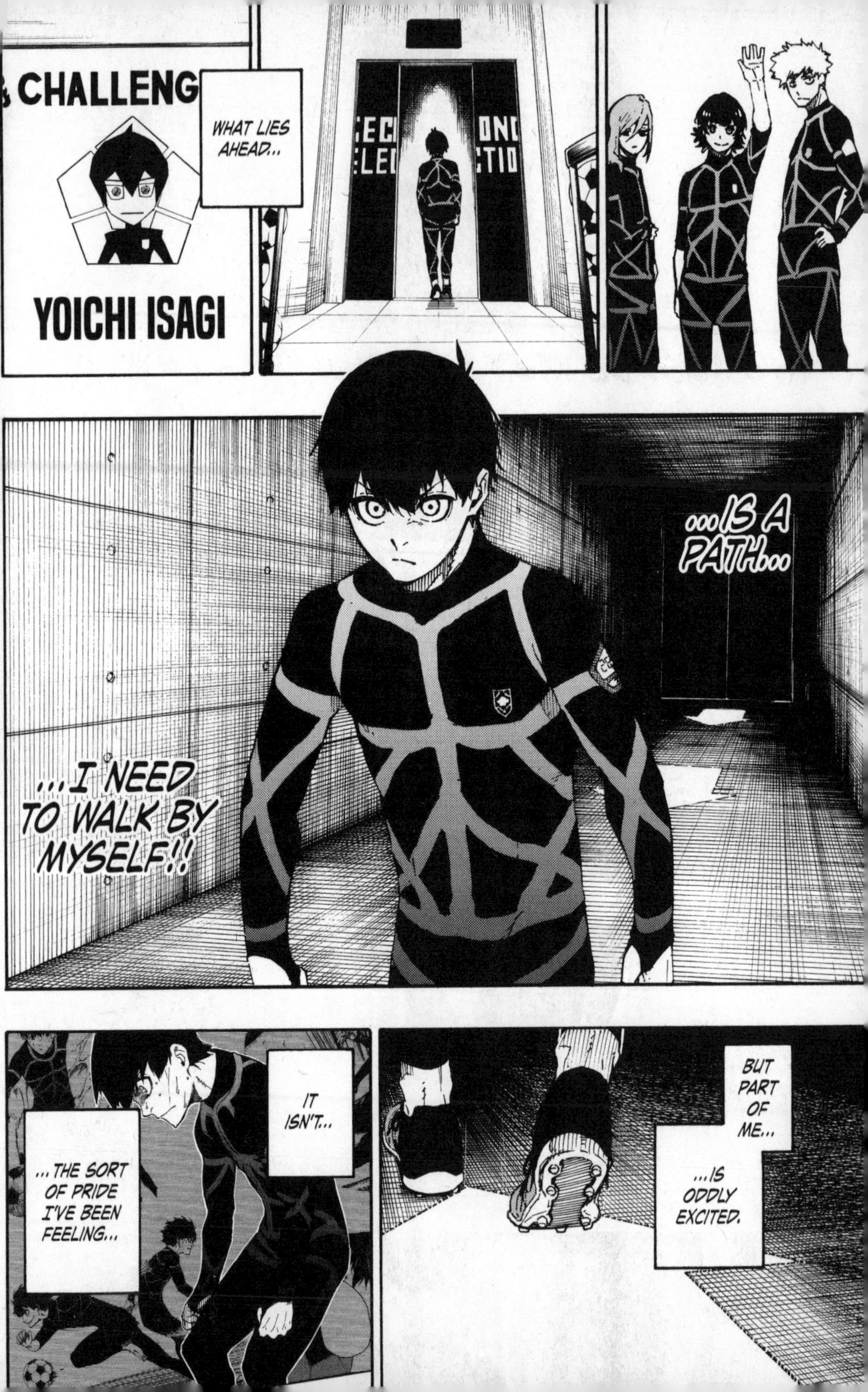
WHAT LIES AHEAD...
& CHALLENG
YOICHI ISAGI
...IS A PATH...
...I NEED TO WALK BY MYSELF!!
BUT PART OF ME...
...IS ODDLY EXCITED.
IT ISN'T...
...THE SORT OF PRIDE I'VE BEEN FEELING...

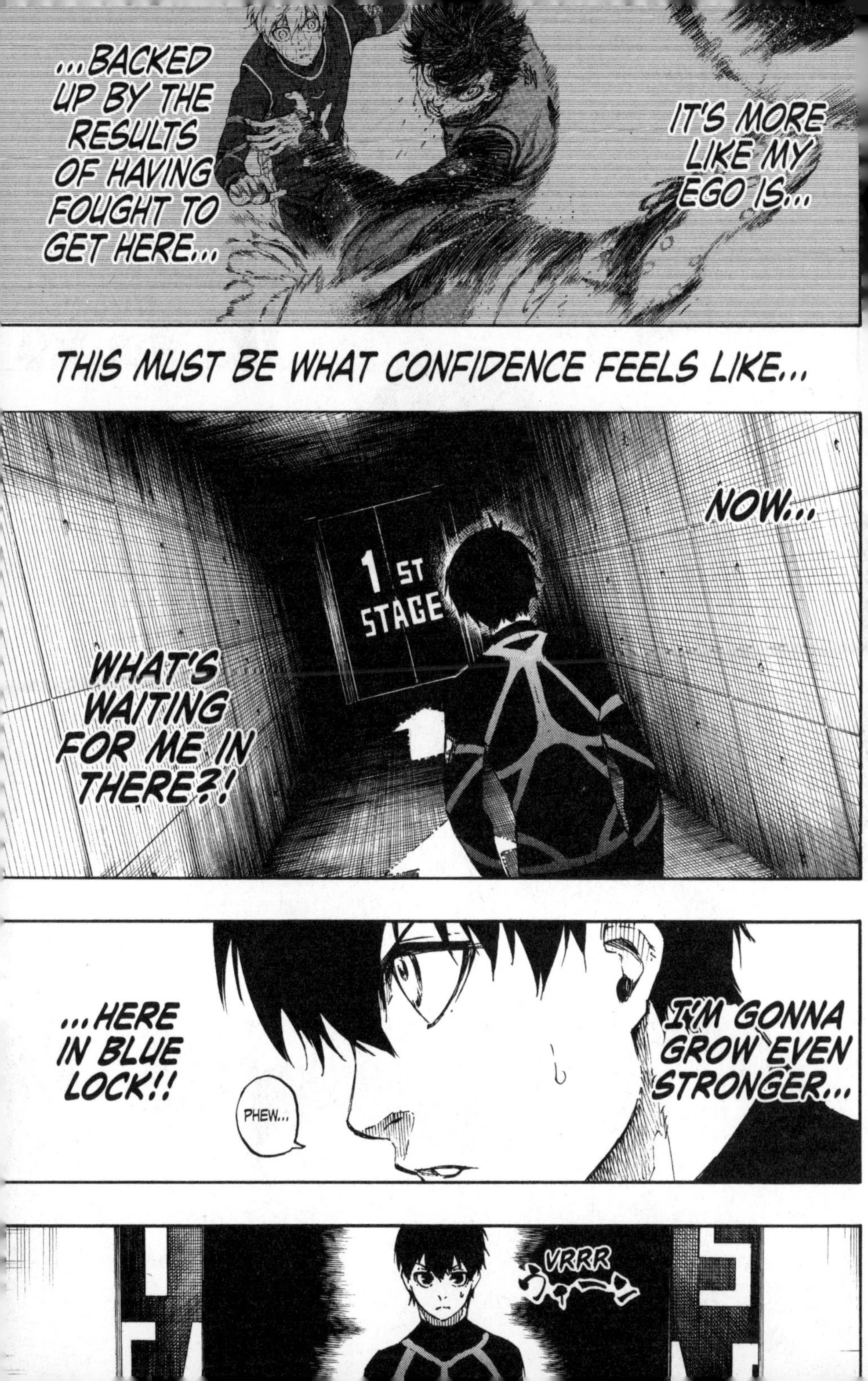
IT'S MORE LIKE MY EGO IS...
...BACKED UP BY THE RESULTS OF HAVING FOUGHT TO GET HERE...
THIS MUST BE WHAT CONFIDENCE FEELS LIKE...
NOW...
1ST STAGE
WHAT'S WAITING FOR ME IN THERE?!
I'M GONNA GROW EVEN STRONGER...
...HERE IN BLUE LOCK!!
PHEW...
VRRR

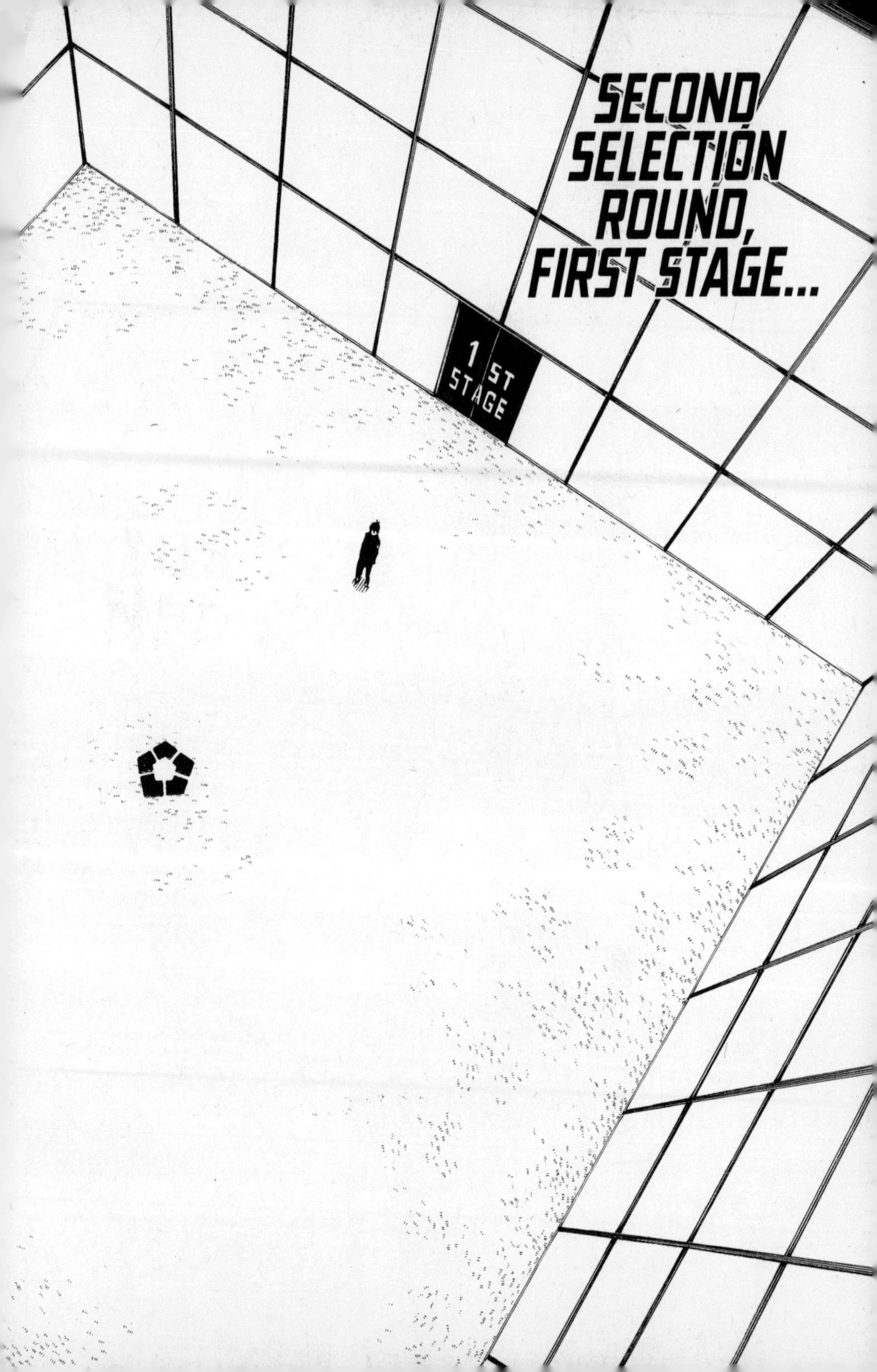
SECOND SELECTIÓN ROUND, FIRST STAGE...
1 ST STAGE

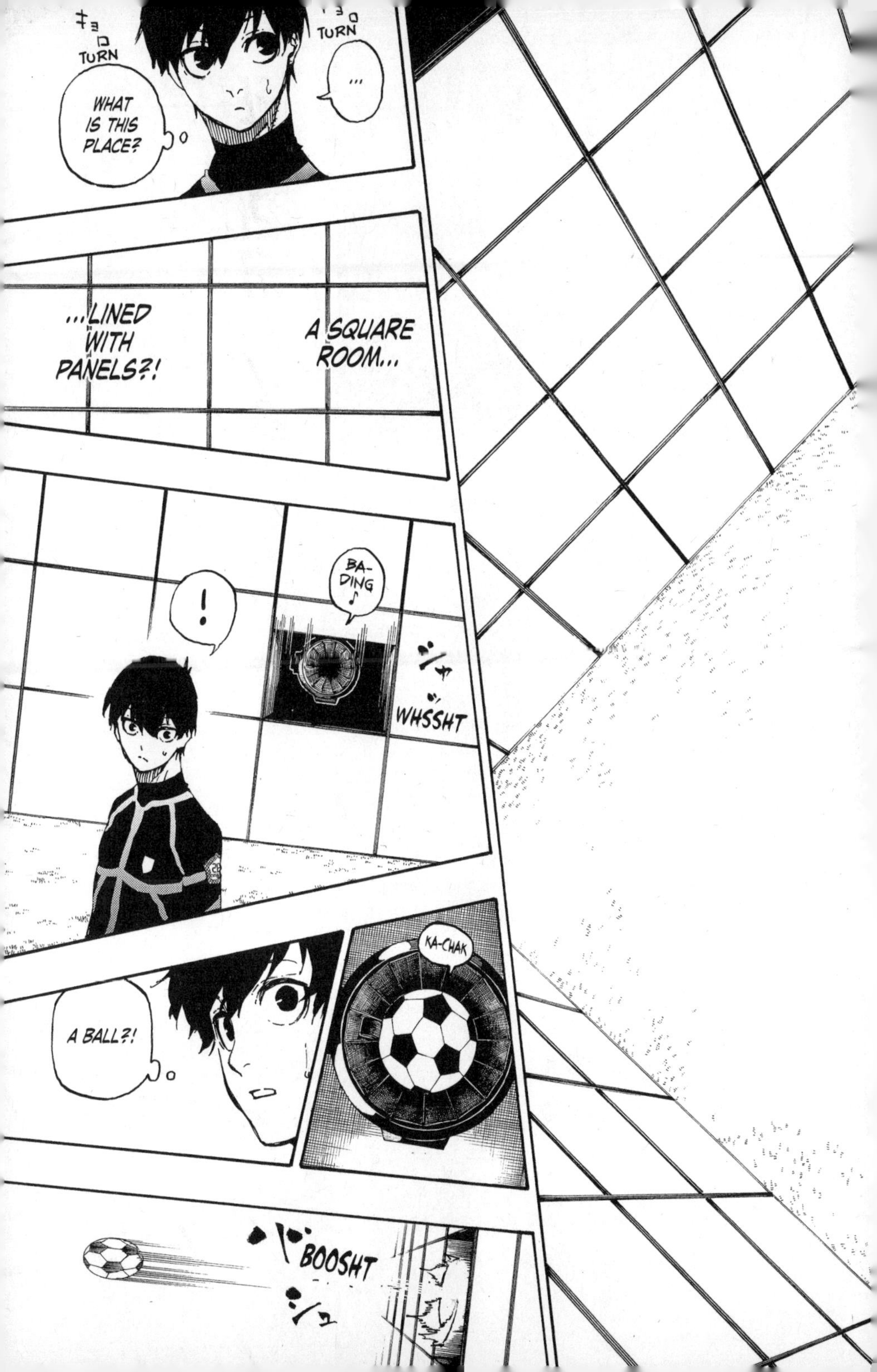
ヨロ
TURN
...
キョロ
TURN
WHAT IS THIS PLACE?
A SQUARE ROOM...
...LINED WITH PANELS?!
ジャ
WHSSHT
BA-DING ♪
!
KA-CHAK
A BALL?!
BOOSHT

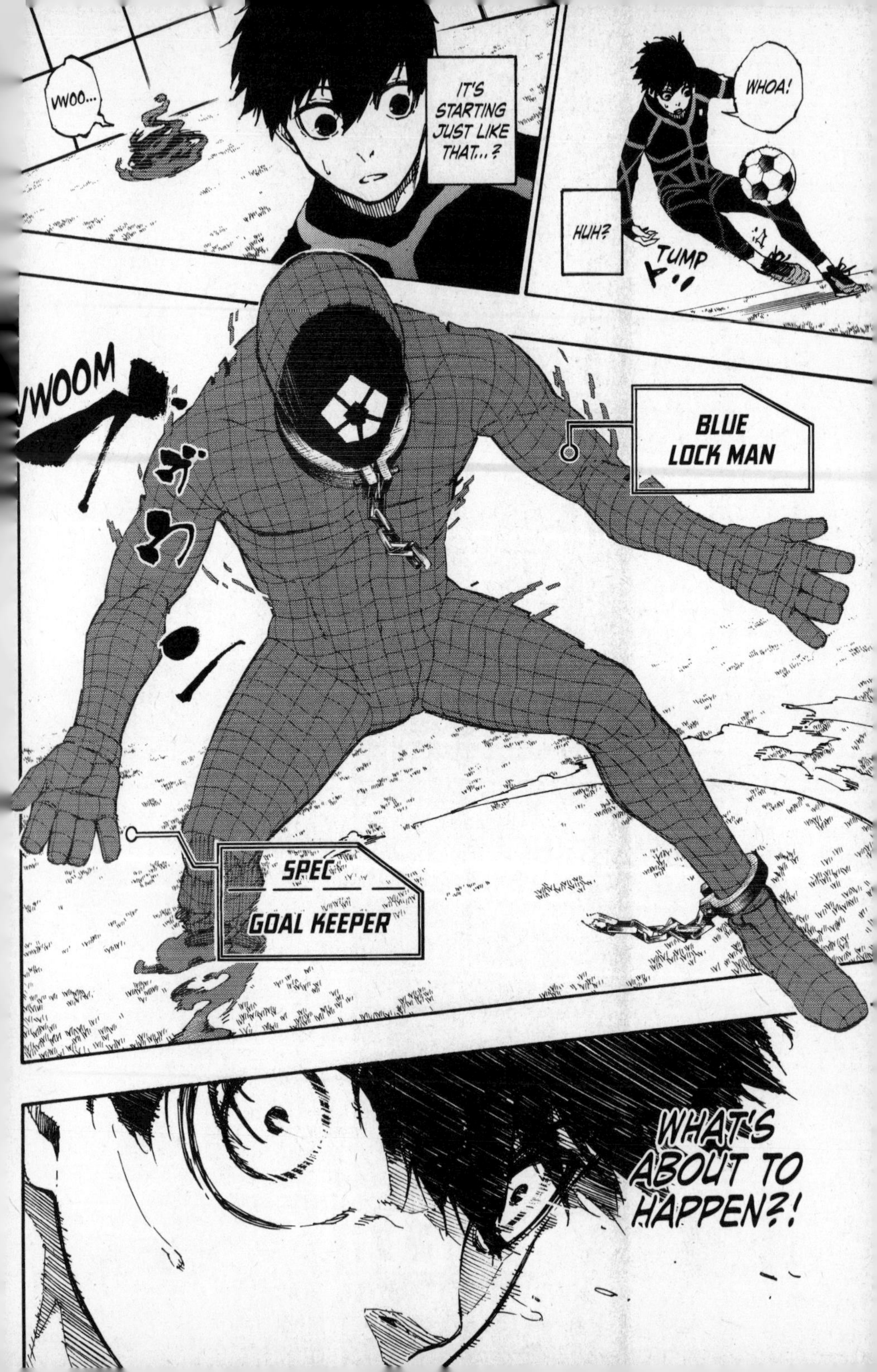
WHOA!
HUH?
TUMP
IT'S STARTING JUST LIKE THAT...?
VWOO...
BLUE LOCK MAN
VWOOM
SPEC
GOAL KEEPER
WHAT'S ABOUT TO HAPPEN?!

# BLUE LOCK
## CONTINUED IN VOL. 6

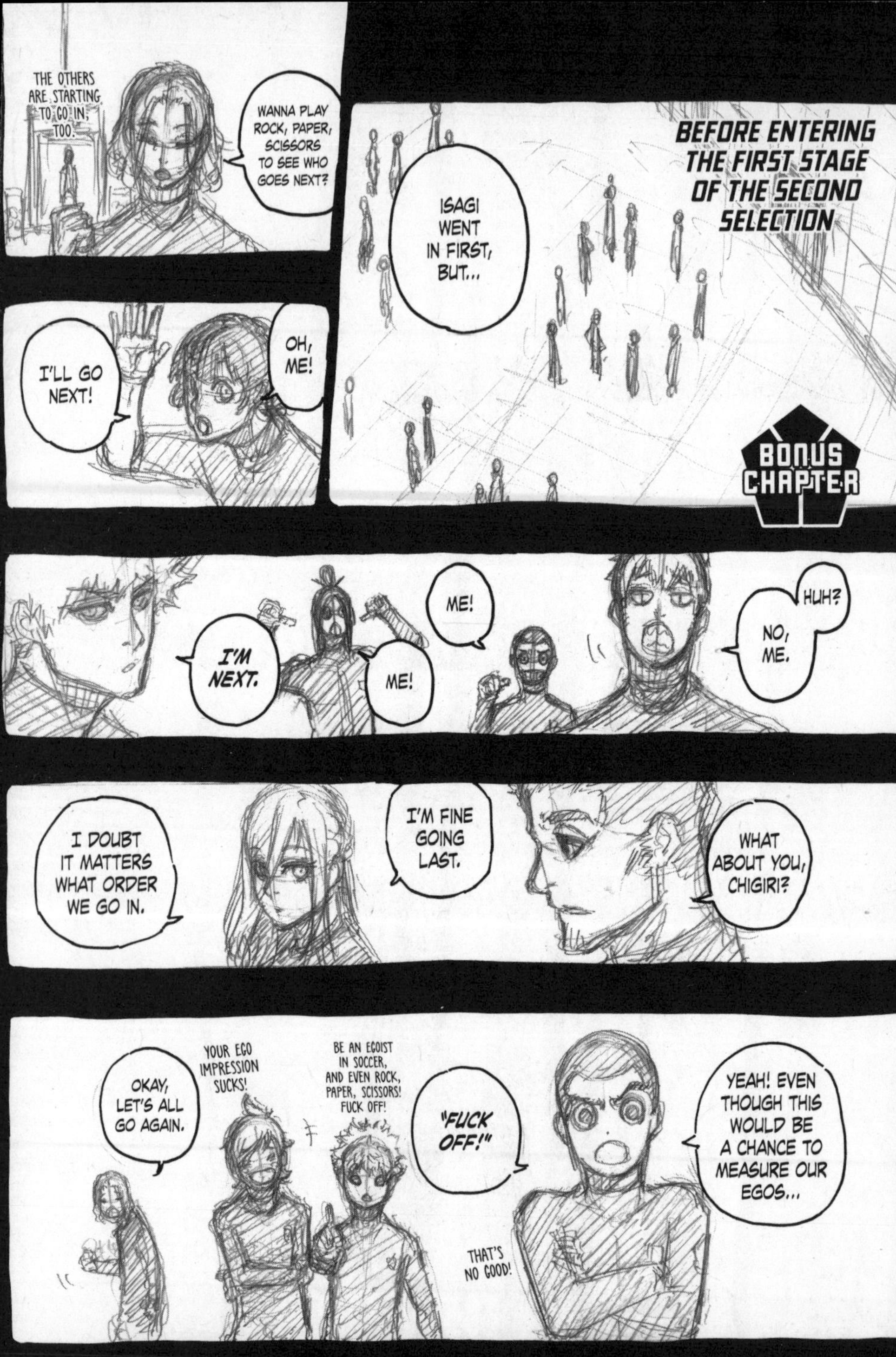
BEFORE ENTERING THE FIRST STAGE OF THE SECOND SELECTION
ISAGI WENT IN FIRST, BUT...
BONUS CHAPTER
WANNA PLAY ROCK, PAPER, SCISSORS TO SEE WHO GOES NEXT?
THE OTHERS ARE STARTING TO GO IN, TOO.
OH, ME!
I'LL GO NEXT!
HUH?
NO, ME.
ME!
ME!
I'M NEXT.
WHAT ABOUT YOU, CHIGIRI?
I'M FINE GOING LAST.
I DOUBT IT MATTERS WHAT ORDER WE GO IN.
YEAH! EVEN THOUGH THIS WOULD BE A CHANCE TO MEASURE OUR EGOS...
THAT'S NO GOOD!
"FUCK OFF!"
BE AN EGOIST IN SOCCER, AND EVEN ROCK, PAPER, SCISSORS! FUCK OFF!
YOUR EGO IMPRESSION SUCKS!
OKAY, LET'S ALL GO AGAIN.

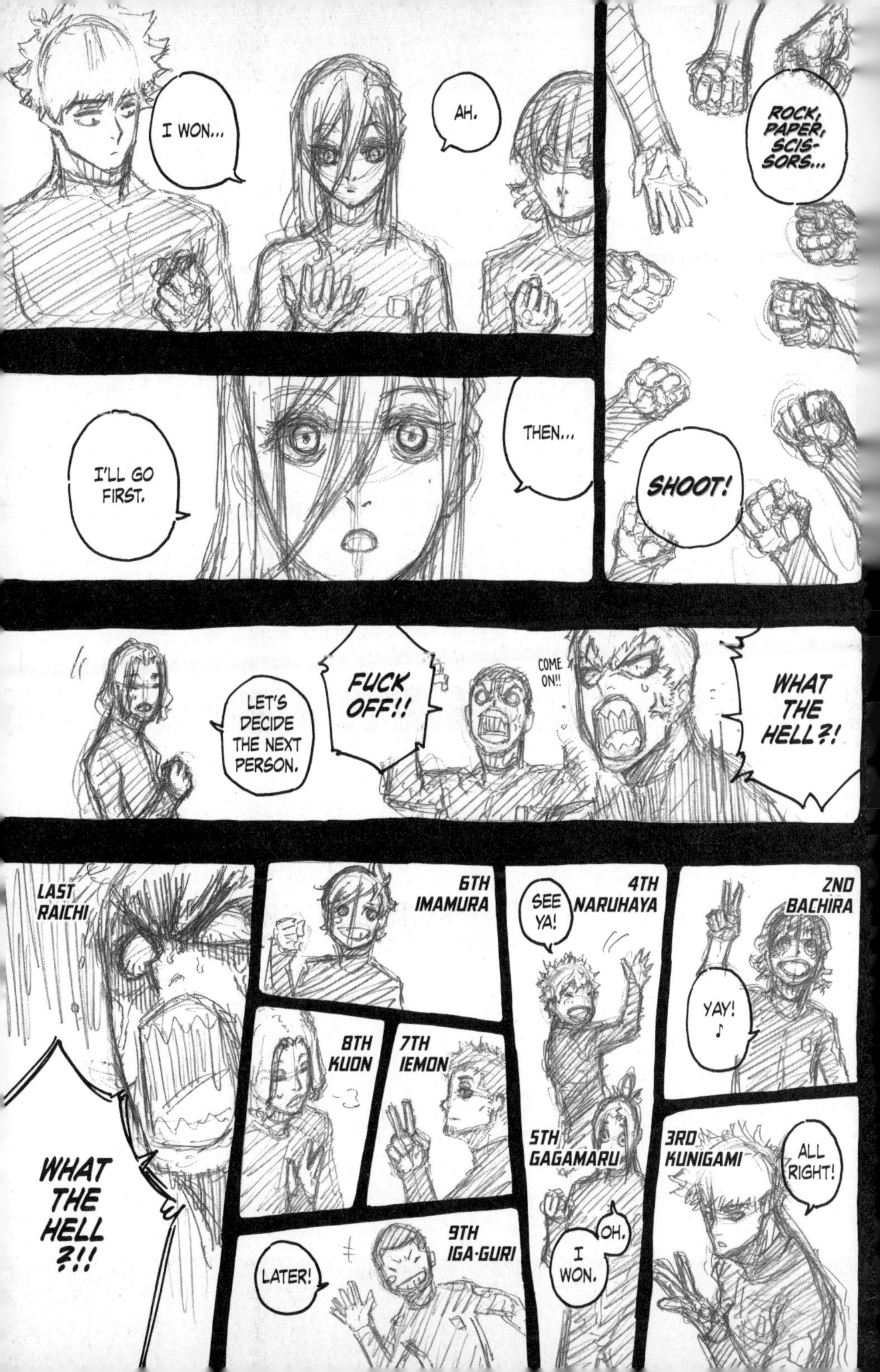
ROCK, PAPER, SCIS-SORS...
SHOOT!
AH.
I WON...
THEN...
I'LL GO FIRST.
WHAT THE HELL?!
COME ON!!
FUCK OFF!!
LET'S DECIDE THE NEXT PERSON.
2ND BACHIRA
YAY! ♪
3RD KUNIGAMI
ALL RIGHT!
4TH NARUHAYA
SEE YA!
5TH GAGAMARU
OH.
I WON.
6TH IMAMURA
7TH IEMON
8TH KUON
9TH IGA-GURI
LATER!
LAST RAICHI
WHAT THE HELL ?!!

| | |
|---|---|
| ◉ STORY | MUNEYUKI KANESHIRO |
| ◉ ART | YUSUKE NOMURA |
| ◉ ART ASSISTANTS | SUEHIRO-SAN FURUMOTO-SAN<br>FUJIMAKI-SAN HARADA-SAN<br>MAEHATA-SAN NAKAMURA-SAN<br>ARATAMA-SAN KONNO-SAN<br>TAKANIWA-SAN SASAKI-SAN<br>SATOU-SAN KAWAI-SAN<br>OTAKE-SAN SEKIGUCHI-SAN<br>(LISTED RANDOMLY) |
| ◉ DESIGN | KUMOCHI-SAN<br>OBA-SAN<br>(HIVE) |

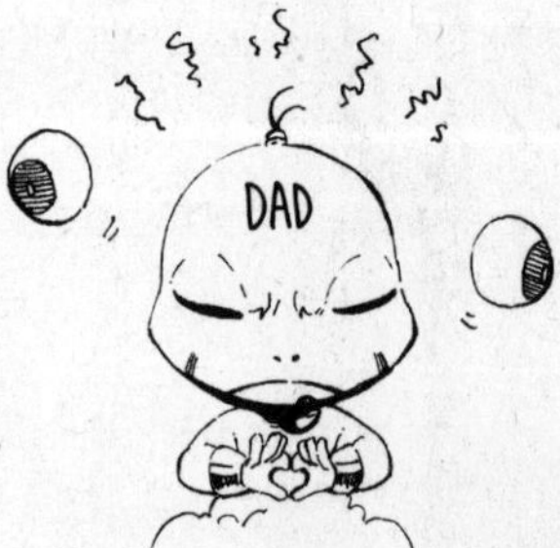
DAD
INK

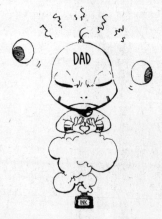

HUMANS SHOULD HAVE AN EXTRA TWO EYEBALLS.
THAT WAY I CAN WATCH MOVIES WHILE I WORK.
I WANNA WATCH ALADDIN...

THANK YOU SO MUCH FOR BUYING VOLUME 5!!

BLUELOCK

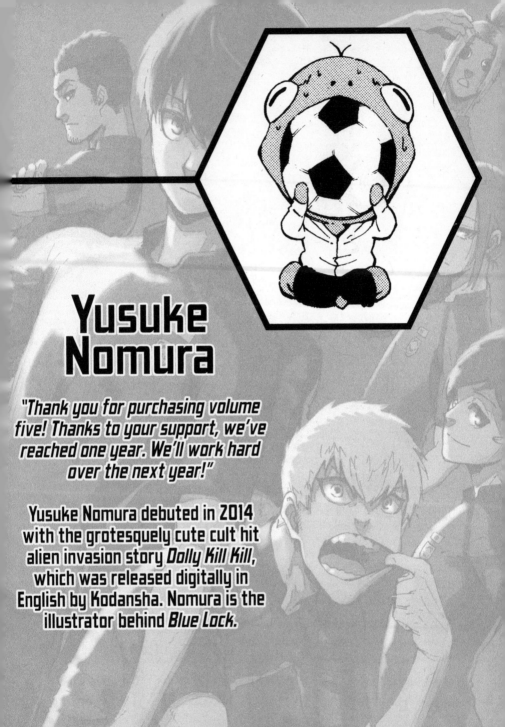

# Yusuke Nomura

"Thank you for purchasing volume five! Thanks to your support, we've reached one year. We'll work hard over the next year!"

Yusuke Nomura debuted in 2014 with the grotesquely cute cult hit alien invasion story *Dolly Kill Kill*, which was released digitally in English by Kodansha. Nomura is the illustrator behind *Blue Lock*.

# Muneyuki Kaneshiro

*"A soccer athlete's prime years is in their late teens to mid-twenties. Seeing those plays is almost like magic. I love seeing it."*

Muneyuki Kaneshiro broke out as creator of 2011's *As the Gods Will*, a death game story that spawned two sequels and a film adaptation directed by the legendary Takashi Miike. Kaneshiro writes the story of *Blue Lock*.

# Young characters and steampunk setting, like *Howl's Moving Castle* and *Battle Angel Alita*

Beyond the Clouds © 2018 Nicke / Ki-oon

A boy with a talent for machines and a mysterious girl whose wings he's fixed will take you beyond the clouds! In the tradition of the high-flying, resonant adventure stories of Studio Ghibli comes a gorgeous tale about the longing of young hearts for adventure and friendship!

Knight of the Ice ©Yayoi Ogawa/Kodansha Ltd.

# SKATING THRILLS AND ICY CHILLS WITH THIS NEW TINGLY ROMANCE SERIES!

A rom-com on ice, perfect for fans of *Princess Jellyfish* and *Wotakoi*. Kokoro is the talk of the figure-skating world, winning trophies and hearts. But little do they know... he's actually a huge nerd! From the beloved creator of *You're My Pet* (*Tramps Like Us*).

Chitose is a serious young woman, working for the health magazine *SASSO*. Or at least, she would be, if she wasn't constantly getting distracted by her childhood friend, international figure skating star Kokoro Kijinami! In the public eye and on the ice, Kokoro is a gallant, flawless knight, but behind his glittery costumes and breathtaking spins lies a secret: He's actually a hopelessly romantic otaku, who can only land his quad jumps when Chitose is on hand to recite a spell from his favorite magical girl anime!

# A SMART, NEW ROMANTIC COMEDY FOR FANS OF *SHORTCAKE CAKE* AND *TERRACE HOUSE*!



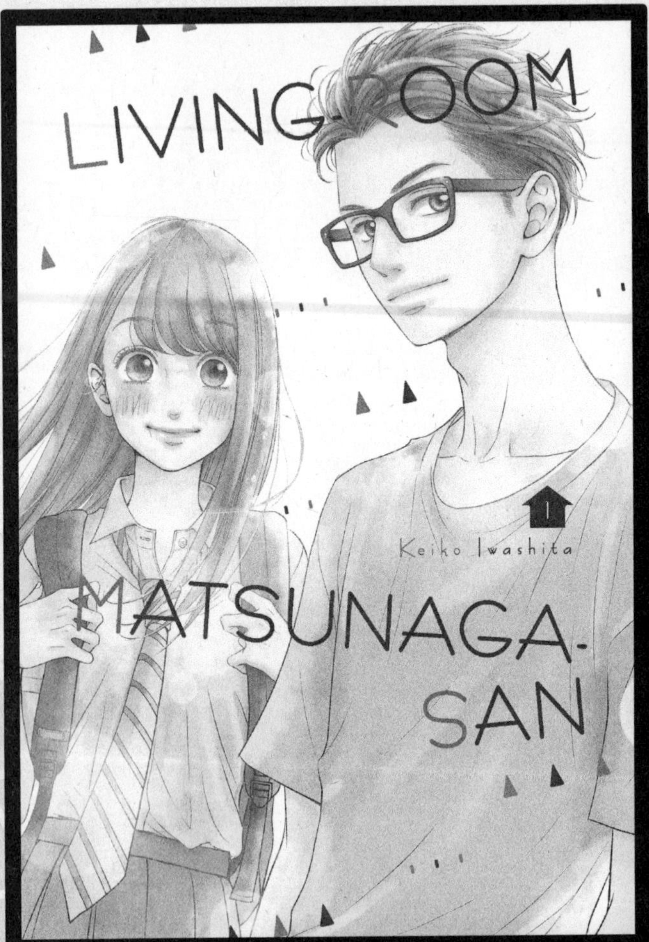
LIVING-ROOM
1
Keiko Iwashita
MATSUNAGA-SAN

A romance manga starring high school girl Meeko, who learns to live on her own in a boarding house whose living room is home to the odd (but handsome) Matsunaga-san. She begins to adjust to her new life away from her parents, but Meeko soon learns that no matter how far away from home she is, she's still a young girl at heart — especially when she finds herself falling for Matsunaga-san.

KC KODANSHA COMICS

# PERFECT WORLD

### Rie Aruga

A TOUCHING
NEW SERIES
ABOUT LOVE AND
COPING WITH
DISABILITY

An office party reunites Tsugumi with her high school crush Itsuki. He's realized his dream of becoming an architect, but along the way, he experienced a spinal injury that put him in a wheelchair. Now Tsugumi's rekindled feelings will butt up against prejudices she never considered — and Itsuki will have to decide if he's ready to let someone into his heart...

"Depicts with great delicacy and courage the difficulties some with disabilities experience getting involved in romantic relationships... Rie Aruga refuses to romanticize, pushing her heroine to face the reality of disability. She invites her readers to the same tasks of empathy, knowledge and recognition."
—Slate.fr

"An important entry [in manga romance]... The emotional core of both plot and characters indicates thoughtfulness... [Aruga's] research is readily apparent in the text and artwork, making this feel like a real story."
—Anime News Network

# The boys are back, in 400-page hardcovers that are as pretty and badass as they are!

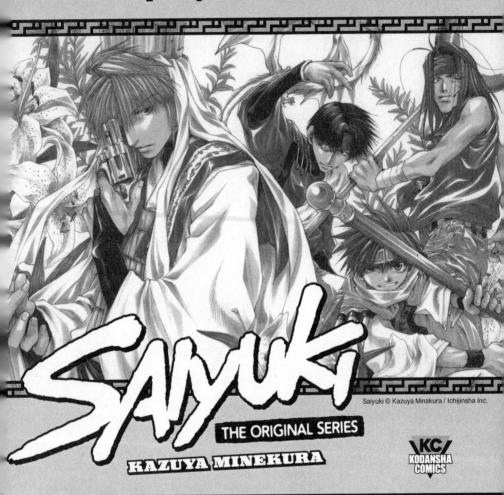

Saiyuki © Kazuya Minekura / Ichijinsha Inc.

## SAIYUKI

### THE ORIGINAL SERIES

#### KAZUYA MINEKURA

"AN EDGY COMIC LOOK AT AN ANCIENT CHINESE TALE." —YALSA

Genjo Sanzo is a Buddhist priest in the city of Togenkyo, which is being ravaged by yokai spirits that have fallen out of balance with the natural order. His superiors send him on a journey far to the west to discover why this is happening and how to stop it. His companions are three yokai with human souls. But this is no day trip — the four will encounter many discoveries and horrors on the way.

## FEATURES NEW TRANSLATION, COLOR PAGES, AND BEAUTIFUL WRAPAROUND COVER ART!

# Something's Wrong With Us

NATSUMI ANDO

The dark, psychological, sexy shojo series readers have been waiting for!

## A spine-chilling and steamy romance between a Japanese sweets maker and the man who framed her mother for murder!

Following in her mother's footsteps, Nao became a traditional Japanese sweets maker, and with unparalleled artistry and a bright attitude, she gets an offer to work at a world-class confectionary company. But when she meets the young, handsome owner, she recognizes his cold stare...

KC/
KODANSHA
COMICS

The adorable new odd-couple cat comedy manga from the creator of the beloved *Chi's Sweet Home*, in full color!

# Sue & Tai-chan

### Konami Kanata

Sue is an aging housecat who's looking forward to living out her life in peace... but her plans change when the mischievous black tomcat Tai-chan enters the picture! Hey! Sue never signed up to be a catsitter! *Sue & Tai-chan* is the latest from the reigning meow-narch of cute kitty comics, Konami Kanata.

# SAINT ☆ YOUNG MEN

## A LONG AWAITED ARRIVAL IN PREMIUM 2-IN-1 HARDCOVER

After centuries of hard work, Jesus and Buddha take a break from their heavenly duties to relax among the people of Japan, and their adventures in this lighthearted buddy comedy are sure to bring mirth and merriment to all!

"Brilliant...the physical comedy and facial expressions will make you literally LOL."
—Sam Humphries
(host of *DC Daily*;
writer, *Green Lanterns*,
*Legendary Star-Lord*)

# THE SWEET SCENT OF LOVE IS IN THE AIR! FOR FANS OF OFFBEAT ROMANCES LIKE *WOTAKOI*

VOL. 1

KINTETSU
YAMADA

Sweat and Soap © Kintetsu Yamada / Kodansha Ltd.

In an office romance, there's a fine line between sexy and awkward... and that line is where Asako — a woman who sweats copiously — meets Koutarou — a perfume developer who can't get enough of Asako's, er, scent. Don't miss a romcom manga like no other!

KC
KODANSHA
COMICS

‹ KAMOME ›
SHIRAHAMA

# Witch Hat Atelier

A magical manga
adventure for
fans of Disney
and Studio
Ghibli!

## The magical adventure that took Japan by storm is finally here, from acclaimed DC and Marvel cover artist Kamome Shirahama!

In a world where everyone takes wonders like magic spells and dragons for granted, Coco is a girl with a simple dream: She wants to be a witch. But everybody knows magicians are born, not made, and Coco was not born with a gift for magic. Resigned to her un-magical life, Coco is about to give up on her dream to become a witch…until the day she meets Qifrey, a mysterious, traveling magician. After secretly seeing Qifrey perform magic in a way she's never seen before, Coco soon learns what everybody "knows" might not be the truth, and discovers that her magical dream may not be as far away as it may seem…

KC
KODANSHA
COMICS

# The beloved characters from *Cardcaptor Sakura* return in a brand new, reimagined fantasy adventure!

RESERVoir CHRoNiCLE
TSUBASA
OMNIBUS
1
CLAMP

TSUBASA
WoRLD CHRoNiCLE: NIRAIKANAI
1
CLAMP

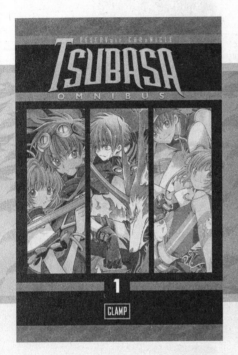

**"[*Tsubasa*] takes readers on a fantastic ride that only gets more exhilarating with each successive chapter."** —Anime News Network

In the Kingdom of Clow, an archaeological dig unleashes an incredible power, causing Princess Sakura to lose her memories. To save her, her childhood friend Syaoran must follow the orders of the Dimension Witch and travel alongside Kurogane, an unrivaled warrior; Fai, a powerful magician; and Mokona, a curiously strange creature, to retrieve Sakura's dispersed memories!

KC KODANSHA COMICS

# The art-deco cyberpunk classic from the creators of *xxxHOLiC* and *Cardcaptor Sakura*!

CLOVER © CLAMP-ShigatsuTsuitachi CO.,LTD./Kodansha Ltd.

Su was born into a bleak future, where the government keeps
tight control over children with magical powers—codenamed
"Clovers." With Su being the only "four-leaf" Clover in the
world, she has been kept isolated nearly her whole life. Can
ex-military agent Kazuhiko deliver her to the happiness she
seeks? Experience the complete series in this hardcover
edition, which also includes over twenty pages of ravishing
color art!

A Kodansha Trade Paperback Original

Published in the United States by
Kodansha USA Publishing, LLC, New York.

Publication rights for this English edition arranged through
Kodansha Ltd., Tokyo.

First published in Japan in 2019 by Kodansha Ltd., Tokyo
as *Buruu rokku*, volume 5.

ISBN 978-1-64651-662-9

Printed in the United States of America.

9 8 7 6 5 4 3 2 1

Original Digital Edition Translation: Nate Derr
Original Digital Edition Lettering: Chris Burgener
Original Digital Edition Editing: Thalia Sutton
YKS Services LLC/SKY JAPAN, Inc.
Print Edition Lettering: Scott O. Brown
Print Edition Editing: Maggie Le
Kodansha USA Publishing edition cover design by Matthew Akuginow

Publisher: Kiichiro Sugawara

Director of Publishing Services: Ben Applegate
Director of Publishing Operations: Dave Barrett
Associate Director of Publishing Operations: Stephen Pakula
Publishing Services Managing Editors: Alanna Ruse, Madison Salters,
with Grace Chen
Production Manager: Jocelyn O'Dowd

KODANSHA.US

 KODANSHA